Qualitative Data Analysis
An Introduction

SAGE has been part of the global academic community since 1965, supporting high quality research and learning that transforms society and our understanding of individuals, groups, and cultures. SAGE is the independent, innovative, natural home for authors, editors and societies who share our commitment and passion for the social sciences.

Find out more at: **www.sagepublications.com**

Connect, Debate, Engage on Methodspace

 Connect with other researchers and discuss your research interests

 **Keep up with announcements in the field, for example calls for papers and jobs**

Discover and review resources

 Engage with featured content such as key articles, podcasts and videos

Find out about relevant conferences and events

Connecting the Research Community

www.methodspace.com

brought to you by

second
edition

Qualitative Data Analysis

An Introduction

Carol Grbich

Los Angeles | London | New Delhi
Singapore | Washington DC

Los Angeles | London | New Delhi
Singapore | Washington DC

SAGE Publications Ltd
1 Oliver's Yard
55 City Road
London EC1Y 1SP

SAGE Publications Inc.
2455 Teller Road
Thousand Oaks, California 91320

SAGE Publications India Pvt Ltd
B 1/I 1 Mohan Cooperative Industrial Area
Mathura Road
New Delhi 110 044

SAGE Publications Asia-Pacific Pte Ltd
3 Church Street
#10-04 Samsung Hub
Singapore 049483

Editor: Katie Metzler
Editorial assistant: Anna Horvai
Production editor: Katie Forsythe
Copyeditor: Elaine Leek
Proofreader: Bryan Campbell
Marketing manager: Ben Griffin Sherwood
Cover design: Jennifer Crisp
Typeset by: C&M Digitals (P) Ltd, Chennai, India
Printed and bound by CPI Group (UK) Ltd,
Croydon, CR0 4YY

Library of Congress Control Number: 2011945803

British Library Cataloguing in Publication data

A catalogue record for this book is available from the British Library

MIX
Paper from
responsible sources
FSC
www.fsc.org   FSC® C013604

ISBN 978-1-4462-0296-8
ISBN 978-1-4462-0297-5 (pbk)

Table of contents

Solutions to the exercises and PowerPoint slides for lecturers are available at www.sagepub.co.uk/grbich2

About the author

Dr Carol Grbich is a Professor in the School of Medicine at Flinders University in South Australia. She is an Epidemiologist and Sociologist and is the author of a number of textbooks on Qualitative Research including *Qualitative Data Analysis: An Introduction 1st* Edition (Sage, 2007), *New Approaches in Social Research* (Sage, 2004) and *Qualitative Research in Health: An Introduction* (Allen and Unwin, 1999), as well as authoring several texts on the Sociology of Health and Illness.

She is also Foundation Editor of the *International Journal of Multiple Research Approaches.*

PART 1

General approaches to collecting and analysing qualitative data

The processes of data analysis in qualitative research are complex. It is not simply a matter of choosing and applying an accepted process such as thematic analysis.

A combination of three key areas is involved:

- the first is to do with you, the researcher – your views and choices in the research journey and the impact of these on the data you collect and analyse
- the second relates to the design and methods used, the quality of the data you have gathered and how you have managed it, and
- the third involves your display of findings and your theoretical interpretation of your analysed data, presented for the reader to assess.

The three Ps – *Person*, *Processes* and *Presentation* – are key issues here.

This book starts from the premise that these three elements are essential to any undertaking of qualitative data analysis, and the examples and strategies presented attempt to indicate how they integrate.

Part 1 introduces you to the background information required for understanding qualitative research. The first chapter deals with research characteristics, investigative areas of research and the role of the researcher, together with his/her influence on the data and finishing with a brief review of the major paradigms that have underpinned qualitative research. The chapter concludes with the important issue of how to evaluate qualitative research.

The second chapter introduces you to the main tools for data collection, transcription and preliminary data analysis – the analysis you undertake while you collect your data. The four most common analytic approaches are then discussed and the range of methodologies currently available for you to choose amongst is displayed. The third chapter deals with one of the newer trends in research: the mixing of qualitative and quantitative approaches, termed multiple or mixed methods.

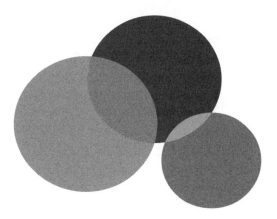

ONE

Introduction

When you undertake a qualitative research study, there are a number of prior aspects that will need addressing: your proposed topic area, is it suitable for the collection of qualitative data?; then yourself, what impact will your prejudices have on the research and how will you treat your potential readers?; and finally, which paradigm would best fit your research question: Realism/postpositivism, Critical theory, Interpretivism/Constructionism, Postmodernism, Poststructuralism or Mixed/multiple methods? Then, having dealt with these decisions, it is always useful to know how to evaluate a piece of qualitative research in order to ensure that your design ticks all the right boxes.

KEY POINTS

- The characteristics of qualitative research
- The best topic areas for qualitative research investigations
- Issues you need to think about prior to commencing research
- Research paradigms
- How to evaluate qualitative research

Introduction

Qualitative research is a fascinating topic. It provides detailed information and can progress knowledge in a variety of areas: it can help assess the impact of policies on a population; it can give insight into people's individual experiences; it can help evaluate service provision; and it can enable the exploration of little-known behaviours, attitudes and values.

Knowledge is a key term here. This can take a variety of forms, and in most cultures there are various claims to knowledge:

1 The first is *tenacity* – this refers to a belief that has been held for a long time, for example doing good to others is viewed as the right thing to do because eventually this good will be reflected back to you; there may be no evidence to prove this is true but we still tenaciously claim that this is so.

2 *Intuition* or our gut feeling is another source of knowledge – for example, we may feel that in a particular situation X is the best thing to do or the right answer; there may again be very little evidence that this is so but if it feels right, we tend to follow that particular path.

3 *Authority* – in particular religious or legal authority provides directions for the way we ought to behave in order to lead a 'good' life … but good for whom? In addition, would another way be more beneficial to us as individuals or as part of a group?

Research tries to step back from knowledge claims developed through tenacity, intuition and authority, by carefully constructing a question and a study design in order to provide the best views of a particular issue so that conclusions can be derived from available evidence. Sometimes findings will challenge the other three sources leading to conflict; for example, when scientists said the earth was not flat but round there was a huge uproar as traditional beliefs about falling off the edge of the world were challenged.

In doing research we try to advance knowledge by aiming to get closer to the 'truth' of the matter while realising that truth is a very elusive concept, which shifts depending on whose truth is being portrayed and whether that 'truth' is:

- *Subjective* (your own view)
- *Relative* (your view compared to others)
- *Objective* (taking a distant perspective)
- *Absolute* (as in philosophical arguments).

So rather than getting too caught up in the notion of 'truth' and the bases of various claims to knowledge in research, instead we seek to reduce uncertainty by using the best and most transparent approaches available.

There are two important aspects to any kind of research: the first is that your data should be collected from the real world … from situations or people involved in whatever the defined research problem is. This real world evidence is termed *empirical* data. Understanding the nature of this data is an *ontological* process and is related particularly to the wider structural and cultural issues that influence claims to truth. Then these understandings need to be further interpreted in a more abstract way using existing theories of knowledge—*epistemology* – to explain your findings about the world and to enable your interpretations to be more globally applied. For example, I might research the experience of being blind by interviewing people who are blind (empirical data). Understanding their experiences would require knowledge of the culture and the health system and other supports available for these people (ontological) while interpreting their experiences might lead me to use the concepts of stigma or normal versus abnormal (epistemology) to make sense of their experiences.

What are the characteristics of qualitative research?

Qualitative research favours certain styles of design, collection and analytic interpretation. The underpinning ideology or belief system asserts that:

- *subjectivity* has value (meaning that both the views of the participant and those of you the researcher are to be respected, acknowledged and incorporated as data, and the interpretation of this data will be constructed by both of you (the researcher is not a distant neutral being)

- *validity* (trustworthiness) is seen as getting to the truth of the matter, *reliability* (dependability) is viewed as a sound research design and *generalisability* is local and conceptual only
- *power* lies predominantly with the researched (who are viewed as being the experts on the research topic)
- *an holistic view* is essential (so the structures impacting on the setting such as policies, culture, situation and context need to be included)
- every study is *time- and context-bound* (so that replication and generalisation are unlikely outcomes).

Which areas are best for researching?

Qualitative research can best help us explore or assess:

- culture
- phenomena
- structural processes
- historical changes.

In more detail, *culture* could involve anything from investigating the behaviours and rituals of a particular tribe or group of people in a particular setting (street kids, pupils or staff in a classroom, patients or clinicians in a hospital ward or an individual in a particular cultural context). *Phenomena* involves detailed investigations over time of a particular experience (for example, marriage breakdown, illness etc.). *Structural processes* might involve investigating policy change and its impact on a specified setting or group (such as increasing taxes or closure of mental institutions). And *historical changes* might involve documented changes in discourses (ways of communicating over time; for example, changes in treatment of an illness as recorded in medical journal articles).

The question focus is usually the *what, how, when, where* or *why* aspects of the chosen topic.

One important issue the qualitative researcher needs to consider prior to commencing research is the choice of research paradigm to work within.

Research paradigms

As researcher, you can choose which of the available broad paradigms (worldviews of beliefs, values, and methods for collecting and interpreting data) that you would prefer to work within.

There are five options:

1 *Realism/postpositivism* (expert researcher documenting reality from a centred position).
2 *Critical theory* (with a focus on class, power and the location and amelioration of oppression).
3 *Interpretivism/Constructionism* (mutual recognition and use of symbols and signs in reality construction).
4 *Postmodernism and poststructuralism* (the questioning of 'truth' and 'reality' and the sources of 'knowledge').
5 *Mixed/multiple methods* (using the best set of tools for the job).

Let us explore each of these in a little more detail.

1. Positivism to realism (postpositivism)

The eighteenth century in Europe was an era, termed the Enlightenment, when positivism (the School of Philosophy that asserts that reality lies only in things that can be seen with the naked eye), optimism, reason and progress became the dominant discourses (ways of thinking, speaking and writing) and all knowledge was believed to be accessible through processes of reason. The 'rational man' was believed to have the capacity to uncover a singular knowable reality through pure understanding and rigorous intellectual reasoning. These processes of broader reason, needed to gain knowledge, included a focus on observation in order to gain 'facts' via scientific deduction. Scientific knowledge gained from observation and based in logical thought processes was seen as having the potential to displace ignorance and superstition, which were the tools of power of the church. Scientific knowledge was seen as having the capacity to facilitate freedom from religious influences and to lead the way to a New World built on the notions of progress and a universal foundation of knowledge.

However, researchers' ability to provide predictable and replicable outcomes and to control variables came under debate as Einstein's theory of relativity and later Heisenberg's theory of uncertainty challenged these views and postpositivism eventuated ... The assumption that a world that could be precisely measured and documented exists independently just waiting for us to gain sufficiently sophisticated tools to discover it, was questioned, and the belief that absolute, knowable truth existed became sidelined and provisional truths became a more likely outcome. The ultimate essence of external reality was also challenged by Sigmund Freud's exploration ([1900]1913) of the unconscious mind as a source of reality construction. He suggested that 'reality' was not only constructed from internal as well as external sources but that this reality changed continually in interaction with the environment, especially in interaction with others, and that what had previously been considered as externally and objectively 'real' was also closely linked to the maintenance of power.

More recently within *postpositivism* it has been argued that scientists are inherently biased by their education and life experiences and that their observations are value-laden and fallible, making errors likely. Our ability to know reality with certainty is thus problematic and no findings can be viewed as absolute or universally generalisable. This has led some positivists to the modified epistemology of realism. *Realism* asserts that structures creating the world cannot always be directly observed and when and if they are observable their genesis is not always clear; thus we also need our creative minds to clarify their existence and then to identify explanatory mechanisms. For example, we cannot see gravity but we know it exists and that it requires a mixture of intuition, various intellectual processes, and the laws of physics in order to clarify the workings of this force. The focus for research in a realist approach involves the identification of the linking of different realisms, for example in nursing, the biological and psychosocial models of nursing can be linked to a biopsychosocial model that has bridging links to interpretations of biological mechanisms and to the psychosocial empirical world as well as to patients' and researchers' influences on these.

Types of research In terms of qualitative research, both postpositivism and realism draw from positivism in that the researcher is seen as occupying a pseudo-objective distant neutral role where their influence in the construction of reality is seen as minimal.

Classical ethnography (see Chapter 4) and Straussian grounded theory (see Chapter 7) are sometimes seen as fitting in to this orientation. Careful description, truthful depiction, studies with clear aims, objectives, a reliable design, a focus on neutrality, objectivity and theory-testing characterise these approaches.

2. Critical emancipatory positions

Changes in the economic system through industrialisation around the turn of the twentieth century led to Karl Marx's critique ([1867]1999) of capitalist exploitation, profit, power and class conflict, being recognised. The outcomes of such economic change became viewed as resulting in societal fragmentation. During the 1960s and 1970s social critics such as feminists identified power imbalances and pointed to the long-term oppression of women by men, while others pointed to inequalities in social justice. Reality was now being viewed as power directed and multiply constructed. The origins of 'truth' were seen as lying in obscure history and/or layered aspects of the present and access required a range of approaches including those beyond the scientific. The simplicity of such notions as the integration of the individual, the power of the author, the universality of knowledge and concepts of uniqueness and originality, came under question.

Types of research In research, critical positions view reality not as existing 'out there' but as being produced by particular exploitative social and political systems comprising competing interests where knowledge is controlled to serve those in power. Issues of race, gender, poverty, politics and culture are seen to shape individual identity. Researchers attempt to identify those who are powerless (usually exploited by those in powerful positions) in order to document their unequal situation and to bring about change through an active process of emancipation through knowledge-sharing or the transformation of society. Any qualitative approach that has taken a critical stance, including grounded theory, phenomenology, ethnography, hermeneutics, sociolinguistics, narratives, and feminist research (see later chapters for these) can fit into the critical emancipatory grouping.

3. Constructionism/Interpretivism

These positions assume that there is no objective knowledge independent of thinking. Reality is viewed as socially and societally embedded and existing within the mind. This reality is fluid and changing, and knowledge is constructed jointly in interaction by the researcher and the researched through consensus. Knowledge is subjective, constructed and based on the shared signs and symbols that are recognised by members of a culture. Multiple realities are presumed, with different people experiencing these differently. The research focus is on exploration of the way people interpret and make sense of their experiences in the worlds in which they live and how the contexts of events and situations and the placement of these within wider social environments have impacted on constructed understandings. The understandings researchers construct and impose through interpretation are seen as limited by: the frames derived from their own life experiences; subjectivity (the researcher's own views and how they have been constructed); and intersubjectivity (reconstruction of views through interaction with others through language and written texts).

Types of research   Qualitative methodologies including grounded theory, phenomenology, ethnomethodology, ethnography, hermeneutics, sociocultural narratives, and feminist research (see Chapters 4–20 for more on these approaches).

4. Postmodernism and poststructuralism

As we moved through the last decades of the twentieth century, unified, powerful, centred individuals with an authoritative point of view became rejected in favour of anti-heroes and complex multidimensional individuals (see Chapters 9 and 14 for more detailed explanations of postmodernist ideas and applications). Literature began to mirror the changes in the economy, science, art and architecture by portraying reality as shifting and uncertain rather than set, and by incorporating multiple perspectives from a range of disciplines such as music, philosophy, psychology, sociology and drama as well as including visual possibilities.

Postmodernism views the world as complex and chaotic and reality as multiply constructed and transitional – unable to be explained solely by grand or meta narratives (such as Marxism and Buddhism, which make universal claims to truth). Postmodernism is very sceptical of such narratives, viewing them as containing power-laden discourses developed specifically for the maintenance of dominant ideas or to enhance the power of certain individuals. The search for reality 'out there' is qualified by the understanding that society, laws, policies, language, discipline borders, data collection and interpretation are culturally and socially constructed. In recognition of this socially constructed world, disruption, challenge and a multiplicity of forms are essential in order to pull these constructions apart and to expose them for what they are. Meaning rather than knowledge is sought because knowledge is limited by 'desire' (lack of knowledge or the imperative to bring about change) and constrained by the discourses developed to protect powerful interests and to control the population's access to other explanations. Truth is multifaceted and subjectivity is paramount.

Poststructuralism, with its emphasis on the fluidity of language and meaning, forms an important subset of postmodernism. It developed as a reaction to structuralism, which sought to describe the world in terms of systems of centralised logic and formal structures. In structuralism, patterns provided meaning and all words were seen as having recognised meanings that could be learned. Language was seen as a system of signs and codes, rules and conventions – and the deep structures that enable a language to operate within a cultural system – were sought. Poststructuralism (see Chapter 14) seeks the deconstruction of the discourses (ways of thinking, speaking and writing) that have been established to control ways of thinking.

Types of research   Most forms of qualitative research now have an established postmodern position: for example, ethnography, grounded theory, action, evaluation research, phenomenology and feminist research. Postmodernism favours descriptive and individually interpreted mini-narratives, which provide explanations for small-scale situations located within particular contexts where no pretensions of abstract theory, universality, or generalisability are involved. Within structuralism and poststructuralism two data analytic approaches have become popular and are available for use by qualitative researchers. The first is discourse analysis, where the dominant ways of writing and speaking about a particular topic become set in place over time and require historical tracking back to identify who has benefited from one particular discourse and how other competing discourses have been marginalised. The second analytic approach is deconstruction, where words are viewed as containing power-laden discourses with multiple meanings requiring careful deconstruction in order to break down artificially constructed boundaries before putting the text back together in transitional form.

5. Mixed/Multiple methods

This is the most recent approach and follows postmodernism's exhortation to cross barriers and to break down boundaries. The two approaches, qualitative and quantitative – for decades seen as poles apart – have now become integrated into mixed/multiple method studies (sometimes called the third wave/third movement). In this situation, they are seen less as two approaches ideologically poles apart and more as an eclectic set of tools which you the researcher – very like the bricoleur (creative handyman) of postmodernism – can use to provide the best answers to your research question. Clearly the issues involved in utilising these very different approaches can be somewhat thorny but this has not prevented researchers from tackling these issues head on and providing ways of dealing with them. The changes in classical physics which provide the underpinning for quantitative approaches, particularly the movement into chaos and complexity theory, have reflected many of the postmodern thought changes seen in qualitative research (Grbich, 2004) and these changes may have facilitated this cooperation. The ensuing paradigm has often become termed 'pragmatism' – a mix of postpositivism and social constructivism, a leaning toward postmodernism, and an emphasis on empirical knowledge, action, triangulation and the changing interaction between the organism and its environments (see Chapter 3 for more detail regarding mixed methods).

Example of paradigm choice

Let us take a research topic, *'An exploration of the lives of young people who are homeless'*, and see how your position as a researcher would differ in each of the above five paradigms:

- *Realism/postpositivism* (expert researcher documenting reality from a centred position). Here an authoritative researcher would assume that truth can be found by gathering detailed accurate observational and interview data of the lives of young people living on the street.
- *Critical theory* (with its focus on class, power and the location and amelioration of oppression). Here the interpretation of the data you collect would focus on power – where does it lie? And the assumption would be that the structures of society (education, health and the socioeconomic influences of the culture) would be determining aspects for a situation where young people became homeless. Action research – working with the homeless to bring about change – might be an outcome.
- *Interpretivism/Constructionism* (mutual recognition and use of symbols and signs in reality construction). Both the aspects of individual choice and lack of choice would be taken into account here as each individual case is explored by you in conjunction with a homeless person.
- *Postmodernism and poststructuralism* (the questioning of 'truth' and 'reality' and the sources of 'knowledge'). Previous explanations would be rigorously questioned and the discourses of

'homelessness', 'begging', 'mental illness' etc. examined and deconstructed. Your assumption would be that the reasons young people are homeless are individual, complex and always changing and no one solution will fit all.

- *Mixed/Multiple methods.* Both qualitative and quantitative data will be needed to see broader aspects of individual circumstances within policy, practice and the views of the wider community.

Evaluation of qualitative research

How can we assess the quality of our qualitative research and that of others? The techniques by which quantitative research are evaluated are not appropriate but sets of guidelines for evaluating qualitative research have been suggested (Kitto et al., 2008) and these guidelines are detailed below seven headings to show the essentials that need to be accounted for in a good piece of qualitative research:

Clarification

- What is the research question/s?
- What are the aims of the research?
- What did the researcher seek to investigate?
- Does the research question reflect what has been investigated?
- Have the aims been translated into the design so that all of them have been accounted for?

Justification

- Why is a qualitative approach the best option to answer this question?
- Why was the particular qualitative research design chosen?
- Why was the study undertaken the way it was? Are the questions, aims and design a perfect match?
- Were any forms of data triangulation evident? For example, multiple sources, i.e., documents, interviews, survey data, observation; multiple methods, i.e., mixing methodologies such as ethnography and phenomenology; and multiple theories, where multiple theoretical and conceptual frames have been applied to the research to enhance insights into phenomena.

Process

- Has ethics approval been obtained?
- Have the techniques of data collection been clearly documented?
- How were participants/settings accessed?
- What sampling techniques have been used to answer the research question?
- Who was interviewed/observed? How often? And for how long?
- What interview questions were asked?
- What was the purpose of any observation/s?
- Which existing documents were accessed? And how were they assessed?
- How was collected data managed?
- Are all the forms of data analysis completely transparent?
- What were the major outcomes of the analytical process in terms of findings?

In more detail, the exposure of what the researcher actually **did** needs to be very explicit.

- How were participants accessed?
- Who were these participants?

- How was rapport achieved?
- Were any sampling techniques used?
- What data collection techniques were used?
- How did interviews occur? Face to face? Telephone? Focus group? Teleconference? Video conference? Email? Skype?
- Who was observed? When? How often? For how long? For what purpose? What existing sets of documentation were collected?
- How was data managed?
- What forms of data analysis were undertaken – transparency of process is essential here.

Representativeness

Notions of comprehensiveness and diversify of results is sought in qualitative research in preference to conformity and homogeneity. An audit trail, monitoring changes and decisions taken in the project, should be recorded in the researcher's diary and made transparent where applicable. In addition:

- Have all the results been reported? Display of results is one aspect of this, and hypertexts to the original data set so the reader can see where your quotes have come from is becoming common.
- Has a holistic answer to the research question been achieved?

Interpretation

Has a conceptual discussion of the results and linkage to existing theory/new theory/models of practice been developed to explain the relevance of findings to a targeted audience or discipline?

Reflexivity

- Has a clear statement of the impact of the researcher's views upon the data and the methods chosen been included?
- How has researcher position and perspectives shaped the vision, slanted the design and questions and affected the interpretation of results? Has the researcher changed previous views on this topic? And has the researcher provided a critique of her/his self in the research process regarding their own history, culture, class, experiences and level of empathy?

Diversity of process, capacity to connect and intertextuality (connections with other relevant sources of influence) as well as the researcher's own epistemological positioning and ongoing response to research outcomes, should also be evident.

Transferability

- Has a critical evaluation of the application of findings to other similar contexts been made?
- How do results match/contradict others on this topic?
- Has the relevance of these findings to current knowledge, policy, and practice or to current research been discussed?
- To what extent are findings applicable to other similar settings, situations and experiences? And to what extent has this study successfully contributed to knowledge?

Newer ethnographic approaches

The newer ethnographic practices (documented in Chapters 10–13) are very challenging to evaluate, assess and/or review as few established criteria exist. The simplest assessment would be a personal one:

- Do you feel that you as the reader have been brought as close as is possible to the voice or images perceived or heard by the researcher?
- **OR,** Do you feel you have been led into a mish-mash or collage of bits and pieces so that you are no closer to experiencing the feelings and emotions of others than you would reading a dry academic text centred wholly in the authoritative voice of the researcher?

Researcher position

Subjectivity is crucial here.

- What have been the experiences of the researcher? Exposure of who the author actually is (past influences, beliefs, values and experiences as well as their responses in all situations) should be available.
- Has the researcher been highly involved as a participant in his/her own right or what has been her/his position?
- How close to the participants' view, voices, emotions and feelings is the display of data and how much 'shaping' (changing or manipulating) has the researcher been involved in?

Process

If the design involved small-scale mini-narratives where *reality* is seen as multiply constructed, multiple methods (both qualitative and quantitative) are often needed to present a holistic view of any situation or experience. *Juxtaposition* will often be called upon to identify voices/perspectives that have previously been marginalised or silenced by powerful discourses. The emphasis will be on the *complexity* of both situations and language – in particular via double coding, irony, paradox, the longevity of particular discourses, discursive practices and deconstruction. The seeking of *multifaceted realities* and the exposure of complex individuals with past lives as well as current issues and experiences, is desirable. There is no assumption of universality or generalisability or even transferability of any findings – these are seen as localised and transitory

Truth – has this been viewed as a complex constructed entity? If so, many voices and many approaches may be required to expose it. Language, discourse and discursive practices obscure truth and need tracking to enable new but transitory representations to emerge. If truth is sought through one individual then the multifaceted nature of that individual is important to demonstrate rather than the display of one simple dimension.

The reader

Has the reader been allowed to interpret data rather than have it interpreted for him/herself by the researcher? The role of the researcher is to take the reader as close to the experiences under study as possible with minimal or no researcher interpretation so the reader can share these experiences.

In addition, the theory of constraints (Agar, 2004: 22–3 adapted) can also be applied to assessing the outputs from the approaches described in Chapters 10–13:

1 *The 'dialogue' consideration.* Is dialogue between the researcher, the participants and the audience facilitated?
2 *The 'scaling' consideration.* Do individual stories promote a broader view of society for the audience?
3 *The 'recognition' consideration.* Is the representation sufficiently 'realistic' so that audiences will recognise themselves in it?
4 *The 'appeal' consideration.* Are the audiences attracted to the style of presentation, narratives and issues?

You can see from this that the assessment of qualitative research is a complex process but general guidelines can be applied to both traditional and to newer approaches. These guidelines need to be flexible in the way they are interpreted so they don't become set in concrete – they need to retain the capacity to encompass and reflect the ongoing changes that are an intrinsic part of qualitative research.

Summary

The paradigms of positivism, postpositivism and realism, critical theory, constructivism/interpretivism, postmodernism and poststructuralism, and mixed/multiple methods provide a complex field for you to navigate. Although each epistemology has achieved dominance at particular times, all are available for you to consider for your own studies. You need to choose the one that best reflects your research question and preferred orientation or you can choose to blend different traditions. In both cases, you will need to be familiar with the traditions on offer so you can adequately justify and evaluate the choices you have made.

Student exercise

You have been asked to evaluate a community phone-in support programme that provides counselling for people facing various crises. It has been funded by the government which is interested to know how useful the programme has been and whether to continue financing it.

Which paradigm would you choose within which to undertake this research and why?

Please visit the companion website **www.sagepub.co.uk/grbich2** for possible answers.

Further reading

Paradigms

Denzin, N. and Lincoln, Y. (eds) (2008) *The Landscape of Qualitative Research: Theories and Issues* (3rd edn). Thousand Oaks, CA: Sage. Part II looks at competing epistemologies (positivist, postpositivist, constructivist, critical theory) as well as specific interpretive perspectives, feminisms, racial discourses, cultural studies, sexualities, and queer theory.

Crotty, M. (1998) *The Foundations of Social Research: Meaning and Perspective in the Research Process.* Sydney: Allen and Unwin. A detailed and accessible discussion of positivism, constructivism, interpretivism, herme-neutics, feminism, critical inquiry and postmodernism is provided here.

Guba, E. and Lincoln, Y. (1994). Competing paradigms in qualitative research. In N.K. Denzin and Y.S. Lincoln (eds), *Handbook of Qualitative Research.* Thousand Oaks, CA: Sage. The chapter by Guba and Lincoln exam-ines various knowledge traditions that are relevant to qualitative research.

Mixed methods

Piano Clark, V. and Creswell, J. (2010) *Designing and Conducting Mixed Methods Research.* Thousand Oaks, CA: Sage. A very accessible how-to text, which also discusses many of the complexities involved in combining methods.

Tashakori, A. and Teddlie, C. (2010) *Sage Handbook of Mixed Methods in Social and Behavioural Research.* Thousand Oaks, CA: Sage. The authors discuss paradigmatic issues, the strengths and weaknesses of mixed methods designs, and provide specific examples as well as demonstrate how to teach and perform collabora-tive research using a mixed methods research design.

Evaluation

Goffman, E. (1974) *Frame Analysis: An Essay on the Organisation of Experience.* New York: Harper and Row. Goffman's book explores the concept of the framing of experience by individuals.

Kitto, S., Chesters, J. and Grbich, C. (2008) Quality in qualitative research: criteria for authors and assessors in the submission and assessment of qualitative research articles for the Medical Journal of Australia. *Medical Journal of Australia,* January 188 (4): 243–6.

MacLaren, G. and Reid, I. (1994) *Framing and Interpretation.* Melbourne: Melbourne University Press. McLaren and Reid show how the different levels of framing influences can impact on researcher interpretation of incidents and events.

References

Agar, M. (2004) We have met the other and we're all nonlinear: ethnography as a nonlinear dynamic system. *Complexity,* 10 (2): 16–24.

Freud, S. ([1900]1913) *The Interpretation of Dreams.* Trans. A. Brill. New York: Macmillan.

Grbich, C. (2004) *New Approaches in Social Research.* London: Sage.

Kitto, S., Chesters, J. and Grbich, C. (2008) Quality in qualitative research: criteria for authors and assessors in the submission and assessment of qualitative research articles for the Medical Journal of Australia. *Medical Journal of Australia,* January 188 (4): 243–6.

Marx, K. and Engels, F. ([1867]1999) *Das Kapital.* Washington, DC: Regnery Publishing.

TWO

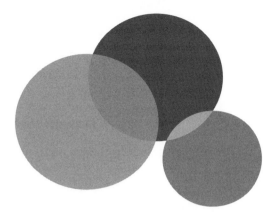

Design methodologies, data management and analytical approaches

In this chapter, the major analytic traditions of qualitative inquiry: iterative; subjective; investigative and enumerative will be discussed and linked to current design methods. How to manage your data and how to undertake preliminary data analysis will also be addressed in some detail.

KEY POINTS

- What constitutes data in qualitative research
- Design methodologies
- Traditions of inquiry and analytic approaches
  - iterative
  - subjective
  - investigative
  - enumerative
- How to match the analytical approach to the data type
- How to prepare data for analysis
  - transcription
  - preliminary data analysis

What can constitute data in qualitative research?

The major data types lie in:

- Face-to-face/telephone interview
- Email and internet interviews
- Focus groups (audio and video)
- Nominal groups
- Delphi groups
- Observation notes, video, webcam, film, photos
- Document collation (existing textual, aural and visual)

Document collation can include information from newspapers, radios, TV, DVD, films, videos, internet chat rooms, policy documents, clinical case histories, photos, drawings, paintings, clothing, graffiti, books, emails and diaries: in short, any information that can shed light on your research question. Be creative and do not be afraid to introduce new data sources. The field is very flexible and finding the best answers for your research question should be your major priority.

Design methodologies

One of your tasks after you have determined your research question is to choose the most useful methodology – ways of collecting and treating your data. There are many methodological options to choose from or to combine in qualitative research designs. Table 2.1 provides a listing of the most commonly used approaches. Each methodology in this table generally comprises guidelines attached to a theoretical underpinning. Your role is to select one or several methodologies that will best help answer your research question. The first option, hermeneutic inquiry, provides the general underpinning for all qualitative research, but it can also be used on its own. It comes from Hans Gadamer's *Hermeneutic Circle* (1975), which relates to the curious researcher who goes out into the field with a question, gathers data in the best ways they can, returns to make sense of his/her findings then returns to the field. This process is repeated in a continuing spiral (iterative) until the research questions are satisfactorily answered and the part answers gathered in the field have produced a creative and meaningful whole.

The major methodological options (listed in Table 2.1) are not static, they provide a feast of continual change.

Table 2.1   Common qualitative methodologies within specific paradigms

Realist/critical paradigm	Interpretivist/Constructivist paradigm	Postmodern (pm)/ poststructuralist (ps) paradigm
	Hermeneutic circle (Gadamer)	
Grounded theory (GT) (Strauss)	Grounded theory (Glaser)	Grounded theory pm
Ethnography: Classical/Critical	Critical	Ethnodrama/auto/cyber
Phenomenology (classical/realist/ transcendental)	Transcendental/heuristic/ hermeneutic	pm/ps
Feminist research (GT, Phenomenology)	Feminist research (Memory work)	pm/ps
Evaluation Summative	Formative	pm/ps
Action research	Participatory action	pm/ps

GENERAL APPROACHES

Traditions of inquiry and analytic approaches

Although certain methodological approaches favour particular analytic approaches, others call on different approaches depending on the research question and purpose. There are four major traditions of inquiry in terms of analytic process: *iterative, subjective, investigative* and *enumerative*. Within each of these fall general design types, which can be used flexibly; some design types occur in more than one tradition while combinations of design approaches and traditions of inquiry can also occur in the same study.

The following is a brief introduction to these four broad types of qualitative analytic approaches, the design of which will be described in greater detail in Chapters 4–20.

1. Iterative inquiry

Iterative/hermeneutic approaches involve seeking meaning and developing interpretive explanations through processes of feedback. This involves a series of actions: defining the question, going out to the field, examining the data collected, adjusting the question/sampling approach/design aspect/data collection tools in light of emerging issues and current literature, subjecting this data to a critically reflective process of preliminary data analysis (see later this chapter) to determine 'what is going on' in order to build up a picture of the data and going back to the field to find out more. These processes are repeated until the accumulated findings indicate that nothing new is likely to emerge and that the research question has been answered. There is recognition within this process that both you and those whom you are researching construct meaning together, and that you will attempt to minimise both your impact on the setting and possible over-interpretation of the situation, in favour of highlighting the views of those researched. Post data collection, thematic analysis often occurs (see Chapter 5). This is a process whereby data is segregated, grouped, regrouped and re-linked in order to consolidate meaning and explanation prior to display. Iterative approaches include the basic hermeneutic approach as well as more defined approaches such as grounded theory, phenomenology, ethnography, oral history, action, evaluation, sociocultural narratives, feminist versions of all of the above, and memory work.

2. Subjective inquiry

Subjective approaches are defined as those where there is a focus on you the researcher and on what takes place within your own thoughts and actions in a specified context. The focus is the collation of your own emotions and experiences. Here you will need to maintain a detailed and critically reflective diary record and be prepared to subject yourself to regular periods of debriefing with a colleague or supervisor. When your experiences are the sole or partial target of the research, you occupy a dual role – that of researcher and researched. Preliminary data analysis is again a key analytic technique, with thematic analysis being a further option depending on how much decontextualising and segmenting you regard as appropriate or desirable. Subjective approaches include: autoethnography, heuristic phenomenology and some postmodern versions of ethnography, grounded theory, feminist, evaluation and action research, where the researcher has chosen to include a significant segment of subjective data.

3. Investigative (semiotic) inquiry

Investigative semiotic approaches involve the uncovering of information relating to languages within cultural contexts. The understanding of signs and symbols is central to this approach, in particular their mythical strength and the embedded power of particular discourses which you will need to disentangle to reveal the original elements as well as to identify arguments that have been marginalised. There is considerable variety amongst the continuum of possibilities relating to analysis of documentation, visuals and body language, varying from the looser ethnographic content analysis approach, which attempts to contextualise the document and to identify and describe the values and attitudes evident, to the precision of some forms of discourse and semiotic analysis, which focus on grammatical structure. But again, the flexibility and the ever-changing nature of qualitative approaches allow you considerable variation, especially when you provide adequate justification. Investigative approaches include: structuralist, poststructuralist, content analysis, feminist research, as well as discourse analysis, conversational analysis and narratives of the sociolinguistic type.

4. Enumerative inquiry

This involves the listing or classifying of items by percentages, frequencies, ranked order, or whatever is useful to the research question. These approaches involve you in the production of 'objective' accounts of the content of verbal, written, or visual texts, the development of codes and categories often prior to analysis, and the definition and measurement of units of analysis. Flow charts, logical reasoning processes, the seeking of links between antecedents and outcomes through identification of ordered (ranked) word frequency, key words in context and incidence counting. The development of previously decided codes can also be seen in the imposition of 'matrixes' (conceptual frames of interlinking variables from which propositions with causal implications have been derived) where you apply this to one case and then further apply it to other cases to develop cross-case analysis. There is an underlying assumption in this process that fully predesigned instrumentation will enhance validity and generalisability. Enumerative approaches are often questioned in qualitative research because of their tendency to atomise and decontextualise the data and the fact that connection does not necessarily equal causation. Approaches include transcendental realism, quasi-statistical and matrix analyses.

These four traditions can be summarised as shown in Table 2.2.

Which analytical approach for which data type?

One of the more difficult areas to grasp is which type of analysis to use with which type of data. The key here is to look at the type of data and be prepared to justify what you are doing and why. However, there are guidelines. If you choose a particular method, such as those in the *iterative/subjective* columns in Table 2.2 it is anticipated that you will be collecting data mostly through interview/observation of others or the self and therefore

Table 2.2 Traditions of design and analytic inquiry

Iterative (hermeneutic)	Subjective	Investigative (semiotic)	Enumerative
Grounded theory	Autoethnographic	**Structural**	Quasi-statistical
Phenomenology Classical/ transcendental	Heuristic phenomenology	**Poststructural**	Transcendental realism
Ethnography	Postmodern versions of iterative approaches	**Discourse analysis**	Matrix analysis
Oral history		**Content analysis**	
Action evaluation		**Conversation analysis**	
Feminist research and memory work	Feminist research		
Narratives – sociocultural		**Narratives – sociolinguistic**	

the dynamics of *interaction* (including your contribution and influence) will impact in questions, sampling, attitude and the nuances of verbal and non-verbal communication. In this situation, you are expected to recognise your contribution AND you are also expected to avoid *imposing* a frame/matrix/set of codes (see Chapter 21) on your data because you want the data to speak for itself initially – so, do not force the data into predefined categories/codes/themes. The analytic approaches you would be expected to consider here would be preliminary data analysis (see below) and thematic analysis (see Chapter 5).

If you are dealing with existing documentation (see Part 4) as in the *investigative and enumerative* approaches (above) then you can use any approach that helps you make sense of the data, including preliminary data analysis and thematic analysis. So, I hear you ask, if you can use any reasonable approach with already existing documentation, why can't you, for example, use content analysis or any other form of enumeration with your self-collected interviews? Well, there is nothing to stop you running these interviews through a content analysis computer package in order to discover the frequency of occurrence of particular words and even the use of these words within a limited defined context (several words on either side of the key word). But, this will not give you properly contextualised themes, and if this is all you do, you will be missing out on achieving the gold standard of qualitative research, which is the detailed analysis and presentation of rich in-depth information via emerging rather than imposed themes.

Summary

From what we have looked at so far in this chapter, you can see that there are a number of signposts along the research path which require your attention as a qualitative researcher before you move into actually conducting data analysis:

- making decisions regarding your research paradigm/s
- seeking the methodology/ies that will best answer your research question/s and the data sources that will provide you with the best information
- choosing the best analytic tradition to use for your completed data set.

Let us assume you have collected some interview/observational data. Now what?

How to prepare interview/observational data for analysis

There are two stages needed here:

- transcription of your data so you can undertake the next stage
- preliminary data analysis.

Transcription

Transcription involves getting the dialogue or narrative off the devices on which you have recorded it and into a document formatted so there is a clear researcher-defined column for notes, as seen below.

Transcription of interview

Researcher's notes

Q. Tony, now that you have been a male primary caregiver for a year how do you think others view you in this role?

A. It's the perception of the division between male and female roles that I find a key to most of the injustice I've encountered during this past year. When it comes to the crunch, most males prefer to be breadwinners; they see this as the more important role. This has also to do with money and title and status.

I remember when my wife graduated from Medical School, amongst the group she was part of, what struck me as odd even then was that the men all looked forward to their futures as doctors and that's natural enough, but there was never any question that they wouldn't work full time. Several were in stable relationships and their partners had started careers of their own. But none of the graduates male or female ever questioned who would stay home should they start a family. There was no question of whose career was expendable. As soon as they had children, both the wives of doctors and the female medical graduates would all give up work and retire to the house.

Source: Grbich, data set: Primary caregiver males

Preliminary data analysis

For many of the methodological qualitative designs (see Table 2.1) the initial analytic stage involves preliminary data analysis. Preliminary data analysis is an ongoing process that is undertaken every time data is collected. It involves a simple process of checking and tracking the data to see what is coming out of it, identifying areas that require follow up and actively questioning where the information collected is leading/should lead you, the researcher. It is a process of engagement with the text, not so much to critique it or to summarise what is emerging from it, but more to gain a deeper understanding of the values and meanings which lie therein.

Regardless of whether the data collected comes from written observations, transcriptions of interviews or the perusal of existing documents, you should undertake this process in order to highlight emerging issues, to allow all relevant data to be identified and to provide directions for seeking further data.

The process with regard to interview data is demonstrated below.

Interview segment of a transcript analysed using preliminary data analysis

Interview segment	Preliminary data analysis
Q. Tony, now that you have been a male primary caregiver for a year how do you think others view you in this role?	
A. Its the perception of the division between male and female roles that I find a key to most of the injustice I've encountered during this past year. When it comes to the crunch, most males prefer to be breadwinners; they see this as the more important role. This has also to do with money and title and status.	*Injustice* – what injustices has he experienced? *I need to check this aspect with him and with other participants.
	Do all men prefer to be breadwinners? *I need to check this with the group.
I remember when my wife graduated from Medical School, amongst the group she was part of what struck me as odd even then was that the men all looked forward to their futures as doctors and that's natural enough, but there was never any question that they wouldn't work full time. Several were in stable relationships and their partners had started careers of their own. But none of the graduates male or female ever questioned who would stay home should they start a family. There was no question of whose career was expendable. As soon as they had children, both the wives of doctors and the female medical graduates would all give up work and retire to the house.	This fits in with the societal view of the nurturing role of women. It also matches with Talcott Parsons's views of instrumental (male) and nurturing (female) societal roles.
	Did Tony have different earlier socialisation experiences than the others in order to want to be a father at home? *I need to follow up with him and the others about this
	*Note to self

There is some diversity within the literature as to how this process of preliminary data analysis might occur, but given that it is idiosyncratic, each researcher must decide what works for him or her. Examples of what other researchers do can be found in the book by Ian Dey (1993), who identified the techniques for early interactive reading of data segments as:

- free association – writing freely regarding words, phrases and topics in order to avoid and release fixed researcher assumptions;
- comparing interviews with own experiences; identifying aspects of the research map – the self, the situated activities, emergent meanings, understandings and definitions, identification of aspects impacting on the contextual setting as well as documenting interactions, history, events, strategies, process and consequences;
- shifting the focus among the levels of data to highlight other areas; reading the data in different sequences; critiquing the data – Who? What? Why? When? So what?
- transposing the data by asking 'What if?' in order to seek new perspectives.

Michele Bellavita (1997: 181) has a similar but looser approach. She allows herself to:

- go over the data segment initially, noting ideas and then trying to create names for chunks of data – listing topics, grouping them, noting exceptions and brainstorming;
- play with metaphors, analysing specific words and employing the 'flip flop' technique (looking at aspects from different perspectives, asking 'Why?' and 'What if?')
- attempt to re-present some of the data in the form of a poem or vignette which may form part of a later display of the overall database.

Face sheets

Each data set that has been transcribed and has undergone preliminary data analysis then requires some form of identification and of summary of this process, such as a face sheet. This is a cover sheet that is attached to the front of your data transcription and identifies the study question, time and place of interview/observation and summarises the main outcomes from your preliminary analysis. The face sheet from the above interview segment would then look like this:

Face sheet: interview with "Tony"

data identifiers

Research question: *How do men experience the role of primary caregiver?*

- Participant profile: age, status: "Tony" 42 years
- Interview/observation/document date: 24/04/07; Interview 2
- Time: 10am – 12.45pm
- Place of interview: Tony's home
- Comments: Daughter Chrissy, 18 months, was present for the first hour before being put to bed

---

Issues emerging from the interview that need to be followed up by the researcher:

- Do all these men experience a sense of injustice?
- Does working part-time make a difference to perceptions of 'injustice'?
- Do all men prefer to be breadwinners?
- Do all women prefer the 'at home' role?
- Do some/all these men prefer the home role to the breadwinner role?
- Investigate the early socialisation of these men.

Summaries of issues emerging

You will find it helpful during data collection to start accumulating emerging issues into potential themes. You do this by summarising supportive data for a particular aspect every 3–5 sessions of interviewing or observation. The advantage of this is that by the end of data collection you will not only have completed the twin processes of preliminary data analysis and judicial summaries but you will be in a position to start interpreting and conceptualising your data.

Following the chapter on mixed methods, the group of Chapters 4–8 will investigate the iterative orientation with regard to specific methodologies that can be used within any of the realist/ critical/ interpretivist/constructivist/ postmodern/poststructural paradigms: namely ethnography, grounded theory, phenomenology and feminist approaches. The analytical tools most pertinent to the postmodern/poststructural traditions will be dealt with specifically in Chapters 9–13. The data dealt with in Chapters 4–13 will be predominantly gathered by the researcher through interview and observation, while Chapters 14–20 will deal with the analysis of documents and other data already in existence.

Student exercise: Preliminary data analysis

Here is a segment of an interview response to the question: 'What are your views on homelessness?'

Well I think it's a terrible thing that in a modern society we have a problem such as this. I don't know though what we can do about it. I want to do something but I don't know what. You are constantly reminded of the problem if you go to town. They are always there asking for money. You don't know though if they really need it or if they are in fact doing quite well from begging. But if you have any caring qualities you can't ignore requests for help, when you have so much yourself.

They say a lot of people choose to live on the streets – well I don't believe that. I think that is an easy thing for the authorities to say – it lets them off the hook. So really I guess the answer to your question is that I am not sure what to think about homelessness. I feel that something should be done but I feel powerless to do anything personally. I think that the time has come for the government to do something. It makes me feel very uncomfortable; I don't know what to do.

Please visit the companion website **www.sagepub.co.uk/grbich2** for possible answers.

Further reading

Qualitative methods

Hennink, M., Hutter, I. and Bailey, A (2011) *Qualitative Research Methods*. London: Sage. An accessible introduction, especially to the iterative approach.

Design and analysis

Denzin, N. and Lincoln, Y. (2011) *The Sage Handbook of Qualitative Research*. London: Sage. A good overall introduction to qualitative methods.

Grbich, C. (2009) *Qualitative Research in Health: An Introduction*. London: Sage. http://books.google.com/books?id=MeMB9wp0p5sC&pg=PA26&source=gbs_toc_r&cad=4#v=onepage&q&f=false (accessed 1 August 2011). A simple introduction to qualitative research.

References

Bellavita, M. (1997). In M. Ely, R. Vinz, M. Downing and M. Anzul (eds), *On Writing Qualitative Research: Living by Words*. London: FalmerRoutledge.

Dey, I. (1993) *Qualitative Data Analysis: A User-friendly Guide for Social Scientists*. London: Routledge.

Gadamer, H. (1975) Hermeneutic circle. *Philosophy & Social Criticism/Cultural Hermeneutics*, 2 (4): 307–16.

THREE

Incorporating data from multiple sources: mixing methods

The mix of qualitative and quantitative data in terms of design, management and presentation will be dealt with in this chapter. The advantage of utilising an innovative mix of data sources is that apart from providing a broader view of the research question, the combination of data allows the reader to view the phenomenon under study from different perspectives.

KEY POINTS

- The advantages of combining quantitative and qualitative data are that you can maximise the impact of both
- For mixed methods to be successful, issues of sampling, design, data analysis and data presentation need careful attention
- Two approaches to mixing methods regarding design are *concurrent* and *sequential*, but other new mixes are emerging
- Does qualitative data miss out in such a mix? And what is the next move?

A brief history of qualitative and quantitative approaches

If we go back in time there appear to be three stages of debate relating to quantitative and qualitative approaches:

1. 'Never the twain shall meet'

Up to the mid-1980s the two approaches were polarised. They were seen as deriving from completely different theoretical underpinnings with very different methods and quite separate orientations; one toward objectivity and the other toward subjectivity. The outcome of this was that people argued fiercely for the superior capacities of one camp or the other and combinations were almost never to be seen.

2. Rapprochement

During the late 1970s philosophical and other differences gave way to a closer examination of possible complementarities between the two approaches and a realisation that although different they could well enhance each other, particularly when run in parallel. This led to a rash of studies within the quantitative tradition where qualitative methods were used as an 'end-on' approach. That is, before developing survey questions a qualitative data set would be collected to identify the 'right' questions, or, after running a survey, some qualitative interviews would be carried out to clarify and expand on 'the reasons behind' some of the statistical results gained. The dangers here lay in oversimplifying the complexities of data analysis and the rigors of theoretical interpretation in the qualitative data set, in favour of a shallow identification of 'emerging issues' or 'recurring themes'.

3. Cooperation and mixing

During the past 25 years as the limitations of both quantitative (in terms of detail) and qualitative designs (in terms of numbers) were recognised and designs to incorporate both equally or as part of a range of mixed method approaches emerged – these ranged from a grab bag of supermarket-type selection of approaches to formal integration of quantitative and qualitative methods. Paradigmatically, postpositivists challenged positivists, and constructivists and critical theorists leapt into the ring, and when the dust settled it was agreed that different methods could be combined and in fact could even drive research under an encompassing but loose paradigm such as *pragmatism* or *transformative action*. Researchers from different fields seeking grant monies found it useful to develop a mixed methods design to enhance the breadth of exploration in a particular project.

What are the major differences between qualitative and quantitative?

Qualitative tends to be seen primarily as an inductive approach using a research question to move from instances gained in the data collection to some form of conclusion, often via comparison with existing concepts or theory. Questions tend to be exploratory and open-ended and data is often in narrative form. Reality is seen as a shifting feast, subjectivity is usually viewed as important and power is shared with the participants who are the experts on the matter under investigation. Analysis predominantly deals with meanings, descriptions, values and characteristics of people and things. The outcome sought is the development of explanatory concepts and models: appropriately theoretically underpinned, uniqueness is favoured and widespread generalisation (apart from logical generalisation – that is from similar instance to similar instance) is avoided.

In contrast *quantitative* is generally viewed as deductive, where the conclusions drawn follow logically from certain premises – usually rule based – which are themselves often viewed as proven, valid or 'true'. Reality is seen as static and measurable, objectivity (distance, neutrality) is important, linearity (cause–effect) may be sought, outcomes are the major focus and pre-specified/developed hypotheses will dictate questions and approach. Researcher control of the total process is paramount, precision and predictability are important and statistical approaches to identify numbers and to clarify relationships between variables will dominate data analysis. Theory testing is the key and generalisation and predictability are the desired outcomes, survey and experimental research being the main design options.

Advantages of combining quantitative and qualitative results

The advantages of a combined approach are:

- clarifying and answering more questions from different perspectives
- enhancing the validity of your findings
- increasing the capacity to cross-check one data set against another.

Other positive outcomes include:

- Providing the detail of individual experiences behind the statistics – the intensive/extensive view. So if, for example, 99% of survey respondents indicate that they are extremely dissatisfied with the resources offered to them by the government to support their role of carer then qualitative interviews can identify in detail what aspects of support the 1 per cent were satisfied with, as well as documenting the experiences of dissatisfaction of the remainder.
- Helping in the development of particular measures – to clarify in detail through the results of qualitative data what the major issues are and then to use the analysis of these responses to refine a survey questionnaire in order to gain more focused results from a larger sample. For example, in the restructuring of a department it would be sensible to find out from all members what they considered to be the positive aspects of the current organisation and what were considered to be barriers to productivity. This detailed information could be used to structure a questionnaire to suggest specific changes which might then be rated for feasibility.
- Tracking stages over time – a multi-staged approach can clarify, from different perspectives, how a situation is progressing. For example: an initial qualitative interview might pick up on the range of stressors faced as couples with children separate, following breakdown of relationships. Three months later an intervention might provide clarification of the long-term roles and responsibilities that each parent needs to take into account regarding their children's care. As well, the financial and emotional costs for each couple can then be calculated at a time which is less stressful than the initial separation period. At six months post separation, a survey could explore the current situation; for those who indicated that things were not working out as planned, further in-depth interviews could tease out their problems and seek solutions.

Philosophical integration of qualitative and quantitative approaches

There are two current options here:

- *Pragmatism* (Rossman and Wilson, 1985), whose origins lie in the works of Charles Peirce, William James and John Dewey. Pragmatism seeks ways through the polarised quantitative–qualitative debate to find practical solutions to the problem of differing ideologies and methodologies. The current movement in pragmatism rejects former polarised positions, focusing instead on the best way to answer a particular research question but with recognition of culture, context, individual experience, the constructed nature of reality, uncertainty, eclecticism, pluralism and the need for creative innovation of method. As well, pragmatism encompasses an instrumental view of theory which endorses the values of praxis, democracy, freedom, equality and progress, but also accepts that bifurcations, infinite loops and provisional truths can emerge within methodological design, analysis and interpretation (Burke Johnson and Onwuegbuzie, 2004). The advantages of pragmatism are that it places a major focus on the research question and that the methods become simply the best tools for providing the most comprehensive answer to the question; thus methods can become hybrid and creative to achieve this goal. The disadvantages are that some topics do not benefit from 'pragmatic' solutions and a focus on applied 'band aid'-style research outcomes with short-term solutions may benefit only a few participants.

- The *transformative paradigm* (Mertens, 2010), where the view is that:
  - multiple realities are shaped by cultural, social, economic and political influences
  - knowledge is historically and socially situated
  - issues of power between researcher and researched need to be explicitly addressed.

  The transformative ethical orientation comprises a strong human rights agenda within notions of beneficence and social justice – with the implication that all research must be for the betterment of humankind. Methods include multiple approaches, multiple methods, techniques and theories, which should provide the basis for action and social change.

Conducting mixed methods research: prior questions

Is your research question one for which mixed methods would be the best approach? If so, which design would be the best?

- A *mutual research* design (Armitage, 2007), involving acceptance that the two approaches come from completely different paradigms, celebrating their differences and keeping them separate within the design process – the 'separate but together' position? Or
- A *mixed methods* design? And if so:
  - At which points will mixing occur – design? analysis? interpretation?
  - What sampling approaches will you utilise from the probability and non-probability suite?
  - How are you going to manage data analysis? Here you can consider *quantitising* – converting qualitative data into quantitative data or *qualititising* – converting quantitative data into qualitative data.
  - To what degree will you qualitatively analyse quantitative data and vice versa?
  - How are you going to display your results – separately? integrated? consolidated?

Mixed method design

Various forms of labelling and terminology have been used for mixed method design: *synergy, integration, triangulation, concurrent, parallel, merging, sequential, exploratory* and *explanatory*. In terms of design, however, this has come down to two broad options: collecting quantitative and qualitative data at the same time, and intermingling sampling and analytical approaches to whatever degree is useful (*concurrent*); and collecting qualitative and quantitative data at different times for knowledge expansion while maintaining paradigmatically separate approaches to whatever degree is seen as useful (*sequential*). A third option, that of mixing concurrent and sequential or mixing named approaches, is also emerging.

1. Concurrent or parallel methods

Here you would consider using multiple reference points, where separate data sets are collected at the same time with the ultimate aim of merging the two data sets, either in a visual display such as a matrix by transforming the data (see quantitising and qualititising data in *crossover/mixed analyses* below) or in the final discussion. Designs might involve using dual sites with the same sampling approach but with different data (quantitative and qualitative) then using the synthesised results to build up a complex picture.

Research example   A concurrent approach can be seen in the study undertaken by Vicki Piano Clark et al. (2010) that examined how the alumni of a Graduate Fellows group, who worked in elementary/middle schools in their districts for 10 hours per week helping to address teachers' needs, perceived the impact of their participation. Data collection was via an online questionnaire with open- and close-ended questions (concurrent qualitative and quantitative data). Data was analysed separately: quantitative with SPSS for descriptive and inferential statistics and qualitative using open coding in MAXQDA (see Chapters 21 and 22). Three merging strategies were trialled in order to develop more precise strategies for researchers:

- *merging via data transformation* (using qualitative findings to develop a quantitative variable and comparing relationships with other variables and developing better variables from combining qualitative and quantitative findings)
- *merging with a matrix* (quantifying difference in qualitative findings, examining these, perusing differences in the quantitative results using a qualitative typology)
- *final discussion merging* (corroborating findings, developing a more complete picture, establishing divergence).

The researchers discovered that different merging approaches suited different research questions but that data transformation merged at data level, matrix at results level, and discussion at the interpretive level.

2. Sequential: explanatory/exploratory

You could undertake a qualitative study to *explore* a particular issue or phenomenon and using an iterative approach you could create hypotheses from these results which you could test using a survey or experimental design. Or, you could develop a short questionnaire survey to elicit key issues that can then be *explained* in depth using qualitative approaches of interviewing and observation. Synthesis of the two sets of results is needed to clarify the dual outcomes and to utilise the increased validity these two approaches provide.

You could also use the sequencing approach at a lower level within questionnaires to provide base data to enable movement into other data sets. For example, using both focused (limited response) quantitative and open-ended (qualitative) questions in a survey permits a more holistic view of the questions to be addressed and allows you to follow up responses:

e.g. Have you received any services from the government?   Yes/No

If Yes, could you name each service and describe your experiences of this service.

These descriptions can then be fleshed out further in a follow up face-to-face or telephone interview, the results of which can then be re-incorporated in a more focused follow up survey.

A typical *sequencing design* could involve:

Stage 1: Representative survey of the population.
Stage 2: Exploratory qualitative interviews or focus groups to tease out the findings of the survey.
Stage 3: Hypotheses generated from stages 1 and 2 are tested in various interventions which are then evaluated.
Stage 4: Participatory action research where the participants take control of the development, implementation and evaluation of the most successful of these interventions.

Research example: quant–qual and qual–quant-qual   Peter Davies and Bob Baulch (2011) used a sequential approach to explore poverty dynamics in rural Bangladesh in a longitudinal study. Already in existence was a rich set of historical data evaluating the short-term impact of microfinance projects, new agricultural technologies and education transfers. This data comprised a number of repeated quantitative surveys and qualitative focus groups and semi-structured interview data. This data was then further extended:

- *the first phase* involved collecting more qualitative focus group data to examine perceptions of change
- *the second phase* undertook a quantitative survey updating the historical surveys
- *the third phase* collected the qualitative life histories of 293 individuals selected from and nested within the quantitative sample to explore poverty transitions.

Comparing data analyses of the different data sets showed more transitions out of poverty in the quantitative than the life history data. This led to a number of queries regarding:

- per capita household expenditure not accurately reflecting economic wealth
- failure of expenditure base transition matrices to indicate how close to the poverty line expenditure actually was
- the cost of illnesses not being reflected in expenditure-based assessment
- changes in household size not being picked up as a factor in moving out of poverty
- recall errors occurring in qualitative data as people tried to remember past events.

In integrating the data, these data mismatches between qualitative and quantitative data were tabled, summarised and sequentially reduced via the application of various explanations. One set of mismatched data is shown in Figure 3.1.

Thus in using mixed data, both sets served to highlight the deficiencies of the other and to clarify weaknesses in poverty assessments.

Research example: qual–quant   Jeffrey Edmeades et al. (2010) used a sequential approach to identify the circumstances surrounding abortion in Madhya Pradesh, India. This study had two phases. The first involved the gathering of an initial qualitative data set (10 focus groups plus 17 key informant interviews plus 41 in-depth interviews using a 'storytelling' technique) to identify key social and cultural factors in the advent, experiences and resolution of unwanted pregnancies. The narrative patterns that emerged from analysis of this data were adhered to and used to shape the questions of the second stage, a subsequent

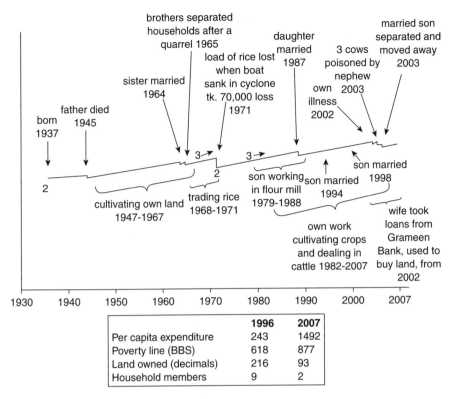

Figure 3.1 **Mismatch caused by diseconomies of scale (70-year-old man) (from Davies and Baulch, 2011, reproduced with permission)**

survey which was then more fluid and conversational than is usual. This sequential structure facilitated gathering information both on individual women and on individual pregnancies, producing high-quality survey data that countered the problem of previous research – that of the under-reporting of abortion providing a more in-depth understanding of these women's motivation for abortion and their problems with societal pressures and access to services, than had previously been available to researchers.

3. Combining concurrent and sequential approaches and other mixes

Concurrent plus sequential Formally putting these two approaches together is a recent innovation, although many researchers will have previously collected concurrent and sequential data within either the qualitative or quantitative traditions or will have moved sequentially among various concurrent data sets in developing and merging analytical procedures (Piano Clark et al., 2010). Donald Nicolson et al. (2011) examined the usability and readability of five patient-focused medication information websites that provided information on the same pharmaceutical drug. They combined concurrent data, which involved sitting with each of the 15 participants and observing their use and understanding of the sites. Participants were encouraged to 'think aloud' and Macromedia captivate – a computer program – recorded voice and monitored online activities. Sequential data (in the form of a post test semi-structured interview) gained participants' views on site accessibility immediately after usage. The researchers found analysing four sets of concurrent data to be demanding of time and energy, but the detailed data, although from only a small group of participants, provided sufficient information to develop evidence-based guidelines for the design and content of the five sites.

Mixing named brands   Some researchers have mixed specific rather than generic approaches. Elizabeth and Andrea Quinlan (2010) put together institutional ethnography and social network analysis to link one personal experience of rape with institutional and textual representations . Data comprised a medicolegal text (sexual assault evidence kit) and one woman's narrative experience – a well-publicised rape case in Canada that led to the writing of a book, *The Story of Jane Doe* (Doe, 2003). From thematic analysis of the narrative and the kit, a map was created using the software program Visualyzer in order to quantitise and simplify the qualitative data and display it via nodes to illustrate relationships between variables and between themes. This allowed the two views of rape to be mapped for comparison exposing the internal structures of both: personal experience is portrayed weblike above the line and the sexual assault evidence kit (hierarchical with no connection between themes) is shown below the line of fault (see Figure 3.2).

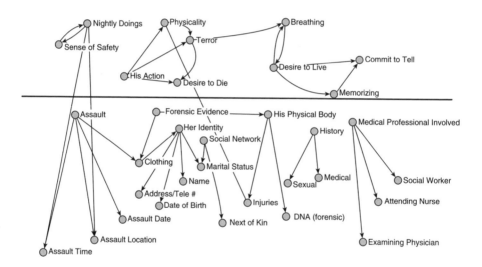

Figure 3.2   The line of fault (from Quinlan and Quinlan, 2010, reproduced with permission)

Issues to consider in attempting to combine data sets

- You need to be familiar with both quantitative and qualitative approaches.
- Mixing of paradigms, data collection, analysis and interpretation takes time and skills to do well.
- Combined designs are more expensive than single designs.
- Are there benefits to converting qualitative to quantitative data?

The main danger is that the time-consuming traditional methods of qualitative analysis may be bypassed or glossed over in favour of quicker but shallower approaches. This would lead to oversimplified results and to researcher-directed rather than data-derived results. Both the qualitative and quantitative data sets must be properly designed, collected and analysed. The quantitative data needs to be systematic with clearly defined variables and with a good sampling strategy to enable reliable predictions, while the qualitative data needs clarification of process, context and culture as well as detailed and rich data properly collected, analysed and interpreted using theory that serves to further illuminate results.

Questionnaires

The order of question type and the numbers of questionnaires may be important. Too much or too many may sensitise participants. In an attempt to ascertain the essential personal qualities of a computer educator, a three-phase sequential approach was used by Pieterse and Sonnekus (2003).

- First, a survey questionnaire was used to incorporate both quantitative and qualitative questions to build up a picture from a sample taken from one location.
- Then, during the second phase the qualitative aspects were integrated into the quantitative items to present a generic picture gained from the first phase and this was then presented to a national sample.
- In the third phase, quantitative findings were integrated into the qualitative questions in an online questionnaire for an international sample of IT Training Groups but with the additional option of a two-way email contact.

These researchers found that the difficulty in providing both qualitative and quantitative questions in the same survey, and in particular putting the closed questions earlier, was that the qualitative information did not appear to add very much in terms of new information, suggesting that the participants had become sensitised to the content and orientation of the earlier questions.

Design

One issue is that of *equality* in the weighting of the data – is the study more qualitatively or more quantitatively focused such that the second approach operates more as an add-on, or minor data set? And is this important in the answering of the research question? And what happens when one set of results contradicts the other? Can these differences be resolved by 'merging' and 'integrating' and if they can does this create more 'truth' or just more cleverly manipulated data?

The issues surrounding the definition and operationalisation of the term *'triangulation'* have been debated for the past 50 years and are still completely unresolved, so the re-imposition of this term in mixed methods does not paper the cracks nor does it give automatic validity to mixed methods (Denzin, 2010). *Validity* of findings has also been an issue and the development of the Instrument Development and Construct Validation (IDCV) tool (Onwuegbuzie et al., 2010) may help here. This is a 10-phase tool covering an interdisciplinary literature review, instrument development and evaluation, and construct validation process and product. Another tool, the Validity Framework (VF) (Leech et al., 2010), provides a five-element approach covering foundational elements and construct validity in qualitative, quantitative, mixed, inferential, historical and consequential data elements.

Crossover/mixed analysis

Crossover analysis involves the use of different lens' on qualitative and quantitative data sets using intersubjectivity, constructivist and postpositivist views, mixing 'objective' with 'multiple realities' perspectives and switching tools – for example using factor analysis on themes derived from qualitative data or a thematic analysis on themes arising from factor analysis, leading to sequential/concurrent mixed analytic approaches in order to expand perspective (Onwuegbuzie et al., 2010) and shifting cases to variables within a three-dimensional framework – case, variable and process/experience (Onwuegbuzie et al., 2007, 2009, 2010).

These authors suggest the following techniques for crossover analysis:

- reducing dimensionality of either data set (quantifying to basics)
- integrating data display (visual presentation of both sets as one)
- transforming data (qual to quant [numerical codes]) and quant to qual [themes]) for analysis
- correlating data (correlating results from quantitising and qualitising)
- consolidating data (merging multiple data sets to create new codes, variables etc.)
- comparing data (comparing findings)
- integrating data (integrating into one or two sets of data)
- using warranted assertion analysis (seeking meta-inferences from both sets)
- importing data (using follow up findings from qualitative to inform quantitative analysis and vice versa). (adapted from Onwuegbuzie et al., 2010: 58-9)

The main problem that arises here is that sampling and data collection have been done with a particular analytic approach in mind and therefore crossing over may be problematic in terms of usefulness. Thick data may (or may not) lend itself to variable analysis and thin closed-ended data may not be productive in terms of thick contextual description – the quantity and depth of information are simply not there.

Interpretation of results

Another issue is that of 'transformation', where the combining or homogenising of data requires a theoretical interpretation that includes both data sets when only one (qualitative) is usually treated in this manner – the other being viewed as 'fact' reflecting 'reality' to prove/disprove a hypothesis. The tendency has been for a low level conceptual interpretation to be undertaken but moves to include multiple frameworks can be seen (Nicolson et al., 2011).

Presentation of dual results

Separate data sets

Is it best to display each data set separately? The difficulties surrounding presentation of qualitative and quantitative approaches lie in their integration, which leads to a very large results section and requires regular summaries of data findings which will need to culminate in a final drawing together of the findings so that the reader can make sense of the diversity presented. An example of this is provided by Duncan and Edwards

(1997), who interviewed 95 lone mothers in three countries (UK, USA and Sweden) and contextualised these interviews within census data. The results are largely displayed in separate chapters (for example, a chapter on social negotiation of understandings followed by one on census data).

Combined data sets

In contrast to the separation of data sets, is it preferable to amalgamate the findings in such a way that a neat display of graphical information occurs, followed by a few carefully chosen qualitative quotes that serve to display the homogeneity (or diversity) of the data gathered? The use of matrixes can serve to bring together variables, themes and cases, as can lists, network diagrams and graphical displays. The totality of this approach may well be neater and more powerful in capturing the reader's attention through the different perspectives presented but it may also result in the complexity of the findings being 'dumbed down' and those findings that are not matched by the other data set somehow dropping off the radar screen. Wacjman and Martin (2002) studied managers in six companies. A questionnaire was completed by a random sample of 470 managers in the six companies together with interviews with 18–26 managers in each company. The data is equally presented, with the quantitative survey results displayed in an extensive single table and alongside this are the career narratives of 136 managers divided into male and female responses and presented as substantial quotes and commentary.

Multiple data sets

Currently the majority of data collected is still within the survey/interview/observation/document analysis framework, with the documents traditionally being written communications, but looking to the field of media images should alert us not only to their possibilities but also to what is being attempted in this field. Luciano Gamberini and Anna Spagnolli (2003) used both qualitative and quantitative data sets to bring together, under the heading of an exploration of human–computer interactions, digital, physical, real and artificial aspects, through three triangulated data sets.

- The first was the *split screen technique*, which allows a synchronised visualisation of different environments on the same screen, in this case the real and the virtual environments a participant is involved in on screen. In this way individual interaction with a computer can be seen on one half of the screen while the other half details the depth view of what is actually happening in the screen as controlled by the individual. This process can be undertaken by individual or multiple users by splitting the monitor into further blocks of two screen displays.
- The second option was the *action indicator augmented display*, which picks up the faster individual interactions with the computer interface, particularly quick hand movements on buttons which are reflected in arrows at the bottom of the screen.
- The third was the *pentagram*, which allows transcription of multiple sequences of events in its own timeline.

Qualitative discourse and interaction analysis were used to analyse these human computer interactions centring on the interactive sequences. Although these can be used as tools to come to a single conclusion they can also serve to provide individual or multi-media displays in their own right, allowing the reader to observe all the data collected and come to their own conclusions.

Summary and critique

Mixed quantitative and qualitative data sets have the capacity to broaden and enrich research questions using styles of synthesis, triangulation and integration. Presentation can be via separate, combined or multiple data set display. The issue you need to be most careful about in combining methods is that your qualitative data is well designed, appropriately collected, analysed and interpreted and not just a set of procedures to enhance a predominantly quantitative design. Norman Denzin (2010) has pointed to the problem of 'poaching' – the grabbing of 'qualitative' approaches (interview, case study, narrative) for the design enhancement of quantitative researchers (this process is often termed 'collaboration', 'consultation' or 'community involvement'). Such researchers have minimal training in qualitative research and this has led to a strong positivist orientation in the mixed methods field with endless quantification of qualitative results. Denzin has suggested that mixed methods is merely a station on the way to a newer paradigm, one a long way from evidence-based research and issues of theory and validity, involving multiple investigators with multiple competencies in multiple paradigms and a focus on multiple approaches, empowerment, social justice and action but recognising that all methods and paradigms are transitional hybrids (Denzin, 2009).

Student exercise

Take the topic of homeless young people and design

1   a concurrent and
2   a sequential

study design using mixed methods.

Please visit the companion website **www.sagepub.co.uk/grbich2** for possible answers.

Further reading
Methodological issues in mixing methods

Bergman, M. (2008) *Advances in Mixed Methods Research: Theories and Applications.* Thousand Oaks, CA: Sage. This edited book covers practical and methodological issues The use of mixed methods in sociology, education, politics, psychology, computational science and methodology is covered.

Qualitative Inquiry (2010) 16: 415 is a special issue on emerging methodologies in the field of mixed methods research.

Design of mixed methods studies

Creswell, J., Fetters, M. and Ivankova, N. (2004) Designing a mixed methods study in primary care. *Annals of Family Medicine,* 2: 7–12. This article evaluates five mixed methods studies in primary care and develops three models for designing such investigations. The authors recommend instrument-building, triangulation and data transformation models for mixed method designs.

Cresswell, J. and Piano Clark, V. (2007) *Designing and Conducting Mixed Methods Research*. Thousand Oaks, CA: Sage. A very accessible basic guide to undertaking mixed methods research.

Gorard, S. and Taylor, C. (2004) *Combining Methods in Educational and Social Research*. London: Open University Press. This book offers basic theorising and extensive practical illustrations of combined research methods.

Analysis of mixed method studies

Teddlie, C. and Tashakkori, A. (eds) (2003) *Handbook of Mixed Methods in Social and Behavioral Research*. Thousand Oaks, CA: Sage. This book covers controversies, cultural issues, transformational and emancipatory research, research design, sampling and data collection strategies, analysing, writing and reading, and applications across such disciplines as organisational research, psychological research, the health sciences, sociology and nursing.

Journals focusing on mixed methods

Journal of Mixed Methods Research, which has a total focus on the mixing of quantitative and qualitative methods.

International Journal of Multiple Research Approaches, which takes the broader approach of multiple methods within either qualitative or quantitative research as well as mixing the two together. Volume 2 Issue 1 (2008) is a special issue on *Computer Assisted Multiple and Blended Research*.

References

Armitage, A. (2007) Mutual research designs: Redefining mixed methods research design. Paper presented at the British Educational Research Association Annual Conference, Institute of Education, University of London, 5–8 September.

Burke Johnson, R. and Onwuegbuzi, A. (2004) General characteristics of pragmatism mixed methods research: A research paradigm whose time has come. *Educational Researcher*, 33 (7): 14–26.

Davies, P. and Baulch, B. (2011) Parekkel realities: exploring poverty dynamics in rural Bangladesh. *Journal of Development Studies*, 47 (1): 118–42. Retrieved from www.tandfonline.com/doi/pdf/10.1080/00220388.20 10.492860 (accessed June 2011).

Denzin, N. (2009) *Qualitative Inquiry Under Fire Toward a New Paradigm Dialogue*. Walnut Creek, CA: Left Coast Press.

Denzin, N. (2010) Moments, mixed methods and paradigm dialogues. *Qualitative Inquiry*, 16 (6): 419–27. Retrieved from http://qix.sagepub.com/content/16/6/419 (accessed June 2011).

Doe, J. (2003) *The Story of Jane Doe*. Toronto, ON: Random House of Canada.

Duncan, S. and Edwards, R. (1997) Lone mothers and paid work – rational economic man or gendered moral rationalities? *Feminist Economics*, 3 (2): 29–61.

Edmeades, J., Nyblade, L., Malhotra, A., Macquarrie, K., Parasuraman, S. and Walia, S. (2010) Methodological innovation in studying abortion in developing countries: a 'narrative' quantitative survey in Madhya Pradesh, India. *Journal of Mixed Methods Research*, 4 (3):176–98. Retrieved from http://mmr.sagepub.com/content/4/3/176 (accessed June 2011).

Gamberini, L. and Spagnolli, A. (2003) Display techniques and methods for cross-medial data analysis. *PsychNology Journal*, 1 (2): 131–40. Retrieved from www.psychology.org/File/PSYCHNOLOGY_JOURNAL_1_2_GAMBERINI.pdf (accessed 1 July 2011).

Leech, N., Dellinger, A., Brannagan, K. and Tanaka, H. (2010) Evaluating mixed method studies: A mixed methods approach. *Journal of Mixed Methods Research*, 4 (1): 17–31. Retrieved from http://mmr.sagepub.com/content/4/1/17 (accessed June 2011).

Mertens, D. (2010) Philosophy in mixed methods teaching; the transformative paradigm as illustration. *International Journal of Multiple Research Approaches*, 4: 9–18. This article counters the pragmatist position with that of transformative action.

Nicolson, D., Knapp, P., Gardner, P. and Raynor, D. (2011) Combining concurrent and sequential methods to examine the usability and readability of websites with information about medicines. *Journal of Mixed Methods Research*, 5 (1): 125–51. Retrieved from http://mmr.sagepub.com/content/5/1/25 (accessed June 2011).

Onwuegbuzie, A., Bustamante, R. and Nelson, J. (2010) Mixed research as a tool for developing quantitative instruments. *Journal of Mixed Methods Research*, 4 (1): 56–78. Retrieved from http://mmr.sagepub.com/content/4/1/56 (accessed June 2011).

Onwuegbuzie, A., Slate, J., Leech, N. and Collins, K. (2007) Conducting mixed analyses: a general typology. *International Journal of Multiple Research Approaches*, 3 (1): 4–17.

Onwuegbuzie, A., Slate, J., Leech, N. and Collins, K. (2009) Mixed data analysis: advanced integration techniques. *International Journal of Multiple Research Approaches,* 3 (1): 13–33.

Piano Clark, V., Garrett, A. and Pelecky, L. (2010) Applying three strategies for integrating quantitative and qualitative databases in a mixed methods study of a nontraditional graduate education program. *Field Methods,* 22 (2): 154–74. Retrieved from http://fmx.sagepub.com/content/22/2/154.full.pdf (accessed 25 July 2011).

Pieterse, V. and Sonnekus, I. (2003) Rising to challenges of combining qualitative and quantitative research. Presented at the 6th World Congress on Action Learning, Action Research and Process Management in conjunction with the 10th Congress on Participatory Action Research, 21–24 September 2003, at the University of Pretoria. South Africa. Retrieved from www.cs.up.ac.za/cs/vpieterse/pub/Challenges.pdf (accessed March 2012).

Quinlan, E. and Quinlan, A. (2010) Representations of rape: transcending methodological divides. *Journal of Mixed Methods Research,* 4 (2): 127–43. Retrieved from http://mmr.sagepub.com/content/4/2/127 (accessed June 2011).

Rossman, G. and Wilson, B. (1985) Numbers and work: combining qualitative and quantitative methods in a single large scale evaluation study. *Evaluation Review,* 9: 627–43.

Wacjman, J. and Martin, B. (2002) Narratives of identity in modern management: the corrosion of gender difference? *Sociology,* 36 (4): 985–1002. Retrieved from http://soc.sagepub.com/cgi/content/abstract/36/4/985 (accessed 9 July 2011).

PART 2

Traditional analytical approaches

In the following chapters, we will examine the tools and analytic procedures that have developed within particular methodological approaches. Although these procedures have a strong historical attachment to the methodology within which they originated, they are flexible entities and can be lifted out, used and adapted to suit the needs of individual researchers in order to answer aspects of a research question. The evolutionary nature of qualitative research means that it is most appropriate that you hunt through the tool box to find the best tool/s for the job at hand and, where none quite fits, be prepared to adapt several in order to seek the best answers to your research question.

However, as most analytical approaches have been strongly linked to particular forms of data collection and may also be underpinned by specific epistemological underpinnings, you will need to know what it is you are adapting in order to see more clearly what limitations and advantages may eventuate. For example, what happens when a particular approach, underpinned by the concepts of symbolic interactionism and designed primarily for observational data, such as grounded theory, is applied to documentation or to interview data? In another situation, you may, for example, have determined that the grounded theory approach (Strauss's version) is the most appropriate for your data analysis but you also want to bring your own voice into the analysis in a subjective manner. The original grounded theory approach you have chosen has embedded in it a neutral researcher position and a third person voice, so some adaptation of the original method and a justification for the insertion and analysis of your own voice would be necessary. Your approach might then be named subjective grounded theory, or quasi-grounded theory, or postmodern grounded theory depending on how the adaptation was made and how you have justified this. The data analytic approaches in Chapters 9–13 may be of greater interest and relevance to you here. You need to investigate the advantages and disadvantages of any approach, to trial new ways of proceeding when disadvantages are found, then to publish the outcomes for other researchers to add to their list of possible choices. In this way the field continues to move forward.

Chapters in this section cover approaches that are more traditional:

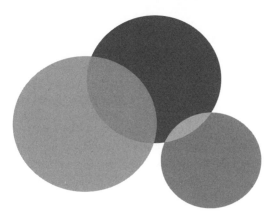

FOUR

Classical ethnography

In this chapter, a traditional ethnographic approach – classical ethnography, which has its origins in anthropology – will be discussed and the techniques of creating summaries, taxonomies, typologies, domain analysis, event analysis and social network analysis will be demonstrated for you.

KEY POINTS

- Background and purpose of classical ethnography
- Analytical tools
  - observation summaries
  - cultural domain analysis (the interconnected groupings of a culture)
  - freelists (identifying what fits into a domain)
  - pilesorts (identifying the internal structure of a domain)
  - triads (identifying the hierarchies within a domain)
  - taxonomies (organisation of knowledge into discrete categories)
  - typologies (classification within groups)
  - frame analysis (deliberate imposition of frames on the data)
  - social network analysis (identification of social relationships)
  - event analysis (intensive analysis of a key event)

Introduction

When to use: When you want to describe a culture and its operation, rituals and belief systems.

Type of research questions best suited: What is the culture of X (a particular hospital ward, a classroom, a street culture, a department, a family group, a tribe, a professional group etc.)?

Strengths: Provides detailed description of the belief systems, values, behaviours and interconnections of whatever has been defined as a 'culture' – a group of people usually with common elements of location/language/purpose.

Weaknesses: Researcher neutrality is often difficult to maintain. Large amounts of observational data are time-consuming and expensive to collect.

Background and purpose

Classical ethnography has strong links with the anthropological tradition of observation of culture in situ. The theoretical underpinnings lean heavily on a combination of structural functionalism and interactive social networks. Structural functionalism focuses on the major structures of a society and how each part contributes via consensus and moves toward equilibrium in the orderly functioning of that society. Change and adaptation are possible with moves toward a new adjusted equilibrium as interactive social networks develop and the society becomes more complex.

The purpose of the classical ethnography is to describe the whole culture (however this has been defined), be it a tribal group or a group of young people living by their wits on the street. Key informants are sought and their voices highlighted. Your role as a researcher is traditionally that of a 'neutral' distant reflective observer (dialoguing between the research process and the product), meticulously documenting observational and visual images, and asking questions in both informal conversation and formal interviews, in order to identify, confirm and cross-check an understanding of the societal structures, the social linkages and the behaviour patterns, beliefs and understandings of people within the culture. This will usually involve you participating for months/years in the setting; learning the language and collecting data. It is usual (where possible) to return to the culture after a period of time (and after the original data has been analysed and written up) to see that nothing has changed and that your 'picture' of the culture is confirmed. Classical ethnography has been linked to colonialism, late nineteenth-century imperialism and 'othering' through imposing your view of culture upon the setting under research. It has also been criticised in that the 'cine shot' approach separates culture from its historical links.

The ethnographers of today have truncated the original process to the 'mini-ethnography' characterised by a shorter time in the field and an eclectic use of data collection techniques, including focus group and face-to-face interviewing, participant observation, surveys and visual and written documentation with options of preliminary, thematic, content, discourse, narrative and conversational analysis (see Chapters 2, 5 and 14–20).

Data collection areas can include:

- the gathering of contextual information
- the delineation of economic, political and social organisations
- the documentation of language, customs and rituals, events, incidents, shared belief systems, attitudes and understandings of events, behaviour and actions.

Analysis of descriptive data is within the interactive tradition and is ongoing in the form of preliminary data analysis, alone or in combination with thematic analysis, so that each set of data informs the next providing feedback in a looped process of building up and confirming the holistic view of the 'culture' under examination.

What is culture?

Ethnographers tend to focus on current culture rather than historical culture by participating in the culture, where this is feasible, in order to gain an insider perspective through participation and observation, or by observing it objectively from an outsider position. Behaviours, beliefs, rituals, interchange with other cultures and language are documented, as well as making comparisons with other cultural groups.

How do you define culture for research purposes?

It really is up to you to place the boundaries around your 'culture'. In physical terms will it be a classroom? A school? A hospital ward? A work department? Or will it be a transient group of homeless people inhabiting a broad area? A religion? Or will it be a queue of people waiting to buy tickets for a show? The definition of boundaries and the focus of the research question are up to you. Usually the defined group will have aspects in common – perhaps language? Purpose? Patterns of behaviour? Rituals? Habits? Beliefs? Interests?

How do you collect and manage field notes?

Once you have determined that you can observe the cultural phenomena you have chosen, you will need to identify the best type of data for the research question. Observational field notes are the most common form of data collected in classical ethnographies, followed by interviewing and document collation. Assuming you have decided to include observational data, the first thing you will need to address is whether the data collection will be:

- *overt* – everyone knows that you are researching so you tend to observe in a more structured manner with a checklist in mind or in hand, or
- *covert* – no one knows you are observing him or her for research purposes and unstructured descriptive data is more attainable. You can train yourself to observe without taking notes/recordings and, following your observation, you can record your data onto audio/video tape or direct to computer via typing or voice recognition programs. Both structured and unstructured data can be collected from any setting.

The following is an example of covert descriptive field data collected while sitting in a hospital clinic waiting room.

RESEARCH QUESTION

Research question: *what is the interaction between staff and patients in the gynaecological clinic?*

Field note observation example

I arrived at the Gynecology clinic at 1.45pm knowing that appointments started at 2pm. This clinic comprises an open room 6 metres by 5 metres with a large circular administrative

(Continued)

---

station in the centre facing patients as they enter. The only entrance to this circular structure lies behind the area facing the public. Two administrative/nursing personnel (female) occupy it both wearing the navy blue hospital uniform of shirt tucked into a knee-length skirt. The clinic consulting rooms (6) run down a corridor behind the central station out of sight and blocked by the high wood-paneled counter (chest height) and the drop-down paneling from the ceiling which leaves an opening of about a metre and a half for interaction. When I arrived there were seven women in the main waiting area; three heavily pregnant wearing loose clothing in shades of pink, white and beige and sitting on higher than usual chairs for ease of getting up; two women of around 50 plus – one wearing a corporate suit of black with a white shirt, the other in a mid-blue track suit, and one elderly woman in a large dark-green cardigan and a navy skirt sitting with a woman in her 40's? who from their conversation about people in common appeared to be her daughter. (she was wearing a sleeveless pink, red and white striped knee-length dress). The television was on and placed high on the wall in the corner facing away from the desk and the consulting rooms and above a toy box – open with toys and children's books spilling over the floor. As each client entered they presented or were asked for their hospital card and the administrator flicked through a pile of buff-coloured A4 manila folders on the waist-high desk on her side of the counter, carefully placing the selected one in a open shelf on the wall while asking the client to take a seat. Apart from the initial 'How can I help?' or 'When is your appointment?' or 'Do you have your card?' eye contact was minimal, the main focus being the card and the notes file,

Source: Grbich data set

Note that the environmental context is described in some detail to set the scene for the interaction focus. Following an hour of observation of the functioning of the clinic, this write up can collect the essence of the interactions through observation and store it for comparison with others taken at different times, on different days or at different clinics in the same or other hospitals depending on whether the research question relates to one or several clinics. Preliminary data analysis (see Chapter 2) would clarify further questions and group the main issues identified.

As the focus of the observation lay in staff–patient interaction, the main points that could be drawn from this segment might be:

- significant physical barriers in the environment separate staff and patients
- verbal interaction with patients in the waiting room is focused and minimal
- consultants are protected from patient view and from direct public access via structural barriers and by the placement of administrative/nursing staff.

These forms of separation maintain a hierarchy of:

- consultants
- administrators and nursing staff
- patients.

In summary, in this setting a hierarchy of consultants, administrative/nursing staff and patients exists and this hierarchy is maintained by the physical layout of the clinic and by a minimalist staff–patient interactive style.

A detailed example of one hour of recorded observational field notes can be found in Taylor and Bogdan (1998: 263, Appendix), involving observation in a state institution in America for people with intellectual disability.

Analytical tools used in classical ethnographies

Preliminary data analysis building to major themes tends to be the mainstay of much of the descriptive observational data collected in classical ethnographies. The trend is to keep the data largely intact where stories or narratives have been gathered; however, where more precise comparable data has been collected, a number of classificatory tools have been developed to further break in to the areas of the defined culture, and these are demonstrated below.

There are three dominant classificatory tools for grouping data: cultural domain analysis (providing the overall big picture label); taxonomies (identifying members of the same grouping); and typologies (putting together aspects with similarities).

Cultural domain analysis

There is a presupposition within cultural domain analysis that domains are structures to which items/entities (symbols of importance as defined by participants) belong and within which there are meaningful links, for example, kinship groups, animals, colours, illnesses, types of knowledge, emotions, cars, computers etc. According to Spradley (1980), the overall process for domain analysis involves:

- initial data collection
- the identification of the major domains of data, which might include the structures and rituals which serve to support, maintain and provide uniqueness to the particular culture under study
- further data collection to elicit more detail or to clarify the types/parts of these domains.

The undertaking of a taxonomic analysis of these domains will serve to identify groupings of subsets and hierarchies and typologising or thematic analysis will clarify selected dimensions of contrast for identified groupings. For example, say a domain was defined by a group of indigenous people as 'indigenous knowledge'; this domain is likely to demonstrate webs of strong internal relationships regarding the types of knowledge regarded as particular to the group. Similarities of what is considered cultural knowledge by the group are likely to be found together with some agreement on the language to be used regarding particular aspects or events within this knowledge. Differences are also likely and may lead to the development of separate or subdomains.

The process of identifying whether or not we have a domain involves:

- finding out which items fit into the domain
- identifying commonalities and relationships
- locating where items fit within the hierarchical structure of the domain
- contrasting one domain with another.

The processes that are available to you for identification of within-domain elements for analysis are: *freelists*, *pilesorts* and *triads*.

Freelists   This approach is used to identify which elements fit into the proposed cultural domain. It involves asking semi-structured questions in group or face-to-face interviews. For example, say the domain being explored in a particular cultural group was 'food' the questions would explore: 'What foods do you eat?', 'What foods don't you eat?', 'When do you eat (certain foods)?', 'When don't you eat (certain foods)?' The views of more than 50 randomly sampled members of the group would be sought in order to attempt to gain consensus (identified through frequency of responses) about what is salient (most important) to the domain in terms of views of food and what should be put into a subdomain or excluded and what level of consensus there is regarding food items. Data is tabulated for order of individual responses and cross-referenced across the group and the frequency of responses, in particular regarding breakfast, lunch, dinner and ceremonial foods, can also be rank ordered and checked against gender, age and status in the group.

Pilesorts   This technique of sorting or piling cards is used to identify the internal structure of the domain – the similarities between and among items and the commonalities and relationships therein. Up to 100 cards are developed from the freelist information gathered with relevant pictures/statements – one card for each food item. In a *single pilesort*, the cards are put in random order and the participants are asked to 'sort' the pile into a number of relevant (to them) categories/piles. For example, they could be asked to sort into 'what goes with what' or into categories, such as 'everyday' and 'ceremonial', or 'morning food' and 'evening food', or 'very desirable food' and 'less desirable food', or whatever piles were relevant to them.

In a *successive pilesort* items are sorted into piles, as in the single sort method, but participants are limited as to the number of piles they can sort into. They may also be required to subdivide these piles until further subdivision is impossible. Responses from the single sort are fed into a matrix showing which item went into which pile to identify the percentages of participants who connected particular items together. Responses from successive pilesorts are used to identify a matrix of individual responses and to compare this with others. The limitation of both free listing and pilesorting is the issue of representativeness – important aspects may be missed if they are only mentioned by one person or a few people when this response may represent an important subgroup within the culture.

Triads   You can use this approach to tease out similarities and identify hierarchies for items in the domain. Combinations of triads – three items – are developed and randomised. The items are presented to the participants as triads and their task is:

either to identify the item that differs most from the other two

or, to order the three items from most to least in terms of an identified aspect.

For example:

Order this list from most to least dangerous in terms of longevity:

raw meat   raw vegetables   yoghurt

Or

Identify the item that differs most from the other two:

goat's milk   cheese   butter   unpasteurised milk

Rank ordered data can be tabulated and matrices of similarities developed for each individual as well as for the overall group so that comparisons can be made. Triads are most useful in clarifying the similarities in small domains where the items are close in kind or meaning, where the strength of individual connections is unclear, or where a proposition needs to be tested. Again, it is essential to clarify and contextualise participants' thought processes and the decisions they have made.

Taxonomies

This form of classification of data involves the organising of similar aspects of knowledge/aspects into discrete categories in a logical manner. Examples of this are the Dewey system of classifying books in libraries, various directories such as phone directories and the Yahoo! web-based system. For example, Bloom's taxonomy of the cognitive domain (1994) involves the following hierarchy of possibilities:

Knowledge
Comprehension
Application
Analysis
Synthesis
Evaluation

In research, you might choose the taxonomic approach to provide categories so that you can compare data across interviews or observations. These categories can either be developed by you or borrowed from some existing source and then applied to the data, or they may come naturally from the data, as in the example below. Apart from applying existing taxonomies it is possible to develop a taxonomy early in data collection and to apply it like a matrix over the database, but it is more usual to mine the data in order to identify and clarify the categories that the data presents.

Example

The following taxonomy was developed from data gathered in order to classify the activities undertaken in a typical day of one father at home and this framework was then loosely applied to the situations of other at home fathers for comparison.

Taxonomy: at home father

Morning before school

Helps wife make breakfast for selves and 3 children
Organises school-aged children and walks them to school

Morning after 9am

Organises youngest pre school child – painting, reading stories, sandpit
Undertakes housekeeping tasks – often shared with child

(Continued)

Breakfast dishes
Bed making
Washing clothes
Sweeping floors
Vacuuming carpets

Takes youngest child to playgroup and stays with her there
Home for lunch

Afternoon

Organises youngest child into play activities
Shopping/continues with housework from morning
Picks up school-aged children and walks them home
Organises play/homework for all children
Starts to prepare tea

Source: Grbich, data consolidation

This data was then further classified into specific tasks and the amount of time spent on each task collated for comparison across the data set.

Typologies

A typology involves classification into one particular group or class. It tends to be used for smaller-scale data than a taxonomy and involves processes of grouping *like* information of particular relevance to the research question.

The process of typology formation involves:

- collating all data relating to the particular issue
- identifying variations, layers and dimensions
- classifying into a type/types (subgroups)
- presenting/re-presenting these to the reader.

For example, I developed a typology of terminology of the language that 25 primary caregiver males used to define and name their at home role. These were first listed as:

Caregiver, child nurturer, housewife, housecleaner, helpmate, my job, father at home, person at home, my career, parent at home, mate (to child), childminder, shared role with partner, fulltime day time child nurturer, child minder.

These terms were then counted, labelled and grouped depending on whether the focus was the child, the home, equality or a job (see Table 4.1).

From this grouping of like responses a summary can be developed: 'This group of primary caregiver men mostly define their role as child carers or house/home persons, with a few seeing the role as achieving equality with their partners or as having a defined/substitute work focus.' This summary then provides the basis for a subheading

Table 4.1 Role definition

Child focus (10)	House/home focus (7)	Egalitarian focus (5)	Work focus (2)
Caregiver (×5)	Housewife (slave to house)	Helpmate (to partner)	My job
Child nurturer	House cleaner	Shared role with partner (×3)	My career
Full-time daytime nurturer of child	Father at home (×2)		
Mate (to child)	Person at home		
Child minder (×2)	Parent at home (×2)		

in the display of results and detailed quotes would be displayed to substantiate this finding.

Frame analysis

The basis of frame analysis lies in the writings of Gregory Bateson (1972) and Erving Goffman (1974), who were interested in how, during social interactions, individuals classify, using meta-cognitive devices (or mental shortcuts) and set parameters, in order to understand information, conversations, narratives, rituals and behaviours and the situational encounters with which they are presented.

Frame analysis is a useful tool you can consider in order to answer the following questions with regard both to yourself and to those whom you are researching:

- What sorts of conceptual and contextual interpretive frames do we place around situations and what sense do we make of them?
- How is meaning and understanding constructed?
- What classifications do we use to frame different kinds of communication/situations and to shape our social lives?
- Frames structure our realities – they can be fixed or emergent and are not so much conscious but unconsciously applied to situations and can be revealed during interaction and communication.

In order to see how this works you may find the following process useful:

1. Draw frames around transcripts of conversation (a frame is the smallest coherent group of words but frames can also be very broad)
2. Group frames into categories and name these
3. Develop larger groupings, often termed galleries (if useful)
4. Interpret and display.

Example

Taking some extracts from interviews with female partners of at home fathers recalling their decision to change parenting roles, a broad framing approach can be applied:

Framing

Interview 1

Well I suppose it happened naturally for us and I don't feel we really planned beforehand for a very long period of time. Because I think we'd gone along for many years thinking that we're going to have children and it didn't happen and when the endocrinologist finally said after about seven years he didn't think we were likely to have children without quite a bit of intervention I decided, well I'll do something. So I got myself into a couple of training pro-grams, sat exams and then I got pregnant. Then I really had to take stock and I really didn't particularly want to stay at home and by that time T had tended to work through a lot of things he wanted to do with his work and we discussed it and he said well perhaps he should stay home and it just fell into place like that.

Interview 2

I suppose it was to do with the pressure on John that started the whole thing in his mind. We were talking about it once and he said 'What would you think if I gave up work?' and I said 'Well if you want to you must do that' and he was travelling a lot and trying to study part-time and trying to be a parent as well. There was a lot of pressure there and I found that being at home, although it was quite relaxing being your own boss, but it was still quite restricting and I'd wanted to do something else and I started doing a course but found that having the alternative of going to work and knowing that our child would be well cared for was a good option so I was quite happy to change over.

Interview 3

It just happened. It's complicated because D came from England and couldn't get a work permit and couldn't get permanent residency so that I took over the breadwinner role and I became pregnant and he became very excited about that and he wanted to be with the baby and it didn't worry me because my job is very convenient and I enjoy doing it. We just stayed as we were. I could just get six months leave of absence not 12 months because I hadn't been employed long enough full-time, so I went back to work when G was only four months of age. But I was able to come home at lunchtimes. So it was really financial and political reasons why we swapped roles.

In terms of frame analysis there are two aspects here:

- the frames indicated by the participants
- the frames imposed by the researcher.

In terms of responses to the question 'How did you come to change roles?' *participants'* frames appear to be:

- natural progression of events over time (interview 1)
- work pressure (interview 2)
- wife's dissatisfaction with the limits of the at home role (interview 2)
- financial and political reasons (interview 3).

In terms of later data analysis and interpretation, the *researcher's frames* appeared to be:

- Interview 1: two frames – convenience and values regarding equal childrearing (drawing from other data provided by this couple)
- Interview 2: work pressure leading to a sea change
- Interview 3: again two frames – political/financial and convenience.

In all cases there was perceived to be an underlying frame of 'fathers' preparedness to participate in childcare' which could be substantiated by 'and he said well perhaps he should stay home' (interview 1); 'What would you think if I gave up work?' (interview 2); and 'I became pregnant and he became very excited about that and he wanted to be with the baby' (interview 3). This was further substantiated by additional data from the interviews with the fathers themselves.

How does the process of frame analysis differ from thematic analysis? It has a great many similarities. The essential difference is that the framing process is a natural one that occurs within the participants' and the researcher's minds but the researcher is more actively aware of the duality involved. The danger on both counts is that these frames may be applied in such a way that they become inflexible and prevent the participant and researcher from identifying other aspects. For example, my desire to frame in terms of 'father's preparedness to participate in childcare' may deflect my attention from the fact that 'work choices' might be a more important frame (from these three families' perspectives). Overall, frame analysis is particularly useful to you in its capacity to clarify your imposition of cognitive frames and the degree to which these are shared between individuals and among groups regarding communications and the events they have experienced.

Social network analysis

Moving from the more formalised approaches of classificatory schemes and identifying and confirming domains and frames, another approach involves the illumination of social structure in groups, systems and organisations through the identification of the webs of social networks evident in the culture under study. This approach allows for greater flexibility in viewing the formation, dynamics, linkages, context and the changing nature of such networks. Social network analysis is particularly useful when the identification of linkages is important; how these operate in terms of patterns of interaction and how individual and group behaviours change over time.

Process

1 Identify the people who constitute the group.
2 Assess the relationships in terms of the focus of the research, for example, lines of power, decision making etc.
3 Produce a graphical analysis – show any changes over time.
4 Confirm with the collection of other data over time.

The following figure from William Whyte's (1955) longitudinal study of a group of street males indicates the results of such an analysis. You can see that the most powerfully networked male in the group is Doc.

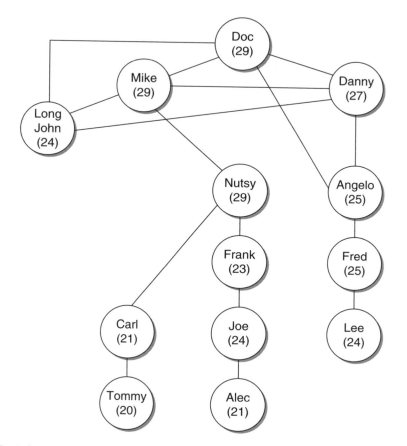

Figure 4.1 Relationships in the organisation of a street corner group: the Nortons, spring and summer 1937 (Figure 2.2 in W. Whyte, Street Corner Society, 1955: 13, copyright 1943 and 1955 by the University of Chicago Press, reproduced with permission).

[Note: Numbers in brackets give the ages of the group.]

Event analysis

When you identify a particular event within a larger base of data collection that requires more detailed explication and highlighting than is provided by preliminary data analysis or thematic analysis, this can be undertaken by employing event analysis:

Process

1 Describe the event – what actually happened? Here the 'voices' presented will be important. Whose perspectives are represented? Is it only that of the researcher? What about the people actually involved in the event as well as bystanders and any relevant others?
2 What are the structural aspects of the event? Time, space, location, context, culture? Again there are a range of perspectives possible here.
3 What meanings and actions can be interpreted in the context? How can what went on be explained?

4   What is the wider impact of the event? Historical links, future potential, or just the impact on those immediately involved.
5   Classify the event/s – either broadly or break them down into separate parts and place them in related groupings for more intense scrutiny, theory development and writing up.
6   How has the researcher's representation of the event been affected by the fieldwork situation? By their limited access to people? Or by their own views developed within their own cultural grouping?

It must be becoming clear to you from the above examples that there is considerable variation in classical ethnography; ranging from the precisely organised classifications and interpretations represented in this chapter to broader less defined or imprecise multiple presentations of data reflecting many views. William Whyte has indicated that for him the experience of data analysis in classical ethnography is a very imprecise process of immersion in the field, muddling around to see what emerges, juggling ideas and waiting for an 'Aha!' or *Eureka!* moment where some of the items, issues and behaviours may start to make sense:

> The ideas that we have in research are only in part a logical product growing out of a careful weighing of evidence. We do not generally think the problems through in a straight line. Often we have the experience of being immersed in a mass of confusing data. We study the data carefully, we bring all our powers of logical analysis to bear upon them. We come up with an idea or two. But still the data do not fall in any coherent pattern. Then we go on living with the data – and with the people – until perhaps some chance occurrence casts a totally different light upon the data, and we begin to see a pattern that we have not seen before. This pattern is not purely an artistic creation. Once we think we see it, we must re-examine our notes and perhaps set out to gather new data in order to determine whether the pattern adequately represents the life we are observing or is simply a product of our imagination. (Whyte, 1984: 3–4)

This more intuitive approach to analysis of classical ethnographic data utilising only immersion, some preliminary data analysis and perhaps some loose thematic analysis, clarifies the breadth of approaches available.

Student exercise: Event analysis

Take an event either in your own life or in your database. Work through the analysis process:

1   Describe the event – what actually happened? Identify perspective.
2   What are the structural aspects of the event – time, space, location, context, culture?
3   What meanings and actions can be interpreted in the context? How can what went on be explained?
4   What is the wider impact of the event – historical links, future potential, or just the impact on those immediately involved?
5   Classify the event/s – break them down into separate parts and place them in related groupings for more scrutiny, theory development and writing up.
6   How has your representation of the event been affected by the situation? Access to people? Or by the views developed within your/their own cultural grouping?

Further reading

Classical ethnographic design and analysis

Becker, H. (1998) *Tricks of the Trade*. Chicago, IL: University of Chicago Press. Full of tactics for problem solving the issues that arise in research from design to analysis. Becker's colloquial style is very readable and he draws upon many years of expertise as an ethnographer.

Fetterman, D. (2010) *Ethnography Step-by-step* (3rd edn). Thousand Oaks, CA: Sage. Useful strategies for dealing with large amounts of ethnographic data.

Madden, R. (2011) *Being Ethnographic: A Guide to the Theory and Practice of Ethnography*. Thousand Oaks, CA: Sage. Classic case studies covering: conversations and interviews; participation and observation of people; writing field notes; turning data and interpretation into stories.

Classification tools

Bernard, R. (ed.) (2000) *Handbook of Methods in Cultural Anthropology*. Oxford: AltaMira Press. Twenty-seven authors describe anthropological fieldwork in practice, providing a comprehensive, description of the methods that anthropologists use, the logic behind them, and the complex problems that field research with humans entails.

Schensul, J. and Le Compte, M. and associates (1999) *The Ethnographer's Toolkit*. 7 volume set. Oxford: AltaMira Press. This book provides a range of tools from research design to data collection techniques and analytical strategies for the novice ethnographer.

Writing classical ethnographic data

Atkinson, P. (1990) *The Ethnographic Imagination: Textual Construction of Reality*. London: Routledge. Atkinson exposes the textual descriptive strategies used in more traditional forms of ethnographic writing.

Wolf, M. (1992) *A Thrice Told Tale: Feminism, Postmodernism and Ethnographic Responsibility*. Stanford, CA: Stanford University Press. Margery Wolf has taken classical ethnographic data of an event which occurred in a village collected 30 years previously and has re-presented it in three different ways: as her own journal record of the event, as the record of her Asian research assistant who has cultural insight into the complexities of the event and as a article for an anthropological journal.

References

Bateson, G. (1972) *Steps to an Ecology of Mind*. New York: Ballantine.

Bloom, B., Englehart, M., Furst, E. and Hill, W. (1994) Excerpts from 'Taxonomy of Educational Objectives, the Classification of Education Goals, Handbook I: Cognitive Domain'. In L. Anderson and L. Sosniak (eds), *Bloom's Taxonomy: A Forty-Year Retrospective*. Chicago, IL: University of Chicago Press.

Goffman, E. (1974) *Frame Analysis: An Essay on the Organisation of Experience*. New York: Harper and Row.

Spradley, J. (1980) *Participant Observation*. New York: Holt, Rinehart and Winston.

Taylor, S. and Bogdan, R. (1998) *Introduction to Qualitative Research Methods* (3rd edn). New York: Wiley.

Whyte, W. (1955) *Street Corner Society*. Chicago, IL: University of Chicago Press.

Whyte, W. (1984) *Learning from the Field: A Guide from Experience*. Thousand Oaks, CA: Sage.

FIVE

Critical ethnographic approaches

Critical ethnography comes out of the classical ethnographic tradition but the notion of 'critical' takes it beyond a descriptive hermeneutic approach to an interpretation dependent on critical theorising. Here the focus becomes identifying where power lies, how it is maintained, and how this might be changed. Feminist and action research approaches are closely linked to this tradition.

KEY POINTS

- Background and purpose of critical ethnography
- Criteria for a critical ethnography
- Carspecken's five-stage process
  - criticisms of Carspecken's approach
- Research examples of contemporary critical ethnographies
- General guidelines for undertaking a critical ethnography
- Thematic analysis

Introduction

When to use: Critical ethnographic approaches are particularly useful when you are concerned about issues of power in society – who has power? How is it distributed and maintained? Are those currently disempowered actually contributing to the maintenance of power imbalances? How are those who are powerless managing to have their voices heard?

Type of research questions best suited: How the identity of X group has been constructed or shaped by such dominant cultural institutions as the media, science, the economy, politics, gender, racism or religion and what has been the contribution of the group to this? Whose interests are being served by current institutional arrangements? Where does power lie in particular societal contexts? How and in whose interest are inequalities being maintained? How could a better balance of power be achieved?

Strengths: A specific focus on power as a concept and on defined theoretical underpinnings relating to power location, such as neo-Marxism and feminist social theory.

Weaknesses: Emancipation has always been a thorny issue – who is in a position to emancipate who? Me? You? Are emancipators any better than religious zealots colonising the lives of others, assuming they have not only all the right answers but that others are lacking in some way? And how realistic is it to expect researchers to promote major social transformation and change? Even if this could be achieved what would an (whose?) ideal democracy look like in terms of equality, justice and freedom?

Background and purpose

The notion of critical ethnography emerged from the University of Birmingham's cultural studies department in the 1970s, where there had been dissatisfaction with classical ethnographic approaches that were seen as ignoring the elements of power within social settings. Rather than just describing what is apparent using observation and interviewing, researchers desired to go beyond this to elicit the whys and wherefores and then perhaps move even further into action to correct power imbalances by alerting participants to the previously unrecognised inequalities they were subject to. The core element of a critical ethnography then became a focus on knowledge – who has it and who does not and what sorts of distortions are being practised and how are these unequal situations being maintained and reproduced? Creating and sharing knowledge about oppression was seen as having the potential to transform unequal social situations and the linkage of left-wing theoretical ideas to actual social situations provided a cutting edge to research praxis. In the move away from classical ethnography, the notion of the 'value neutrality' of the ethnographer was also questioned. In critical ethnography, the researcher moves from the fairly static position of 'observer' of the classical ethnographer to a more active analytical position where terminology such as 'location of power', 'ideology', 'hegemony', 'alienation', 'domination', 'oppression', hierarchy,' 'exploitation under capitalism', 'empowerment' and 'transformation' become important terms. History, politics and the economics of a situation dominate explanations and interpretation is largely through the critical theory tradition via Karl Marx and Jürgen Habermas, and through the principles of feminism, particularly the concepts of oppression, empowerment, liberation and social justice.

Criteria for a critical ethnography

A critical ethnography should meet the following criteria:

- Power and the location of power and oppression must be key issues.
- Emancipation and social transformation of inequality and oppression suffered by participants needs to be addressed by some form of liberating action.
- Identification of the author/researcher and how are they are influencing the data collection, design, analysis and interpretation must be adequately addressed.
- An abstract level of understanding of the political, economic and social aspects of the culture must be gained through interpretation using critical theory.

Hypothetical example

If we take the research question *What can be done about homelessness?* we can see how these issues might play out in a critical ethnography. The underlying assumptions behind such a question would be that the current political and economic systems in many developed countries are based in capitalism whereby profit is the driving force and fewer and fewer workers are forced through multiskilling to produce more and more surplus labour (where the value of producing the product is less than the value of the product produced) in order to enable higher profit margins to be gained. This means that those workers with limited qualifications or variations in style, gender, age, race, levels of mental and physical health etc. may be considered unemployable in certain areas. As a researcher, you could gather data through observation and interviewing a range of key people, including people who are homeless, and undertake a discourse analysis of policy documents. This data should clarify the problem and show if, where and why homelessness has occurred, how it is perpetuated, what is currently being done about it and what the experience of homelessness is like. The data analytic tools you might choose would probably include preliminary data analysis (Chapter 2), thematic analysis (below) and discourse analysis (Chapter 20). Application of the critical theory of Karl Marx (profit capitalism), Max Weber (economic rationalism) and Jurgen Habermas (distorted communication for power maintenance) could provide a critical interpretation. From the information gained, you could suggest solutions to the problem of homelessness or you could conduct focus groups with key figures in the welfare industry and with homeless people in order to create awareness and action to develop possible solutions. The feeding back of information and solutions to all participants would be assumed to go some way to supporting an emancipatory stance but you could also choose to become involved in action research (where you work either with people who are homeless to promote their agendas and help them to undertake collective action, or you could work with the government to change policy and implement solutions).

Changes in critical ethnography

Between the 1970s and the 1990s the *ethnographic hermeneutic approach* detailed above dominated data collection and *critical theory* provided the interpretation. There was a strong emphasis on empowerment and action research was occasionally incorporated.

In 1996, Phil Carspecken further developed a detailed five-stage process underpinned by ideas of William James, John Dewey, George Mead, Anthony Giddens and others but in particular Jürgen Habermas's notions of communicative action. This approach has subsequently become the mainstay for critical qualitative research in general and for critical ethnography in particular.

Five stages of critical ethnography

1 Build a critically reflective primary record of thick description using a hermeneutic iterative approach to make sense of what is going on in the setting. This is termed *monological data* involving only the researcher as s/he unobtrusively collects observational data through note taking, audio and videotaping of events, behaviours and rituals.

2 Preliminary reconstructive analysis or researcher interpretation (away from the field) is then undertaken regarding what has been gathered.

3 Preliminary data analysis and thematic analysis can be used here to identify power location, role relations, meanings and cultural values as well as validity.

4 *Dialogical data* (collected in collaboration with participants) should then be gathered through interviews and focus groups. The data is examined to discover system relations between specific sites and these findings are linked to the wider social, political and economic contexts.

5 Findings are then considered 'in relation to general theories of society, both to help explain what has been discovered in stages 1 to 4 and to alter, challenge, and refine macrosociological theories themselves' (Carspecken, 1996: 172).

Although this approach (apart from the specifics of stages 4 and 5) differs little from the general qualitative hermeneutic iterative approach, it has been criticised by Colin Holmes and Wendy Smyth (2011).

Criticisms of Carspecken's approach

- The original critical ethnographic approach, with its emphasis on political and social activism, has become depoliticised through its transfer to the American context.
- Carspecken's theoretical underpinnings for his stages are selective and eclectic, resulting in a grab bag of philosophically derived terminology, most with little connection to their original context, thus creating confusion.
- The 'critical' nature of interpretation (stages 4 and 5) appears to have minimal links with interpretive explanations from actual critical theorists.
- The process of researcher neutrality of stage 1, involving reflection of personal values and biases, does not appear to inform the research in any critical way.
- The lack of overt links to the ethnographic tradition makes the term critical ethnography misleading.

Recent research undertaken in the critical theory tradition appears to have either encompassed Carspecken's five stages as described earlier or developed creative adaptations.

Research examples of contemporary critical ethnographies

Pre Carspecken: the authoritative researcher

Kathleen Bennett (1991) investigated the relationship between students' Appalachian cultural background and their Grade 1 classroom-reading program which was supposed to meet the written goal of being culturally sensitive. Data was collected by classroom observation and formal and informal interviews within the classroom setting, including audiotaping of small group reading sessions, staff meetings and District Education meetings, and this data was analysed thematically. Analysis of student report cards, district curriculum guides, absentee records, achievement scores, and criterion-referenced test scores was also undertaken. Bennett found: that the ideology of stratification was embedded in the reading program (top, average and slow with a continuum of creative-structured tasks) creating different experiences for different students; that this was reinforced by rigid educational policies and the limited resources provided by the district; and that the reading program did not meet the goal of cultural appropriateness and in fact was in conflict with the Appalachian culture by presenting only a white middle class curriculum. There was no place for the use of children's natural language patterns or life experiences in the process of learning to read. In addition, large class sizes, rigid district policies and insufficient funding as well as the beliefs they had been taught about how children learn, hindered teachers' autonomy. Giroux's theory of reproduction of the dominant culture through the schooling system was used for interpretation. Lack of success in learning to read was the outcome for two-thirds of the Appalachian children involved. The identification of racial inequality and structural impediments to change were reported to the Appalachian people as well as to the education authorities to begin to raise awareness in order to start the process of pressure for change.

Following Carspecken

Terry Robertson (2005) explored corporate domination within the classroom. He directly transposed Carspecken's five-stage approach to explore the question: 'How does the public school system reinforce corporate processes that determine the perceptions of students toward themselves as well as student perceptions toward socioeconomic conditions to which they are destined?'

Stage 1 involved direct but flexible observation with recording devices, note taking, peer debriefing and participant checks to ensure validity of the observed data,

Stage 2 involved grouping aspects of the data and searching for instances of power (themes of normative, coerced and interactive power) and identifying aspects of the culture. Further participant checks and peer debriefing were undertaken to maintain validity of interpretation.

Stage 3 involved undertaking the collection of interview data using 2–5 leading interview questions then developing probing questions from these. Interviews were audio recorded for validity and questions sought to link the two data sets of interview and observational data. More peer debriefing and participant checks were undertaken.

Stages 4 and 5 sought explanations of meaning through theoretical concepts linking systems of power, subordination, corporatism and fascism to provide answers to questions concerning class, race, gender and politics.

The major thematic results documented were: the imposition into the school setting of the language of capitalistic corporatism and the advent of the corporate model in education, both of which appear to be displacing democratic principles of freedom and critical scholarship. Robertson called on teachers to band together to counter this trend.

Creative adaptation: co-researchers in liberation

Michele Knight et al. (2004) examined the diversity of practices utilised by poor, black, working class and Latina/o families to support their children in going to college. The researchers used critical ethnography to explain data from 27 cases collected over one year. Twenty-four college-bound students (ninth grade) involved in the study were co-researchers, chosen through a community selection process and trained. The research assumptions in the study relating to critical ethnography were:

- that power and inequality would be actively sought out and that issues of race, ethnicity, gender and class oppression would be found
- that there would be a dialectic between data collected and theory building, and
- that researcher and researched had an obligation to act upon and change any oppressive conditions uncovered.

Data was collected through observation (school classrooms and activities and the broader school social culture), interviews and story and counter-story collection (students, families – interviewed by students, teachers), focus groups (students) and the production of written documentation (school policies regarding support for access to college). Data was analysed iteratively and thematically in an ongoing process and the co-researchers provided member checks regarding validity. The dynamics of race and power were theorised by researchers, co-researchers (Latina/o and Spanish) and their families.

Outcomes included a need for reconceptualisation of family versus parent involvement with the need for inclusion of the wider family as potential supports, not just parents; the need for the school to accept and work differently with non-participant families; and the need for a multidirectional model of school support that encompasses an academic, social and political focus, including counter-stories of race, class and gender oppression in the development of culturally relevant processes that were racially inclusive rather than exclusive..

Guidelines for collection and analysis of critical qualitative/critical ethnographic data

From the above examples, it is possible to develop some general guidelines:

Data collection

- Construct your question around the issue of power – how is it manifest? what structures influence or determine situations? and how are unequal situations maintained by both structures and participants?
- Note your own power relations with participants and how these and your values change as well as how they impact on the data. Practice reflexivity of your own frames (ethnicity, class, age, gender, discipline theories) at all stages of data collection and interpretation and be transparent regarding how these are impacting on data collection and interpretation.
- Plan to collect extensive data from both the etic (outsider) and emic (insider) positions in your chosen setting. Collect multiple data sources: observational, verbal, visual, documents, questionnaires (mixed methods) etc. in order to gain the broadest view of the context. Seek diversity and counter-stories to illuminate the holistic view rather than homogenous outcomes.

Data analysis

- Use both preliminary data and thematic analysis approaches to explore links between local culture and the political, social, economic and global institutions and forces that dominate your research setting.

- Your critical assessment of the diversities and complexities of the locations and workings of power relations in your chosen settings should result in recommended strategies for, or personal/ participant action toward, empowerment and social justice.
- The complexity of critical ethnographic data can be presented through narratives, dramatic dialogues, multiple voices, layered mixed data and participant-generated visual and oral/aural data (see Chapter 24 for other ideas).

Summary

The majority of research that has been undertaken within critical ethnography has occurred in situations where socioeconomic inequality and oppression are likely to be found, in particular within the institutional structures of workplaces, schools, hospitals and in underdeveloped countries. Working with participants as co-researchers is one way of creating understandings of and helping to alleviate identified oppression while production of reports with recommendations for change can also be very effective if targeted to the right audiences.

As you will have noticed, following preliminary analysis the majority of critical and classical ethnographies have undertaken *thematic analysis* as their main data analytic approach, so a detailed demonstration of this technique is now presented.

Thematic analysis

Thematic analysis is a process of data reduction and is one of the major data analytic options in qualitative research. By the time preliminary data analysis (see Chapter 2) has been completed (the focus being questioning of the data during collection) and all the data is in, it is likely that you will have a fairly clear idea what the database contains in terms of issues that are becoming evident and you will have had the opportunity to explore aspects that initially may not have been considered central to the research question/s. Whether you are labelling the process thematic analysis, coding or a combination of both (see Chapter 21 for a discussion on terminological confusion) the following stages will be involved:

1 Read and re-read your database.
2 Recall your research questions, your theoretical frameworks, your methodology and the literature you have reviewed, and decide what is most appropriate to do with your data: rigorous segmentation? intact case studies/narratives providing the basis for a poetry/a dramatic performance/a pastiche (quilt) of voices?
3 Underline/colour key segments and/or write descriptive comments alongside in the margins where further insight is useful.
4 Group like segments.
5 Attach overarching labels and identify subgroupings.
6 Conceptualise these groupings and link with literature and theory.

Using the label 'thematic analysis' rather than 'coding', this process is conducted when a data set is complete, and one of the reasons it is not often detailed in textbooks is because it is particularly idiosyncratic. It can involve a focus on repeated words or phrases, individuals, cases or narratives, the construction of intact narratives or case studies or collating evidence of answers to the research question/s. Labels may be imposed by you derived from previous relevant literature, which you have reviewed, from evidence within the area being studied or from your gut feelings as well as from the views of those being observed or interviewed. However, despite the temptation for researchers to impose labels early in the process, qualitative research insists that the data should speak for itself initially before researcher-designed labels are over-imposed.

Process

The process is one of reducing the data into meaningful groupings that are easier to manage. There are three options:

1 *block and file* approach, if you wish to keep the data largely intact
2 *conceptual mapping* for a broad overview, or in combination with (1)
3 *segmentation*, used when close examination of fragmented data is desirable.

The following example demonstrates the block and file approach to responses to a question addressed to men in intact nuclear family groupings who are staying home to care for their young children. The question was: *'Why did you decide to stay home?'*. The block and file approach for five responses to this question appears below.

Block and file approach

Step 1: Identify relevant data and list   The following are five out of 25 interview responses to the question for male primary caregivers *'Why did you decide to stay home?'*

I've always worked from home and initially we just shared our baby's care while my wife attended university part time. In the second year she went full time studying elsewhere at night and weekends because our baby was so wakeful. Because of these factors we decided to put our daughter into day care from 9am to 2pm weekdays so we could both get some work done and I took over the rest of the day and at night.

We had always planned that my wife would look after our first child during the first 12 months then she would go back to work and I would take over until the next child arrived. But I had trouble using my qualifications and had to take up taxi driving, working 12–13 hours a day for 4 years, no holiday or sick pay, and even working those hours I couldn't make as much as my wife so our original decision made sense when the second child came along and here I am.

Well my wife had been at home for 12 years over 4 children, then I was retrenched and she found full time work so I decided to stay home with our one-year-old and start to set up a secondhand book business from home.

We didn't plan to share parenting. I worked full time and helped out when I was around, got up during the night. After 3 months my wife went crazy and said she was sick of being home. My job was giving me migraines and my wife was offered a good job so we rapidly reversed roles. We both see this as a permanent change.

I was just going crazy at work, the same old shift work routine day after day. I was just desperate to get out and my wife had loved her job as a receptionist so we decided to change for a bit and see how it went

Progression	Pre planned	Workforce change	Desire for change
1 I've always worked from home and initially we just shared our baby's care while my wife attended university part time. In the second year she went full time studying elsewhere at night and weekends because our baby was so wakeful. Because of these factors we decided to put our daughter into day care from 9am to 2pm weekdays so we could both get some work done and I took over the rest of the day and at night.	2 We had always planned that my wife would look after our first child during the first 12 months then she would go back to work and I would take over until the next child arrived. But I had trouble using my qualifications and had to take up taxi driving, working 12–13 hours a day for 4 years, no holiday or sick pay, and even working those hours I couldn't make as much as my wife so our original decision made sense when the second child came along and here I am.	3 Well my wife had been at home for 12 years over 4 children, then I was retrenched and she found full time work so I decided to stay home with our one-year-old and start to set up a secondhand book business from home.	4 We didn't plan to share parenting. I worked full time and helped out when I was around and got up during the night. After 3 months my wife went crazy and said she was sick of being home. My job was giving me migraines and my wife was offered a good job so we rapidly reversed roles. We both see this as a permanent change. 5 I was just going crazy at work the same old shift work routine day after day. I was just desperate to get out and my wife had loved her job as a receptionist so we decided to change for a bit and see how it went.

The responses have been kept intact and if overlapping occurs, this is not an issue. The headings given may stay in this form but will probably change as new data is added and consolidation and the development of new columns is desirable. For example the column 'desire for change' may need to be broken down into 'female partner's situation' and 'male partner's situation' or even further into 'work situation' or 'home situation' as more data is added.

The advantage of a block and file approach is that you can keep fairly large chunks of data intact and once your headings are finalised you can move into data display of themes, with easy-to-access quotes and case studies. The disadvantages are that you end up with huge columns of data, which can become unwieldy.

Conceptual mapping

Conceptual mapping is another way of tracking the outcomes of thematic analysis. This approach is useful when a broad overview or a quick view of a specific aspect is required.

More than one map will need to be developed in order to represent different parts of the database. Figure 5.1 shows a conceptual map of one response to the question *'What is your view of homelessness?'* presented earlier in Chapter 2.

> Well I think it's a terrible thing that in a modern society we have a problem such as this. I don't know though what we can do about it. I want to do something but I don't know what. You are constantly reminded of the problem if you go to town. They are always there asking for money. You don't know though if they really need it or if they are in fact doing quite well from begging. But if you have any caring qualities you can't ignore requests for help, when you have so much yourself.
>
> They say a lot of people choose to live on the streets – well I don't believe that. I think that is an easy thing for the authorities to say – it lets them off the hook. So really I guess the answer to your question is that I am not sure what to think about homelessness. I feel that something should be done but I feel powerless to do anything personally. I think that the time has come for the government to do something. It makes me feel very uncomfortable; I don't know what to do.

You can see from visual display that the major themes relate to personal responses and to a view that this the government's problem to solve. One of the issues with conceptual maps is that they very easily become heavy with key information. In this example you would probably develop several conceptual maps as more data was added; one for government activities as a solution, another for the emotions and feelings homelessness provokes and another for the experiences and choices of people who have become homeless.

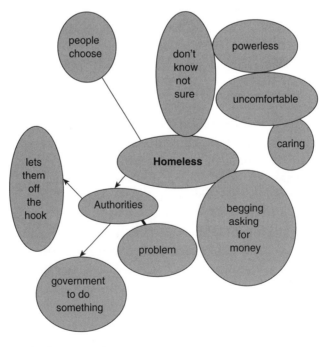

Figure 5.1   A conceptual map

Conceptual mapping provides a simpler more flexible (although potentially more decontextualising) picture of issues emerging. The advantage of the conceptual mapping approach is that you have a neat and brief summary overview of the issues that are emerging; the disadvantage is that these brief words and phrases tend to oversimplify and decontextualise issues and you need to keep going back to the database to get the fuller story. However, a combination of the block and file and conceptual mapping – moving between detail and overview – can help to minimise the disadvantages.

The advantages of both styles are that the data is now in a form from which theoretical interpretation and early writing up can be contemplated. You could take the outcomes of each approach and attempt to summarise or to re-present the data in poetic, narrative or case study format in order to excite your reader.

Segmentation/fragmentation

Here the key words or phrases from several/a set of responses are underlined/listed and then tabled/grouped and a thematic label attached to the column. These are working columns and labels and as the data mounts up new columns and labels will be developed and some columns will merge with others.

Process First *list* the key words from your participant responses. In this case the responses come from a group of parents to the question *'What were your experiences with doctors in trying to get a diagnosis'* as they tried to clarify why their young child was not developing normally:

> rude and abrupt, 'I haven't time to answer your questions', 'He's retarded … try an intervention program; some it helps, others it doesn't', the paediatrician was nice … but gave no advice on where to go, he didn't even tell me there was a disability nurse at the hospital, information isn't given freely, absolutely atrocious – referred to damaged brain separate to the child, he didn't refer to the services at the hospital let alone outside, total lack of information, there is a lack of coordination of services when a disability is diagnosed, it should be a function of the hospital to provide a support base and link to community services, absolutely atrocious – I was told she had curvature of the spine and that is all I was told, we were strongly advised to put her in a home as she would only ever be a vegetable.

Then sort and group these words under appropriate labels:

> **uncaring attitude**: rude and abrupt, 'I haven't time to answer your questions, 'He's retarded … try an intervention program; some it helps others it doesn't', absolutely atrocious – referred to damaged brain separate to the child, we were strongly advised to put her in a home as she would only ever be a vegetable

> **unhelpful attitude**: the paediatrician was nice but gave no advice on where to go, he didn't even tell me there was a disability nurse at the hospital, I was told she had curvature of the spine and that is all I was told

> **connection to services**: information isn't given freely, he didn't refer to the services at the hospital let alone outside, total lack of information, he didn't even tell me there was a disability nurse at the hospital, there is a lack of coordination of services when a disability is diagnosed, it should be a function of the hospital to provide a support base and link to community services.

Then develop a summary:

Summary: Doctor's communications with this group of parents of a young child with developmental delay have been uncaring and unhelpful, providing poor information and failing to connect parents either with existing hospital or community services.

The advantage of word-by-word, line-by-line segmentation and fragmentation is that data is meticulously examined. The disadvantage lies in decontextualisation, requiring recontextualisation from the database.

Comparing the three approaches, the overall results are similar, but greater context can be retained with the block and file approach while conceptual mapping provides a broad overview and segmentation, a focus on detail. These analytical tools are yours to choose from and you can use some or all in one study depending on what you want to do with your data.

Student exercise: Thematic analysis

Take the following two responses and block and file them:

Response 1:

For the first 10 months no one helped. I went to several doctors and a paediatrician. The paediatrician was very rude and abrupt. He told me 'He's retarded. I haven't time to answer your questions; I'm on the phone to the physiotherapist. I hope I haven't ruined your weekend. Try an intervention program; some kids it helps, some it doesn't.' The second paediatrician we saw at X hospital was nice but hasn't given us advice on where to go. I have to go and find everything myself. He didn't even tell me there was a developmental disability nurse at the hospital. Its not a very caring hospital. Information is not given freely. They don't bother to remember a child's name – don't give any extra attention. I wouldn't leave my child overnight there. I did once, he was in a very bad way when I came back in the morning. They told me he was very spoilt.

Response 2:

We finally were referred to a paediatrician at 6 months. He was absolutely atrocious – he treated the situation as though it was a damaged brain independent of the child. He didn't refer to the services in the hospital, let alone outside. There was a total lack of information as to what cerebral palsy was. There is a lack of coordination of services when disability is diagnosed. It should be a function of the hospital to provide a support base from which to move out into the community to whichever services are most appropriate.

Please visit the companion website **www.sagepub.co.uk/grbich2** for possible answers.

Further reading

Example of critical ethnography

Myers, M. and Young, L. (1997) Hidden agendas, power, and managerial assumptions in information systems development: an ethnographic study. *Information Technology & People*, 10 (3): 224–240.

Using critical ethnography, this paper discusses the development of an information system in mental health. Available at www.emeraldinsight.com/journals.htm?articleid=883478&show=abstract (accessed 10 July 2011).

Maxwell, Y. (2011) *A Realist Approach to Qualitative Research*. Thousand Oaks, CA: Sage. Maxwell applies critical theory to social and educational research with a focus on the researcher and the collection of objective data in a realist style.

Critical ethnography process

Carspecken, P. (1996) *Critical Ethnography in Educational Research*. New York: Routledge. Carspecken's approach to critical ethnography is delineated here.

Madison, D. (2011) *Critical Ethnographic Method, Ethics, and Performance* (2nd edn). Thousand Oaks, CA: Sage. This text focuses on ethics, and the performance, art and politics of fieldwork in critical ethnography. Theory and method are linked and include queer theory, feminist theory, and critical race theory, Marxism and phenomenology. Data collection techniques are covered and three fictional ethnographic case studies demonstrate the interdependence between theory and method and the significance of social theory, ethics, and performance.

Social network analysis

Alexander, M. (2013) *Introduction to Social Network Analysis*. London: Sage.

References

Bennett, K. (1991) Doing school in an urban Appalachian first-grade. In *Empowerment Through Multicultural Education*. Albany: New York. ch 1.

Carspecken, P. (1996) *Critical Ethnography in Educational Research*. New York: Routledge.

Holmes, C. and Smyth, W. (2011) Carspecken's critical methodology – a theoretical assessment. *International Journal of Multiple Research Approaches*, 5 (2): 146–54.

Knight, M., Norton, N., Bentley, C. and Dixon, I. (2004) The power of black and Latina/o counter stories: urban families and college going processes. *Anthropology and Education Quarterly*, 35 (1): 99–120.

Robertson, T. (2005) Class issues: a critical ethnography of corporate domination within the classroom. *Journal for Critical Education Policy Studies*, 3 (2) October. Retrieved from www.jceps.com/?pageID=article&article ID=52 (accessed 21 April 2012)

SIX

Feminist approaches

Feminism is a perspective with a set of principles that inform research approaches. These principles have heavily influenced qualitative research regarding researcher–researched relationships and notions of accountability. Feminists use a variety of approaches, including ethnography, phenomenology, grounded theory, hermeneutic, action and evaluative research, postmodern and poststructural approaches, within which feminist principles are applied. One specific methodology which has been developed and which incorporates and demonstrates feminist principles is memory work and this is discussed in detail later in this chapter.

KEY POINTS

- Feminist principles can be applied to all forms of qualitative approaches from ethnography to poststructuralism
- The empowerment and emancipation of female participants through the research process is an essential but contentious aspect
- These principles demand different relationships with participants in terms of equity in data collection and interpretation
- Memory work is a feminist method that has been developed and widely used to illuminate women's life experiences and help them relieve their contribution to their own oppression

---

Introduction

When to use: When undertaking research where the position of women in society is of primary importance.

Type of research questions best suited: Why do women earn less than men in most professions? Why are women the major carers of children and the elderly in most societies? Why do so few women achieve senior positions in organisations?

Strengths: A focus on inequality and a capacity to empower women.

Weaknesses: Does not take into account the diversity within males and focuses only on them as a homogeneous group controlling the patriarchal structures that disempower women. Achievement of empowerment and emancipation tend to be presumed rather than demonstrated or evaluated in the research process.

Feminist principles

Although the content of the set of principles of feminist research has been hotly debated by feminists of various epistemological and political leanings, there is general agreement on the following aspects:

- that there is inequality in our society which has been constructed along gender lines and this has left women as a group subordinated to men in terms of socioeconomic status and decision making power; structural and cultural expectations and practices continue to reinforce these inequalities
- that current modes of knowledge disadvantage women by devaluing their ways of knowing and their forms of knowledge construction
- that highlighting the experiences of women through research and allowing their voices to be heard may go some way to making these inequalities more widely recognised and may also encourage political action to redress oppressive practices, and
- that transformation of society through empowerment (the capacity to be able to assert personal power through having and making choices) and emancipation (freedom from the control of others) of women, particularly those participating in research, is seen as a desirable outcome.

Within feminist qualitative research these principles demand different relationships between researcher and participants in terms of equality, empowerment and data interpretation.

The researcher and the researched

The relationship between the researcher (usually female, although some males have utilised feminist approaches) and the researched (women) seeks to conform to the following guidelines:

- non-exploitative relationships between you and those you are researching
- exposure of your position and your personal biography in relation to the position you take on the topic. Your emotions and values and how these impact on your view of reality need to be addressed as well as how this view of reality will be managed in the data gathering, analytical and interpretative phases
- the voices of the researched should be heard in their own words and ownership (and interpretation) of narratives should be shared between you and your participants in an egalitarian manner.

These guidelines have produced some interesting dilemmas. Ideally, your relationships should be as equal and as non-exploitative as possible. However, those who undertake research are usually educated students, academics, community or government researchers and inevitably these people will maintain control over the topic, the design, the analysis, and the final interpretation of data. Techniques used by researchers which may minimise differences between you and those you are researching have included divulging aspects of your self by clarifying who you are, what your interests in the topic are, how you plan to conduct the research and what you hope to do with the data contributed by participants. Friendships with participants have also been seen as a desirable outcome but the short-term shallow relationships that usually develop during research can hardly be glorified with the term 'friendship'.

How do these guidelines play out in practice?

Issues of equality   In a study of self-reclamation in the process of leaving an abusive conjugal relationship, Marilyn Merritt-Gray and Judith West (2011) collected the stories of six survivors of abuse living in geographically isolated areas, returning to involve each in the refinement of the emerging framework gained through a grounded theory analytical approach. The focus on the women as 'survivors' rather than 'victims' enabled a different perspective to emerge, allowing emphasis on the women's active management of the abusive situation. While waiting to break free, these women underwent three phases of reclaiming the self: relinquishing parts of self; minimising abuse; and fortifying defences before they achieved the final stages of moving out and moving on.

Here the researchers have tried to minimise differences, but appear to have taken control of the initial analytical process then presented the outcomes to participants for their agreement or assessment in an attempt to share power.

Empowerment of participants

The whole concept of emancipation and empowerment of participants raises several issues you need to grapple with. What does this actually mean? And for whom? Who is actually emancipating who? And from what? And what would this look like in terms of outcomes? These terms together with 'consciousness raising' have overtones of a superior position inhabited by the researcher to which participants might aspire. This places you as researcher in the space occupied by early Christian missionaries, who with religious zeal set out to convert the 'natives' to a culture and a set of beliefs that they perceived to be of a higher order than those of the 'primitive' natives.

You will find the oppression that women are seen to experience can be better addressed if the following are in place:

- recognition of the value-driven nature of research and the practice of reflexivity
- a research agenda driven by participants
- a focus on improvement of participant's lives (rather than on achieving researcher publication) as the major outcome
- inclusion of a diversity of participants, including 'elites'
- use of language that is recognised and meaningful to participants
- contextualisation and substantiation of data so readers can make their own judgments rather than you presenting a single 'truth' for their acceptance or rejection
- presentation of ways in which women may improve their situation.
  (Adapted from Wadsworth 2001: 4–5)

In feminist participatory action research, empowerment of participants is seen as being gained through their participation in and reflection of the research process and through transformation of their perspectives via challenging new ideas provided by the researcher. However, participating in research has not always (nor even often) led to life changes of the transformatory type, and is a greater understanding of one's oppression necessarily empowering? Power differentials still remain an issue, particularly where knowledge of the research process with regard to planning, interpretation, analysis and the writing up of the results and discussion, are concerned. Do participants want to be involved in these time-consuming processes anyway?

Feminist approaches to data analysis and interpretation

This often involves a direct imposition of feminist frames, as in the above example on domestic violence. With less direct imposition but with a specific agenda, Melissa Fisher (2010) explored documentary evidence of the challenges to gender roles on Wall Street over 60 years via the examination two women's networks – The Financial Women's Association and the Women's Campaign Fund (now Forum). She found that active and creative tactics had been applied and that these networks had shifted the sites of their spatial tactics for visibility over time from using downtown financial spaces like the stock market and the organisation of events to celebrate women's achievements in male-dominated industries to using the press, feminist performance artists' autobiographical storytelling and the 'democratic' professional–managerial spaces throughout Manhattan. One example of this was an event at Christie's auction house where a dozen women on ladders appeared in the middle of the room talking about the history of the women's movement and the need for female representation in government. This ladder piece of performance art brought feminism into political and corporate institutions such as Wall Street, challenging its perceived inequality, discrimination, and social and gender injustice. Within the postmodern/poststructural tradition, disruption of traditional research practice forces a process of reflexivity onto the viewer/reader, thus minimising researcher control of the interpretive process and re-emphasising participants' views.

To show in more detail how feminist principles have been applied in research I have chosen the method of *memory work*. Although feminist principles can provide the underpinnings for any kind of qualitative approach, there is only one actual 'method' that is uniquely feminist.

Memory work

The feminist narrative method of memory work was developed from the work of Frigga Haug and her collective in the late 1980s. It uses an emancipatory feminist focus within the critical theory of Marxism and social constructivism to help women rewrite memories of past oppression in order to liberate themselves. The underlying assumption is that women's oppression has occurred as part of their (unrealising) collusion with the wider (male) society to enter into societal roles and positions of lesser value than those occupied by men. As women go through life they are seen as experiencing various important events and their memories and the reconstructions of these form a critical part of the construction of the self. This identity construction then feeds further into the interpretation of later events as they occur – reinforcing and justifying particular positioning. In memory work the group processes involve tracing back aspects of women's work and gender relations through memories in order to demonstrate how the women have taken an active part in oppressive female socialisation processes. Identification of the construction and reconstruction of memories in the presentation of self in a patriarchal culture and should result in considerable adaptation and change for the women involved. The outcome sought is transformation via increased awareness of their contribution to the exploitations they have experienced.

The role of the researcher

In pursuing notions of equality, you are required to become part of the group of participants under study, so although you have a facilitating role you are also examining and exposing your own life experiences and subjecting these to the gaze of the other participants (usually referred to as co-researchers) as well as to your own critically reflective analysis.

The method

There are three main stages:

1 Involves the tracing of memories and the identification of processes of construction from each co-researcher's perspective.
2 The group then takes the collective memories and seeks to understand how each memory has come to be constructed in this particular way and how interaction within the wider society, including through the responses of other women, has reinforced their oppression. Common themes are then drawn out across the memories of the group.
3 The application of theoretical constructs to the memories occurs to facilitate a new interpretation. This is usually managed by you in the position of researcher.

Let us look at each of these in more detail, and using the basic processes developed by Crawford et al. (1992).

1. The tracing of memory and re-presentation of it in written form   All participants identify a particular episode in their lives relevant to the topic of the research and write several pages about it. Sometimes it helps to write it initially in the first person to try to get inside the experience but ultimately the third person voice will represent the final product, i.e. 'Jane (pseudonym) went to … and Jane felt this or did that …' Participants are asked to describe the episode as vividly as memory permits to show the impact it had on them at the time, bringing in state of mind, mood, emotions, sound, smells, the environment etc. This helps to start distancing the participant from the action or event and allows the beginnings of another perspective to form. As much circumstantial and other detail as possible is encouraged, including anything that may seem trivial and inconsequential. Neither explanations nor interpretations are sought, just pure description.

2. Collective examination of memories to identify social meanings   This is a recursive process involving moving from the memories to cross-sectional analysis and back again. The participants in the group now discuss each memory in turn and question 'What did you mean by ...? And 'Did you experience that ...?' in order to clarify meaning. As the memories have focused on a particular topic and people's experiences of this, connections across the memories are sought and compared but, more especially, lack of connections and differences are highlighted and these are not to be contextualised within that person's biography. Clarification of ambiguities and any identified omissions are also sought – the silences and unsaid/unwritten aspects that might be expected to be there but which are missing from the written memory are often very revealing of issues of deep significance that have been too painful or too problematic to be written.

You then seek general societal explanations – the myths and clichés that have currency amongst media discourses and the general public together with new concepts from such sources as Marxism, critical psychology and Michel Foucault as well as a range of feminist theorists. At this point the memories may be rewritten to be more inclusive of missing aspects or they may not, depending on the group.

3. Reappraisal of memories   The general societal explanations identified in discussion in the second stage are then related and situated within academic literature and the group of women takes part in this process. Their autobiographies should then have the capacity to illustrate how the formation of identity and the production of self within a particular social context have contributed to the reproduction of a particular societal order. The provision of a bridge between experience and theory will enable the development of new discursive frameworks. The disruption and destabilisation of past interpretations should break their continuity and provide the potential for transforming and liberating the women involved.

Studies using memory work

Researchers using memory work approaches have come from such diverse fields as tourism, business, marketing, health, psychology, sociology, women's studies, education, cultural studies and management and have included the topics of female sexualisation (Haug, 1987); women's negotiation of heterosexuality (Kippax et al., 1988); menstruation (Davies, 1990); emotion and gender (Crawford et al., 1992); older women's well-being (Mitchell, 1993); the experiences of women leaders (Boucher, 1997); literacy and numeracy (O'Conor, 1998); links between bodies and the landscape (Davies, 2000); female sexuality (Farrer, 2000); customer service (Friend, 1997); leisure experiences (Friend et al., 2000); educational learning and assessment (Rummel and Friend, 2000); emotions and learning mathematics (Ingleton, 2000); profeminist subjectivities among men (Pease, 2000); women's speaking positions (Stephenson, 2001); tourism experiences (Small, 2003), the patriarchy of aid agencies (Sangtin Writers and Richa Nagar, 2006) and gendered spaces (Bryant and Livholts, 2007).

The following examples explicate processes, dilemmas and adaptations of this form of research.

Adding an additional stage

Bronwyn Davies (2000) provided a more autobiographical focus than the original method described by Haug (1987), seeing the processes of writing and sharing and rewriting and reinterpreting as blurring the boundaries that normally separate researcher and researched. She has added a preliminary stage to the process which involves the group in choosing the topic to be explored and discussing it verbally in terms of individual stories and current societal/cultural interpretations – rather like a pre-focus group. This process leads to uncovering the stories that are behind the more obvious stories that may spring to mind, forming the basis of more detailed written memories.

Truncated stages

Lorraine Friend (1997) has truncated the method by following the first two stages only. She asked women to write about a 'nasty retail clothing shopping experience' then went straight to individual and cross-textual comparison. The group discussions were taped and the researcher separately further analysed these and the interpretations were fed back to the participants to confirm accuracy. The separating out of the theoretical phase allows participants to share memories and identify sociocultural explanations but may well limit any emancipation or transformation.

Adding reflective interpretation

The writing in the third person to create a more distant perspective can be seen here in an autobiographical study of life challenges (Lapadat et al., 2010):

Job loss (Ruby)

When she arrived at work that summer morning, she saw her boss. It flashed through her mind that it was odd for her boss to be at work when she was supposed to be on vacation, but she was too weary to ponder this. Instead, she consciously avoided her boss and tried to quietly slip upstairs to her office. But her boss had been purposefully waiting for her. Her boss called to her, I need to talk with you, she said. They walked towards the meeting room. Her boss held a file.

This is going to be bad, said her boss. She heard this and thought I'm so tired of hearing that, if I never have to hear that again, I will be so happy. They were in the room, the door was shut, they sat at the table, and her boss opened the file and read: effective immediately your employment is terminated. Her boss looked up, give me your keys, she said. She gave the keys to her boss. Her boss continued reading. You have lost the confidence of the management team. She heard those words and thought, well, the management team has lost my confidence, too. Her boss was still reading. You may choose to be fired, or you may choose to resign and I will accept your letter of resignation.

A choice, she thought, a choice? This is no choice. Everything was unreal, dreamlike. Time had frozen. Her body had frozen, her blood had frozen.

(Lapadat et al., 2010: 83)

These researchers adapted the original memory work approach slightly focussing it more to an autoethnographic style with an interpretivist underpinning using narrative, reflexive and thematic analyses, as in the final stage of Ruby's writings, where reflection and understanding of one's own contribution to one's life events can be seen.

> Often we will not immediately see, understand, or interpret what is going on around us, even though our bodies and minds may be sending us signals. We are caught up in responsibilities, expectations (real or imagined or imposed), and perhaps we do not see a solution until some outside action becomes the catalyst for change ...

> Various experiences or memories shape us and carry us through life challenges. This in turn contributes to our maturity, confidence and ability to adapt to situations, events or emergencies. It's as if these memories are catalogued and filed in our minds as touch-stones for future reference: to help us understand or make meaning from our experiences, to inform us when similar situations arise, to share with others who may learn from us, and for healing. (Ruby)

> (Lapadat et al., 2010: 97–8)

Emphasis on theorising

Overt political theorising has also been added. The Sangtin collective used memory work to tackle social change in India and the obstructive domination of aid agencies (Sangtin Writers and Richa Nagar, 2006). A collective of seven voices of rural women employed as activists in their own rural communities by a large donor-driven non-government agency for developing countries, sought to understand their lives and work at family, community and global levels in order to clarify future directions. Three years of data was based on diaries, interviews and conversations among the collective. Together their diverse personal stories revealed larger themes and questions of sexism, casteism and communalism, and showed how the aid agency both nourished and stifled local struggles for solidarity. The Hindi edition of their book, *Sangtin Yatra*, published in 2004, created controversy that resulted in a backlash against the authors by their employer, who tried to silence them and claim ownership of their voices. In the above publication Richa Nagar addresses the dispute in the context of the politics of NGOs and feminist theory, articulating how development ideology employed by aid organisations serves to disempower those it claims to help.

Lia Bryant and Mona Livholts (2007) also reincorporated theorising using dialogue to develop interpretations relating to landscape, movement, fear, agency and differentiation of gender relations across and within spaces in the connection of memories and emotions of gendered spaces to explain the three dominant themes that had emerged: gendered bodies and landscapes – space in unfamiliar spaces; movement and restricted spaces – place and time in travel; and disrupting space and time – via material media and telephones.

Criticism of memory work

Criticisms of the memory work approach have included:

- Using friends/close acquaintances to form the group is not always ideal – some women may find it difficult or even impossible to discuss deep or buried emotional issues which may change others' perceptions of them in negative ways.

- Women who have no background in academic theory may either become subjects and experience minimal emancipation or transformation or they may prefer not to use academic theories to interpret their lives and this will impact on emancipation and analysis of memories.
- The group may tend to indulge in primitive psychotherapeutics in the sharing of memories, which is not productive.
- The focus on Marxist frameworks tends to produce a particular explanation of individual action as conformity rather than resistance, which may not sit well with group interpretations. Studies that have emphasised resistance and coping, despite the restrictions of a patriarchal culture, tend to have a more positive outcome for participants than those that emphasise women as victims.

Jenny Onyx and Jennie Small (2001: 779–81) indicate other issues that have emerged from use of the method over time:

- The status of the individual's memories becomes somewhat problematic when they are challenged and reconstituted by the collective. To what extent can painful and personal memories be deconstructed and what if this process is not an emancipatory one for the individual?
- What happens when the individual refuses to accept the collective's analysis or the whole collective rejects the researcher's theoretical frames as explanations too foreign to be of relevance to their lives?
- How are differences of opinion to be maintained and managed in the group process?
- Is it really possible to share ownership with a researcher who will also ultimately gain through publishing the work?
- In terms of analysis and final publication, what happens to the material from the first and second stages? Are these just discarded as not fitting the needs of academia and publishing? Where do they best fit?
- Whose voices are being silenced, particularly when issues of academic credibility are important?
- What happens to notions of emancipation and transformation when the groups are more interested in sharing than theorising their experiences?

Clearly the analytical processes in memory work will depend on the collective: their capacity for subjective, reflective discussion and their preparedness to take on the literature in terms of more abstract interpretations. But the issues surrounding both memory work and feminist research will continue to be hotly debated.

Summary

Feminist principles relating to empowerment and emancipation of women, who are seen as unequal to men in most societies, are well entrenched across research practice. Some of these principles, in particular the equalisation of power relations between researcher and researched, have become mainstream practice in qualitative research although varying degrees of equality can be observed here. The contentious issues in feminist research continue to relate to who has the most power and control over the research design, data collection and analysis together with the issues of empowerment and emancipation of participants. Even if these issues have not been solved, the levels of transparency involved in feminist research have provided a clear insight into the complexities of practice and fuelled debates across all versions of qualitative research.

Further reading

Feminist principles and methods

Hesse-Biber, S. and Leavey, P. (2007) *Feminist Research Practice*. Thousand Oaks, CA: Sage. A large number of feminist researchers have contributed to this text. Feminist empiricist, feminist standpoint and postmodern perspectives are explored, amongst others.

Pascale, C. (2011) *Cartographies of Knowledge: Exploring Qualitative Epistemologies*. Thousand Oaks, CA: Sage. The focus is gender inequality, violence against women, body image issues, and the discrimination of 'other/ ed' marginalised groups. Feminist ethnography, oral history, focus groups, content analysis, interviewing, survey and mixed methods research concerned with feminist social justice, critical race, and poststructural approaches are included.

Memory work

Haug, F. (1999) *Female Sexualization* (trans. E. Carter). London: Verso. This collective work explores the sexualisation of women's bodies, charting the complex interplay of social, political, and cultural forces which produces a normative 'femininity'.

References

Boucher, C. (1997) How women construct leadership in organisations: a study using memory work. *Gender, Work and Organisation*, 4 (3): 149–58.

Bryant, L. and Livholts, M. (2007) Memory work as a reflexive methodology in exploring the gendering of space. *International Journal of Qualitative Methods*, 6 (3): 29.

Crawford, J., Kippax, S., Onyx, J., Gault, U. and Benton, P. (1992) *Emotion and Gender: Constructing Meaning from Memory*. London: Sage.

Davies, B. (1990) Menstruation and women's subjectivity. Paper presented at the Australian Sociological Association (TASA) University of Queensland: Brisbane.

Davies, B. (2000) *(In)scribing Body/Landscape Relations*. Walnut Creek, CA: AltaMira Press.

Farrer, P. (2000) Relinquishment and abjection: a seminanalysis of the meaning of losing a baby to adoption. Unpublished doctoral dissertation, University of Technology, Sydney.

Fisher, M. (2010) Wall Street women: engendering global finance in the Manhattan landscape. *City & Society*, 22 (2): 262–85. Retrieved from http://onlinelibrary.wiley.com/doi/10.1111/j.1548-744X.2010.01042.x/full (accessed 3 August 2011).

Friend, L. (1997) Understanding consumer satisfaction and dissatisfaction of clothing retail encounters. Unpublished doctoral dissertation, Otago University, New Zealand.

Friend, L., Grant, B. and Gunson, L. (2000) Memories. *Australian Leisure Management*, 20 (Apr–Jun): 24–5.

Haug, F. (1987) *Female Sexualisation: A Collective Work of Memory* (trans. E. Carter). London: Verso.

Ingleton, C. (2000) Emotion in learning – a neglected dynamic. *Research and Development in Higher Education*, 27: 86–9.

Kippax, S., Crawford, J., Benton, T., Gault, U. and Noesjirwan, J. (1988) Constructing emotions: weaving meaning from memories. *British Journal of Social Psychology*, 27 (1): 19–33.

Lapadat, J., Black, M., Clark, P., Gremm, R., Karanja. L., Mieke, M. and Quinlan, L. (2010) Life challenge memory work: using collaborative autobiography to understand ourselves. *International Journal of Qualitative Methods*, 9(1): 78–104. Retrieved from https://ejournals.library.ualberta.ca/index.php/IJQM/article/view/1542/6496 (accessed 13 July 2011).

Merritt-Gray, M. and West, J. (2011) *Reclaiming Self: A Feminist Grounded Theory of the Leaving Process in Abusive Conjugal Relationships*. Virginia Henderson Nursing Library. Retrieved from http://hdl.handle. net/10755/176899 (accessed 11 November 2011).

Mitchell, T. (1993) Bridesmaids revisited: health, older women and memory work. Unpublished masters thesis, Flinders University of South Australia.

O'Conor, C. (1998) Assessment and us: a memory work project. *Literacy and Numeracy Exchange*, 1: 53–70.

Onyx, J. and Small, J. (2001) Memory work: the method. *Qualitative Inquiry* 7 (6): 773–86.

Pease, B. (2000) Reconstructing heterosexual subjectivities and practices with white middleclass men. *Race, Gender and Class*, 7 (1): 133–45.

Rummel, A. and Friend, L. (2000) Using memory work methodology to enhance student learning. Proceedings of the 25th International Conference, The University of the Future and the Future of Universities: Learner Centered Universities for the New Millennium. Frankfurt Germany. pp. 326–30.

Sangtin Writers and Richa Nagar (2006) *Playing with Fire: Feminist Thought and Activism Through Seven Lives in India*. Minneapolis, MN: University of Minnesota Press.

Small, J. (2003) Good and bad holiday experiences: women's perspectives. In M. Swain and J. Momsen (eds), *Gender, Tourism, Fun?* Elmsford, NY: Cognizant Communications Corp.

Stephenson, N. (2001) If parties are battles, what are we? Practising collectivity in memory work. In J. Small and J. Onyx (eds), *Memory Work: A Critique*. Working paper series. School of Management, University of Technology, Sydney, Australia.

Wadsworth, Y. (2001) What is feminist research? Paper presented at Bridging the Gap: Feminists and Participatory Action Research Conference, Boston. June. Retrieved from www.wnmu.org/gap/wadsworth. htm (accessed 13 April 2006).

SEVEN

Grounded theory

Grounded theory is an approach that was developed in the 1960s in order to generate theory from observations of real life as these were occurring. This chapter looks briefly at three versions of grounded theory: Barney Glaser's version; the multiple processes inherent in the form of grounded theory developed by Anselm Strauss; and the constructionist approach developed by Kathy Charmaz.

KEY POINTS

- Grounded theory is a useful approach when the microcosm of interaction in poorly researched areas is the focus of the research question
- There are three main versions of grounded theory
  - Straussian, which has a focus on fragmentation of data through a three-stage coding process
  - Glaserian, which is closer to field-based/hermeneutic qualitative research with a lesser emphasis on coding, and
  - Charmaz's constructionist approach, which more closely links researcher with participants
- Like all qualitative approaches, grounded theory has developed into a number of different versions either through dilution of the original approach, by combination with other approaches or through the inclusion of a new orientation such as postmodernism

---

Introduction

When to use: When there is little or no prior knowledge of an area, when the microcosm of interaction in particular settings is to be observed and all related aspects need to be explored and when there is a need for new theoretical explanations built on empirical knowledge to explain changes in the field.

Type of research questions best suited: Those relating to interaction between persons or among individuals and specific environments.

Strengths: Can really tease out the elements of the operation of a setting or the depths of an experience.

Weaknesses: Too much fragmentation of the data (Straussian version) may lead to loss of the bigger picture.

Grounded theory: underlying assumptions

The grounded theory perspective locates the phenomena of human experiences within the world of social interaction. The assumptions underpinning grounded theory come originally from symbolic interactionism and presume that reality is a constructed and shifting entity and social processes can be created and changed by interactions among people. There is a focus on the construction of self within the social processes of society, through interaction in the social world. 'Meaning' is achieved through the use of symbols, signs and language, and our ability to take the position of others and interpret our own actions from that position through the two phases of consciousness; the 'I' (the uninhibited self) and the 'me' (the societal controls reflected in the attitudes, values and behaviours of significant others). These symbolic interactionist underpinnings derive from George Mead as well as from the writings of John Dewey and Charles Peirce. These writers emphasised change, action and interaction in social settings and the construction of meaning through our reflections on both the phenomena and on our own roles. The focus in grounded theory then becomes life as it is actually happening – the empirical, social world 'out there'. This world is viewed as comprising many different layers, as well as public and private views.

Grounded theory, like ethnography, uses the inductive approach (which relies on observations to develop understandings, processes, laws and protocols) and ultimately aims for construction of substantive and formal theory. The grounded theory approach emerged in the mid 1960s and was the brainchild of two academics: Barney Glaser (a psychologist) and Anselm Strauss (a sociologist) (Glaser and Strauss, 1967). It was seen as a way of shifting researchers from theory directed to theory generating research using observations of reality to construct both meaning and theories that were relevant to the mid-twentieth century rather than those that had been developed for the late nineteenth century. The primary focus then became the investigation of the context of the setting within which the day-to-day lives of people were occurring – their interactions, their behaviours and their constructions of reality, which were further reconstructed through researchers' frames of reference. A secondary agenda of Glaser and Strauss involved exposure of the processes of qualitative data analysis in order to demonstrate that these were close in meticulous practice to those of the quantitative tradition and therefore were worthy of consideration.

The formal aims of grounded theory are to generate an analytic substantive schema through processes of theoretical sensitivity (awareness of and application of existing theory) which, after comparison with other substantive areas, can become formal theory (Grand). The approach is best used for small-scale environments and micro activity where little previous research has occurred. Although Glaser and Strauss jointly devised this approach, they soon parted company and developed different emphases in their approaches to data analysis (Glaser, 1978; Strauss, 1987) – Strauss to stage-based coding and Glaser to a more general hermeneutic approach and these have firmed up into two very different approaches, a summary of which can be seen in Table 7.1.

The Glaserian approach to grounded theory

From Table 7.1 it becomes evident that Glaser is opposed to what he sees as 'fracturing' the data through the various stages of coding and prefers the constant comparison of incident to incident and incident to emerging concepts in order to enable the development of new theoretical explanations rather than framing data with existing conceptual positions. Glaser indicates that through open coding, theoretical sampling and constant comparison the answers will emerge. Glaser's approach would be closer to a more meticulous version of the form of preliminary data analysis, previously described in Chapter 2, followed by a grouping of emerging categories derived from empirical data which are then combined with a close reading of relevant literature in order to facilitate the constant comparative process of indicator to concept. The researcher 'should simply code and analyze categories and properties with theoretical codes which will emerge and generate their complex theory of a complex world' (Glaser, 1992: 71). He sees the difference between grounded theory and the management of the data from field research not as the highly organised turning of a huge pile of data into themes and categories but as a looser process of generating connections and ideas and explaining them theoretically.

In more detail, the focus for Glaser is the substantive problem to be researched, its variations and its categories (those emerging and those it is linked to). He suggests you seek for the underlying patterns amid the many perspectives that participants present. These can be identified by adding an abstract layer of conceptualisation, which helps to distance you from the data, and should allow you to see patterns more clearly. He rejects the constructivist orientation, with its interacting interpretations between you and participant, as inappropriate for grounded theory, seeing your role as researcher (although inevitably biased) as one of greater passivity in the receiving of data, and

Table 7.1 Grounded theory: differences between Glaser and Strauss

Characteristic	Glaser	Strauss
Style	Discovery	Verification
Question	Problem + variations	Dimensionalising and critiquing
Process	Emergent directions	Coding and hypothesis testing
Literature review	Ongoing from first category identification	When categories emerge – if desired
Coding	Constant comparison	Three levels of data fracturing
Open coding	Words, lines, sections	Words, lines, paragraphs
Axial coding	Unnecessary	Meticulous procedure
Selective coding	Core variables only	Core categories to other categories
Theory	Theory generation	Theory verification

one where there is minimal intrusion of your own predilections as you go about the constant comparative process (Glaser, 2002). Glaser avoids reviewing the literature until the first core variables or categories have been identified, then literature relating to these categories should be examined and any further categories should be explored as they emerge.

Theoretical sensitivity is one area where Glaser has held stronger views than Strauss. According to Glaser, 'sensitivity is necessarily increased by being steeped in the literature that deals with both the kinds of variables and their associated general ideas that will be used' (1978: 3), and these ideas can be derived from a range of disciplines.

The processes that help to enable this to occur are:

- *theoretical sampling* – the process whereby you concurrently collect, code and analyse/interpret data in an ongoing process
- *memoing* – the development of theoretical and conceptual links and their relationships within the empirical data which serve to transcend this data and are made each time you move into coding the data collected
- *saturation* – an awareness that no new information is emerging
- *substantive coding* – theoretical codes that conceptualise how substantive codes relate to each other and consolidate the story emerging from the data, which will form the basis of the final written version.

Example

This example comes from the *Grounded Theory Review,* an international journal that emerged from Glaser's website and which publishes Glaserian-style grounded theories. Thulesios and Grahn (2007) explored sickness absences in Sweden using 130 interviews, data from meetings, conferences and literature, plus sick leave data from a cohort of 196 people. In the Glaserian tradition interviews were not recorded but field notes were gathered. The cyclic process of comparing incidents, creating categories, memo writing and linking to theoretical codes developed the theory of 'reincentivising' work and identifying incentives and 'traps' (repair and release) in the journey back to work.

The Straussian approach to grounded theory

Anselm Strauss indicates that in his version of grounded theory the first step is for you to raise generative questions from your insights in order to develop concepts and propositions and to explore their relationships. Provisional linkages can be made and verified using real-life data.

The processes involved in Strauss's version of grounded theory involve the following.

Dimensionalising and subdimensionalising

The earliest work occurs on the research question itself. Refining it involves you in a basic operation of making distinctions in terms of dimensions and subdimensions. For example, Strauss developed the question *'How does the use of machines in intensive care units affect interaction between staff and patients?'* – the dimension of mind–body connection. Such mind–body connections can be either internal or external to particular body parts and can be further subdimensionalised into levels of discomfort and safety issues. This process helps to open up the research question and to gain insights into the areas where data needs to be collected.

Open coding

You must undertake this process every time data is collected. Open coding involves word-by-word, line-by-line analysis questioning the data in order to identify concepts and categories which can then be dimensionalised (broken apart further). Core to this process is the concept-indicator model where analytical concepts are drawn from empirical indicators in the data by comparing indicator to indicator. A conceptual code is then developed and the indicators are further compared to this. Changes may be made to these codes until a process of saturation is achieved and no new information is emerging regarding the properties of the category or code. The words 'code' and 'category' tend to be used interchangeably by Strauss but he does define category as a distinction emerging from the process of dimensionalising and indicates that codes surround a core category and strengthen it.

Strauss has suggested that the following guidelines may be useful in undertaking open coding:

- Look for 'in vivo' (within the data) codes and attach existing concepts (from your own discipline) to these
- Name each code
- The application of the following questions will gain broader dimensions:
  - What is going on here?
  - Why is this being done?
  - What if this or that changed?
  - What would be the outcome of any change?
  - What category does this incident indicate?
- Locate comparative cases
- Account for all data in the coding process.
  (Adapted from Strauss, 1987: 30–32)

This constant critiquing of data should enable you to break open the text and lead you to seek specific examples of this or that aspect (theoretical sampling) in a process of induction (inferences from observations), deduction (reasoning from general to particular instances) and verification (double-checking or cross-checking against other data). Strauss has provided pages of his initial stream of conscious thought undertaken during open coding, a small part of which is shown below to illuminate the process.

Open coding as a stream of thought

"*She changed ...*" This is a task [drawn from common experience]

"*She changed ...*" She is doing the task by herself. This apparently does not require any immediate division of labour [a category drawn from technical literature]. However there is a division of labour involved in supplying the blood, an issue I will put aside for later consideration [raising a general question about that category]

(Continued)

"*... the blood transfusion bag*" "Blood transfusion" tells that this is a piece of equipment, the bag and its holder requires supplies [category]. Again, a fascinating issue, about which I can ask questions in a moment.

Let us look at the 'changed' qua task. What are its properties or what questions can I ask about its properties? Is it visible to others (the dimension here being visible–invisible). It seems like a simple task so it probably doesn't take much skill. It's a task that follows another (replace one bag with another). It seems routine – it doesn't take long to do. Is it boring or just routine? It isn't a strenuous task either and certainly it doesn't seem challenging. How often must she do this in a day's work? That is, how often does it take for the blood to get transfused into the patient? Or, perhaps, how much time is allowed to elapse before new blood is actually transfused into the patient between each bag? Or does that depend on her assessment of the patient's condition? What would happen if they temporarily ran out of the bags of blood? [Implication of safety for the patient which will be looked at later]. I would hypothesize that if there is no immediate danger, then replacing it would have low salience. But if there were potential danger for certain kinds of patients, then there would be organisational mechanisms for preventing even a temporary lack of blood bags. Well I could go on with this focus on the task, but enough.

(Strauss, 1987: 60;. reprinted with permission)

The processes of opening up the data through the twin processes of constantly questioning the data and then comparing the data with other empirical data and linking to conceptual frameworks can clearly be seen here. To show what not to do Strauss also reproduced an example of open coding undertaken by one of his students:

Open coding: version 1

"*Our society is so locked into the physical*"... when you've got a major deviation you have got to come to terms with it, what's meaningful, what's bullshit. While someone else may be dealing with feeling too fat, for example, if your whole body is different, you've got to come to terms with it. It can be a liberating experience, a time for reassessment

"*Our society*" ... "*Our society is so locked into the physical*"... this implies a notion of some big "Society", with a capital S, as opposed, perhaps, to what she or some others might think. Anyway I think it implies that there is another way of looking at things than "our society" does. "Our society" is a powerful, impersonal, abstract entity. Normative and impersonal.

"*is so locked into*" Locked – this is a very strong word. It suggests a strong connection. Not just "partial to" or "accustomed to" but "locked into". Sounds permanent, restricting, involuntary, certain.

"*the physical*" Physical – as opposed to psychological, emotional, spiritual. Notions of beauty, perfect bodies, magazine ads. Not various standards of beauty, but one. Does not imply being understanding and tolerant of physical differences, but being locked into one standard of physical perfection. Judging people physically.

(Strauss: 1987:153; reprinted with permission)

The problem in version 1 is that the student has not questioned the data but simply summarised it – there is no opening up of the debate nor looking to see where other data aspects will need to be pursued.

The following version 2 is an attempt to demonstrate how the same data could be treated within Strauss's guidelines:

Open coding: version 2

'Our society' contains an assumption that all those within a defined location or racial boundaries see themselves as one homogenous group – but are they homogenous? and are all views shared? Most societies are very diverse in terms of race, colour, age, gender roles, ability, disability and social and political views (I think diversity may be a key concept here). But what does diversity mean, particularly with regard to people with disabilities and their views? And how does any variety in views impact on policy? funding? and on individuals both abled and disabled? Is it different when the media portrays the 'heroically disabled' or is it notably silent regarding disability?

'is so locked into the physical' reinforces the notion of a cohesive society? Have societies always favoured the physically perfect? What about the notion of 'special gifts' from a higher being and the Paralympic Games – or are these viewed as imitations of the real heroes, the physically abled?

'Locked' links to 'unlocked'. But how 'locked' is locked? What does 'unlocked' look like? When has the physical been of lesser importance or unlocked? or mental abilities seen as a substitute for a lack of physical capacity? An example of this could be Stephen Hawking? What other forms of diversity or variety of approach are evident?

Theoretical memos

You will need to write these up every time data is collected and open coded and they become a record of identification of both indicators and categories from the database and of the link with concepts (which may come from the literature or be imposed by you). Memos are a descriptive record of ideas, insights, hypothesis development and testing.

The purpose of memoing is to:

- follow the pathway from indicator to concept
- develop the properties of each category
- identify hypotheses relating to categories
- link categories and generate theory.

Memos emphasise conceptual and theoretical processes and are consolidated over time. The detail of what is being observed and reflected on by you as researcher can be seen in the following example.

Example memo: spiritual care

I observed nurse F. working with a woman who had 'locked in syndrome' after having had a stroke. One week ago she was a healthy active 36-year-old woman with two young children, now

(Continued)

(Continued)

she could not communicate with her family at all. Visiting hours were a real trial to her, causing her and her family great sadness. Mrs C. was unable to move or speak, she could not even shed a tear when she cried. Nurse F. went into Mrs C.'s room before her husband arrived to visit. She gave Mrs C.'s hair a brush and washed her face and cleaned her teeth. She sat next to her and stroked her hair and talked soothingly with her informing her quietly about the day's weather, the latest news on what was happening while she stroked her. Nurse F. asked Mrs C. questions and looked carefully at her eyes for answers. She told Mrs C. she would find out how her family were coping at home and what support they could get while she was in hospital. She ended her time spent with Mrs C. by giving her a hug and quietly whispered a joke in her ear. Mrs C.'s eyes lit up. Nurse F. left the room turning to Mrs C. and giving her a smile, a wink and a 'thumbs up' sign and then went about her other tasks.

(Van Loon, 1995: 79–80; reprinted with permission of the author)

Axial coding

Axial coding involves you in taking one core category that has emerged in open coding and linking it to all the subcategories that contribute to it, as seen in Figure 7.1.

Figure 7.1   Axial coding: spiritual care (Van Loon, 1995, reproduced with permission)

Selective coding

Selective coding is where you validate the relationship between a nominated central core category such as spiritual care by the drawing together of additional categories of context, conditions, actions, interactions and outcomes together with the focusing of memos and the generation of theory regarding this category.

Integration

This involves you in the final putting together of the two major files – the empirical data and the theoretical memos both of which have been building up along parallel lines and should now be ready to be put together more formally within the conceptual sets which have been identified. In some cases a series of operational mapping diagrams are developed in the process of sorting data and moving it toward consolidation of memos and integration in preparation for writing up illustrative data and constructing case histories.

Formal theory

This is a much later stage involving many years of research in a number of related fields. Glaser and Strauss (1971) identified the core category 'status passage' which they said was in the process of moving from substantive (empirical research) to formal theory through the ongoing process of theoretical sampling and selective coding of a range of status passages in literature and other documents. Examples such as single–married, defendant–prisoner, pregnant woman–mother, married man–divorced man, dying–death, all have an emphasis on the processes of transition.

Both Glaser (Burgess, 1982: 225–32) and Strauss (1987: 241–2) indicate that the process of developing a formal grounded theory is as follows:

- identify the core category to be developed
- open code and write memos of an example of the data in which this category occurs
- theoretically sample in a range of different areas
- continue until a wide range of sources have been covered.

Evaluation of Glaser and Strauss's grounded theory

What are the criteria for evaluating substantive/formal theory? In their earliest work, Glaser and Strauss agreed that the following provided a guide for assessment:

- *Fit* – the link between the theory and the arena where it will be used to provide insight needs to be clear.
- *Understandability* – will the theory be meaningful to those who don't work in the area from which the data has been collected?
- *Generalisability* – the theory needs to be meaningful in a large range of areas.
- *Control* – does the theory empower users in the field with knowledge to improve their situation? (Adapted from Glaser and Strauss, 1967: 237)

Criticisms of Strauss's grounded theory

Anselm Strauss's version of grounded theory has received several criticisms:

- There is a focus on a quasi-objective centred researcher with an emphasis on hypotheses, variables, validity, reliability and replicability. This contrasts with the move away from this more quantitative form of terminology in recent qualitative research approaches.
- Existing theories cannot be ignored by avoiding a literature review; the researcher invariably comes to the research topic bowed down under the weight of intellectual baggage from his/her own discipline.
- There is a focus on a complex method and confusing and overlapping terminology rather than data. The meticulous three-stage coding process with associated data fragmentation may lead the researcher to lose track of the overall picture that is emerging.
- Poorly integrated theoretical explanations tend to be the outcome where data is linked conceptually and early to existing frameworks. Concept generation rather than substantive or formal theory may be the best outcome.

Charmaz's constructivist grounded theory

More recently, Kathy Charmaz (2000, 2006) has adapted the original versions to create a 'constructivist' emphasis. The differences between her approach and those previous versions of Glaser and Strauss lie in:

- *the relationship between researcher and researched*: here she challenges the previously 'objective' nature of the relationship between researcher and participants bringing them closer to a situation of partnership in the data generation process and she also refocusses on researchers and their critical reflective role in the recognition and management of their biases (which she felt was missing from Glaser's approach); and
- *data accountability*: Charmaz suggests that immersion in and transposing raw data into memos is one way of keeping close and accountable to data (maintaining participants' voices). In addition, using non-scientific writing styles closer to the literary options available in postmodern approaches will also forefront the voices of the researched.

Criticisms of constructivist grounded theory

The formal advent of this approach (Charmaz, 2000) sparked a fairly heated debate between Glaser and Charmaz. Barney Glaser (2002) has referred to the approach as totally misrepresenting his version of grounded theory and commenting on the notion of 'bias', which he says he treats as another variable and that this together with the constant comparative process linking data with existing and emergent theory makes bias transparent. He also asserts that constructivism legitimates 'forcing' the data to the researcher's view. More recently (2009) he has accused Charmaz of just 'jargonising' – creating meaningless labels to be added to the original grounded theory approach for self-aggrandisement. Interestingly, an assessment of constructivism within classical grounded theory (Mills et al., 2006) discovered strong elements of constructivism, so word games and blinkered positions on both sides of the debate may well be an issue here. Although both protagonists have mediated their positions slightly over the past decade (Charmaz to pragmatism and Glaser recognising that 'latent patterns' or structural influences do exist in the data), the battle continues.

McCreaddie et al. (2010), who examined pain management of drug addicts in acute care settings, provide an example of constructivist grounded theory. Interviews with 11 drug users and five focus groups of nurses (n = 22) were undertaken. The core category developed was 'moral relativism', which clarified the clash between the drug users expectations of caring, compassionate treatment and acceptance of their 'rituals', with the hospital's expectations and 'rituals', which created challenges for both groups and impacted on the outcomes of pain and withdrawal management.

Method modification

General changes

Dimensional analysis has replaced coding (Schatzman, 1991) in order to bring the researcher's focus back from linear procedures (such as those suggested by Strauss) to the data itself through the use of an explanatory matrix. Each story is subjected to a process of reflection regarding attributes, dimensions and consequences and all dimensions can influence analysis. The potential of grounded theory as an integrative mechanism, particularly through the use of the Straussian guidelines for the constant comparative process, the processes of axial coding and the notions of 'fit' (accurate representation of the experience) and generality (applicability to a range of situations) to bring together evidence from both qualitative and quantitative studies for health practitioners and policy makers, has also being explored (Dixon-Woods et al., 2004)

Combinations

Many new versions of grounded theory are now evident, including 'quasi' grounded theory where the original Straussian approach has been modified so that perhaps only open coding or some form of this is incorporated. Grounded theory and Heideggerian hermeneutics (seen as interpretation of the understanding of in-depth human experiences gained via intuitive embodied knowledge of our culture) have been combined to explore nursing practice (Wilson and Hutchinson, 1991). Here the Straussian approach has been added to the hermeneutic immersion in the data to clarify themes and includes the reading of related scholarly documents – an outcome somewhat closer to the Glaserian tradition. Glaserian grounded theory and Husserlian phenomenology have also been combined (Baker et al., 1992). Here the participants' experiences of the world provide the major focus and the processes of intense reflection of experiences (bracketing) is followed by open coding from the emerging codes and categories which are then linked to a conceptual framework. Caroline Oliver (2011) has melded Bhaskar's critical realism with its objective independent reality and grounded theory (all versions) together as a framework for social work research to bridge the divide between theory and practice.

Postmodern moves

A postmodern feminist orientation, combined with Straussian grounded theory (Wuest, 1995), has been used to displace symbolic interactionism which initially underpinned the original grounded theory process. The feminist orientation provides an emphasis on multiple explanations of reality and a critical framework for exploring the shifting issues of power, knowledge, truth, gender, class, race, socioeconomic location, education and sexual orientation. The processes of reflexivity and the fluid nature of the conceptual framework utilised, are said to provide sufficient breadth in the constant comparative process. Postmodern and poststructural possibilities in grounded theory have also been explored by Star (1991).

Summary

Grounded theory has proved very popular in qualitative research. Whether you undertake the meticulous three-stage coding approach, the more general hermeneutic approach, the constructivist approach, or any creative variations or combinations, this methodology allows you to look in depth at interaction in particular contexts to see how people define and experience situations. In grounded theory, as in ethnographic approaches, the flexibility of the qualitative field allows you to be creative and to add on aspects of other approaches in order to access the information you require to answer your research question.

Student exercise

Take the memo below and subject it to a process of open coding – a rigorous questioning of the data, in particular regarding the nurse's interaction with the patient.

I observed nurse F. working with a woman who had 'locked-in syndrome' after having had a stroke. One week ago she was a healthy active 36-year-old woman with two young children, now she could not communicate with her family at all. Visiting hours were a real trial to her, causing her and her family great sadness. Mrs C. was unable to move or speak, she could not even shed a tear when she cried. Nurse F. went into Mrs C.'s room before her husband arrived to visit. She gave Mrs C.'s hair a brush and washed her face and cleaned her teeth. She sat next to her and stroked her hair and talked soothingly with her informing her quietly about the day's weather, the latest news on what was happening while she stroked her. Nurse F. asked Mrs C. questions and looked carefully into her eyes for answers. She told Mrs C. she would find out how her family were coping at home and what support they could get while she was in hospital. She ended her time spent with Mrs C. by giving her a hug and quietly whispered a joke in her ear. Mrs C.'s eyes lit up. Nurse F. left the room turning to Mrs C. and giving her a smile, a wink and a 'thumbs up' sign and then went about to her other tasks. (Van Loon, 1995:79– 80; reprinted with permission of the author)

Please visit the companion website **www.sagepub.co.uk/grbich2** for possible answers.

Further reading

Glaser and Strauss's grounded theory

Glaser, B. and Strauss, A. (1967) *The Discovery of Grounded Theory*. New York: Aldine Publishing. This is the first joint text on the operation of Grounded Theory.

Glaser, B. and Strauss, A. (1995) *Status Passage: A Formal Theory*. Walnut Creek, CA: Sociology Press. A useful model for generating formal theory showing that many studies can be theoretically sampled for their properties of status passage and comparatively analysed in order to develop formal theory.

Glaser's grounded theory

Glaser, B. (1978) *Theoretical Sensitivity: Advances in the Method of Grounded Theory*. Walnut Creek, CA: Sociology Press. **Glaser explores the intricacies of the generation of new theoretical constructs from empirical data.**

Glaser, B. (2005) *The Grounded Theory Perspective III: Theoretical Coding*. Walnut Creek, CA: Sociology Press. **The focus here is on the processes of developing theoretical codes; sorting memos and making sense of developing theoretical perspectives.**

Strauss's grounded theory

Strauss, A. (1987) *Qualitative Analysis for Social Scientists*. Cambridge: Cambridge University Press. **A very accessible text in which Strauss exposes the detail of all the processes of Grounded Theory.**

Strauss, A. and Corbin, J. (1990) *Basics of Qualitative Research: Grounded Theory Procedures and Techniques*. Thousand Oaks, CA: Sage. Accessible introduction to grounded theory study with chapters on getting started; the uses of literature; various forms of coding processes; theoretical sampling; memos and diagrams; writing up; and criteria for judging a grounded theory study.

Strauss, A. and Corbin, J. (eds) (1997). *Grounded Theory in Practice*. Thousand Oaks, CA: Sage. Provides examples of the Straussian form of grounded theory method.

Charmaz's grounded theory

Charmaz, K. (2005) Grounded theory in the 21st century: applications for advanced social justice studies. In N. Denzin and Y. Lincoln (eds), *Handbook of Qualitative Research* (3rd edn). Thousand Oaks, CA: Sage. pp. 505–35. The focus is on the investigation of 'invisible' structures in systems, resources, hierarchies and policies using a constructivist approach.

Puddephatt, A. (2006) An Interview with Kathy Charmaz: On constructing grounded theory. *Qualitative Sociology Review*, II (3). Available at www.qualitativesociologyreview.org/ENG/Volume5/QSR_2_3_Interview. pdf (accessed 21 January 2011). This interview seeks to tease out the differences between Charmaz's approach and that of Glaser, in particular Glaser's criticisms of Charmaz's constructionist approach.

References

Baker, C., Wuest, J. and Stern, P. (1992) Method slurring: the grounded theory/phenomenology example. *Journal of Advanced Nursing*, 17: 1355–60.

Burgess, R. (ed.) (1982) *Field Research: A Sourcebook and Field Manual*. London: George Allen and Unwin.

Charmaz, K. (2000) Grounded theory methodology: objectivist and constructivist qualitative methods. In N. Denzin and Y. Lincoln (eds), *Handbook of Qualitative Research*. Thousand Oaks, CA: Sage.

Charmaz, K. (2006) *Constructing Grounded Theory: A Practical Guide Through Qualitative Analysis*. London: Sage.

Dixon-Woods, M., Agarwal, S., Young, B., Jones, D. and Sutton, A. (2004) *Integrative Approaches to Qualitative and Quantitative Evidence*. London: National Health Service.

Glaser, B. (1978) *Theoretical Sensitivity: Advances in the Method of Grounded Theory*. Walnut Creek, CA: Sociology Press.

Glaser, B. (1992) *Basics of Grounded Theory Analysis*. Walnut Creek, CA: Sociology Press.

Glaser, B. (2002) Constructivist grounded theory? *Forum: Qualitative Social Research*, 3 (3): Art.12. Retrieved from www.qualitative-research.net/fqs-texte/3-02/3-02glaser-e.htm (accessed 21 January 2011).

Glaser, B. (2009) *Jargonising: Using the Grounded Theory Vocabulary*. Walnut Creek, CA: Sociology Press. See also http://www.groundedtheory.com/ and YouTube presentations and interviews at http://www.youtube.com/watch?v=r6RpQelvS1k&feature=player_embedded (accessed 21 January 2011).

Glaser, B. and Strauss, A. (1967) *The Discovery of Grounded Theory*. New York: Aldine Publishing.

Glaser, B. and Strauss, A. (1971) *Status Passage*. London: Routledge and Kegan Paul.

McCreaddie, M., Lyons, I., Watt, D., Ewing, E.,Croft, J., Smith, M. & Tocher, J. (2010) Routines and rituals: a grounded theory of the pain management of drug users in acute care settings. *Journal of Clinical Nursing*, 19 (19–20): 2730–40.

Mills, J., Bonner, A. and Francis, K. (2006) The development of constructivist grounded theory. *International Journal of Qualitative Methods*, 5(1). Retrieved from www.ualberta.ca/~iiqm/backissues/5_1/PDF/MILLS.PDF (accessed 21 January 2011).

Oliver, C. (2011) Critical realist grounded theory: a new approach for social work research. *British Journal of Social Work*, May. Published online 22 May 2011; doi: 10.1093/bjsw/bcr064.

Schatzman, L. (1991) Dimensional analysis: notes on an alternative approach to the grounding of theory in qualitative research. In D. Maines (ed.), *Social Organisation and Social Process: Essays in Honour of Anselm Strauss*. New York: Aldine de Gruyter.

Star, S. (1991) The sociology of the invisible: the primacy of the work of Anselm Strauss. In D. Maines (ed.), *Social Organisation and Social Process: Essays in Honour of Anselm Strauss*. New York: Aldine de Gruyter.

Strauss, A. (1987) *Qualitative Analysis for Social Scientists*. Cambridge: Cambridge University Press.

Thulesios, H. and Grahn, B. (2007) Reinventing work: a grounded theory of work and sick leave. *Grounded Theory Review*, 6 (2): 47–6. Retrieved from www.groundedtheoryreview.com/documents/GTReviewvol6no2.pdf (accessed 21 January 2011).

Van Loon, A. (1995) What constitutes caring for the human spirit in nursing? Unpublished masters thesis, Flinders University Australia.

Wilson, H. and Hutchinson, S. (1991) Triangulation of qualitative methods: Heideggerian hermeneutics and grounded theory. *Qualitative Health Research*, 1: 263–76.

Wuest, J. (1995) Feminist grounded theory: an exploration of the congruence and tension between two traditions in knowledge discovery. *Qualitative Health Research*, 5 (1): 125–37.

EIGHT

Phenomenology

Phenomenology is an approach that attempts to understand the hidden meanings and the essence of an experience together with how participants make sense of these. Essences are objects that do not necessarily exist in time and space like facts do, but can be known through essential or imaginative intuition involving interaction between researcher and respondents or between researcher and texts. This chapter attempts to expose the varieties of underpinnings in phenomenology and to clarify data collection and analytical procedures.

KEY POINTS

- Phenomenology involves exploring, in depth, experiences or texts to clarify their essences
- There are several different forms of phenomenology: classical, realistic, transcendental, existential, hermeneutic and heuristic
- Modifications of phenomenological approaches have been undertaken

---

Introduction

When to use: When the rich detail of the essence of people's experiences of a phenomenon is to be explored, described, communicated and possibly interpreted. Phenomena about which there is little in-depth data, for example, domestic violence, high-risk leisure activities, sexual ecstasy, near death experiences etc., are preferred topics.

Type of research questions best suited: What has been the in-depth experience of X for you?

Strengths: Can document detailed changes in feelings and experiences over time.

Weaknesses: The form of phenomenology being used is not always clear. Bracketing is difficult to do and it is also very hard to judge when this process is complete.

Classical phenomenology

One of the underlying issues prompting the genesis of classical phenomenology was a concern that the foundations of knowledge needed to be placed upon reality as it could be consciously interpreted. It was assumed that humans exist in the world in a state of wakeful consciousness with little awareness of each other, separated by processes of socialisation and other social constructions. These constructed ways of being; it was thought, could be identified, and suspended, allowing a refinement of consciousness to occur and enabling us to access the essential aspects of experiences in order to increase our knowledge base.

Edmund Husserl introduced the method of classical phenomenology in his book *Ideas 1* (1913), calling it 'the science of the essence of consciousness' ([1913]1982: 33). The focus is first-person experiences and the trait of intentionality (direction of experience towards things in the world) seen as the means by which an established world of objects or an established way of seeing is brought into being. Intentionality also refers to the way the researcher uses established objects and ways of seeing to judge and analyse experiences. The definition of an 'object' was that 'any subject whatever of true predications is an object' ([1917]1981: 3), thus all phenomena are objects. Husserl confirmed this by saying: 'To every object there corresponds an ideally closed system of truths that are true of it and, on the other hand, an ideal system of possible cognitive processes by virtue of which the object and the truths about it would be given to any cognitive subject' (Husserl, 1917: 3). Objectivity and subjectivity were clearly combined here and the anticipated outcome was that knowledge would be grounded and enhanced by this approach.

At the lowest level, how we see, hear, understand, and intuitively experience everyday objects/phenomena such as sleeping, working, loving or hating defines meaning for us. Husserl saw meaning as being created by the mind and seen through actions that have been directed toward these objects via a process of intentionality using concepts, ideas and images meaningful to that individual. However, only objects that allow a process of critical reflection from the outside through phenomenological reduction or bracketing of the natural world were seen as useful for study so that we can disconnect the world's 'taken for granted' reality, concentrate on the structures of our conscious experience, and gain a state of pure consciousness or ego. The disengaged consciousness can then be directed toward a specific focus leading to a dual state of conscious awareness and reflective consciousness in which the essence of the phenomenon will become evident.

This reflective consciousness facilitates the complete transformation of conscious experience and intentionality as the object of reflection. The essential structure of the experience will then be brought to light through the essence of pure transcendental experiences. These essences of appearances and emotional experiences of phenomena gained through intuition are what researchers should be seeking. For example, if my consciousness is directed toward someone such as a male person, visually my experience will include size, shape, clothing, face shape, hairstyle. However, my visual experience of this person will also be coloured by my intentions in directing my consciousness toward this person and by whether he is viewed as a stranger, a brother, a lover, a child or a focus for research. These visual and emotional responses provide content and meaning or the sense of my experience.

This form of reality is referred back to consciousness and forward to meaning in a two-way process that seeks the ideal meaning. The 'ideal meaning' of an object remains, even though the physical object may be destroyed or may have died. The two 'realities' – the physical object and the ideal meaning – are both necessary (or at least need to have existed at one time) to comprehend meaning. In other words the actual spatial and temporal 'thing', together with the memories, feelings and multivisual pictures associated with that 'thing' comprise the whole. There is also an underlying assumption that an experience's structure may sit on an invisible base of concealed meaning that must be intuited. Experience involves the dynamic engagement of the ego and provides a focus on positional consciousness and the intentional relation of the object. This consciousness is viewed as a self-contained, self-sufficient entity existing apart from and continuing beyond the physical world. The disengaged consciousness can then be directed toward a specific focus leading to a dual process of conscious awareness and reflective consciousness. This reflective consciousness involves the complete transformation of conscious experience and intentionality, as the object of reflection.

Our natural day-to-day approach to intuiting experiences and creating meaning involves observing, describing and conceptualising or theorising them in the process of creating explanatory meanings that may be lightly linked to relevant concepts. If we formalise this approach and add phenomenological reflection to these natural processes, a phenomenological approach is achieved. Pure phenomenological reflection (bracketing) involves undertaking 'to accept no beliefs involving Objective experience and, therefore, also undertake to make not the slightest use of any conclusion derived from Objective experience' (Husserl, [1917]1981: 3). The putting aside of experiences of the particular phenomenon and the placing of brackets around the objective world should eventually enable a state of pure consciousness to emerge which will clarify our vision of the essence of the phenomenon and enable us to explore the structures and 'truths' that have constituted it.

So what aspects of the structure of conscious experiences should you as researcher be seeking in intuiting objects? According to Husserl (1917), fantasy, imagination, memory, emotion, action and their representations in language and culture are a useful starting point. Issues of perception, a capacity for self-reflection, intersubjectivity, temporal, cultural and linguistic awareness, and a capacity to identify intentionality, meaning and action in yourself and others are also obviously essential here. The changing modes and your changing perceptions of unified phenomena add further complexity to this process as higher forms of consciousness are built. Husserlian phenomenology thus is an attempt to use a rigorous method to study experience both objectively and subjectively by going as close as possible to the experience of the things themselves.

The major outcomes sought in phenomenology are the description of the structures of consciousness of everyday experiences as experienced at first hand. The grand theoretical frames from various academic disciplines are notably absent in interpretation and only description is highlighted.

Processes of phenomenological reduction

If you decide to undertake a classical phenomenology, the process of bracketing out your worldviews through phenomenological reduction could involve:

- identifying the phenomenon or object
- identifying a recent experience of your own of this phenomenon in terms of how it appeared to you

- taking certain features of this experience and developing variations on aspects of this bracketed experience and then deleting these from the object
- continuing this process until you arrive at the essence or essential features of the object.

Say, for example, that the phenomenon you wanted to research was the experience of grieving. You may have had a recent experience of the loss of a personal item or person of value to you – this experience is then separated out, examined and explored in terms of possible variations and then discarded as potentially biasing the exploration of the experiences others may have had of grieving – although ultimately some aspects of your experience may well be highlighted by respondents.

Michael Crotty has clarified the process of bracketing more precisely by developing a step-by-step approach:

1 Develop a general question (for example: What is the experience of being HIV positive?) Ask more specific questions about your knowledge of and attitudes to what it is to be HIV positive (What do I think of this? What do I think this experience would be like?)
2 Move back further, and remove all theoretical perspectives (the stigmatisation of men who are gay), symbols (such as the Grim Reaper) and constructs ('safe sex practices') as well as your own preconceived ideas, experiences and feelings regarding the topic under research.
3 Prepare to re-confront the phenomenon with a blank sheet, rather like taking the position of an alien from a distant planet.
4 Focus on the phenomenon and become open and passive.
5 Set reasoning aside, listen carefully and allow yourself to be drawn in, in a sustained and receptive manner.
6 Document a detailed description of the experience based on answers to the question: What does the experience appear to be now?
7 Examine this description, considering the question: Does it arise from my own experiences or from past knowledge or my reading? All aspects that can be seen to have come from other sources must be abandoned.
8 Locate the experience's essence and identify and critique the essence's elements. Ask yourself the question: Would the phenomenon still stand without any of these?
9 Negotiate the essence's elements with those observed/interviewed. (Adapted from Crotty, 1996: 158–9)

Data collection: intuiting and disclosure

Following the processes of phenomenological reduction, your intuiting (through close observation and listening) should enable the essence of the phenomenon to become more visible, allowing you to build up a picture over time in terms of emerging patterns, relationships and interconnections. Data that seeks lengthy first-hand exposure of the complex layers of human experience can be collected by you from a range of sources via:

- interviewing (of those who have first-hand experiences) but in a non-structured manner so that initial responses to open-ended questions lead you and your respondent in the direction of the respondent's experiences; you should return several times to seek clarification of issues raised by your respondent or to explore further potential aspects that are becoming illuminated

- observation (bathing in the experience as it occurs – observing the human experiences both of yourself and of others)
- reading documentation, including literature, poetry, biography, material culture etc. (immersion and re-immersion in the relevant texts under exploration, seeking the perspectives of others regarding these texts, meanwhile recording your own understandings and experiences) and
- identifying and deconstructing discourses.

Data analysis

You should use descriptions to uncover the essence of the phenomena. Each text allows the uncovering of different layers of interpretation, which are constructed by you from within your social locations and cultural influences. These have to be identified in the analytical process. Meaning lies in the identification of the dominant themes in the encounter between you and your participant through a light form of thematic analysis where the data is kept largely intact. In-depth case studies are systematic, detailed and reflective and you will avoid comparing one case with another. The overall process will then involve:

- bracketing out your own experiences
- entering a dialogue with individual participants (or engaging with an existing text)
- reflecting on what you have gained through reading and re-reading and through journaling your thoughts, including any questions and responses
- identifying the major themes from the narratives/texts using processes of preliminary data analysis and/or thematic analysis of the block and file variety
- questioning the data and any emerging assumptions so that new descriptions and new conceptualisations are then more likely to arise.

Description of the experience's essence is gained through intuition and reflection and thematic analysis should reveal different perspectives that can be written up, through the use of metaphor or through conceptual linking. You must aim to reflect as closely as possible the essence of the experience. If you are certain that the description and interpretation correctly reflect experiences and that the reader will be able to recognise the experience's description as mirroring aspects of their own experience of the same phenomena, then credibility is enhanced.

Example

In an attempt to create specific steps for you in undertaking applied phenomenological analysis of the Husserlian variety for explication of interview transcripts, Stuart Devenish (2002) utilised a combination of methods to undertake a form of thematic analysis as follows:

Stage 1: ideographic mode (the gathering of closely connected ideas, words or concepts) from each transcript:

1 Identify categories of meaning from experiences by constructing a 'research key' of categories and subcategories related to the research question to highlight and isolate the themes and

experiences occurring in the transcripts. This key will be expanded as more transcripts are perused.

2 Isolate 'natural meaning units' – phrases with a single meaning – and number these according to categories in the research key.
3 Select themes that are central to the experiences of participants and write a phenomenological comment on each central theme.
4 Write a succinct subnarrative of the individual's experience of the phenomenon and relate it to the interpretive themes selected.

Stage 2: nomothetic mode (the search for abstract principles)

1 Collate succinct subnarratives and interpretive themes and use concept maps to place the interpretive themes into related 'fields' indicating interconnections around the phenomenon being researched.
2 Rank interpretive themes in order of importance (frequency × intensity) and group meta-themes and sub-themes.
3 Identify explicative themes (those that appear to have a primary referential character) using bracketing of your own thoughts and biases followed by creative writing through 'free variation' to multiply possibilities.
4 Write creatively using your own embodied experience of the phenomena together with information from the literature to enhance phenomenological description of interpretive themes key to the phenomena.
5 Distil explicative themes into one final phenomenological description to form the conclusion of the research.

(Adapted from Devenish, 2002: 5-6)

Forms of phenomenology

Various forms of phenomenology have developed over time. These approaches have been separated out to provide ideal types so that their differences are clearer for you to see but overlapping is common and you can see that some of the originators appear in more than one strand. Four of the major streams are as follows.

1. Classical/realistic/transcendental phenomenology (Husserl)

As clarified in the previous segment of this chapter, this stream describes:

• the structures of the world and how people act and react to them, in particular the structure of consciousness, intentionality and essences in an external world
• how objects are constituted in pure consciousness
• how these constitutions can be identified through processes of phenomenological reduction.

An example of transcendental phenomenology can be seen in the exploration of male rape in non-institutional settings (Pretorious and Hull, 2005). The broad approach was guided by Moustakas (1994: 81) and involved: phases of epoche (the suspension of previously held theories, ideas etc. via phenomenological reduction, in order to connect at the consciousness level); imaginative variation (reading and re-reading of interviews to identify the essences of the phenomenon, division of the data into parts based in meaning, clustering of themes for each participant and developing of individual descriptions); and synthesis of texture and structure (integration of the whole). Findings indicated that rape is an unexpected occurrence, often violent, massively invasive, and with traumatic outcomes for the victim resulting in anger, self-blame and the unravelling of self-image. Disclosure is difficult but can lead to reconstruction of the self and life changes, although for some the burden is a heavy one and is difficult to remove.

2. Existential phenomenology (Jean Paul Sartre, Martin Heidegger, Maurice Merleau-Ponty, Clark Moustakas)

This stream questions Husserl's essences as problematic regarding their associated layer of consciousness, which was seen to underpin experience, as not necessarily being based in human experiences of everyday life, but as being some form of cerebral reconstruction. Sartre particularly emphasised reflection on the structure of consciousness using the issues of freedom and choice and the concept of the 'other' and Merleau-Ponty (1945) provided a focus on bodily selves, embodiment, the body experience and its reflection in the mind.

Existential phenomenology sees consciousness not as a separate entity but as being linked to human existence, particularly in relation to the active role of the body and to freedom of action and choices. In this manner, essences became part of human experience. People are inextricably immersed in their worlds (called by Heidegger *Dasein* or 'being-in-the-world'). Existentialism has a focus on the issues of in-the-world existence (which Sartre saw as preceding essence), in particular 'being', which provides an absolute beyond the essences that are being sought. 'Intentionality' links humans with their physical contexts. Within these contexts (lifeworld – mundane daily occurrences, place – temporal and spatial location, and home – a location and a state of mind in a particular situation) humans have the capacity to respond and react to the situations and to relationships with others they confront/meet/are attached to in their worlds. In these worlds the notion of 'free choice' is seen as an individual responsibility not to be left to the group or society. The choices and responsibilities that are possible, the physical and intellectual experiences (actions, emotions, etc.) that will eventuate and the interconnectedness of individuals in 'being in the world' all provide a focus for 'being'. 'Nothingness' through death is viewed as the final outcome.

These writers also disagreed with Husserl that a process of phenomenological reduction was possible because of one's own interconnectedness in the world. They saw complete reduction as impossible because one must first experience oneself as existing in order to experience other aspects. As individuals we are inseparably part of the world. The fact and nature of our existence must affect our conceptualisations of any essences. Intentionality to these authors is revealable simply by involvement in the world, a focus on contextual relations and allowing things to show themselves rather than utilising processes of bracketing. The difference in approach here from the classical phenomenology of Husserl lies in the broad movement from the abstract to the real – the meanings for being must be uncovered first – in contrast with Husserl's movement in classical phenomenology from the real to the abstract.

TRADITIONAL ANALYTICAL APPROACHES

Example: existential phenomenology

Joaquin Trujillo (2004) has used existential phenomenology to explore the human significance of crack cocaine abuse through conducting over 50 first-hand interviews with recovering and active cocaine users. To participate in the study respondents had to be able to communicate adequately and to have had experience of using crack cocaine. Trujillo found that for these user respondents there was a significant change in the structure of being. There had been a move away from inter-human significance and a transfer from being with others to being with crack. This had resulted in a focus on the self in the attempt to achieve a situation of being high but free of craving. In the process of data analysis large chunks of interview texts are presented to support the author's interpretation of this theme within the existential tradition.

3. Hermeneutic phenomenology (Martin Heidegger, Hans-Georg Gadamer, Paul Ricoeur and Max Van Manen, Amedeo Giorgi)

This stream investigates the interpretive structures of experience of individuals or texts, whether public, private, in the form of art or in other material forms such as buildings. The interpretive focus in hermeneutics can occur either from the outside – from the perspective of the 'objective' researcher, or from the inside – with a focus on interaction between the interpreter and text (Heidegger). The integration of part and whole in terms of overall interpretation is essential. Everyday transaction predominates and 'being' (existence) is the overarching hidden aspect that becomes evident via the activities of 'beings' (individuals). Bracketing does not occur but you will need to keep a reflective journal recording your own experiences, personal assumptions and views. It is also recognised that co-construction of the data between you and your respondent is occurring and that the outcome involves a continuous conversation.

Example: hermeneutic phenomenology

In exploring the process of becoming a Professor, Friedrich (2010) used a hermeneutic approach drawing on the writings of Van Manen. One person was interviewed for three hours using open-ended questions. The interview was then read and experiences specific to the phenomenon under discussion identified. The meanings of each segment were sought through the process of translating the interviewee's words into those of the researcher using a zigzag process (Colaizzi, 1978) between the interview and others accounts of a similar experience to produce themes of experience. The themes developed indicated feelings of competence and incompetence in the identity development of an academic: initially emphasising incompetence by self-measurement against experienced others; developing an early sense of competence, which increases over time and with experience as activity becomes purposeful and effective. An example of the detailed and non-edited transcript quotes presented is:

> Because I was still in this period of "I can't talk like a real [academic," I was] standing there around this pool at this conference, but I don't know if I should go up and stand by [a large group of veterans]. ... Then, I ran into [Professor] Barbara Goshen, who is ... a friend

of my friend, Nora, so for some reason I didn't picture her as a professor who I should shmooze with ... [yet] ... she's an English Ed person at [another university]. ... I just said, "Barbara, I'm Nora's friend Janis ...". And she's like "Oh my God." ... We're chatting on and on, and she was maybe a little bit drunk maybe, and ... she was like "Well, come to dinner, and here are all my friends." ... I almost said "Oh, I changed my mind," but then I went and I had such a great time. ... It was a moment where I realized professors are regular people, you know? And that maybe I was someone who could do this. ... [S]o that was ... [a] moment of feeling competent in a situation where I had felt really incompetent. (Friedrich, 2010: 7–8)

The next stage of development involved a move toward coping with multiple roles.

The key criterion for trustworthiness in phenomenology overall, lies in whether a reader in 'adopting the same viewpoints articulated by the researcher, can also see what the researcher saw, whether or not he agrees with it' (Giorgi, 1975: 96). Your role as researcher is to provide transparency of process and to bring the reader as close as possible to the experiences and structures of the essences being displayed and this will depend on creativity of re-presentation and display of information gained.

4. Heuristic phenomenology

This approach (Moutsakas, 1994) recognises and highlights the experiences and insights of the *researcher* and their experiences in the world in an autobiographical manner. The orientation is meaning, essence, and experience and the researcher can be the sole focus, or co-researcher, as part of the group under research. There is an underlying assumption that the researcher has inhabited or currently inhabits the world/experience under exploration – not just superficially but intensely.

The heuristic process of phenomenological analysis described by Moustakas (1994: 120–22) includes six stages:

1 *Engagement* or becoming at one with the research question through self-awareness and self-knowledge. This involves: self-dialogue (one's own experiences), tacit knowing (that which lies beneath intuition), intuition (that which is between explicit and tacit knowledge), indwelling (going inwards for a deeper understanding), focusing (on the central meaning of the experience) and examination of the internal reference frames formed (created from knowledge and experience).
2 *Immersion*: the researcher becomes totally involved in the world of data and the experiences gained.
3 *Incubation*: intense concentration on knowledge expansion through increased awareness, intuitive or tacit insights and understanding.
4 *Illumination*: an active knowing process to expand the understanding of the experience through a breakthrough.
5 *Explication*: reflective actions and a comprehensive construction and depiction of the core themes.
6 *Creative synthesis:* bringing together and displaying data creatively to show the patterns and relationships of the essences of the experiences.

From interview recordings, very detailed notes are taken and the results verified. Essential components are collated, clustered and mapped and thematic matrices are developed.

From these, composite depictions can be formed leading to the development of exemplary portraits and finally creative synthesis puts it all together and re-presentation in story, poetry, artwork etc. occurs.

Research Example

Spirituality has been a key theme in heuristic phenomenology. Jennifer Barnes (2001) explored her own meditation experiences while Meath Conlan (2004) utilised Moustakas's approach meticulously to informally interview 17 co-researchers regarding their experiences of spirituality after exploring his own views in detail. He found that spirituality referred to practices and learning beyond self-centred positions of power and control, and to experiences that enhance meaning, wholeness, wisdom, virtue, joy and harmony with life. Conlan contends that daily life is informed by 'spiritual' engagements and practices and that these may provide a way of discovering or recovering the sacred in ordinary situations and events and can also help to strengthen consciousness and nurture human development.

Modification of phenomenological approaches

Current modes of phenomenological analysis indicate that this approach is very flexible and that Husserl's classical orientation has in the main shifted either towards a hermeneutic, heuristic or an existential approach where some form of bracketing may or may not occur depending on whether the 'essences' are seen as harder to separate out from the human generated discourses that constitute them. Various forms of descriptive writings wherein relevant persons can identify the 'essences' are then seen as a sufficient outcome.

Display

Peter Willis (2004) has, however, pointed to the problem whereby more traditional descriptions can dull essences, creating boredom in the reader. He suggested that in the description of 'lived experiences' a 'living text' would be more appropriate – one that uses metaphor or draws the reader in closer to the experience by utilising a range of literary approaches such as the autobiographical reflections and stories introduced by Moustakas (1961) in his descriptions of the excruciating loneliness which he experienced when he had to make decisions about the treatment of his seriously ill daughter. Willis suggests fiction, poetry and graphic and visual arts are appropriate ways of data presentation and these options have been reinforced by Clarke Moustakas (1994). Creative synthesis using poetic forms of writing may result in intensifying attention but may also generate more critical reader appraisal. There is an element of risk here in that certain disciplines may find creative approaches problematic despite the fact that literary portrayals have been common in some disciplines for many years and are now accepted practice within the postmodern tradition (Grbich, 2004).

Incorporation of other qualitative approaches

The incorporation of other methodological approaches, such as grounded theory, has been utilised as an analytical tool by Knight and Bradfield (2003) in their exploration of the experience of being diagnosed with a psychiatric disorder. Apart from the overarching focus provided by the study aim, research questions included:

'What does the label mean for the individual being labelled?'
'How does the labelled individual understand that meaning?'
'How does the individual respond to that meaning in his/her world?'
'How does the individual understand the label and its impact on his/her experience of self in relation to others?'

Three people who fitted the criteria of the study were interviewed. Interview data was subjected to the three-stage coding process of Anselm Strauss – open, axial and selective coding – and the construction of models and theoretical propositions occurred using the constant comparative process. Further processes involved converting diagrams into narrative form to expose the tensions identified within and between the codes generated and abstract conceptual frameworks. The authoritative voice of the author presented the findings and discussion with interspersed quotes from the three participants. In terms of interpretation, the existential tradition dominated.

Another study loosely situated with links to the psychological, critical ethnographic and action research traditions explored the needs experienced by sufferers of late stage AIDS in KwaZulu–Natal (Rabbets and Edwards, 2001). Twelve respondents from an AIDS care centre were recruited and interviewed using non-directive interviewing techniques (no set format, following the lead of the interviewee). The general approach to data analysis involved the collation of first-hand experiences where the essential research question was 'What are your needs as a person with late stage AIDS?' This was followed up later by 'Can you tell me more about your needs as a person with late stage AIDS?'. From the detailed responses gained, reflective generative practice, which provides a focus on relevance and an emphasis on empowerment, was used to conceptualise the key issues and guide community interventions.

Modification of Giorgi's existential approach

In a study of the phenomenon of 'being in community' Carl Holroyd (2001) used Schweitzer's (1998) adaptation of Giorgi's (1977) approach for identifying the meaning structures developed through the two people being interviewed. Six stages were involved: intuitive/holistic understanding of raw data (epoche/bracketing then reading and re-reading interview transcripts); summarising data from each participant to develop natural meaning units and central themes in the construction of constituent profiles; developing a thematic index to identify overall major themes; searching the thematic index for interpretive themes (oriented to psychology) to explain the findings; and describing meanings and summarising the interpretive themes.

Summary

Phenomenological approaches involve you in intensive sampling of a small group and the detailed exploration of particular life experiences over time. Depending on the version of phenomenology undertaken, bracketing may or may not occur and the inclusion of other analytical approaches may be added on. Your final display varies from descriptive narrative to the more creative poetic/dramatic/literary displays of the postmodern tradition.

Student exercise: Bracketing

Try doing this exercise out loud with a partner who can challenge you.

1 Take the topic of the sexual habits of gay males who are HIV-positive.
2 Identify your view, biases and prejudices on this topic.
3 Undergo a process of bracketing to see if you can identify, address and remove all your preconceived ideas.

Further reading

Beginning phenomenology

Moran, D. (2000) *Introduction to Phenomenology*. London: Routledge. A history of phenomenology in the twentieth century is provided, including the versions of Husserl, Heidegger, Merleau-Ponty, Sartre and Derrida. A very useful text for beginners.

Classical/realistic/transcendental phenomenology

Husserl, E. (1981) 'Phenomenology' Article written by Husserl for the *Encyclopaedia Britannica* in 1927. Trans. Richard Palmer. McCormick, Peter and Elliston, Frederick, A. (eds) *Husserl: Shorter Works*. Notre Dame, IN: University of Notre Dame Press, pp. 21–35 This article provides a clear summary of Husserl's ideas including epistemology, ontology, language theory and objectivity.
Smith, B. and Woodruff Smith, D. (2003) *The Cambridge Companion to Husserl*. Cambridge: Cambridge University Press. A series of essays that explicate Husserl's thought.

Existential phenomenology

Heidegger, M. (1962) *Being and Time*. San Francisco, CA: Harper. The meaning of everyday life and the meaning of being is explored in this book.
Merleau-Ponty, M. (2004) *The World of Perception* (trans. O. Davis). London: Routledge. This is the translation of seven radio lectures given by Merleau-Ponty in France in 1948. Suitable for both beginners and more advanced scholars.
A website called Mythos and Logos dedicated to the exploration of existential phenomenology can be found at www.mythosandlogos.com/ (accessed 26 July 2011). It contains online essays and a comprehensive set of links.

Hermeneutic phenomenology

Van Manen, M. (1990) *Researching Lived Experience: Human Science for an Action Sensitive Pedagogy*. Albany, NY: State University of New York Press. The focus here is everyday lived experience, the hermeneutic approach, reflection and thematic analysis and writing up in narrative form.

Heuristic phenomenology

Moustakas, C. (1994) *Phenomenological Research Methods*. Thousand Oaks, CA: Sage. This book presents an historical overview of phenomenological research methods with an emphasis on hermeneutic, empirical and heuristic approaches as well as their philosophical underpinnings.

New forms of phenomenology

Chan-fai Cheung (2009) *Kairos: Phenomenology and Photography*. Hong Kong: Edwin Cheng Foundation Asian Centre for Phenomenology. This is the first book to take account of the increasing role of visual texts in phenomenology and links these with phenomenological theory.

Watkin, C. (2009) *Phenomenology or Deconstruction? The Question of Ontology in Maurice Merleau-Ponty, Paul Ricoeur, and Jean-Luc Nancy.* Edinburgh University. Watkin shows that when phenomenological tradition goes beyond Husserl or Heidegger to take into account Derrida's poststructuralist critique of ontology new readings of 'being' and 'presence' expose limits in traditional readings of both phenomenology and deconstruction.

References

Barnes, J. (2001) The lived experience of meditation. *The Indo-Pacific Journal of Phenomenology,* 1 (2). Retrieved from www.ipjp.org/index.php/component/jdownloads/view.download/15/35 (accessed on 21 April 2012).

Colaizzi, P (1978) Psychological research as the phenomenologist sees it. In R. Valle and M. King (eds) *Existential Phenomenological Alternatives for Psychology.* pp. 48–71. New York: Oxford University Press.

Conlan, M. (2004) The experience of spirituality in everyday life. Doctoral thesis, University of South Australia.

Crotty, M. (1996) *Phenomenology and Nursing Research.* Melbourne: Churchill Livingstone.

Devenish, S. (2002) An applied method for undertaking phenomenological explication of interview transcripts. *The Indo-Pacific Journal of Phenomenology,* 2 (1). Retrieved from http://www.ipjp.org/index.php/component/jdownloads/view.download/17/45 (accessed 21 April 2012).

Friedrich, T. (2010) Becoming 'member enough': the experience of feelings of competence and incompetence in the process of becoming a professor. *The Indo-Pacific Journal of Phenomenology,* 10 (1). Retrieved from http://academicpublishingplatforms.com/downloads/pdfs/ipjp/volume1/201107180155_thomas_friedrich_10e10.pdf (accessed 24 July 2011).

Giorgi, A. (1975) An application of phenomenological method in psychology In A. Giorgi, C. Fischer and E. Murray (eds), *Duquesne Studies in Phenomenological Psychology,* Vol. 1. Pittsburgh, PA: Duquesne University Press. pp. 82–13.

Giorgi, A. (1997) The theory, practice and evaluation of the phenomenological method as a qualitative research procedure. *Journal of Phenomenological Psychology,* 28: 236–60.

Grbich, C. (2004) *New Approaches in Social Research.* London: Sage Publications.

Holroyd, C. (2001) Phenomenological research method, design and procedure: A phenomenological investigation of the phenomenon of being-in-community as experienced by two individuals who have participated in a community building workshop. *The Indo-Pacific Journal of Phenomenology,* 1 (1). Retrieved from www.ajol.info/index.php/ipjp/article/view/65725 (accessed 24 July 2011).

Husserl, E. ([1913]1982) (Ideas 1) *Ideas Pertaining to a Pure Phenomenology and to a Phenomenological Philosophy* (trans. F. Kersten [1931]). Dordrecht: Kluwer.

Husserl, E. ([1917]1981) Inaugural Lecture at Freiburg im Breisgau 'Pure Phenomenology, Its Method and Its Field of Investigation' (trans. R. Welsh Jordan). In Husserl's *Shorter Works* (ed. Peter McCormick and Frederick A. Elliston). Notre Dame, IN: University of Notre Dame Press.

Knight, Z. and Bradfield, B. (2003) The experience of being diagnosed with a psychiatric disorder: living the label. *The Indo-Pacific Journal of Phenomenology* 3 (1). Retrieved from http://www.ipjp.org/index.php/component/jdownloads/view.download/20/55 (accessed 21 April 2012).

Merleau-Ponty, M. (1945) *Phénoménologie de la Perception.* Paris: Gallimard.

Moustakas, C. (1961) *Loneliness.* Englewood Cliffs, NJ: Prentice–Hall.

Moustakas, C. (1994). *Phenomenological Research Methods.* Thousand Oaks, CA: Sage.

Pretorious, H. and Hull, R. (2005) The experience of male rape in non-institutionalised settings. *The Indo-Pacific Journal of Phenomenology,* 5 (2). Retrieved from http://www.ipjp.org/index.php/component/jdownloads/view.download/25/80 (accessed 21 April 2012).

Rabbets, F. and Edwards, S. (2001) Needs experienced by persons with late stage AIDS. *The Indo-Pacific Journal of Phenomenology,* 1 (2): 1–9.

Schweitzer, R. (1998) Phenomenological research methodology: a guide. Paper presented at a phenomenological seminar. Edith Cowan University of Western Australia.

Trujillo, J. (2004) An existential phenomenology of crack cocaine abuse. *Janus Head,* 7 (1): 167–87.

Willis, P. (2004) From 'the things themselves' to a 'feeling of understanding': finding different voices in phenomenological research. *The Indo-Pacific Journal of Phenomenology,* 4 (1). Retrieved from www.ipjp.org/index.php/component/jdownloads/search?Itemid=318 accessed (21 April 2012).

PART 3

Newer qualitative approaches

The following section examines in detail what the impact of the postmodern and poststructuralist theoretical changes outlined in the paradigm section of Chapter 1 have had on the field of qualitative research.

In general, there has been a major shift away from the centre stage position of the researcher as the key authoritative voice to one that gives participant's voices greater space and allows the reader to take a more prominent role in interacting with data and coming to their own individual conclusions regarding the data displayed. This shift has also allowed for a greater focus on the written/performed text which then becomes; 'a multidimensional space, in which a variety of writings, none of them original, blend and clash' (Barthes, 1977: 146). Your power as the writer then lies in your capacity to mix writings, to play with ideas from a variety of perspectives, to become a poet/actor in your own right and to display information and voices in such a way as to encourage many interpretations. You become the eye of the text – the facilitator of the display of voices, including your own, and the illuminator of the text through reflexive/reflective/refractive critique.

This shift has involved recognition that you, as researcher, are a complex and constructed historical entity with multiple personae that shape both the data collected and its interpretation and presentation. These personae shift among those of author, academic, student, storyteller, pillager, recycler of ideas, and cyborg – the crossing of boundaries among person, nature and machines. Reflexivity is now essential and you must view your role and the processes of data collection and interpretation in a critical and detached manner through close scrutiny of what you know and how you know it in your development of knowledge claims. *You* become the focus and there is an assumption that reflection on the self (looking and re-looking) is essential in understanding the self and the identification of the discourses which have impacted on the lenses through which you view the world. This self-referential interrogatory process is both inwardly and outwardly reflected/refracted to the reader and is usually recorded in diary form then re-presented in poetry, drama or narrative. The audience then has access to your real life experience.

Chapter 9 details the impact of postmodern influences then four of the newer approaches, three with links to ethnography, which have emerged from these changes, will be explored:

Chapter 9 Postmodern influences on society and qualitative research
Chapter 10 Autoethnography
Chapter 11 Poetic inquiry
Chapter 12 Ethnodrama and performative art
Chapter 13 Cyber ethnography and e-research

Reference

Barthes, R. (1977) *Image–Music–Text*. London: Fontana.

NINE

Postmodern influences on society and qualitative research

The advent of postmodernism has had an ongoing influence on society, culture, and research. With regard to the latter, a critical questioning of the roles of researcher and reader and a strong emphasis on self reflectivity and subjectivity as well as a focus on small scale research without generalisation have been important outcomes.

KEY POINTS

- Background to postmodernity
  - o definitions
  - o key authors
  - o underlying beliefs
  - o data display
- Changes in society reflecting postmodern influence
  - o architecture
  - o literature and knowledge
  - o art and film
  - o politics
  - o economics
  - o culture and individuals
  - o time and space
- Changes in qualitative research following postmodern influences
  - o theory and research styles
  - o truth and reality
  - o validity and reliability
  - o reflexivity
  - o position of the author/researcher
  - o position of the reader
  - o objectivity and subjectivity
  - o sampling
  - o data analysis
  - o ongoing issues of contention

Background to postmodernity

Definitions

Postmodernity/postmodern literally means the time following modernity or the modern era, while *postmodernism* is the identifiable ideological position that developed from modernism, including further development of ideas, forms of communication, and perceptions and beliefs.

Key authors

Writers whose ideas illuminate this era include: Roland Barthes, Jean Baudrillard, Jacques Derrida, Gilles Deleuze, Umberto Eco, Felix Guattari, Luce Irigary, Julia Kristeva, Jacques Lacan, Jean Francois Lyotard and Richard Rorty.

Underlying beliefs

Although many books have been written about postmodern beliefs, the core elements can be summarised as:

- everything is transitional and non-finite in nature
- capacity exists to dialogue with other contexts in time and space
- the search for reality 'out there' is qualified by a recognition that the tools, language and processes of discovery (as well as the interpretations and actions of individual researchers) are socially and culturally constructed and require further examination
- not only are research processes subject to social construction, but other social processes such as morals and laws are also constructed discourses that have served to maintain the power bases of particular groups
- borders (disciplinary, research approaches, country and culture) are also constructions that can be crossed, incorporated or reconstructed.

Data display

In order to make sense of these constructions, disruption, challenge and a multiplicity of sources are essential. Displays of results in postmodernism incorporate: irony, playfulness, illusion, pastiche, parody, brilliance, an emphasis on improvisation, satire of others and the self; the use of a variety of visual, textual and other genres; multiple narrators and voices as well as fragmented and open and closed forms to break the boundaries of genres and to encourage the audience to see and see through, to participate in events and to interpret experiences gained at (almost) first hand.

Changes in society reflecting postmodern influence

Architecture

Architecture was one of the first disciplines to incorporate postmodern influences. Charles Jencks (1980a: 214) has described architectural postmodernism as dialoguing on a range of fronts, as being pluralist or double-coded, 'one half modern the other as something linked with an attempt to communicate with both a wide public and a dedicated minority, mostly architects'. To Charles Jencks (1980b), buildings comprise signifiers – or signs that can be read. This capacity to emit multiple and contradictory messages is what makes a building postmodern. From the early 1970s some buildings can be seen evoking 'dialogue' with classical influences.

An example of this can be seen in Charles Jencks's Cape Cod 'face house', where a 'Medusa head' – a human like head shape with the characteristics of a Medusa – has been placed on top of the building in order to evoke a more intense dialogue between past and present and between humans and their places of residence.

Literature

In literature, irony and parody have become popular. Plots and characters are played with and ideas and relationships have been replayed in different situations and different eras. An example of social construction, ambiguity and the playful proliferation of meanings can be found in *Mary Swann* by Carol Shields (1990). The text is divided into five sections, four of which reveal the contextual environments and subsequent perspectives of four people whose lives have in some way fleetingly come in contact with the work or person of the main character, Mary Swann, a poet long dead. The four perspectives are juxtaposed then amalgamated when all four meet at a symposium. The character of the invisible Mary Swann is constructed from the four accounts which in turn have been created by secondary sources, fantasy relationships, non-existent biographical material and insight gained in a brief one-hour meeting with one person just prior to Mary's death. Mary's continuing 'existence' becomes constructed by and interwoven with the lives of the four characters, impacting significantly on each. When all four come face to face for the first time, reflection, refraction and distortion construct new possibilities for the lives of all five characters.

Knowledge

The assumptions, developed under modernity, that the universe is ordered and completely knowable by observation (once sufficiently advanced tools have been developed) and that an objective reality exists, give way to a view that the universe is chaotic and unknowable. As social constructions and questionable discourses are increasingly seen to dominate knowledge, meanings become recognised as individual creations, which require interpretation and negotiation. If all we can be sure we know are individual and situational constructions, then absolute knowledge becomes unattainable, and all knowledge becomes relative and subject to negotiation.

Art and film

The impact and sensory experience of the image on the viewer rather than an emphasis on the artist's meaning or someone else's interpretation provides the postmodern focus in art. Sensation and surface replace depth and interpretation. Participation by the audience becomes paramount. The role of the art reviewer also changes from centred critic dispensing judgements to one who acts as a channel – exposing the energy of the piece through the impact of the work on this particular person.

One form of art that has emerged from this tradition is that of bricolage. The bricoleur (the artist/handyman) uses whatever materials are at hand – existing bits and pieces which are then put together to create something new. An emphasis on recycling to create new forms can be seen in Tom Fruin's (2002) quilt constructed from the different coloured plastic (drug) bags left by cocaine addicts on the streets of New York. In film, a number of other postmodern influences can be seen. The aspect of time is evident in *Blade Runner* (Scott, 1982), where the Replicants live in an era of compressed time, a life span of four years. Surveillance and the mechanical monitoring of pupil response to emotion, is used to separate Replicants from humans. Hyperreality and simulacra (the Replicants) abound with the juxtaposition of humans and Replicants in a situation where Replicants (supposedly emotion-free) are seen to be developing more emotional capacity than their human creators. The creation of avatars with their capacity to re-embody the alter ego and provide another aspect of an existing persona in another dimension, provides a form of virtual space travel and challenges both time and place.

Politics

In the postmodern world, centralisation of power disappears. Decentralisation and micro-politics dominate and interest groups, minority groups and social movements become local and situational. These groups include families, communities, ethnic groups, commercial institutions, and religious and sporting groups. The focus on the local and particular may result in political action being very effective in a decentralised system. This form of local organisation does not mean that these groups will necessarily always be independent units endlessly jockeying for their place in a global system. Amalgams of smaller groups may emerge and re-emerge in different combinations for particular purposes.

Economics

Globalisation, multinationalism, transnationalism and consumer capitalism with a strong focus on commodity consumption and marketing can be seen taking over. Post-Fordist production values emphasise multiskilling and an endlessly flexible workforce where casual, part-time, and work-from-home structures grow. Outsourcing and subcontracting become endemic. Within larger organisations, smaller specialised teams/groups can be seen taking charge of narrowly focussed areas of production. Boutique products – small-scale, unique and with limited markets – became fashionable. As the service sector increases, the practical aspects of skills and training become more highly valued than the older style broad general education. The skills now most highly valued include those that facilitate the production and consumption of commodities; managerial, computing and electronic, plus those of skilled service providers.

Culture

Cultural pluralism emerges more strongly as the overarching national ethos becomes less important. The dominance of high culture with its emphasis on depth, meaning and value is disrupted and replaced by popular culture with an emphasis on superficiality, presentation and re-presentation (image saturation) and hybrid amalgamations (such as opera and pop stars). Hyperreality and simulacra (copies without originals) abound. For example, the

Virgin Mary exists in the form of many simulacra (she may or may not ever have existed in the flesh, however despite this no human form of this person nor drawing nor statue based on the real person is now known to be in existence). Simulacra often become more powerful than the actual living/non-living entities or experiences they represent.

As we move into advanced capitalism, virtual/hyperreality or simulacra take over. Reality is constructed (for example, TV 'reality' shows) and endlessly copied and recopied, and the images of disaster on television become more real than reality.

Individuals

In the modern era, the individual was socialised into a continuum of groups starting with the family and reinforced by education and work settings. Here the focus was fitting the individual into the belief systems of existing groups – tangible, identifiable and continuing entities with particular values that could be taught. In the postmodern era, individuals are still seen as social beings constructed by the systems or networks they inhabit, but these comprise many socialising contexts with different meanings and practices and through interaction in these, individuals become situated, symbolic beings. For example a female person becomes situated geographically, culturally, sexually, educationally and with regard to work position as well as in terms of sports and other interests. But in each of these contexts another facet of personality is called on to be creatively constructed in situ and added to as other contexts impinge. The individual has creative reflexive capacities and can control the impact of the ideology of each social context, incorporating aspects that they are most comfortable with.

In the postmodern era, the groups one inhabits are seen as more transient in nature with less continuity and a greater emphasis on internal and external transformation and change in values. Fragmentation dominates and group power is lost to changing passions, processes of the law and the political issues of the moment. Fluidity and diversity of discursive forms can only be momentarily captured and any issues are dealt with at the local level.

There is an emphasis on individual growth, on a variety of alternative forms of the traditional nuclear family unit, on arrangements other than marriage and on couples other than the male–female pair. Androgyny and polymorphous sexuality become more widely accepted. The view of self as a social construction evolves from similar views of reality and truth. We construct, deconstruct and decentre ourselves. The self is not a fixed entity, it can change from situation to situation, moment to moment. Individuals experience and recognise multiple and conflicting identities, both in themselves and in others.

Time and space

The changing signs of time and space facilitate action. A fluid movement among future, past and present, fragments linear time. History and place interweave with other times and other locations and the secure model of a child within a family within a community, gives way to a centred individual with multiple identities and subjectivities and with many social bonds – discursive practices or 'language games'. Some bonds remain relatively intact over time; others join, break, and rejoin elsewhere in an endless network of possibilities.

Changes in qualitative research following postmodern influences

Theory and research styles

There is considerable scepticism toward the metanarratives of religion, research and economic, political and philosophical theory, which are seen as historical epistemologies with no capacity to provide privileged discourses nor universal explanations. Ironic deconstruction of these narratives is viewed as one important way of removing their power. Emphasis on the explanatory power of metanarratives has been downplayed in favour of descriptive documentation of specific processes.

Postmodernism favours 'mini-narratives', which provide descriptive explanations for small-scale situations located within particular contexts where no pretensions of abstract theory, universality or generalisability are involved.

Truth and reality

Truth, reason and logic are also seen as being constructed within particular societies and cultures, providing illumination of meanings within these specific cultural understandings. Realities are multiple. All are subject to endless formation, reformation, construction and reconstruction, including those of the self, family and the groups we are aligned to. Individual interpretation is paramount, there is no objective reality, and truth and reality lie in the changing meanings we construe regarding our own subjective perceptions of our life experiences.

If truth can only be temporarily constructed through dialogue negotiated in interaction, then any claims to valid knowledge will also be subject to negotiation. The outcome of this will be many truths. But are all people's knowledge claims equal? How will dialogue progress? Whose 'truths' will be enacted? Those with greater power will certainly want to insist that their claims to truth have greatest value and, in addition, can be imposed through legislation, media access, or force if necessary. Will all information be available for critique? Or will some still be controlled or distorted by webs of power?

If the assumption that truth is multifaceted, that reality is multiply constructed and that large-scale research which homogenises differences is no longer appropriate, are accepted, we fall back on smaller-scale depth research with multiple data sources and individual narratives. These narratives must then be considered as providing only a narrow illumination of the chosen topic – a constructed reflection which is time- and context-bound, a momentary impression of 'truth', a truth limited by the constructions and interpretations of both researcher and researched, a truth that is fluid in its capacity to shift and change with further time and other contexts.

Validity and reliability

Such terminology as the qualitative versions of 'trustworthiness' and 'dependability' give way to indicating how individually constructed views, which are relative to time and context, match or vary from others in the cultural/social group under investigation. No single view nor group of views can be privileged over any others. All are 'valid'. Subjectivity becomes paramount, multiple identities are accepted and it is assumed that any individual will comprise multiple subjectivities and that these may shift, form and reform in unpredictable ways. Different contexts with different situations and different people allow different identities to be constructed or foregrounded. Laurel Richardson (1994) suggests 'the central image is the crystal, which combines symmetry and substance with an infinite variety of shapes, substances, transformation, multidimensionalities, and angles of approach' (1994: 522) reflects and refracts understandings in the creation of more complex understandings. The researcher and the researched are no longer identifiably separate, they interweave their constructed meanings in a delicate dance of recognition and interpretation as the same narratives are told and re-told, presented and re-presented for the reader to become involved with.

Reflexivity

Reflexive subjectivity and the politics of position replace objectivity. Self-reflexivity involves a heightened awareness of the self in the process of knowledge creation, a clarification of how one's beliefs have been socially constructed (self-revelation) and how such frames/values as age, gender, ethnicity, religion, social class, education etc. are impacting on interaction, data collection and interpretation in the research setting. Styles of reflexivity relevant to postmodern research in the attempt to transcend differences include:

1 reflexivity as self-critique – history, power, culture, class, experience and empathy
2 reflexivity as process, emphasising diversity, connectedness and intertextuality; and
3 subjectivist reflexivity, situated in epistemological positioning.
   (Adapted from Marcus, 1992: 5).

To these can be added reflexivity in the response of the researcher to the responses of the public to her/his constructed product.

The researcher cannot be separated from his/her background, life experiences and memories (frames), which inevitably filter impressions of the actions and behaviour of others. It is important to recognise that the self is not a clean slate waiting to be written on. We interact, react, incorporate and shift in a never-ending process. Tracking all these changes precisely would be a mammoth project in itself but identifying major shifts and their outcomes is not difficult, and in the intersubjective process, essential.

The key here is not to see oneself as a static centred object but as interlinked with others and undergoing processes of change. There are several selves in this process – the central historically constructed self, the self that is currently undergoing change and another self, the reflexive observer of this process. The strong focus on self-disclosure in this form of research has been criticised by Clive Seale (1999), who has suggested that the exposure of bias and multiple selves through the confessional stories of the researcher may simply serve as a distraction from poor research. This comment, although legitimate in terms of one reader's response, has echoes of the 'expert' researcher standing in judgement on the universal 'quality' of research – a meaningless concept in this context and derived from modern hegemonic discourse (dominance of one way of thinking over other views).

Position of the author/researcher

As researcher you can choose a position along the continuum from centred (authoritative) to decentred (off-stage facilitator) for the whole study or you can move flexibly between these two polarised positions. As authority slips away, the dominant voice of the researcher is replaced by the voices of participants, voices from other texts, or your own 'eye'/'I' speaking in your own right. Certain techniques are available in order to enable you to achieve such decentring:

- presenting views through the eyes of others who speak directly to the audience
- incorporating the views of others with your views which are represented through your own lens but with transparency of process
- replacing the dominant voice of the researcher by the voices of participants, voices from other texts, or your own subjective 'eye'/'I' speaking in your own right.
- highlighting both your biases and the sources of information that have influenced textual construction by bringing the footnotes and secondary sources up into appropriate places in the body of the text
- hyperlinking quotes to the complete original interview (which can also be viewed as a hard copy appendix) so the reader can view the broader content and the intertextual nature of the document
- deconstructing (pulling apart) previously accepted maxims
- recycling of ideas
- resisting closure.

Position of the reader

The reader used to be perceived to have only a passive role and some research still maintains this assumption, presenting information for the reader in such a way s/he either accepts the authority of the researcher or challenges it if sufficiently well informed. In general, it is now assumed that the reader has a more active role and is encouraged to use the text produced by the researcher as one of many sources in the construction of a response to this information. The reader is seen as having the capacity to participate, to interact, to interpret and to respond to the information displayed.

To encourage the widest possible reading of your text and to ensure that your reader's role is an active one, you as author can include:

- open reading approaches such as gaps in the text (to be filled in by the reader)
- paradoxes (apparently true yet contradictory statements to prompt responses)
- complexity (the inclusion of many different layers of voices).

It is assumed that each reader will take away something different from your text and further interpretations and deconstructions will occur in an ongoing manner. The formal incorporation of readers' comments within second and third editions of books serves to emphasise active participation in the generation of new meanings and this is part of the ongoing transformation of the text.

Objectivity and subjectivity

In postmodern research, subjectivity replaces or is incorporated within objectivity.

With the interconnection between subject and object and agent and agent, objective reality – snapshot approaches of discrete objects of study – disappears and intersubjectivity (shared consciousness/agreement/disagreement) emerges. Intersubjectivity leads to an examination of language as one of the main forms of communication with others and as a constraining aspect in social construction. The simple and easily identified 'subjects' of modernity – portrayed as one- or two-dimensional people, be they researchers or participants, with identifiable attributes, integrated within a stable context and following a defined and predictable life-path, are replaced by decentred, layered, unstable, fluid, fragmented, schizophrenic individuals made up of many selves. Fuzzy objects with dynamic and overlapping boundaries loosely interconnected and with emergent patterns exhibiting stability and instability, dominate.

Sampling

There is recognition that individuals are changing entities and that a quick snapshot bounded by time and context is all that can be achieved. Maximum variation/heterogeneous sampling will certainly allow for the combination of elements from a variety of sources and facilitate mixing them into a collage/pastiche in order to contrast various views/experiences. However, more appropriately, complex/chaotic systems will need initial articulation as will their interactions with other systems. Then a situational sampling approach, the focus of which is to give insight into system operation from a number of vantage points, should occur, tailored to issues of equal representation of all aspects.

Analysis

Analysis of each data set will produce unique results. Should a study be replicated over time (although there is little advantage to this in qualitative research except to document change), any differences in results will be explained by the assumption that the researcher is viewing/sampling from a different position. It is important to avoid the modern search for universals and absolutes as local complex explanations are seen as more relevant (Bauman, 1993).

Ongoing issues of contention

Postmodern beliefs and practices have produced many criticisms. The main ones are:

- that the pulling apart of situations and the deconstruction of discourses may lead to nihilism (or nothingness) and the collapse of knowledge
- that the rejection of objectivity and a lack of certainty make it too difficult for researchers or readers to come to any solid conclusion
- that montages of social reality are too limited to provide information upon which policy decisions can be made
- that the rejection of grand narratives and logic and rationality lead to very limited theoretical explanations

- that privileging and marginalising, although rejected as an approach, are also tools of post-modernists and that the rejection of truth has not stopped postmodernists seeking their own versions of truth.

Summary

In summary, the essentials that can be taken from postmodernism and the aspects that have influenced the qualitative research approaches covered in the next four chapters are as follows.

1 Postmodernism favours 'mini-narratives', which provide explanations for small-scale situations located within particular contexts where no pretensions of abstract theory, universality or generalisability are involved.

2 The emphasis on the explanatory power of metanarratives has been downplayed in favour of descriptive documentation of specific processes.

3 Individual interpretation is paramount, there is no objective reality, and truth and reality lie in the meanings we construe regarding our own subjective perceptions of our life experiences. These narratives must then be considered as providing only a narrow illumination of the chosen topic – a constructed reflection that is time and context-bound, a momentary impression of 'truth', a truth limited by the constructions and interpretations of both researcher and researched, a truth that is fluid in its capacity to shift and change with further time and other contexts.

4 Reflexive subjectivity (the constantly reflective and self-critical processes undergone by the researcher at all stages of the research process both here and in constructionism/interpretivism) replaces objectivity. Self-reflexivity involves a heightened awareness of the self in the process of knowledge creation, a clarification of how one's beliefs have been socially constructed and how these values are impacting on interaction, data collection and data analysis in the research setting.

5 Truth, reason and logic are seen as being constructed within particular societies and cultures, providing illumination only of meanings within specific cultural understandings.

6 Realities are multiple. All are subject to endless formation, reformation, construction and reconstruction, including those of the self, family and the groups we are aligned to.

7 The terminology of 'validity' and 'reliability' gives way to indicating how individually constructed views, which are relative to time and context, match or vary from others in the cultural/social group under investigation. No one view or group of views can be privileged over any others. All are 'valid'. Subjectivity becomes paramount, multiple identities are accepted, and it is assumed that any individual will comprise multiple subjectivities and that these may shift, form and reform in unpredictable ways. Different contexts with different situations and different people allow different identities to be constructed or foregrounded. The researcher and the researched are no longer identifiably separate, they interweave their constructed meanings in a delicate dance of recognition and interpretation as the same narratives are told and re-told, presented and re-presented for the reader to hook in to.

8 Postmodernist forms of display characteristically seek and incorporate: irony, playfulness, illusion, pastiche, parody, an emphasis on improvisation and satire targeted to others as well as the self, and the use of a variety of visual, textual, and other genres. Multiple narrators and voices as well as fragmented and open and closed forms are used to break open the boundaries and to encourage the audience to see and see through, to participate in events and to interpret experiences gained at (almost) first hand.

9   Montages (collages) of sound, text and music and an emphasis on fragmentary images invite
    readers to participate, to contribute from their own experiences and to take away challenging
    images for integration with their own life experiences. Complex individuals displaying different
    aspects of their personae are favoured over simple two-dimensional characters. There is an
    emphasis on multiple voices providing multiple perspectives but offering no finite answers.

So, how has postmodern thought influenced research designs and the ways that research
is approached? It is becoming clear that the principles of postmodern research are sliding
quietly but determinedly into the mainstream, challenging, subverting and becoming
part of accepted practice. In many qualitative projects objectivity, certainty, legitimation
and predictability are not sought. In place of these, doubt, chaotic possibilities, complex
interconnected systems, multiple selves and multiple critiques of findings in the transformative process, replace rationalism, closure and simple hierarchies. A more holistic
but unbounded approach is evident. The metanarratives, which have driven intellectual
thought in the past, are severely questioned and largely discarded in favour of smaller
local explanations.

Further reading

Postmodernism – history

Barthes, R. (1977) *Image–Music–Text*. London: Fontana. Barthes explores the relationship between images and
    sound as well as clarifying the changing position of the researcher (author) and the move away from structural
    analysis.
Baudrillard, J. (1988) Simulacra and simulations in Jean Baudrillard. In *Selected Writings* (M. Poster, ed.). Stanford,
    CA: Stanford University Press. A detailed discussion of the replacement of reality by symbols and signs – a perceived
    reality more 'real' than the original.
Lyotard, J. (1979) *The Postmodern Condition: A Report on Knowledge* (trans. G. Bennington and B. Massumi).
    Manchester: Manchester University Press. A good background document to postmodernism.

Basics of postmodernism

Rosenau, P. (1992) *Postmodernism and the Social Sciences: Insights, Inroads and Intrusion*. Princeton, NJ: Princeton
    University Press. Rosenau critically examines the limitations and controversies of the postmodern paradigm.
Sarup, M. (1993) *An Introductory Guide to Post Structuralism and Postmodernism* (2nd edn). New York: Harvester.
    A very accessible introduction to the basics.

Impact of postmodernism
and poststructuralism on research

Alvesson, M. and Skoldberg, K. (2009) *Reflexive Methodology: New Vistas for Qualitative Research*. London: Sage.
    Provides a focus on the impact of postmodernism and poststructuralism in qualitative research.
Chaffee, D.G. (2010) Structuralist and post-structuralist social theory. In *Routledge Companion to Social Theory*.
    Oxford: Routledge. pp. 73–85. A good introductory chapter on poststructuralism.
Grbich, C. (2004) *New Approaches in Social Research*. London: Sage. Explores the implications of postmodernist
    and poststructuralist ideas on research.

Postmodern practice

Gubrium, J. and Holstein, J. (2003) *Postmodern Interviewing*. Thousand Oaks, CA: Sage. Very detailed on all
    aspects of postmodern interviewing.
Hesse-biber, S. and Leavy, P. (2011) *The Practice of Qualitative Research* (2nd edn). Thousand Oaks, CA: Sage.
    Postmodernism, poststructuralism and queer theory are explored in some detail.

References

Bauman, Z. (1993) *Postmodern Ethics*. London: Blackwell.

Fruin, T. (1997–2002) *Quilt*. Armory Show 2002, New York.

Jencks, C. (ed.) (1980a) Post modern classicism: the new synthesis. *Architectural Design*, 42. London: Lenister Gardens.

Jencks, C. (1980b) The architectural sign. In *Signs, Symbols and Architecture*. Geoffrey Broadbent, Richard Bunt & Charles Jenks (eds). Chichester: John Wiley and Sons.

Marcus, G. (1992) Cultural anthropology at Rice since the 1980s. Provost Lecture, February. Retrieved from www.ruf.rice.edu/~anth/provost.html (accessed 19 July 2011).

Richardson, L. (1994) Writing: a method of inquiry. In N. Denzin and Y. Lincoln (eds), *Handbook of Qualitative Research*. Thousand Oaks, CA: Sage.

Scott, R. (1982) *Blade Runner*. 117 minutes, USA Columbia: Tri Star Productions.

Seale, C. (1999) The quality of qualitative research. *Qualitative Inquiry*, 5 (4): 465–78.

Shields, C. (1990) *Mary Swann*. London: Harper and Collins/The Fourth Estate.

TEN

Autoethnography

Current moves have been away from the extreme realist position of researchers as neutral observers, which can sometimes be seen in classical and critical ethnographies where you stand apart from the setting and meticulously document the culture in an 'objective' manner through observations, interviews and the examination of existing documentation. This chapter follows autoethnography, a highly subjective approach where you as researcher become the major focus of data collection within particular cultural contexts.

KEY POINTS

- Your experiences are the main focus of the research study
- An in-depth analysis of your activities, feelings and emotions within particular cultural contexts is facilitated by this approach
- You need a well-developed capacity for critical reflexivity in order to avoid the pitfalls of self-indulgence
- Your capacity to present data innovatively and to create an impact on the reader by bringing them in close to your experiences is very important

---

Introduction

When to use: When the focus is the self in various contexts.

Type of research questions best suited: The experiences of your own life.

Strengths: Very powerful data, which if carefully re-presented allows the reader to get close to individual experiences.

Weaknesses: Potential for you to become over-subjective and self-indulgent and to lose the capacity for critical self-reflection.

Definition and process

The word autoethnography derives from *auto* (self), *ethno* (culture) and *graphy* writing/ presentation (presentation of the self within the culture/s you inhabit):

> Autoethnography is an autobiographical genre of writing and research that displays multiple layers of consciousness, connecting the personal to the cultural. Back and forth ethnographers gaze, first through an ethnographic wide-angle lens, focussing outward on social and cultural aspects of their personal experience; then, they look inward, exposing a vulnerable self that is moved by and may move through, refract, and resist cultural interpretations. (Ellis and Bochner, 2000: 739)

The link between autobiography and ethnography is evident as you move from an internal examination of yourself, including your emotions and feelings, to an external view of yourself within a sometimes conflictual cultural context where your performances need to be deconstructed. The wide-angle lens approach, zooming in and out of situations in order to examine and critique them with an analytical reflective critique, is what distinguishes autoethnography from narrative (a story with a beginning, middle and an end).

You tend to focus on the self in interaction with others in situations where there are conflicting emotions or cultural restraints. A dialogue between you as researcher and you as the focus of the research is often exposed as you move from insider to outsider position. Voiceovers, third person voice or the subjective 'I' are often used to indicate the position you are taking. This source of the self as the major focus of data collection has been criticised as being self-indulgent but these criticisms are usually based on judging autoethnography with the criteria of earlier more traditional forms of qualitative research.

It has been suggested that the following need to be in place for an autoethnography to be considered:

1 The existence of a personal experience as part of a group or culture and the capacity to create sufficient distance in order to write and analyse this experience. This account may include elements of:

cultural conflict

being different or an outsider or experiencing 'othering'

strong emotional feelings/epiphanies

the mundaneness of everyday experiences/activities

2 Others may be interviewed and documents may be introduced to contextualise and extend the account.

3 The account is usually written for an audience (and therefore requires well-developed writing/ re-presentation skills).

(Adapted from Ellis et al., 2011)

Autoethnographic example

Autoethnographies aim to create dual experiences of individual and cultural activity for both you as the researched and for your readership. The following example demonstrates the outside-looking-in approach fostered by the use of the third person voice to provide distance while clarifying emotions and cultural context.

First story

It's 1969. She's on her high school senior trip to Florida. She's a white girl from a small, rural, southern town, attracted to Jesse, one of only two African American males on the journey. Prior to lights out the first night, students go for a walk on the beach. Immersed in talking about being Black in a White world, she and Jesse wander away from the others.

"You always remember you're Black," Jesse says. "People's responses remind you."

"What was it like growing up?" she asks.

"We had no money. My father left when I was a baby, so I was raised by my ma and grandma. Then my mother remarried. Once I woke up and my step-daddy had a butcher knife to my throat."

"Oh, my God. What did you do?"

"I ran outside. In the freezing cold, with no shoes, in my underwear. I got frostbite on my toes."

"What had you done to make him so angry?"

"Nothin'. He was drunk. And he was always jealous that my mother loved me more than him. That's all. Just jealous."

"We better go back in," she says, noting that everyone else has disappeared. She wonders what people will think about their being out in the dark … together … alone.

She leads the way into the room where the other students have gathered. She feels she has nothing to be embarrassed about since her time with Jesse was so innocent. What she feels does not matter when all eyes turn on her and she experiences the deadly silence of all voices stopping – at precisely the same time. She has never felt such hostile attention before. Jesse, who has, hesitates before walking into the same treatment a few minutes later. In those few silent, enraged moments, she knows viscerally a little of what it feels like to be Black in a White world – just a little.

(Excerpted from Ellis, 1995a: 152–3)

Approaches to data collection and analysis

Many autoethnographies are mono or solo affairs but duo (two researchers) or collaborative autoethnographies are starting to emerge. A study of bulimia (Ellis et al., 1997) involved three collaborative researchers where the last two named academics were/had been bulimic and they document, review and analyse their thoughts and feelings as they interview each other. They interweave their thoughts with their mutual interview data, together with documentation written by each of the three authors after a dinner together (a clearly complicated form of interaction for all three). This process not only clarifies the previously hidden world of each researcher's mind in the reflexive process but also reveals to the reader much more starkly the insider views of the issues and contexts of bulimia as experienced by two sufferers. The contrasts provided within the spaces between Carolyn (as the non-bulimic researcher) and Christine and Lisa (as the bulimic researchers/interviewees) provide considerable insight. Carolyn Ellis points out the interesting dilemmas and risks of exposure of this process, in particular that the need to protect one's self-image may well lead researchers such as academics and those in the public domain, to release limited or sanitised information.

If you start data analysis of a preliminary type early with this kind of data, you will be able to develop and identify concepts, themes and propositions but the richness of the data will depend on the extent to which you as both researcher and researched are prepared to engage with the text both emotionally and intellectually through journal keeping. The opportunity to debrief with supervisors and colleagues or partners is also important. One approach to troubling the text during analysis involves identifying the level of analysis at which you are working and then applying a theory that operates at a different level. For example, you could view your individual interpersonal data through system-based theories such as feminism or Marxism to clarify the impact of structural influences on the constructed nature of your behaviour. Re-presentation of often minimally analysed (but often edited) data is essential as the impact on the reader is of high importance.

Examples of autoethnography

Karen Brown's (1991) classical ethnographic study of Mama Lola, a voodoo priestess in Brooklyn, led Brown eventually to undergo initiation into voodoo practice herself. This shifted the study from classical to autoethnography as she became part of the group under study, enabling the documentation of observations of herself as community member and herself as researcher in this setting. Brown started to write herself into the story of Mama Lola so that in the final book she appears in two voices, one an academic voice and the other a more personal reflective voice.

Autoethnography of the self as the primary phenomenon under study can be seen in Carol Ronai's (1992) experiences of the difficulties she faced in becoming an erotic dancer (age, feminist views, body changes post motherhood etc.,) in order to access and study other erotic dancers in a strip bar. Her twin roles as researcher and dancer allowed her to move with ease from one role to the other and to layer her observations with a critical analysis of her own experiences. Carolyn Ellis and Art Bochner (1992) go further and provide dual autoethnographies of the emotions and ambiguities each experienced in discovering their pregnancy and undergoing the decision and the procedure to terminate this. These experiences were re-produced as a dual-voiced dramatic production and presented at a conference to provide reflections on their own streams of consciousness and to explore the link between 'emotional, cognitive and physical experiences' (1992: 5) in an attempt to understand internal subjectivity through response and resistance to external social discourses. The text enters very personal territory where many researchers would fear to tread, preferring to remain silent regarding their participation in matters formerly regarded as private.

Michael Hemmingson (2009) used an autoethnographical approach to explore the experience of the sudden death of a friend and former lover and to describe his experience of attending her memorial service. He presents his inner thoughts of confusion and uncertainty while exposing as dialogue the conversations he took part in. This dialogue was created from his memory and from notes taken shortly after the service. The epiphany he experienced may well act as a turning point in his life as he now vows to be happier, more sociable and less of a hermit. Much of this change appears to have been facilitated by the experience of forgiveness from the dead person's friends who previously had seen him as exploiting her. The whole autoethnography is contextualised within the cultural rituals surrounding death in the American culture.

Data collection

Data can come from a variety of sources:

- personal memory – which may come from notes or just memories of a powerful event, the details of which are imprinted on your mind
- self-observational data – where you chronicle events close to their actual happening through observing yourself in situ
- self-reflective data – maintaining a detailed critically reflexive journal of thoughts and feelings – emotional self-disclosure responses
- other sources – this might include any audio, visual or written documentation relating to the events being recorded.

Writing autoethnography

The process of collecting data for autoethnographies is often a very time-consuming and emotionally complex process and may involve you in years of writing and rewriting in order to gain distance from or to get closer to the data. Karen Brown (1991) documenting the life of a Mexican woman and Ruth Behar (1993) spent up to 12 years collecting and writing their data and Carolyn Ellis took nine years to come to terms with a lost relationship and to find the right voice to do justice to her feelings. Ellis indicated that the story of her relationship with her husband who had died of emphysema (Ellis, 1995b) was interspersed with the horror of her brother being killed in a plane crash at around the same time. This double tragedy led her to a need 'to understand and cope with the intense emotion I felt about the sudden loss of my brother and the excruciating pain I experienced as Gene deteriorated. I wanted to tell my stories to others because it would be therapeutic for me and evocative for them' (2004: 126). She found it necessary to keep notes of the process of writing, in order to re-address the voices of participants and find a comfortable way of communicating.

The documentation of this process led Ellis to accumulate considerable data including:

- field notes of the relationship both during the illness and up to two years after her husband's death
- field notes of the illness processes from eight months prior to his death
- interviews with family and friends
- medical case notes
- personal diaries
- travel logs.

Carolyn was the object, subject and researcher and she also wrote the final version of this practice in the first person as she attempted to move from realist ethnography to literary narrative in her search for the right 'voice' to clarify both her personal experiences and understandings, and the sociological significance of these events.

Ellis focused on emotions and feelings (narrative truth rather than historical facts), moving from past to future, incorporating alternative versions, photos of family graves and her own multiple voices in an open text that emphasised ambivalence and contradiction as outcomes. The process of constructing such autoethnographies is documented in more detail in Tierney and Lincoln (1997: 127-31).

In exploring the role of the emotional in understandings of landscape Jacob Bull and Michael Leyshon (2010) used visual data to study anglers' verbal accounts of fishing trips. Disposable cameras were sent to the participants with instructions to photograph or film their experiences of rural life via fishing. The visual data derived from photograph stills and videos taken by the anglers were used as the basis of a narrative process created to explore the tensions, complexities and inconsistencies of everyday life experienced in these contexts. The frames of memory and identity provided a more abstract level of discussion of these stories.

Data analysis

The narrative aspect of autoethnography leads, apart from preliminary questioning through preliminary data analysis (see Chapter 2), to the maintenance of intact stories either briefly edited or re-presented in some creative manner such as poetry, narrative or drama.

Data presentation

Dramatic form

One presentation of an autoethnography used a three-voiced dialogic, multivocal dramatic form in Loreen Olson's (2004) re-construction of the identity of a battered woman (herself). This is performed on stage with two women sitting on stools behind a translucent white curtain. The first voice is provided by the narrator who in a voiceover provides the literary and statistical context of abuse for women and the theoretical and methodological framework for the study. The stage light then focuses on the first woman – the author as woman next door who presents her story of her experience of abuse and her journey to reconstruct herself as an independent being. As she does this she uses the second woman, the author as academic voice, to critically reflect her experiences and to locate these within existing literature. The three women – narrator, author as woman next door and author as academic – speak sometimes in unison, sometimes over each other and sometimes alone/alternating reflection and refraction on the content. In the final scene the three women appear on stage, move together, overlap and become one.

Dialogue

You can find presentation of a largely dialogical interaction in Carolyn Ellis's (2003) description of reluctant grave tending with her mother. This is written in the 'I' of the author interspersed with reflections on the people whose graves are being tended, photos of family graves, personal reflections regarding the ritual and quotes from other writers on this topic:

> Mom watches me walk back to the car. "I don't like those yellow flowers in Rex's vase," she says. "They don't go with the red ones."

"They look okay," I say, wanting her to feel satisfied. What difference does it make? They're only plastic flowers, I think to myself. (2003: 5)

Ellis links this experience to her mother's death a year later and notes how the ritual of grave tending has been continued on in this family, through the female members, and how this ritual of love, helps to give meaning to their loss.

Poetic re-presentation

A briefer form of display using poetic re-presentation can be seen in Jeannie Chiu's (2004:4) reported autoethnographies of the Hmong people. The example below exposes some of the difficulties of assimilation:

they are deaf when I speak

they clothe me in the old ways that I cannot understand

traditions that have become too heavy

I have worn them on my back for too long

As woman and as child

I know I cannot stay

Buried voiceless

Single voice – multi personae

The use of multivocal vignettes (Mizzi, 2010) where the author discloses multiple subjectivities through changing voice tags is demonstrated in the next example, where an employee (self) is walking home with a visiting senior member of the organisation (James).

Multivocal vignettes

As we pass by several dark streets, James begins a new topic. "I had an interesting conversation with Riyadh today." Riyadh is another Project Assistant, a very friendly fellow who is well-liked around the office.

I peer back at James. "Oh yeah?"

"He asked me if you were gay."

"Really? What did you tell him?" James knows I'm gay but he has kept it from everyone else in the office.

"I told him that it was nobody's business and that was not the type of question that should come up in a professional context. But I also realize that he is a generally open person, so I also told him that is a question he needs to ask you if he had a genuine reason why he needs to know." I immediately feel mixed about this response.

Homophobic Control Voice: When such a common response is given in a professional setting, I do not see how it benefits the "suspect" gay man. I notice some anxiety around this response because it just locks out discussions of sexuality altogether at the expense of learning

(Continued)

(Continued)

about relationships of power and difference. Furthermore, given how the workplace is often constructed along heterosexist lines, I do not seem entirely convinced that straight guys who have their sexuality under question are treated in the same way.

Homophobic Control Voice/Safety Voice: I wonder how I will respond if Riyadh comes asking me. James has now put me in an awkward situation.

Educator/Safety Voice: I question just what he is actually protecting: the integrity of the organization by having a gay person work in a deeply homophobic society or my actual "secret." My fear focuses on the ramifications about what could happen if my "secret" becomes public knowledge and how it might affect my contract renewals.

Counter-Voice: Perhaps James is protecting me and this is the only way he knows how to do it. After all, James and I are friends, as well as colleagues.

Employee Voice: My thoughts also circulate around where to proceed with James over this one. I know that he has positive intentions, but, perhaps, he could have probed why Riyadh was asking the question and what Riyadh's response would be if it were a "yes."

"I guess that is the best way to handle it, but I don't know what I would say if he did come to me asking," I clarify.
James keeps walking and doesn't offer much.
(Mizzi, 2010, reproduced with permission)

Assessment of autoethnographies

Evaluation criteria for assessing autoethnographic writing include assessment of:

- The contribution of the writing to our increased knowledge of social life
- the style of presentation – is it satisfyingly complex?
- Reflexivity – has the author been able to move between inside and outside subjectivities?
- The emotional/intellectual impact this has had on you as the reader and how close the text has drawn you into events and emotions? Is it believable?
- Is the author credible in terms of the experiences described?
- Can the reader make sense of the story in terms of their own/others' life experiences?
(Adapted from Richardson, 2000:15-16 and Ellis et al., 2011)

Criticisms of autoethnographies

- It is too indulgent, self-absorbed and introspective (insufficiently 'objective' and insufficiently analytical).
- Is exposing the experiential emotions of the self and others 'real' research? Or just obsessiveness?
- Have others given proper permission to be part of your stories (ethics)? Writers are not always sufficiently careful in protecting the privacy of others who are linked in to the story being told.
- How authentic is the voice of the researcher – researched?
- In centring oneself, one highlights one's own role and marginalises those of others – doesn't this lead to a lack of perspective balance, or worse still colonising, making others' narratives of lesser value?
- Discussion of very personal events may create a situation of vulnerability, especially for well-known authors.

Summary

Despite criticisms, autoethnography allows you to go deep into your emotions and life experiences. Through reflexivity you can move from insider to outsider positions and back again in the connecting and situating of your emotions within culture. Skilful re-presentation can draw the reader close to where you have been.

Student exercise

1 Using personal memory data, write up a significant personal experience from your life ... use third/first person voice to do this, explaining what the circumstances were and why the experience has been important.
2 Re-present your experience as a two-person dialogue between yourself and your sceptical self who stands aside and comments critically on your interpretation

Further reading

Autoethnography – general

Bochner, A. and Ellis, C. (eds) (2002) *Ethnographically Speaking: Autoethnography, Literature and Aesthetics.* Walnut Creek, CA: AltaMira Press. A collection of 27 conference papers.

Criticisms of autoethnography

Buzzard, J. (2003) On auto-ethnographic authority. *The Yale Journal of Criticism,* 16 (1): 61–91. This article provides a detailed critique on the perceived problems of autoethnographic texts.
Delamont, S. (2007) Arguments against autoethnography. Paper presented at the British Educational Research Association Annual Conference, Institute of Education, University of London, 5–8 September. Available at http://www.cardiff.ac.uk/socsi/qualiti/QualitativeResearcher/QR_Issue4_Feb07.pdf page 2 (accessed 2 March 2011).

Ethical challenges

Chatham-Carpenter, A. (2010) 'Do thyself no harm': protecting ourselves as autoethnographers. *Journal of Research Practice* 6 (1). Available at http://jrp.icaap.org/index.php/jrp/article/view/213/183 (accessed 2 February 2011). A discussion of the ethical challenges and vulnerabilities experienced in an autoethnography of anorexia.

Autoethnography practice

Behar, R. (1993) *Translated Woman: Crossing the Border with Esperanza's Story.* Boston, MA: Beacon Press.
Brown, K. (1991) *Mama Lola: A Voodoo Priestess in Brooklyn.* Berkeley, CA: University of California Press.
Cole Robinson, C. and Clardy, P. (2010) *Tedious Journeys: Autoethnography by Women of Color in Academe.* New York: Peter Lang. An exploration of the experiences of women of color in predominantly White institutions.

Autoethnography method

Ellis, C. (2004) *The Ethnographic I: A Methodological Novel About Autoethnography.* Walnut Creek, CA: AltaMira Press. This text captures the changing nature of this cross-disciplinary genre by presenting a textbook in novel form.
Ngunjiri, F.W., Hernandez, K.C. and Chang, H. (2010) Living autoethnography: connecting life and research [Editorial]. *Journal of Research Practice,* 6 (1): Art. E1. Available at http://jrp.icaap.org/index.php/jrp/article/viewArticle/241/186. This is a special issue of *Journal of Research Practice* on autoethnography (accessed 4 March 2011).

Tamas, S. (2008) Writing and righting trauma: troubling the autoethnographic voice. *Forum Qualitative Social Research*, 10 (1): Article 22. Available at http://nbn-resolving.de/urn:nbn:de:0114-fqs0901220 (accessed 2 February 2011). A discussion of the difficulties as an autoethnographer writing about grief and loss.

Tenni, C., Smyth, A. and Boucher, C. (2003) The researcher as autobiographer: analysing data written about oneself. *The Qualitative Report*, 8 (1). Available at www.nova.edu/ssss/QR/QR8-1/tenni.html (accessed 4 March 2011). The authors suggest a number of strategies including collaborative analysis, forms of grounded theory and alternative forms of representation such as poetry, art and drama.

References

Behar, R. (1993) *Translated Woman: Crossing the Border with Esperanza's Story*. Boston, MA: Beacon Press.

Brown, K. (1991) *Mama Lola: A Voodoo Priestess in Brooklyn*. Berkeley, CA: University of California Press.

Bull, J. and Leyshon, M. (2010) Writing the moment: landscape and the memory image. *Spatial Practice*, 10: 125–48.

Chiu, J. (2004) 'I salute the spirit of my communities'. I: Autoethnographic innovations in Hmong American literature. *College Literature*, 31 (3): 43–56.

Ellis, C. (1995a) The other side of the fence: seeing black and white in a small southern town. *Qualitative Inquiry*, 1: 147–67.

Ellis, C. (1995b) *Final Negotiations: A Story of Love, Loss, and Chronic Illness*. Philadelphia, PA: Temple University Press.

Ellis, C. (2003) Grave tending: with Mom at the cemetery. *Forum: Qualitative Social Research*, 4 (2). Retrieved from www.qualitative-research.net/fqs-texte/2-03/2-03ellis-e.htm (accessed 24 July 2011).

Ellis, C. (2004) *The Ethnographic I: A Methodological Novel About Autoethnography* (Google eBook). Roman Altamira.

Ellis, C. and Bochner, A. (1992) Telling and performing personal stories: the constraints of choice in abortion. In C. Ellis and M. Flaherty (eds), *Investigating Subjectivity: Research on Lived Experience*. Newbury Park, CA: Sage. pp. 79–101.

Ellis, C. and Bochner, A. (2000) Autoethnography, personal narrative, reflexivity: researcher as a subject. In N. Denzin and Y. Lincoln (eds), *Handbook of Qualitative Research* (2nd edn). Thousand Oaks, CA: Sage Publications. pp. 733–68.

Ellis, C., Adams, T. and Bochner, A. (2011) Autoethnography: an overview. *Forum: Qualitative Social Research*, 12 (1): Art. 10. Retrieved from www.qualitative-research.net/index.php/fqs/article/viewArticle/1589/3095 (accessed 23 July 2011).

Ellis, C., Keisinger, C. and Tillman Healy, L. (1997) Interactive interviewing: talking about emotional experience. In R. Hertz (ed.), *Reflexivity and Voice*. Thousand Oaks, CA: Sage.

Hemmingson, M. (2009) Anthropology of the memorial: observations and reflections on American cultural rituals associated with death. *Forum: Qualitative Social Research*, 10 (3): Article 6.

Mizzi, R. (2010) Unravelling researcher subjectivity through multivocality in autoethnography. *Journal of Research Practice*, 6 (1): Art. M3. Retrieved from www.jrp.icaap.org/index.php/jrp/article/view/201/185 (accessed 4 April 2011).

Olson, L. (2004) The role of voice in the (re) construction of a battered woman's identity: an autoethnography of one woman's experience of abuse. *Woman's Studies in Communication*, 27 (1): 1–33.

Richardson, L. (2000) New writing practices in qualitative research. *Sociology of Sport Journal*, 17: 5–20.

Ronai, C. (1992) 'A night in the life of an erotic dancer/researcher', in C. Ellis and M. Flaherty (eds), *Investigating Subjectivity: Research on Lived Experience*. Newbury Park, CA: Sage. pp. 79–101.

Tierney, W. and Lincoln, Y. (eds) (1997). *Representation and the Text: Re-framing the Narrative Voice*. Albany, NY: State University of New York Press.

ELEVEN

Poetic inquiry

Poetic inquiry is one response to the crisis of representation and audience connection through the advent of postmodernism. Poetic inquiry draws on poetic artistic forms to more authentically express human experiences. It has links with phenomenology and hermeneutics in its exploration of the depths of experience.

KEY POINTS

- Poetic inquiry is a form of qualitative research that incorporates poetic forms as data display
- The researcher participates creatively in the reframing of data in order to bring the reader as close as possible to the original researcher/participant experiences of emotions and feelings
- Data can come from your own memories and journal notes or from visual, observational, interview and any other forms of documented data
- Poetic re-presentation can take any form but tends to derive from

  o researcher response to public issues
  o researcher memory or journal data, or from transcripts of gathered data

---

Introduction

When to use: Particularly useful for exploring individual experiences or feelings, whether those of self or other or both. It is often used in autobiography, autoethnography and narrative inquiry.

Type of research questions best suited: Primarily those relating to participant feelings and emotions. Studies where data has been reframed in poetic form include:

What has been the impact of cervical cancer created by diethylstilbestrol on the lives of young women? (Bel and Apfel, 1995)
How do managers feel about losing their jobs? (Brearley, 2000)

How does it feel to be a mother? (Barg, 2001)
What is the experience of being a terminal cancer patient? (Kendall and Murray, 2005)
Does writing poetry improve research skills? (N.G. Wiebe, 2008)
What is the experience of love? (P.S. Wiebe, 2008)
What is the experience of recovery of a methamphetamine addict? (Sameshima et al., 2009).

Strengths: Very useful for communicating emotions and feelings sourced from memory, interview, observational, visual and textual documents, and from researcher responses.

Weaknesses: There is always the potential of the researcher colonising the data through re-presentation of selective perspectives to suit their own beliefs and values or to create desired outcomes. Transparency of process is essential to counteract this and to demonstrate how much of the focus comes from the researched and how much from the researcher.

Definition

Poetic inquiry is a form of qualitative research that incorporates poetry in some way as a component of an investigation. It requires the researcher to participate creatively in the reframing of data in order to bring the reader as close as possible to the original researcher/participant experiences.

Process

The reframing/reforming of data may depend on whether it is to be read, spoken aloud, performed publicly, or sung. It also depends on the source of the data that has been transformed, the levels of participant collaboration and the stage of the research project.

For example, will the poetry be derived from:

- Researcher response to existing literature or to current social or political events?
- Researcher's field notes and/or their autoethnographical data?
- Participants' interview transcripts created separately by the researcher or collaboratively between researcher and participants?

Poetic inquiry creates a third voice – one that is neither that of the researcher nor the researched but is a combination of the two. The researcher largely undertakes the shaping of this third voice unless a collaborative project has been negotiated. Bricolage is favoured – seeking for bits and pieces from a variety of sources with which to create something to draw the reader in while also exposing the presence of the researcher – bridging the separation between researcher and researched by bringing the reader close to gained/shared experiences. The process involves the researcher hunting through the data seeking words, phrases and paragraphs to collate into themes, which capture the essence of the experiences. The choices made expose both researcher and researched, demonstrating their interconnectedness.

In more detail and noting that the researcher can undertake this process alone or collaboratively with the participant/s:

1 Read the transcripts during data collection and undertake preliminary data analysis so that you gain information on all aspects of the research question.
2 When all the data is in, re-read the transcripts together with any other data gathered (observations, visual and written documents) and make notes identifying themes.
3 Develop files of the themes noted, keeping to the words of the participants if data is in interview transcripts or videotapes.
4 Order and reorder these themes.
5 Transform them into the poetic or combined styles that best portray the response to the research question.
6 Read aloud or display to others to gauge the effect.

Example of process

The following is part of a transcribed interview (left-hand column) while the identification of the essence of the transcript relating to 'responses of others' is being grouped under the theme of gender division (right-hand column) in the early stages of poetic transformation:

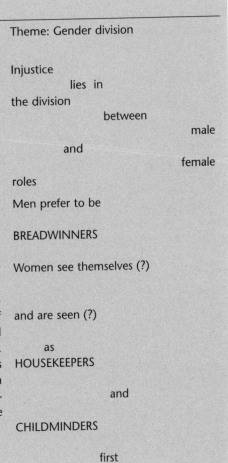

Interview response to	
Q. How are others responding to you in your father at home role?	Theme: Gender division

It's the perception of the division between male and female roles that I find a key to most of the injustice I've encountered during this past year. When it comes to the crunch, most males prefer to be breadwinners; they see this as the more important role. This has also to do with money and title and status.	Injustice
	         lies in
	the division
	           between
	                  male
	    and
	                  female
	roles

I remember when my wife graduated from Medical School, amongst the group she was part of what struck me as odd even then was that the men all looked forward to their futures as doctors and that's natural enough, but there was never any question that they wouldn't work full time. Several were in stable relationships and their partners had started careers of their own. But none of the graduates male or female ever questioned who would stay home should they start a family. There was no question of whose career was expendable. As soon as they had children both the wives of doctors and the female medical graduates would all give up work and retire to the house	Men prefer to be
	
	BREADWINNERS
	
	Women see themselves (?)
	
	and are seen (?)
	
	    as
	HOUSEKEEPERS
	              and
	CHILDMINDERS
	            first

Further data from this interview and other sources will clarify the questioned areas of perceptions regarding women's roles and the pattern of poetic representation will consolidate into something the researcher feels captures both the essence of the response and the reader's attention.

Data re-presentation

Taking the options for data sourcing mentioned above, namely researcher response, researcher notes, or gathered data, each of these will now be illustrated.

Researcher response to literature or political/social events

This poem was written by Monica Prendergast in 2009 in response to a speech given by Donald Blumenfeld-Jones in his role as Vice-President of Division B [Curriculum Studies] at the annual meeting of the American Educational Research Association, April 2006

i
the scholar dances
to silence

(middle-
aged crackling
of joints ...
the thump jump
of bare feet
on conference-
carpeted floor)

the sound
of breath
magnified
by the microphone

in returns
to breathless
speech

a visceral push

the body's need

to breathe
the dancing scholar's
insistent urge
for articulation

ii
in the dance
(its curved
contractions

its carved

extensions)
live mirror-

shattered

scatterings
of memory

my mother-in-law
dancing too
in found spaces

(living rooms &
backyard
gardens)
a joyful photograph
taken by my father
the morning
of our wedding
(6/18/88)

barefoot on the grass
behind her house
arms sun-spread
Saskatchewan sky—
high in
simple pleasure
both now
are missing
the dancer
the photographer

cancer-stricken
and stolen

iii
the scholar dances
his struggles
his joys
fills space
intensely
immersed
inside
the shape
of art
/
the art
of shape

fills space

touches loss

(the cracks
grief creates)

dangerous mosaics
caught in

broken memories
life

(breath
death
breath)
life.

(Prendergast, 2009: 1373–5)

The portrayal of the sound and rhythm of the speech and the drifting of the mind of the researcher to other connected memories are displayed here. The shifting of individual words or groups of phrases across or down the page forces the reader to read in a particular manner allowing word groupings or order to mimic the sound in real life. Take for example the last five lines. They focus on life and the essence of life – the breath. Breathing is simulated by the short, truncated one-word lines – breath – death – breath as a inset/subset of life.

Author's field notes or personal diary record or memory

Lynn Butler-Kisber (Butler-Kisber and Stewart, 2009) wrote a cluster of poems around the time of her parents' deaths and her associated experiences of death and dying as a way to come to terms with these issues and to share them with a wider audience:

Fani

You sat

diminished

breathless on the couch

The cough

a ripple that interrupted

erupted

wracking every sinew

Your luminous gaze

chided my inner thoughts

bathed me in warmth.

Gently, you said,

'I thought

I would be one of those miracles,

I won't.'

Like giving birth

taking death is slow

an arduous argument

between spirit and body

(Butler-Kisber, 2008: 7–8)

NEWER QUALITATIVE APPROACHES

Interview transcripts

The following comes from interviews with Dona Juana, an 86-year-old Puerto Rican professor, researcher and educator. Corrine Glesne (1997) used 10 hours of interviews to create a number of verse portraits of the participant. She undertook thematic analysis and filed the coded segments into broad areas like 'experiences of racism', 'self-perception' etc. Then within each theme she sought to identify the 'essence' of the experience using only the spoken words of the participant, rather like a photographer pointing the camera at a different angle to portray a different aspect of the person without changing the actual image – just shifting the light source.

That Rare Feeling

I am a flying bird
moving fast
seeing quickly
looking with the eyes of God
from the tops of trees

How hard for country people
picking green worms
from fields of tobacco,
sending their children to school
not wanting them to suffer
as they suffer
In the urban zone
students worked at night
and so they slept in school.
Teaching was the real university

So I came to study
to find out how I could help
I am busy here at the university
there is so much to do
But the university
is not the Island

I am a flying bird
moving fast, seeing quickly
so I can give strength,
so I can have that rare feeling
of being useful.

(Glesne, 1997: 202–3)

Kate Connelly (2010: 36) has suggested the following guidelines for the transformative process:

- The words must be those of the interviewees – participant-voiced.
- Repetition can be used when the occasion warrants extra clarity or emphasis, or to highlight an issue.

- Trailing off, or pausing to slow down a narrative, or enjambment – where people spoke quickly and without breaks, can to be shown where relevant (researcher decision).
- Stumblings or inarticulateness and searching for expression, should be re-presented as they appear in the transcript.

Types of poetic form

There are as many creative options available to you as you can envisage, some of which are defined below and illustrated using as a basis the previous poem from Glesne:

Haiku: a poem written in three unrhymed lines of five, seven, and five syllables. This form can be repeated. A Haiku version of one aspect of Glesne's poem could be:

> *Flying bird am I*
> *moving fast seeing quickly*
> *giving strength useful*

Narrative poetry: a story portrait with a beginning, middle and an end in any form, but usually close to the spoken word;

> *The metaphor I would use to describe myself*
> *would be that of a flying bird.*
> *A bird can move fast above the trees and see a lot of territory –*
> *being a flying bird would make me feel like a God, one who could alleviate*
> *the suffering of the people below by giving strength to those in need.*
> *Giving strength would make me feel useful.*

Cinquain: this is a poem with five lines:

Line 1 has one word (the title)	Strengthening
Line 2 has two words that describe the title	Helping others
Line 3 has three words that tell the action	A flying bird
Line 4 has four words that express the feeling	Supporting those in need
Line 5 has one word, which recalls the title	Sharing

Tanka: a poem of 31 syllables divided into 5 lines of 5–7–5–7–7 syllables

> *I'm a flying bird*
> *Moving above the tree tops*
> *Seeing with God's eyes*
> *Sharing spiritual power*
> *Giving strength to those in need*

Heroic couplet: two successive lines of rhymed poetry in iambic pentameter

> *as I flew high and fast above the trees*
> *I gained the strength to help all those in need*

Quatrain: a stanza of four lines, where lines 2 and 4 must rhyme

> *I am a flying bird*
> *moving fast above the trees*

NEWER QUALITATIVE APPROACHES

seeing the world with the eyes of God
while others work upon their knees

Lyrical: rhyming poetry about personal thoughts or feelings that can be sung (originally with a lyre)

As I fly above the trees
I speed across the land
Beneath me is the breeze
and there the workers stand

Other options are:

Canzone: a lyrical poem with 5–6 stanzas and a shorter concluding stanza.
Free/blank verse: using rhymed/unrhymed lines with no fixed pattern mimicking ordinary English language speech. The original poem by Glesne is an example of this form.
Prose poetry: combines prose and poetry for emotional effect. sometimes with metrical overtones.

Visual images of art or photography that interplay, or a prose-based essay that includes poetry woven throughout, can also be very effective. The purpose of combining techniques is to achieve synthesis, reflection, refraction and crystallisation.

New forms of representation

Repetition for effect

The following example from Melisa Cahnmann (2003: 33) shows how repetition can pick up on a range of interview responses and present them for emphasis.

SO MANY PLATES SPINNING
The principal says our test scores are
ABYSMAL.
because tests don't show progress.
because politicians aren't educators.
because everyone is not created equal.
because of IQ.
because other schools have a top that
pulls up the scores.
because the school board doesn't want to
hear.
because 30% have Spanish as a first language.

Dissertations in poetic form

Peter Wiebe (2008: 32–4, 52) has written his doctoral dissertation on love in poetic form with commentary. The following are some segments, excerpted at random:

Abstract 1

a brief summary...
to help the reader quickly ascertain the paper's purpose.

Boy meets girl.
Girl loves boy.
Family and friends intervene.
Boy dies.
Girl dies.

32

Since this dissertation is clearly not that, then this must simply be this, and I can't call it that. But if that is what I'm supposed to do, what am I going to do with this? Not really a real problem if this doesn't exist because it's not that.

Abstract 2

an abstract always appears
at the beginning of a manuscript, acting as the point-of-entry. Worthy man seeks promotion.
Nepotism followed by Murder.
Bad dreams.

The trouble with abstracts is the same as the trouble with Haikus.

The Problem with Haiku
Of all the things I
Wish would be, the one that most occurs to me is ...

Abstract 3

Abstraction and indexing services
are available for a number of academic disciplines,
aimed at compiling a body of literature for that particular subject.
Boy loves girl. Girl rebuffs boy. Boy goes crazy. Girl goes crazy. Crazy girl commits suicide.

Crazy boy kills parents.

What follows, in a word, is "poetry" that has been
collected,
    sifted,
        shaped,
            mused on, ordered, reordered,
                lived into,
                    written into,
                       written on,
                         written from,
                           performed, etc.

I have used whatever artful means available, like a bricoleur.

A range of other styles are also incorporated in this thesis: various poetic forms, letter writing, anecdote, narrative, a quiz and emails.

Combinations of various forms of re-presentation in the style of the bricoleur, are becoming popular. Jennifer Lapum (2008: 20–21) has used poetry, reflective text and photos in a form of autoethnography of her journey to cultivate a research identity:

Illustration 3:   Introspection © **Gary C. BARJAROW, 2006 (reproduced with permission)**

Mere acknowledgment of self.
Traditional bracing of me.
Objectifying it. Compartmentalizing it. Pushing it out of my mind.
Burying it into the bottom of my being.
Nearly out of reach
unleashing "self" …
uprooting that which is ingrained
understandings arising
truth
fading
notions of objectivity
dissipating
struggling to extricate self
engaging self
confusion looms heavily
—a way of being faltering
bridling biases
guarding the personal
—an illusion unsound
representing self without subsuming my essence
—an illusion faltering
a struggle to rid myself of me
vacillating between ways of thinking
cast,
into disarray
potent convictions to savor this immersion

(Continued)

(Continued)

> hold strong
> anticipating the demise of my struggle as though an end exists
> fortunate
> my thinking isn't paralyzed
> gazing at this endless path further into the abyss I proceed unleashing
> self
> letting my story sway my next move
> spiraling
> daunting
> exposed—
> I gaze inward

The undeniable struggle in the above poem was initially disturbing because I was unfastening myself from a dominant paradigm that I was comfortable with because of tradition, but uncomfortable with because it demanded a way of thinking and being that did not engage all facets of self. Within the dominant discourse of science, I am expected to step out of and suspend self. But self is not an entity that can be contained and sculpted in place. Like sand, it can be imprinted, molded, changed, with the shifting winds, sifting sands.

www.qualitative-research.net/index.php/fqs/article/view/397 (accessed June 2011)

Practising to be a poet

General guidelines for improving researcher capacity to write in poetic forms:

- Keep a poetry journal – write down ideas, snippets of overheard conversations, phrases that catch your attention.
- Read poetry and find the styles you like best – imitate these.
- Practise some of the styles listed in this chapter.
- Follow the rhythm of the language you hear around you where words/phrases are repeated for emphasis – 'because', 'and', 'one has to be so careful', 'why', 'why not' etc. – in order to build and emphasise rhythm.

Summary

Poetic inquiry is one of the most recent new forms of re-presentation, with many exciting options of poetic form and combination formats available for the start of your own creative journey.

Student exercise 1: Writing practice

Observe a situation for a period of time.
Write it up under the following three headings

1 What did you see?
2 What was your response to this situation?
3 What feelings did you experience?

Take the same observation and rewrite it up from three different perspectives

a   The perspective of the individual most involved
b   Your own perspective observing with intent to record
c   The perspective of a casual bystander

Write the first two in the first person and the third perspective in the third person

Student exercise 2: Free verse

Choose a topic and write down 10 key words that seem to you to be the most relevant or most related to some aspect of this topic. Use each of these words as a basis to write a 10-line free verse poem. Keep the lines short, with a maximum of six words per line – preferably less.

Further reading

Poetic inquiry – background

Forum: Qualitative Social Research Thematic Issue on performative arts including poetic inquiry. *Forum: Qualitative Social Research* 9 (2) (2008). Available at www.qualitative-research.net/index.php/fqs/issue/view/10 (accessed 12 March 2011).

Barone, T. and Eisner, E. (2011) *Arts Based Research*. Thousand Oaks, CA: Sage. A useful basic text.

Butler-Kisber, L. (2010) *Qualitative Inquiry: Thematic, Narrative, and Arts-informed Perspectives*. London: Sage. Foundational information about both traditional and arts-based qualitative methods.

Prendergast, M., Leggo, C. and Sameshima, P. (2009) *Poetic Inquiry: Vibrant Voices in the Social Science*. Rotterdam: Sense Publishers. This edited volume outlines the use of poetry to collect data, analyse findings and represent understandings in multidisciplinary qualitative research investigations.

How to write poetry

http://thewordshop.tripod.com/forms.html (accessed 14 March 2011). Has some useful links on how to write in particular poetic forms.

Dekel, G. (2008) Wordless silence of poetic mind: outlining and visualising poetic experiences through artmaking. *Forum Qualitative Social Research*, 9 (2): Art. 26. Available at www.qualitative-research.net/index.php/fqs/article/view/384 (accessed 12 February 2011). The paper explores the 'poetic silence' that occurs in the moments before the poem is written, and the three elements that characterise the process of poetic activity: thought, emotion, and inner knowledge. Short films are included to clarify the process of visionary poetry.

Faulkner, S. (2010) *Poetry as Method: Reporting Research Through Verse*. San Francisco, CA: Left Coast Press. This book takes an interdisciplinary approach to using and creating poetry for conducting and reporting social research. It includes examples of poetry, interviews of poets, and practical exercises.

References

Barg, R. (2001) Rebirthing mother. In L. Neilson, A. Cole and J. Knowles (eds), *The Art of Writing Inquiry*. Halifax, NS: Backalong Books. pp. 115–24.

Bell, S.E. and Apfel, R.J. (1995) Looking at bodies: insights and inquiries about DES-related cancer. *Qualitative Sociology*, 18, 3–19.

Brearley L. (2000) Exploring the creative voice in an academic context. *The Qualitative Report*, 5 (3 & 4). Retrieved from www.nova.edu/ssss/QR/QR5-3/brearley.html (accessed 21 April 2012).

Butler-Kisber, L. and Stewart, M. (2009) The use of poetry clusters in poetic inquiry. In M. Prendergast, C. Leggo and P. Sameshima, *Poetic inquiry: Vibrant voices in the social sciences*. Rotterdam: Sense Publishers.

Cahnmann, M. (2003) The craft, practice and possibility of poetry in educational research. *Educational Researcher*, 32 (3): 29–36. Retrieved from http://edr.sagepub.com/content/32/3/29.full.pdf+html (accessed June 2011).

Connelly, K. (2010) 'What body part do I need to sell?': Poetic re-presentations of experiences of poverty and fear from low-income Australians receiving welfare benefits. *Creative Approaches to Research*, 3 (1). Retrieved from ahttp://search.informit.com.au/fullText;dn=063632578460773;res=IELHSS (accessed June 2011).

Glesne, C. (1997) That rare feeling: Re-presenting research through poetic transcription. *Qualitative Inquiry*, 3: 202–21. Retrieved from http://blogs.ubc.ca/qualresearch/files/2007/11/202.pdf (accessed 8 February 2011).

Kendall, M. and Murray, S. (2005) Tales of the unexpected: patient's poetic accounts of the journey to diagnosis of lung cancer – a prospective qualitative serial study. *Qualitative Inquiry* 11 (50): 733–51.

Lapum, J. (2008) The performative manifestation of a research identity: storying the journey through poetry. *Forum: Qualitative Social Research* 9 (2): Art. 39. Retrieved from www.qualitative-research.net/index.php/fqs/article/view/397 (accessed June 2011).

Prendergast, M. (2009) The scholar dances. *Qualitative Inquiry*, 15: 1373. Retrieved from http://artfulresearch creations.yolasite.com/resources/Prendergast%20M%20the%20scholar%20dances%20QI%2015-8%20 2009%5B1%5D.pdf (accessed 14 February 2011).

Sameshima, P., Vandermause, R., Chalmers, S. and Gabriel (2009) *Climbing the Ladder with Gabriel: Poetic Inquiry of a Methamphetamine Addict in Recovery.* Rotterdam: Sense Publishers.

Wiebe, N.G. (2008) Mennocostal musings: poetic inquiry and performance in narrative research. *Forum: Qualitative Social Research*, 9 (2): Art. 42. Retrieved from www.qualitative-research.net/index.php/fqs/article/viewArticle/413/897 (accessed 14 March 2011).

Wiebe, P.S. (2008) What I meant to say about love: a poetic inquiry of un/authorized autobiography. Doctoral dissertation University of British Columbia. Retrieved from www.researchgate.net/publication/29735059 (accessed 14 March 2011).

TWELVE

Ethnodrama and performative art

Ethnodrama and performative art provide further examples of the shifts in the roles of researcher and participant. Here the researcher becomes a dramatist while the participants share often very personal life experiences with the purpose of changing audience perceptions.

KEY POINTS

- Ethnodrama is a powerful tool for highlighting cultural aspects and the perspectives of disempowered people
- The skills of a playwright or theatre producer are essential and need to be developed or brought in
- The dialogical aspect of performance should bring together diverse perspectives and can be an important vehicle for change

---

Introduction

When to use: When you have data that can be presented in dramatic form. The educative function of this performance is important.

Type of research questions best suited: Those with wider political and social ramifications where information dissemination or behaviour change are important. Topic areas where ethnodramas have been developed include stories of vulnerable or violated people, and health studies in particular those related to people with a disability, HIV/AIDS, substance abuse and mental health issues.

Strengths: Powerful stories that affect the audience, often challenging long-held beliefs and leading to changed social and political views.

Weaknesses: The researcher also needs the skills of a playwright and stage director (or needs to co-opt these) in order to develop data into a successful performance.

Ethnodrama

The primary objective is to educate and/or to bring about change in your audience by using ethnographically derived data to present economic, political and social issues in dramatic form. Both ongoing hermeneutic and critically reflective processes are involved in construction and application

Background

The use of theatrical documentaries can be traced back in radio to the 1950s (Mienczakowski, 1995), but it was not until the mid 1980s that a research-based ethnographic form of theatre developed. One strong influence in the transition from static to active presentations can be seen in the advent of *relational aestheticism* in art. According to Bourriaud (2002), relational aestheticism encompasses practices in which people come together in social spaces to participate in a shared activity. In ethnodrama these principles can be translated and have been applied as the use of improvised interactive, collaborative performances in creative social spaces which involve the public and benefit relationships across the community. Here, the actors, research participants, writers and audience are envisaged as the community who are experiencing dialogical intersubjective encounters (Bakhtin, 1984). There are also educational and empowering elements involved through the provision of space for disempowered citizens whose voices have previously been marginalised or silenced. Through joint encounters, meaning is collectively elaborated and negotiated.

The move toward presentation of data in staged performances is also one option you can consider in autoethnography, but performance texts in the form of ethnodrama have another dimension. The performance of such texts has been described as something that 'can contribute to radical social change, to economic justice, to a cultural politics that extends critical race theory' (Denzin, 2003: 187). The anticipated outcomes of ethno dramatic presentations are therefore quite different from those of autoethnography, where the purpose is to share and connect with the audience in a situation where the boundaries between the actor and the audience become blurred. In ethnodrama, although the boundaries between actor and content are also often blurred, the performances are vivid and dramatic and seek to educate by creating an emotional catharsis in the audience. Situations are presented with the view of confronting the audience and challenging their positions in such a way as to lead to an *epiphany* – an acute realisation with the potential for emancipation and empowerment. In health, this approach has been used to display: the powerlessness experienced by people with traumatic brain injury (Mienczakowski et al., 1996); the process of undergoing detoxification (Mienczakowski, 1996); and the experience of schizophrenic illness (Mienczakowski, 1992). Following a performance, open discussions between the actors and the audience occur in order to consolidate the impact, seek consensual validation of the perspective provided and to provide further data to lead forward into either community action or script revision or both. In addition, support counsellors and further information are usually available for those who may need this.

Process

In an ethnodrama you convert data gained from relevant participants into a dramatic performance. The scripts that are produced in ethnodrama derive from a compilation of interviews, observations and documentation gathered in the field which you then put together and recreate into poetry, fiction, dance, music, visuals etc., keeping as close to the original voices, actions and visuals as possible, in order to produce a polyphonic narrative collage. This narrative can be interspersed with your own voice to provide voiceovers or clarifying comments – the whole being amalgamated in such a way that the audience is drawn in as time and space shift and change in the collage.

The overall process of writing an ethnodrama involves you in developing the plot around which the 'play' will evolve, working on the characterisation and development of the personae of the actors, and scripting the dialogue and the stage movements. Decisions have to be made as to whether a solo dramatic monologue will be the major format, or whether a dialogue between two or more characters to provide more than one perspective in an interactive mode will be more effective, or whether both monologues and dialogues will be used, situated within a number of case studies, scenes, or collages using a multiperspective frame and a range of theatrical techniques. How many scenes to include is another question. Three seems to be common, with a prologue and epilogue to tie it all together. It is clear that in many cases the average ethnographer may not have sufficient stagecraft skills to develop such a performance and may seek to gain these prior or organise to work with someone already skilled in these areas.

Your dramatic outcome is more like a reflexive or performative interview (Denzin, 2001: 24) involving a 'dialogic conversation that connects all of us' to the wider moral community – involving an interpretive relationship of the text by the audience via its performance. The actors in these performances, although often (but not necessarily) different people from your participants, may also have experienced the situations and emotions they are portraying, given that we are all 'co-performers in each others' lives' (Mienczakowski, 2000: 2). Further validation may be gained from interaction between the two groups and with consumer groups if these are relevant to the topic. As the aim of ethnodrama is to create plausible and meaningful accounts – *vraisemblance* – the process of validation usually involves scripts of the performance being made available to the audience prior to the performance and discussions being held afterwards with actors, key informants in the field, audiences and theatre personnel in an ongoing interactive process. From these discussions, which provide further data, the next performance is adjusted. In this manner the drama is not a fixed but an evolving product that may bring together and examine a wide variety of perspectives, from those of individual sufferers to those of professionals, policy makers and government. You can see that you as the author of an ethnodrama will become largely a facilitator and a manager of readjustment of the text as the process of vraisemblance proceeds.

Developing performance texts

Details of how to convert narrative texts into performative texts are hard to come by, but Saldaña (2003: 220–24), as a theatre arts specialist who has undertaken successful conversions of qualitative data into dramatic scripts, provides some guidance:

1 *Develop the story line* – in ethnodrama the story line refers to the sequential progression of events within the plot, so in *Finding My Place: The Brad Trilogy* (Saldaña and Wolcott, 2001) the three separate scenes of 'Description', 'Analysis', and 'Interpretation' had a 'Prologue' and an 'Epilogue' added for context. Chronological linearity is usual but not essential in ethnodrama.

2 *Take out the essence* of field notes, interview transcripts and journal entries to maximise dramatic impact. The following is an example of this reduction Saldaña (2003: 224).

Taking out the essence

Original transcript

Barry: And I remember going to see the shows. I remember the interviews afterwards, sitting out on the grass, talking about what we thought about the shows, and what we thought about the longitudinal study. I remember always having interns sitting in the back of the class, watching us do drama.

Johnny: What shows do you remember?

Barry: I remember a lot of the Childsplay stuff. [Childsplay is a local professional touring theatre company for young audiences.]

Johnny: Any particular titles or images come to mind?

Barry: I remember 'Clarissa's Closet', which was interesting because I performed that last year. And I was thinking, 'You know I've seen this, I've seen this, it was Childsplay came did it.' And I also remember one about, I recall an Oriental setting, there were masks, uh, I don't know much about it, like journeying something.

Johnny: Any other images?

Barry: I remember them coming out and taking their bows and then talking to us after the show, and the energy they had, and just the raw energy and everything. They were answering questions and they seemed to be having so much fun just being there, and I think that's when I first decided I wanted to be an actor. So I saw that and it was an amazing feeling, there was just energy, you could see it, it was emanating from them, and just from having done this show. And it was just a show for a bunch of elementary kids, and yet it was still, it was a show, you know? And it was, that was when it first, I first started thinking, 'Hmm, this is something I want to look into.'

Edited version

Barry: And I remember going to see the shows, a lot of Childsplay stuff. I remember them coming out and taking their bows and then talking to us after the show.

And the energy they had! They were answering questions and they seemed to be having so much fun just being there. And I think that's when I first decided I wanted to be an actor. It was an amazing feeling! That was when I first started thinking, 'Hmm, this is something I want to look into.'

---

3 *Keep the numbers of actors to the minimum required to tell the story effectively.* Each character should be adequately developed to show their character via what they say, what they do, and through what others directly or indirectly say or how they act towards them. Further indications can be shown through voiceovers.

4 *Decide from whose perspective the story is to be told* – which individual/s? and should this change? And if so where in the tale? And how? Or should there be multiple vignettes, monologues and small group scenes in juxtaposition?

5 Decide whose story it is and *what role the researcher should play* – leading character with monologues? invisible voiceover ? chorus member? comic relief? extra? or totally absent story re-teller?

6 *Use theatrical artefacts* to send messages to the audience rather than overusing language – for example, stage settings, or a white cane to indicate vision impairment, expensive clothes to indicate wealth etc.

(Adapted from Saldaña, 2003: 220–24)

Examples of ethnodrama

Some forms of ethnodrama are presented for display and general discussion – illuminating various principles or aspects of people's lives only – while others fall into the mode of critical ethnodrama, with an action research component fostering change through protracted dialogical exchange.

Information and discussion examples validity issues

One very often cited ethnodrama that falls into the first category (illuminating aspects of lives for discussion) was *Finding My Place*, which sought to create a provocative account in order to 'provide a level of insight and understanding into human social life' (Saldaña and Wolcott, 2001: 5). This is a double-edged title involving a situation where two actors both found 'places'. This drama tracks the relationship between an academic, Harry Wolcott, and a 19-year-old unemployed male, Brad, whom Wolcott discovers living in a cabin situated at the edge of his 20 acre property. Later, Harry, who had become sexually involved with the squatter, Brad, interviews him for a case study and develops his life history. Brad is diagnosed as a paranoid schizophrenic and institutionalised for two years. Following this, he returns to Harry's house, trashes and burns it, and is caught, tried and imprisoned. Brad indicates that he hates the older man and goes to prison still threatening him. The overall purpose of the ending of this dramatic performance is to forefront the contentious notion of validity. This notion is taken up and thoroughly critiqued by Schreiber et al. (2001), who assert that Harry Wolcott's behaviour was unethical in having sex with a research participant, particularly one who is dependent on the researcher for his survival. The portrayal of Wolcott as the victim and Brad as the predator in this power-laden performance is seen as extremely divisive in terms of audience impact.

Cultural mores: alcohol   In another example of an ethnodramatic performance within the information and discussion mode, the purpose was to challenge the way young audiences and student participants felt about substance abuse in the Australian culture. In particular, gendered drinking cultures were examined along with the implications of peer pressure in drug-related settings. The following piece of data provides some insights:

> *Voice over/narrator*: You know. Women are the silent drinkers, especially in Australia. It's the male thing – drinking. It's accepted, you know? Aussie macho drinkers. Even the adverts. You know the one?

Friend: I've got some bad news for you, your best mate has run off with the bride.

Bridegroom: Oh shit!

Friend: I've got some other bad news. He took the beer with him!

Bridegroom: What! The bastard!

(Mienczakowski, 1997: 368)

The quirky humour of the Australian male is used here to demonstrate cultural dependence on alcohol in social occasions and provides some insight into the basis of alcohol abuse in this culture.

Critical action ethnodrama: examples music therapy

Within critical ethnodrama action research, the life experiences of a group of people with developmental disabilities was explored (Snow et al., 2008). Data was collected via focus groups, interviews, ongoing creative music, art, dance groups and playback theatre, where stories were told, played back and creatively re-enacted first by researchers and student volunteers and later by the informants themselves. These workshops formed part of the developmental ethno dramatic process. Agreement to participate involved participants in becoming researchers – providing ongoing feedback on the content and presentation of the script. Performances were held first for health professionals then for caregivers, educators and social workers and finally for family and the general public. A multivocal dialogical follow up process involved feedback questionnaires distributed after each performance and subsequent audience discussions were videotaped. These tapes were then discussed with the informants/actors to identify potential revisions to the script. More public and overseas performances are planned.

Detox Another ethnodrama also within the critical action research style (Mienczakowski and Morgan, 1993) highlighted the experiences of people undergoing detoxification. This was written largely for health professionals and opens with a scene derived from an informant's description of herself at a night beach party. A teenage girl stands alone drinking Bourbon. An adjacent slide show echoes her drinking posture showing images of this girl and other women drinking alone and in a range of drinking contexts. The girl then dances alone to music and is approached by an intoxicated male who offers her a bottle and tries to have forced intercourse with her. His advanced drunken state and her vomiting prevent this occurring. For this project, actors spent time in a detox centre paired to staff in order to get a sense of the organisation and typical behaviours within the setting in the move into character (Mienczakowski, 1992). The evolving ethnodrama was performed in a variety of settings including clinical workplaces and university campuses and included a range of health promotion activities undertaken by health professionals during the intermission, including: alcohol and drug counselling sessions, and demonstrations of the effects of drugs, the processes of withdrawal, breathalyser tests, photos of drug-induced motor vehicle accidents, and follow up educational kits for schools and teenagers. Scripts of the potential performance were made available prior to performances and comments encouraged. Script extracts were also incorporated into school and university teaching curricula and feedback was fed into the performances. Press and television coverage were also sought to widen public debate and to put pressure on health organisations to take account of changes the community felt ought to happen.

Criticisms of ethnodrama

Quality

Without help or special playwriting skills, researchers may not be able to translate their data into powerful dramatic presentations and may only achieve poor quality theatre or unedited monologues.

Ethics

Bringing case studies to the public arena may provoke ethical dilemmas, especially if individuals can be identified or play themselves. Johnny Saldaña (1998) has documented this in relation to the difficulties of including negative aspects of individual characters who play themselves on stage where there may be complex outcomes for them regarding other people's changed views; in this case resulting in a suicide attempt. Other studies have indicated that community members recruited into ethnodrama, where they become informants and/or actors, often experience considerable periods of uncertainty but that self-confidence does develop over time even although uncertainties may persist (Snow et al., 2008; Schipper et al., 2010).

Evaluation of ethnodrama

Is the creation, enacting and publishing of an Ethnodrama sufficient? In evaluating an ethnodrama we may need to call on different principles from those applying to more traditional research (see Chapter 1). Kip Jones (2007) falls back on Bourriaud's relational principles in suggesting the following as key criteria for evaluating whether the ethnodrama created has been adequate:

- What level of participation do key participants have in the creation of their stage characters and the dialogical negotiation which follows a performance?
- What levels of interactivity are planned or have occurred with the audience and with relevant public groups in the co-creation of outcomes through dialogical exchange ?
- Do performances succeed in bringing people of different perspectives together to the extent that exchange and collaboration can occur?
- What are the outcomes of these interactions in terms of change?
  (Adapted from Jones, 2007)

The dialogic encounter

It is easy to receive validation of ethnodramatic performances when responses are positive or when only minor negotiations eventuate, but what happens when validation is minimal and major controversy develops? Are researchers and actors actually prepared for what this might mean in terms of their carefully constructed performances? Do you document this and pat yourself on the back for your liberal stance in listening? Or do you do something about these comments? After several years of data collection Sheryl Cozart et al. (2003) produced an ethnodrama of schools participating in an A+ program. Although well received at an educational conference it was not well received when performed for teachers from these schools, forcing the authors/actors to completely reconsider and rewrite their perspectives from flat depictions of the situation to complex ones with multiple meanings. The question then arises as to whose interpretation is dominating? Who has control over the perspectives being presented? Is it the insiders (the teachers?) or the outsiders (the researchers?) and how can these be adequately balanced in a strongly oppositional environment? Should all stakeholders be involved in writing the scripts and if so how can the polyphonic nature of the script be maintained so that bland consensus is not the likely outcome?

New forms

Using the world wide web as a stage

The ethical issues of use of the World Wide Web to collect data from participants in public spaces without their consent have been discussed by Kip Jones (2007a). He uses as an example his own experience in 1965 of going to a club with friends and being asked to shift tables because a royal party was coming – Princess Margaret and Lord Snowdon. Jones opportunistically used this situation to record non consensual observations of the parties' behaviour and these were later reformatted and displayed on YouTube (Jones, 2007b:10).

Morphing: autoethnodrama

Autoethnography and ethnodrama have also been combined in a performative exploration of self in terms of identity, healing and wholeness in the reconciliation of sexuality, race and spirituality (Callier, 2010). Data was collected via autoethnographic methods (poems, journal entries and monologues – recollected conversations etc.) and staged as an ethnodrama. The thesis storyline contained: prologue (poetic form) journey, writing to live, reflections of recovery and epilogue, and the ethnodrama was constructed using framing, juxtaposition, and polyvocality. The latter was achieved by Callier by splitting his biographical voice amongst other characters and interspersing voices from media clips. The performative script was divided into five movements: the ending is the beginning; silent no more; affirmation through community; out through text coming out to self, coming out to others; and don't box me in.

Ethnodramatic articles

The use of theatrical performances as a basis for article writing can be seen in Mindy Carter's (2010) teacher monologues, where an autoethnodramatic orientation is used to document teaching experiences. The article is presented in the following dramatic format:

Prologue

ACT 1 Theoria

Scene 1 introduction

Scene 2 specifics

Scene 3 final notes

Scene 4 the start

Scene 5 understanding theatre as research

ACT 2

Scene 1 towards praxis

Scene 2 merging of the intertextual voice

Scene 3 insights and understandings

ACT 3 Poesis

Scene 1 the songs

Scene 2 analysis as poesis

Scene 3 new knowledge in communion

The text comprises a reflective discussion around the story of one student 'Rose' – a conglomerate of self and students encountered as a teacher, to represent the overwhelming emotional experiences of the author as a beginner teacher. This forms the basis of a reflective exploration of the use of theatre in research creating an interactive dialogue among the multiple personae of – artist, teacher, researcher, a/r/tographer – and the research paper under construction.

Creating a film from data

Jocelyn Woo (2008) translated her research findings regarding Singaporean youth into a social-realist narrative film that has engaged multiple audiences. She found that socialisation into a materialist culture imposed by family, government and educational institutions and reinforced by the media and everyday social relations, had created limited options for these young people. The movie, called *Singapore Dreaming*, is a 105-minute narrative feature produced for theatrical release, DVD and TV. The story centres around six members of the Loh family – parents and two children and the children's respective partners – revealing their materialist discursive environment.

Summary

Ethnodrama is a very useful tool used primarily for highlighting marginalised voices and exposing previously unexplored life experiences for the purposes of insight as well as for social and political change. Ethnodramatic creation requires not only the skills of a researcher but also those of a dramatist if it is to have strong impact. The researcher also needs to come to terms with the dialogical nature of the beast to be prepared to interact, to listen to actors, participants and the wider community and in a collaborative manner to modify both script and performances in an ongoing process.

Further reading

Ethnodrama and performance ethnography – background

Denzin, N. (2003) *Performance Ethnography Critical Pedagogy and the Politics of Culture*. Thousand Oaks, CA: Sage Publications. The focus is performance ethnography and autoethnography.

Denzin, N., Lincoln, Y. and Smith, L. (2008) *Handbook of Critical and Indigenous Methodologies*. Thousand Oaks, CA: Sage. This book covers a range of innovative approaches including ethnodrama.

Hesse-Biber, S. (2006) *Emergent Methods in Social Research*. Thousand Oaks, CA: Sage. Both autoethnography and ethnodrama are covered here.

Creating ethnodramas

O'Toole, J. and Ackroyd, J. (2010) *Performing Research, Tensions, Triumphs and Trade-Offs of Ethnodrama*. Stoke-on-Trent: Trentham Books. Excellent insight into the trials and tribulations of creating and staging an ethnodrama. Five groups of researcher/performers offer their projects up for critical examination.

Examples of ethnodrama

Pelias, R. (2002) For father and son, an ethnodrama with no catharsis. In A. Bochner and C. Ellis (eds), *Ethnographically Speaking: Autoethnography, Literature and Aesthetics*. Walnut Creek, CA: AltaMira Press. pp. 35–43.

Saldaña, J. (2005) *Ethnodrama: An Anthology of Reality Theatre*. Walnut Creek, CA: AltaMira press. Seven ethnodramas are included here with foci on marginalised identities, abortion, street life and oppression.

References

Bakhtin, M. (1984) *Problems of Dostoyevsky's Poetics* (trans. C. Emerson). Minneapolis, MN: University of Minneapolis Press.

Bourriaud, Nicolas (2002) *Relational Aesthetics*. Dijon: Les Presses du Reel.

Callier, D. (2010) Acting out: a performative exploration of identity, healing and wholeness. Masters thesis, University of Illinois Urbana–Champaign. Retrieved from www.ideals.illinois.edu/bitstream/handle/2142/16927/1_Callier_Durell.pdf?sequence=3 (accessed 4 April 2011).

Carter, M. (2010) The teacher monologues: an A/r/tographical exploration. *Creative Approaches to Research* 3 (1): 42–66.

Cozart, S.C., Gordon, J., Gunzenhaiser, M., McKinney, M. and Petterson, J. (2003) Disrupting dialogue: envisioning performance ethnography for research and evaluation. *Journal of Educational Foundations*, 17 (2): 53–69.

Denzin, N. (2001) The reflexive interview and a performative social science. *Qualitative Research*, 1 (1): 23–46.

Denzin, N. (2003) The call to performance. *Symbolic Interactionism*, 26 (1): 187–207.

Jones, K. (2007) How did I get to Princess Margaret? (And how did I get her to the World Wide Web?). *Forum: Qualitative Social Research*, 8 (3): Art. 3. Retrieved from www.qualitative-research.net/index.php/fqs/article/view/281/617 (accessed 30 March 2012).

Mienczakowski, J. (1992) *Syncing Out Loud: A Journey into Illness*. Brisbane: Griffith University reprographics.

Mienczakowski, J. (1995) The theatre of ethnography: the reconstruction of ethnography into theatre with emancipatory potential. Qualitative Inquiry, 1: 360–75. Retrieved from http://qix.sagepub.com/content/1/3/360 (accessed 4 May 2011).

Mienczakowski, J. (1996) An ethnographic act: the construction of consensual theatre. In C. Ellis and A.P. Bochner (eds), *Composing Ethnography: Alternative Forms of Qualitative Writing* Walnut Creek, CA: AltaMira Press. pp. 244–64.

Mienczakowski, J. (1997) Theatre of change. Research in Drama Education, 2 (2): 159–73.

Mienczakowski, J. (2000) Ethnodrama: performed research: limitations and potential. In P. Atkinson, A. Coffey, S. Delamont, J. Lofland and L. Lofland (eds), *Handbook of Ethnography*. London: Sage.

Mienczakowski, J. and Morgan, S. (1993) *Busting: The Challenge of the Drought Spirit.* Brisbane: Griffith University reprographics.

Mienczakowski, J., Smith, R. and Sinclair, M. (1996) On the road to catharsis: a theoretical framework for change. *Qualitative Inquiry*, 2 (4): 439–62.

Saldaña, J. (1998) Ethical issues in ethnographic performance text: the 'dramatic impact' of 'juicy stuff'. *Research in Drama Education*, 3 (2): 181–96.

Saldaña, J. (2003) Dramatizing data: a primer. *Qualitative Inquiry*, 9, (2): 218–36. Retrieved from http://qix. sagepub.com/cgi/content/abstract/9/2/218 (accessed 26 April 2011).

Saldaña, J. and Wolcott, H. (2001) *Finding My Place: The Brad Trilogy*: Performance draft. Tempe, AZ: Arizona State University Department of Theater.

Schreiber, R., Rodney, P., Brown, H. and Varcoe, C. (2001) Reflections on deconstructing Harry or when is good art bad science? Letter to the Editor. *Qualitative Health Research*, 11 (6): 723–4.

Schipper, K., Tineke, A., van Zadelhof, E., van de Griendt, C. and Widdenshoven, G. (2010) What does it mean to be a patient research partner? *Qualitative Inquiry*, 16 (6): 501–10.

Snow, S. and D'Amico M. (2008) Interdisciplinary research through community music therapy and performance ethnography. Recherche interdisciplinaire: musicothérapie communautaire et ethnographie de la performance. *Canadian Journal of Music Therapy*, 14 (1): 30–46.

Woo, J. (2008) Engaging new audiences: translating research into popular media. *Educational Researcher* 37 (6): 321–9. Retrieved from http://edr.sagepub.com/content/37/6/321.full#ref-2.

THIRTEEN

Cyber ethnography and e-research

Cyber ethnography is a recent development in qualitative research involving the exploration of the development of digitally mediated identities within existing online communities.

KEY POINTS

- Cyber ethnography is one of the newer forms of qualitative data collection
- There are complex issues of access, ethics and analysis to be addressed
- Data is rhizomatic (goes off in unpredictable directions)
- The use of avatars creates multiple personae

When to use: When internet interaction is to be examined or the internet used.

Type of research questions best suited: What are the forms of content, interaction and communication at a particular site or sites? How do individuals respond to particular issues? How do people construct, present and negotiate themselves in online forums?

Strengths: Collects 'real' data as it occurs with minimal influence from the researcher.

Weaknesses: Ethical issues. Superficial presentations of participants may occur if the data is very thin or incomplete and follow up is difficult.

Cyber ethnography

The rapid integration of technology into our lives has changed forays into the internet from occasional ventures to daily use – we now log on to mobile phones, emails, Facebook, work web pages and online forums anything from several times a week to several times a day. The question of separation of real life and virtual life has to be re-adjusted toward a view encompassing integration of these two worlds. But there can be danger in such integration because once we stop separating out the virtual from the real we have to look at what integration might imply. Steven Downing (2010) has studied online computer gaming using text, voice chat and surveys and suggests that mimicking 'real' behaviour such as stealing from others, bullying, inflicting gratuitous violence and killing people 'for fun' may have the capacity to desensitise individuals and allow such behaviours to cross from virtual to real-life activity. Previous research regarding the influence of television programmes on children has clearly indicated that the impact of violent programmes is either short term or minimal as children appear to have little difficulty separating real from fantasy worlds. But, another example (Dibbell, 1993) shows how extremely negative online interaction likened to the self appears to have the capacity to affect participants' real-life states of mind. This situation involved one user perpetrating online sexual violence (rape) to other users' avatars in a text-based 'living room' where the other users characters were violated. This behaviour continued for several hours in a particularly aggressive manner, until an experienced user was able to contain and then exclude the intrusive user from access to the site. One of the violated personae reported being in tears of post-traumatic stress as she posted a message on the site asking that the violator be punished.

Acceptance that online and offline situations can be inextricably interlinked regarding both technological and social contexts in a supplementary rather than an exclusionary manner has led to the development of the concept of '*cyborg*' – a cybernetic organism (that is, an organism that has both artificial and natural systems capable of extending human capacity). The implicit notion of collapsing the boundaries of the aspects comprising the cyborg allows an unbounded flow from organic to technological to occur and for complexities to develop at different levels. Each cyborg can then be a hybrid amalgam of identity and artifact with no fixed start or conclusion to either the cyborg entity, to 'reality', or to 'cyberspace', all of which become changing spaces where unfinished realities can take various social forms .

Michel Foucault's concept of *heterotopia* ([1967]1984) is another term that has emerged in this field. Foucault used the term for a variety of situations: spatio-temporal prisons (such as care facilities for the elderly) and children's imaginary worlds. These heterotopic spaces have the capacity to mirror, reflect and distort both real and imagined experiences. In the following quote Foucault separates out the functions of heterotopias from utopias:

> I believe that between utopias and these quite other sites, these heterotopias, there might be a sort of mixed, joint experience, which would be the mirror. The mirror is, after all, a utopia, since it is a placeless place. In the mirror, I see myself there where I am not, in an unreal, virtual space that opens up behind the surface; I am over there, there where I am not, a sort of shadow that gives my own visibility to myself, that enables me to see myself there where I am absent: such is the utopia of the mirror. But it is also a heterotopia in so far as the mirror does exist in reality, where it exerts a sort of counteraction on the position that I occupy. From the standpoint of the mirror I discover my absence from the place where I am since I see myself over there. (Foucault, [1967]1984)

The aspects of reconstitution reflection, refraction and change place this concept alongside and in support of those of the cyborg and the theories of complexity. Cyberspace clearly provides the ability for users to get to know themselves in different ways and to develop aspects of their various personae in an anonymous fashion that may help reconstruct both online and offline personae in a positive manner.

Process

The traditional ethnographer who analyses existing written/visual data and goes into a 'field' to 'participate' to whatever degree s/he determines is necessary in order to gather good data, has shifted to a different kind of field where anonymity and privacy dominate, where no one is seen or even identifiable except in carefully chosen words and where observation may only be of online text with no visuals, no sound apart from the clicks of mice and keys, and no defined location. In this situation, interaction is no longer face-to-face but technologically mediated. Traditionally, breadth of observation and time in the field were key factors in authenticating accounts, and although these terms are still relevant they have been replaced by items such as 'thread-length' and role in the site (member/avatar or lurker). The researcher still has to spend time in the field and immerse themselves in their chosen role, observe meticulously, collect further data sources and negotiate the final interpretation with the participants. It has been suggested that in cyberspace the libraries of books of traditional ethnography are replaced by libraries with people on the shelves rather than texts and that these people will use the web like a stage but without the confining parameters of time and space (Teli et al., 2007) but a stage where there is no scripted dialogue, unfinished discourse and flexible movement to online and offline sites.

Access and ethics

Access to potential participants can be complex – do you become a member of a site and actively participate in your own right? Many sites have strict administrative rules and access is limited to those with justified bona fide interests but others are sufficiently flexible to allow interested persons to create avatars with persona accommodated to the focus of the site in order to participate. Or, you could hover anonymously in a public access area but the more private sites do not have these areas and access is limited to members only. You could also approach the administrator of the site and explain your purpose as a researcher and seek permission to enter. This is clearly the most ethical way of going about it but you may have to approach several sites before a controller will be prepared to seek and gain member consent for you to enter and participate. Participant privacy and anonymity will normally have to be protected, as in most research, as many of these sites are safe places created for individuals to divulge feelings, emotions, concerns etc. Member entry will also make it easier to participate in your own right and to seek offline meetings for further interview data. If you can only gain access to public arenas, how ethical is 'lurking' anonymously? And how much data will you be able to gather regarding sensitive topics? And if you do gain that kind of data, how will you use it?

In terms of ethics committees (although this varies from country to country) after some discussion, most will usually accept that legitimate entry as a researcher into sites discussing very private matters such as sexuality, drug habits, etc. will disturb these sites and members may well dissipate, limiting the researcher's access. In these situations ethics committees should be prepared to give permission for you to enter anonymously but may require you to expose your intent before you finally leave the site and in this situation you will have to be prepared to delete data from individuals who refuse permission. If you do not wish to communicate with potential participants on an existing site, Facebook has the facility for you to create a research page to attract and inform potential participants of your study and for you to communicate with them and receive agreement to participate. The old-fashioned physically signed informed consent should also be something for negotiation with ethics committees as privacy and distance may lead this to becoming an obstacle for the research to proceed.

Data collection

The focus in cyber ethnography is primarily the study of relationships among people within online environments. Researchers collect individual and collective subjectivities in the construction and understanding of a particular culture. Data sources include text based forums, personal web pages, webcams, video blogs (vlogs), video animation, and social network and networking sites such as Facebook, Myspace, Cyworld and YouTube. Researchers often enter sites in their own right or anonymously, employing an observational role in order to minimise their impact. Once in, you can collect data on such aspects as: content of discussions, the numbers of monthly postings, message lengths, thread links and gaps between the emergence of these and their being picked up and disappearing from the site, the numbers of members, and any demographic details that are available. In online sites the anonymity factor operates allowing people to disclose quite private information. More in-depth information, interviews, questionnaires and focus groups can be possible both on and offline but these require you to reveal both yourself and the participants in the move to a more 'visible' place.

Some basic questions that might be useful in providing direction for the collection of data in cyber ethnography are:

- How do people construct and present themselves on a particular site?
- How do people engage with each other?
- How do they negotiate what it means to be part of the site?
- How do they engage with new media?
- How are meanings and accounts framed, shared and monitored?
- How do people transcend the limits of internet media framing?
- How do they extend the boundaries between online and offline encounters?

Data analysis and presentation

The process of data collection involves you in identifying a transitional and changing community through textual postings and then making some sense of these postings. Preliminary data analysis may help identify the gaps but filling these gaps may require you to go offline to collect additional data not feasible in many cases. This leaves the researcher with thematic analysis (Chapter 5), coding (Chapter 21) or just editing narratives down to their essentials. Data presentation can also utilise multimedia and polyphonic juxtaposition of 'voices' together with different narratives from other sites. Apart from the rhizomatic (non-hierarchical with multiple entries and exits) nature of the data other problems you may experience with analysing this kind of data include the lack of homogeneity of the population to be studied, the inability to determine the extent of its diversity and the development of different cultures at each site which make comparisons difficult. Details of who the contributors are can often be inaccessible or non-existent and the quoting of comments without participant consent or the agreement of the group of individuals who may have assisted in the social construction of particular positions, is problematic and time-consuming to gain.

Should you impose an analytic frame and sequence the data in order to follow a particular thread? Or should you allow the generally chaotic nature of the data to follow its own patterns? Certainly the former is better in terms of the construction of a simple picture of communication at the site where certain foci of communication may be presented but the latter presents a truer picture of some of the types of communication that occur.

The tracking of discourses that develop at particular sites is another analytic option.

Research examples: member

Member: multiple data sources on- and offline Willem de Koster (2010) was able to add to his data set by gaining offline data. He used administrator consent to access a 300-members-only site ('RefoAnders') developed for Dutch protestant homosexuals and after monitoring and participating in the site for a year de Koster invited members to undertake a face-to-face interview with him. Accessing 15 people for these interviews was made easier by the fact that forum members also regularly organised recreational activities for the forum group either in public (bowling, dinners etc.) or in 'living room gatherings' held in rented locations. Thematic analysis of the interviews clarified and revealed two types of participants:

- lonely singles or unhappy marrieds living a double life of stigma and isolation; and
- supported individuals who were seeking practical everyday information on how better to manage their emotionally complex lives.

For the first group the online community provided much-needed support and was a retreat – a virtual community where they felt protected and safe – and for this group issues of privacy and secrecy dominated their concerns re the research. For the second group personal contacts, friendships, information, and affirmation were the dominant gains sought from membership. Concerns regarding privacy were minimal and public debate was encouraged. De Koster suggests that online forums provide spaces for Goffman's (1959) 'backstage performances' where stigma can be revealed, covert skills developed, and support and advice given and received.

Member: mixed methods   Micheala Fay (2007) used qualitative and survey methods to undertake internet research on a website of feminist academics, in which she herself was a legitimate participant, to investigate the concept of 'home belonging' and its fit in contemporary mobile lives. She gained permission from the group and undertook textual thematic analysis gained from total immersion in the group, sent out a structured survey questionnaire analysed via descriptive statistics, and kept notes of her own critically reflective involvement in the forum as well as undertaking two face-to-face interviews. For both Fay and de Koster access to the site and to data was facilitated by membership.

Member: on a site for teenagers   The position of being a member has its own dilemmas, particularly when the users may well be under age for giving consent to participate in research. Heather Battles (2010) was a member of a public Message Board site aimed at American, Australia and Canadian female adolescents for discussions about the human papilloma virus (HPV) vaccine. This public site carried warnings that privacy was not possible so personal information should be restricted. She could have posted an open message to all participants so that individuals could withdraw or seek deletion of their comments, but she thought this might open the website to unethical players. She could perhaps have gained individual adolescent and parental consent but this might have been very time-consuming and difficult so she chose to gain permission from the administrator and to email the 72 participants to inform them about the study, giving concerned contributors the opportunity to withdraw their data. She chose to position herself as an unnamed member (pseudonym only) and she protected the site by not naming it and the contributors by not divulging names, user names nor using verbatim quotes that could identify the site or the users. Analysis of the 136 replies gained over a 3-month period was by limited manual coding to identify persistent threads.

Lurker

The lurker   Brett Billman (2010) inhabited the lurker role over a period of 3 weeks, investigating communication processes and embodiment in cyberspace in monitoring the MightTMenFTM channel, a video and discussion site for transmen – those undergoing gender transitions in four countries. He also monitored other female-to-male sites. All were public sites where transgendered and transitioning individuals post their stories to gain a wider audience and to enhance public understanding. Because of this, the researcher did not seek permission to collect these vlogs but he did alter usernames to protect privacy. The videos and the subsequent discussions form the major part of the results and are reproduced unedited. Billman found the site provided participants with a bridge to link the performances trialled on site with 'meatspace' behaviours (offline), thus blurring the boundaries between the two in the creation of new identities.

Member and lurker   A study of South Asian Women's email discussion list (SAWNET) by Radhika Gajjala (2002) highlights further some of the problems of researching internet sites you are part of. She sent out a questionnaire to one site where she was an active member and also observed at a second site for people of Indian culture where she acted as a 'lurker' and did not actively participate in the discussions. She sent her completed paper from both sources – questionnaire and observations – to the SAWNET site. The women members protested that they were unhappy about being researched and analysed, that permission would have to be gained from each individual member to use their messages and that no generalised statements regarding group activity were to be made. These demands then prevented the research from continuing. Gajjala suggests that researchers need to find ways to disrupt their own authority as ethnographers. She also raised the following key questions for debate:

- How important are partial truths, any betrayals and exposure of bias of the researcher?
- What or who constitutes an online community, how this is decided and who has control of the group?
- Is a forum email list a public or private space?
- What is the status of intellectual property in these situations?
- How long should a vote to prevent researchers entering and taking data from a site last?
- What is to be the status of participants – texts or informants?

Further problematic issues were revealed in another study, by Ward (1999), who followed the Cybergirl Web Station and Women Halting Online Abuse (WHOA), both of which were 'read-only' sites. Ward found that the notions of 'culture' and 'community' were very problematic on these sites. She also discovered that a 'virtual community' was neither absolutely physical nor virtual but was illusionary and that participants' relationships with groups tended to be short term and transitory. In addition, the dialogic process allowed participants considerable freedom to define their own reality and to pose questions to the researcher. This led to an open reflexive methodology of the feminist kind involving dual interpretation between researcher and researched.

Permitted lurker   Researchers are treading a very fine line where ethics are concerned, in order to avoid intruding on the class reunion site of a group of friends who 20 years before had been students together in India but were now migrants scattered over the world. In order to bypass some of the problems listed above, Teresa Davis (2010) chose to lurk with permission on the basis that she might become a participant. This allowed her to follow discussions and gave her access to all previous discussions. She avoided the conflict of exposure (with potential to taint the data) and not disclosing while participating (unethical) by only using past data produced during the year prior to her joining the site. Data comprised archived messages including, files, photos and the group calendar. This data was thematically ordered from the discussion threads, then coded and arranged chronologically and interpretations cross-checked by the friend who as part of the forum had facilitated Davis's entry.

E-research: using the internet for data collection

Constructing sites specifically to collect data especially from geographically dispersed participants whom you would like to interact with each other and/or with you is another use of the internet. Samantha Crompvoets (2010) created an anonymous online discussion board where participants who had agreed to be part of her study could log on at any time, post comments to questions and respond to others. She was seeking to gain the personal and professional discourses of overseas-trained doctors undergoing re-training from remote locations. There was no written consent gained but participants opted in via participation but could withdraw at any stage although their comments would remain part of the study unless they themselves deleted them. Webwiz software was set up and moderated and maintained by the researchers' university; the site was thus internet-based but not live to other people. Such a site can then be used as a locked filing cabinet for storage and security. Crompvoets found that there was minimal interaction among participants who just responded to her questions but who were clearly watching and reading the responses of others at certain times. From the researcher's perspective this tool was inexpensive, easily modified with questions being added as required, and the anonymity factor made the introduction of sensitive issues easy.

Criticisms of cyber ethnographic research

Ethical issues

The major criticism lies in the ethical complexities. Should the ethical standards that apply to offline research also apply to online research? As the examples above illustrate there is clearly division of opinion where publicly accessible sites are observed. If offline ethics are to apply to online studies, permission to use content may be very difficult to obtain from all participants, as some may not be able to be traced. Permissions to access some sites may require several levels of agreement, for example teenagers, guardians, the forum in general and the administrator. Taking publicly posted data for research purposes without going through any form of permission will always be ethically problematic. Should it be assumed that conversations on online sites are public or private? Despite the use of pseudonyms, there still may be sufficient information to identify people or their stories may be traceable to individual identification through search engines.

Data quality

Other problems lie with the data: the boundaries of the online field are difficult to define in a rhizomatic world. Where do they start and where would be a good place to finish? Access is also problematic particularly into sites that may be regarded by some members as private spaces. Authoritative findings are difficult to gain when information is fragmented and follow up cannot easily be undertaken, particularly from the lurker position. Insiders as members may have better access to data but their potential exploitation of participants may lead to resentment and a sense of betrayal. The dynamics of power between researcher and researched in terms of interpretation are well and truly on the researchers side and negotiated collaborations are rare except in specifically feminist sites. Where does power lie when a participant does not want to participate in research but when extrication of their voice would create large holes in threaded conversations?

Summary

Cyber ethnography is an exciting new field and the internet is worthy of investigation as an independent cultural form or as an integral part of online and offline lives. Issues of ethics, data quality and data analysis still need to be addressed. Analysis is largely a loose form of thematic grouping (see Chapter 5) and coding (see Chapter 21) followed by data display when this is permitted.

In summarising these chapters on the newer forms of qualitative research practice, autoethnography provides a focus on the self as subject of the research; ethno drama constructs dramatic performances and can provide political and social challenges; and cyber ethnography explores via the observation and analysis of online (and offline) communication. Like all qualitative research, these approaches require meticulous collection of data, careful analysis and interpretation, and creative forms of display, such as those seen in poetic inquiry, in order to impact on the reader or the audience.

Student exercise

Find a public access website on a topic of interest to you, take a lurker (observation only) position and watch for a week. Download or print the threads if this is possible, and identify the major themes that are occurring.

Further reading

Cyber ethnography – background and practice

Dicks, B., Mason, B., Coffey, A. and Atkinson, P. (2005) *Qualitative Research and Hypermedia: Ethnography for the Digital Age* (New Technologies for Social Research series). London: Sage. Investigates how digital technologies potentially transform the ways in which we do research and explains how to conduct data collection, analysis and representation using 'hypermedia'.

Enochsson, A. (2005). A gender perspective on Internet use: consequences for information seeking. *Information Research*, 10 (4): 95–112. This article explores the different voices used by males and females and the consequences of this for information seeking.

Zweerink, A. Ethnography online: 'natives' practising and inscribing community. *Qualitative Research*, 4 (2): 179–200. The article provides an analysis of the methodology used to study a community created by an Internet website which was devoted to following a particular television program.

Kozinets, R. (2009) *Netnography: Doing Ethnographic Research Online*. London: Sage. A survey of online research, ethics and practice relating to researching of blogging, videocasting, podcasting, social networking sites and virtual worlds.

Research examples

Bortree, D.S. (2005). Presentation of self on the Web: an ethnographic study of teenage girls' weblogs. *Education, Communication & Information*, 5 (1): 25–39.

Kozinets, R. (2001) The field behind the screen: using Netnography for marketing research in online communities. Looking at the symbolism and activities of online consumer groups. Available at http://kozinets.net/__oneclick_uploads/2009/07/field_behind_round4.pdf (accessed 14 November 2011).

Wilson, B. and Atkinson, M. (2005) Rave and Straightedge, the virtual and the REAL: exploring online and offline experiences in Canadian youth subcultures. *Youth and Society*, 36 (3): 276–311.

References

Battles, H. (2010) Exploring ethical and methodological issues in internet based research with adolescents. International Institute of Qualitative Methodology. Retrieved from http://ejournals.library.ualberta.ca/index.php/IJQM/article/viewArticle/5017 (accessed 15 November 2011).

Billman, B. (2010) Re-producing masculinities on Youtube: a cyberethnography of the mightTMenFTM channel. Doctoral dissertation, Graduate College of Bowling Green State University. Retrieved from http://etd.ohiolink.edu/view.cgi/Billman%20Brett%Ned.pdf?bgsu1276644001 (accessed 21 April 2012).

Crompvoets, S. (2010) Using online qualitative research methods in medical education. *International Journal of Multiple Research Approaches*, 4 (3): 206–13.

Davis, T. (2010) Third space or heterotopias? Recreating and negotiating migrant identity using online spaces. *Sociology*, 44 (4): 661–7.

De Koster, W. (2010) Contesting community online: virtual imagery among Dutch orthodox protestant homosexuals. *Symbolic Interaction*, 33 (4): 552–77.

Dibbell, J. (1993) A rape in cyberspace. Retrieved from www.juliandibbell.com/articles/a-rape-in-cyberspace/ (accessed 21 April 2012).

Downing, S. (2010) Online gaming and the social construction of virtual victimization. *Eludamos Journal for Computer Game Culture*, 4 (2): 287–301. Retrieved from http://www.eludamos.org/index.php/eludamos/article/view/vol4no2-11/196 (accessed 10 May 2011).

Fay, M. (2007) Mobile subjects, mobile methods: doing virtual ethnography in a feminist online network. *Forum: Qualitative Social Research*, 8 (3): Art. 14.

Foucault, M. ([1967]1984) Des espaces autres, trans. J. Miskowiec as 'Of other spaces (1967), Heterotopias', *Architecture/Mouvement/ Continuité*, October 1984. Retrieved from http://foucault.info/documents/heteroTopia/foucault.heteroTopia.en.html (accessed 30 March 2012).

Gajjala, R. (2002) An interrupted postcolonial/feminist cyberethnography: complicity and resistance in the 'Cyberfield'. *Feminist Media Studies*, 2 (2): 1–16. www.cyberdiva.org/erniestuff/sanov.html (accessed 26 April 2011).

Goffman, E. (1959) *The Presentation of Self in Everyday Life*. New York: Anchor Books.

Miller, D. and Slater, D. (2000) *The Internet: An ethnographic approach*. Oxford: Berg. ch. 1.

Teli, M., Pisanu, F. and Hakken, D. (2007) The internet as a Library-of-People: for a cyberethnography of online groups. *Forum: Qualitative Social Research*, 8 (3): Art. 33.

Ward, K. (1999) Cyber-ethnography and the emergence of the virtually new community. *Journal of Information Technology*, 14: 95–105.

PART 4

Analytic approaches for existing documentation

Analysis of all documents within the qualitative domain is all about *shaping*: how social, cultural and political events together with individual and group understandings have shaped what is said and written, and how these influences can be tracked through natural conversations and stories, collected through observation or, as in this section, identified in the perusal of existing documents. These documents can include a wide variety of artefacts from policy documents, case history notes, newspaper articles, clothing styles, body art, graffitti, paintings, photography, television programmes, chat room conversations and advertisements. You will find that although the analytical approaches for analysing these documents such as content analysis, conversation analysis, narrative analysis and discourse analysis overlap and sometimes duplicate each other, each one has a particular orientation – a distinctive flavour that identifies it as a discrete entity. For example, content analysis involves taking large documents and coding and categorising their contents; while conversational analysis focuses on conversation sets and turn-taking – the effect of one response on another; narrative analysis focuses on stories told by participants; and discourse analysis can cover conversations and stories as well as including analyses of media and other documentation of a written or visual nature in the tracking of discourses. The techniques for analysing existing documentation are underpinned by two strong theoretical positions (structuralism and poststructuralism) and these are discussed briefly in the Chapter 14, providing a background and the setting for the principles underlying the management and analysis of existing documentary data sets using the approaches explored in the other chapters:

FOURTEEN

Structuralism and poststructuralism

Documentary analytic approaches have been heavily influenced by theoretical shifts in structuralism and poststructuralism. This chapter explores the shifts in structuralism and outlines the criticisms of this mode of thought which then formed the basis for the growth of poststructuralism.

KEY POINTS

Structuralism

- Individuals and entities were viewed as system produced and representative of an era or type
- In language, meaning was seen as lying within the text where the signifier (written word) attributed meaning to the signified (object or concept) in an easily visualised manner

Poststructuralism

- The finite meanings of structuralism were queried and it was argued that each word could be linked to multiple meanings
- In pulling the text apart to find these meanings, Jacques Derrida suggested deconstructing it and Michael Foucault suggested identifying the powerful discourses and tracking them historically

---

General principles of structuralism

Structuralism became a dominant mode of thought in France in the 1960s. The ideas that can be termed structuralist sought to describe the world in terms of systems of centralised logic and formal structures that could be accessed through processes of scientific reason. Individual objects were viewed as being part of a greater whole. Psychologists concentrated on the structures of the mind and sociologists emphasised the societal institutions that formed the individual. Nothing was seen to be of itself, for example a particular building was seen less an individual entity, and more a representative of an architectural style based at a particular point in time in a specific culture and reflecting identifiable values. Similarly, people become seen as objects/products with the self and the unconscious being classified and constructed by their webs of cultural networks, perceptions and values. This allowed people to be seen largely as mechanical organisms produced by systems, and with defined needs, predictable behaviours and actions. Thus the underlying forms, structures and processes of construction and transmission of meaning, rather than the content, became the main focus.

Language, signs and meaning

Under structuralism, language was seen as a key process in the creation and communication of meaning. It was viewed as a self-referential system – all perceptions and understandings were seen as being framed by words. Meaning lay within the text, a coherent and unified structure derived from pattern and order, and analysis simply involved uncovering these patterns and ascertaining their meaning through the particular order in which they have been constructed.

Much of this view derived from the early twentieth-century work of a Swiss linguist Ferdinand de Saussure (1857–1913) who, in viewing language as a system of signs and codes, sought out the deep structures, the rules and conventions that enable a language to operate at a particular point in time. He saw individual words as arbitrary signs with meaning only in relation to other signs in the cultural system. Within each rule-based language system (langue) the linguistic sign is the spoken or written word (the signifier) which attributes meaning to objects, concepts and ideas (the signified – the mental picture produced by the signifier) in the construction of reality. For example, the word 'rain' produces a mental image of rain falling. We recognise the meaning of the word rain not from the word in itself but from its difference to other similar sounding words such as 'pain' and 'lain' which produce different mental pictures. In comprehending meaning we also utilise the difference between rain and similar concepts such as 'hail, 'sleet' and 'snow' as well as opposing concepts such as 'drought'. Meaning is seen as being structured through binary opposites. As Saussure said, '… in the language itself there are only differences, and no positive terms … the essential function of a language as an institution is precisely to maintain these series of differences in parallel … the language itself is a form, not a substance' (1916: 166).

Acceptance of the assumption that through signifiers and signifieds reality is socially constructed and that any utterance (parole) is meaningful only in relation to other words within the larger cultural system in which all of these have been constructed, became widespread. Binary oppositions were sought to clarify meaning and were seen to provide a localising (within specific cultures) focus and the interrelationships among signs were viewed as crucial in the analysis of language. Some signs were seen as embodying broader cultural meanings and were termed 'myths' – these were viewed as having the capacity to operate as signifiers at a second level of signification or connotation (Barthes, 1957). For example, a Ferrari sports car is a mythic signifier of wealth and a particular lifestyle. Saussure called the structural analysis of the meanings of signs and codes of textual and material culture in terms of underlying structures 'semiology' (1907–11, 1983) and Roland Barthes (1964) continued this terminology while Charles Peirce called it 'semiotics' ([1894]1998).

Texts

The focus on signs, signifiers, codes (the frameworks in which signs make sense), and order and meaning through repetitions of patterned relationships, enabled texts and cultures to be 'read' using semiotic or other structural forms of analysis. Here construction of meaning, representation of reality and the privileging of binary opposites is integral. Everything then became 'text', both the author and the reader are also viewed as social constructions, and the ways of presenting 'reality' within 'cultures' was meticulously documented. In literature, reading carries with it certain conventions and expectations – words, style of presentation, type of narrative etc., to which the reader responds in the construction of the story (parole). Within structuralism, however, each literary work is further seen as part of the broader institution of literature (langue), which is also intricately intertwined in the cultural system.

Structuralist positions

Key figures in various disciplines became very involved in structuralism. In psychology, Jacques Lacan used the analogy of language and the binary oppositions of the 'subject' and 'other' to examine the development of the structure of the unconscious (Lacan, 1957: 36–7). He suggested that the 'I' was broader than the centred 'ego' of Freud and that the unconscious was fragmented and dispersed. This focus on deep rather than surface structures has similarities with modernity and in particular the works of Marx and Freud with their de-emphasis on individuals as powerful agents and their focus on unconscious motivation and the power of societal structures in constraining action.

Roland Barthes, who was a literary critic, outlined the process of analysis of 'objects' in terms of a search for their functioning rules; 'The goal of all structuralist activity, whether reflexive or poetic, is to reconstruct an "object" in such a way as to manifest thereby the rules of functioning (the "functions") of this object … Structural man [sic] takes the real, decomposes it, then recomposes it' (Barthes, 1972: 214–15).

In the construction of myths, the anthropologist Claude Lévi-Strauss personified the elements of the process into two intellectual approaches: the 'bricoleur' (the odd-job man, who re-uses the bits and pieces at his disposal in devious and creative ways) and the engineer (who can access scientific thought, concepts and theories). But despite the different approaches, both are constrained by the need of order and structure in the creation of knowledge. The scientist 'is no more able than the "bricoleur" to do whatever he wishes when he is presented with a given task. He too has to begin by making a catalogue of a previously determined set consisting of theoretical and practical knowledge, and of technical means, which restrict possible solutions' (Lévi-Strauss, [1962]1966: 19).

Lévi-Strauss used binary oppositions to identify the underlying structures of phenomena and to track their interconnections with other parts of the culture or to compare systems of 'myth' across cultures. For example, he investigated the meanings attached to raw or cooked food across a number of tribal cultural groups. He wrote, 'That which constitutes a society and a culture is a universal code that runs through the culture and the institutional and behavioural forms of that society … This universal cultural system objectively exists, structuring mental processes as well as social' (Lévi-Strauss, 1963: 202–12).

However, this view of the usefulness of some signs in determining universal cultural values would have to be questioned. Returning to the example of the Ferrari sports car, this mythic signifier would have minimal use, meaning and quite different value to the pygmies of the Congo forests in comparison to the value and meaning it might hold for the elite of Milan. This focus on the universality and centrality of structures and signs

even across cultures also tended to diminish the role of history and context in constructing and influencing current values and behaviours.

Criticisms of structuralism in the transition to poststructuralism

In developing arguments regarding the limitations of structuralism, and in a similar process to that between modernity and postmodernity, many authors were actually shifting
the field forward and at the same time providing the foundations of what would later be
termed poststructuralism.

Is there meaning beyond the text?

Jacques Derrida challenged the notion from Saussure that meaning was to be found in the
difference between particular words and other concepts in the language system by emphasising both the simultaneous referral and deferral of meaning. He supported this view in his
statement 'There is nothing outside of the text {there is no outside-text, *Il n'y a pas de hors-
texte*}' (Derrida, 1976: 158). This meant that textual signifiers did not relate to any clear centred 'reality' or 'signified' outside the text, they simply slid away toward multiple possibilities.

Roland Barthes also asserted that structural analysis could not seek meaning beyond
the text itself: '"What takes place" in a narrative is from the referential (reality) point of
view literally nothing; "what happens" is language alone, the adventure of language,
the unceasing celebration of its coming' (Barthes, 1977: 124). In his essay 'Death of the
author' Barthes suggested that the author did not have total control of textual meaning
and had no greater insight into the text than the reader. This allowed the notion of free
play of meanings to be developed but also emphasised the impossibility of originality
under structuralism where the text becomes a product of the system and any possibility
of uniqueness is lost. 'We know now that a text is not a line of words releasing a single
"theological" meaning (the "message" of the Author–God) but a multidimensional space in
which a variety of writings, none of them original, blend and clash. The text is a tissue of
quotations drawn from the innumerable centres of culture' (1977: 146).

Jean Baudrillard (1993) also emphasised the death of the possibility of originality in the
recycling of images by referring to Andy Warhol's (1962) repeated identical paintings of
Marilyn Monroe's face, and Jacques Derrida shared Friedrich Nietzsche's critique of the level
to which 'truth' had descended under structuralism:

> What, then, is truth? A mobile army of metaphors, metonyms, and anthropomorphisms –
> in short, a sum of human relations which have been enhanced, transposed, and embel-
> lished poetically and rhetorically, and which after long use seem firm, canonical,
> and obligatory to a people: truths are illusions about which one has forgotten that
> this is what they are; metaphors which are worn out and without sensuous power;
> coins which have lost their pictures and now matter only as metal, no longer as coins.
> (Nietzsche, 1911: 46–7; quoted by Spivak in the preface to Derrida, 1976: xxii)

The problems of binary opposites

Jacques Derrida (1976) pointed out that when deconstruction of texts is utilised, binary
opposites (each of which always contains traces of the opposing entity) collapse, articulating

the difference between space and time and making nonsense of Saussure's precise systems of meaning (for example the opposites 'male' and 'female' have both linguistic and biological traces). Luce Irigaray (1985) also strongly critiqued the limited social frames that binary opposites imposed, in particular the binary opposites of 'penis' – 'vagina'. She notes that this privileging of the male organ has led to a phallocentric orientation for all sexuality. Her concern lies with female sexuality and gender, which are seen to have been rendered invisible, except through the male 'gaze' or dissolved into reproductive activities. 'There is only one sex, the masculine that elaborates itself in and through the production of the "Other" (p. 18). Irigaray suggests that removal of this binary opposition is essential in order to shift female dependence on male versions of their sexuality. The subsequent reduction of the focus on distant male 'vision', substituting instead female 'touch' – 'woman takes pleasure more from touching than from looking' (p. 26) would allow for a physically closer form of sexuality, greater fluidity of language and multiple interpretations.

Signs and signifiers and the problem of desire

Jacques Lacan, like Derrida, emphasised relations between signifiers (rather than signifier and signified like Saussure) and further added into the debate the concept of desire through alleging that the sense of self, 'I', is constructed through the symbols of language. Without language we cannot perceive the difference between others and ourselves. Thus, language develops around a lack, a separation from the other that creates desire (desire of the Other – the arena that all else relates to or gains relevance from). Lacan sees the unconscious as being structured like a language and made up of signifiers. Because of this, signifiers have no fixed identity or reference points. They shift and change continuously. Desire becomes insatiable, comprising difference and lack '... an element necessarily lacking, unsatisfied, impossible, misconstrued' (Lacan, 1981: 154). The self tries to create meaning in order to make sense of individual being.

Julia Kristeva similarly criticised linguistics as having 'no way of apprehending anything in language which belongs not with the social contract but with play, pleasure or desire' (Kristeva, 1986: 26). Kristeva saw the 'speaking subject' (a person capable of both conscious and unconscious motivation) involved in the creation of two levels of meaning: semiotic (internal individual processing) and symbolic (signs). Kristeva suggested another form of analysis – semanalysis (a combination of psychoanalysis and semiology), which utilises signifying processes rather than sign systems. Here she is seeking the movement of unconscious desire into language: '... the language of dreams and the unconscious ... is not identical to la langue studied by linguistics; it is however, made in this langue ...' (1989: 272).

The position of the individual

The contentions surrounding 'desire' and the movement beyond the language system can also be seen in the work of the French philosopher Gilles Deleuze and the psychoanalyst Felix Guattari (1977), who also criticised psychoanalysis on the grounds that it had become stuck in a limited Oedipal frame which prevented recognition that individuals are resistant, fragmented, constantly shifting among multiple positions and assemblages and not solely locked into familial and predictable roles. In moving toward an active rather than a passive individual, Deleuze and Guattari further criticised psychoanalysis for its view that 'desire' was psycho-symbolic and negative – always seeking something that is absent. They re-conceived desire as creative, active involvement in the world. The process by which the self is constructed and subjectivity created involves embodiment and resistance (termed nomadology). The resistant and reflective self (termed the body without organs), in taking in the social environment, counteracts the possible domination (territorialisation) of the self by powerful social forces. The self is continually being constructed and deconstructed through further involvement in and the incorporation of aspects of other texts and social contexts (intertextuality), and thus individual styles shift and change.

Territorialisation is seen as an active process involving creative involvement in taking in new ideas (deterritorialisation) to allow new connections to be formed (reterritorialisation) in the production of another form of the body without organs (the 'virtual' dimension of a body with its collection of traits, connections and affects). Building on these ideas, Deleuze and Guattari critiqued the view posited by Marx that capitalism is a powerfully integrated hierarchical system dependant for its functioning on cohesive and clearly delineated class and familial groupings, by suggesting that this system is actually schizophrenic in operation. In order to maximise profits, the societal structures of the family, church and state have been deterritorialised and reterritorialised into new groupings, for example, farm labour was freed up and took on new skills in order to become industrial labour and the extended family became a nuclear family with greater flexibility of movement to travel to where the jobs were.

To make greater sense of these processes, Deleuze and Guattari introduced the concept 'rhizomatic' to explain the infinite nature of change:

> the rhizome connects any point to any other point, and its traits are not necessarily linked to traits of the same nature; it brings into play very different regimes of signs, and even nonsign states ... It is comprised not of units but of dimensions, or rather directions in motion. It has neither beginning nor end, but always a middle (milieu) from which it grows and which it overspills ... . It has multiple entranceways and exits and its own lines of flight. (Deleuze and Guattari, 1987: 21)

This notion of the rhizome, capable of constant adaptation, shifted the field light years away from previous finite vertical hierarchies.

The issue of the broader cultural concepts and the individual

Michel Foucault (1972) introduced a broader political perspective into the study of texts and countered the flexibility of Deleuze and Guattari by re-emphasising the arguments regarding the construction and control of people via signs and symbols. He took a more negative and bounded view of self-construction within which he sought to expose the history of claims to truth by indicating that there were identifiable and underlying structures underpinning the human condition which could be observed objectively. He challenged the documentation of events as single, value-free, disinterested narratives, emphasising instead the historian's political and cultural interpretations in writing and rewriting for different audiences. He asserted that any event requires multiple narratives in order to approach the many perspectives through which it has been constructed/experienced and that the discourses of power must be traced back in time and exposed so that future patterns can become clearer. Foucault exposed the manner in which the state had created particular powerful discourses such as 'madness' and 'sexuality' and how through sovereign and disciplinary power and using the metaphor of the arterial system, these ideas had filtered down to the (largely unresisting) population and had become the basis of their understandings and explanations (written and inscribed on their bodies). In this situation, he demonstrated that language would not necessarily be reflecting reality and the location of 'truth' could become very controversial. In tracing the discourses, hidden or buried truths are not sought; the search itself is an active process of detection and creation.

Foucault also emphasised that the death of the author left this position open to other possibilities, such as the emergence of other 'voices'. He utilises Nietzsche's historiographical approach – genealogy, to access knowledge (the hidden voices) that have not been recorded, in order to expose the hidden power plays, the memories and knowledge that have been covered over in the maintenance of powerful interests by dominant institutions. 'Geneology, … seeks to re-establish the various forms of subjection: not the anticipatory power of meaning, but the hazardous play of dominations' (1984b: 83). 'The search is directed to "that which was already there", the image of a primordial truth fully adequate to its nature, and it necessitates the removal of every mask to ultimately disclose an original identity' (1984a: 78). Despite these challenges, Foucault still tends to fall back on the underlying structuralist dichotomies 'powerful' and 'powerless' to frame discourses and there is an inbuilt assumption that the discursive practices associated with particular discourses may become governed by rules. The influences of structuralism have obviously been pervasive.

Many of the critics mentioned above came from the structuralist tradition and have been responsible not only for initiating the move into poststructuralism but also for the continuity and linking of this newer approach with that of structuralism. As time passed, the overall focus shifted from the structures that generate meaning, to documenting how the generative capacity provided by the framing and content of the texts themselves was displaced by the possibility of an endless deferral of meaning amongst a range of signifiers.

Post structuralism

Language

Here, there is rejection of the existence of deep structure or form and it is no longer accepted that the language system is stable and closed with signs that have clear meanings, instead signifiers dance in an endless play of meaning with no relation to any integrated centre. Thus there is no one all-encompassing explanatory concept such as 'god' or 'science', which can explain the genesis and operation of the universe.

However, there is an acceptance in poststructuralism that our major mode of communication is through language and recognition that the meanings signified by signs are conventions. Further, there is recognition that existing discourses structure and limit the way we think, read, and write, that the language we use and the discourses and tropes (metaphors) within which we think prevent us from seeing the genesis and development of ideas as the power-laden discourses that they really are. A process of naturalisation has taken place, which has smoothed over the discourses making them appear to be transparent and 'truthful'. However, the privileging of certain discourses and texts allows exposure to take place and formerly hidden aspects to emerge.

Truth

There is considerable scepticism about this concept. Knowledge is viewed as unreliable if it comes solely from language. History and the discourses they have been a part of, influence meaning. There is no absolute truth beyond or beneath the text. Reality is fragmented and diverse, and analysis has tended to highlight texts, language, history and contextualised cultural practices.

Meaning is fluid; it is focused either within the text or between and among texts. All that we can know is textual and related to discourses. There is constant referral of meaning, the signifier/signified breaks down and everything becomes a signifier with neverending possibilities. This allows many readings of the text to occur thus emphasising that the original writing may change meanings over readers, time and culture.

Criticisms of poststructuralism

Poststructuralism has been criticised regarding the complexities that it provides. In particular:

1 How will the contradictions between culture and science be explained without recourse to the language claims of structuralism?
2 The decentring of the author doesn't take into account the fact that the author still composes the structure of the text, has selected the 'voices' and manipulated the direction of interpretation. Although deconstruction should clarify this, it is a lengthy and painstaking process.
3 The lack of finite conclusions through the constant deferral of meaning also presents difficulties in terms of evaluation and policy decisions.
4 Are discourse analysis and deconstruction any more than an older authorial desire to appropriate a text (however momentarily)?
5 There is a tendency toward nihilism – endless deconstruction can very quickly lead to meaninglessness.

Research applications

Two arenas of poststructuralism currently dominate the field: Michael Foucault and 'discourse' (see Chapter 20) and Jacques Derrida and 'deconstruction' (see Chapter 15). Neither Foucault nor Derrida has provided precise instructions as to how the processes of analysing discourse or undertaking deconstruction might be carried out in research, but they have left some strong indications of the general principles and processes that could be followed. Those relating to deconstruction will be demonstrated in the next chapter.

Further reading

Semiotics – basics

Chandler, D. (2007) *Semiotics: The Basics* (2nd edn). London: Routledge. This book provides an easy-to-read, jargon-free introduction to the study of semiotics from Saussure and Freud to Lacan, Eco and Derrida. Daniel Chandler's 'Semiotics for Beginners' is available online. The text is closer to the first edition of his book. It covers structuralism, sign systems, and poststructural deconstruction. Plenty of examples are provided. www.aber.ac.uk/media/Documents/S4B/semiotic.html (accessed 1 May 2011).

Johansen, J. and Larsen, S. (2002) *Signs in Use: An Introduction to Semiotics.* London: Routledge. An accessible introduction which presents semiotics as both theory and set of analytical tools: code, sign, discourse, action, text, and culture. Numerous examples are included, from traffic systems to urban parks.

Poststructuralism – basics

Belsey, C. (2002) *Poststructuralism: A Very Short Introduction.* A simple but concise introduction to poststructuralism from Ferdinand de Saussure to today.

Sarup, M. (1993) *An Introductory Guide to Post-Structuralism and Postmodernism.* Athens, GA: University of Georgia Press. This is a comprehensive but basic introductory text – a good place to start for those with no previous knowledge in these areas.

Williams, J. (2005) *Understanding Poststructuralism.* Chesham, Bucks: Acumen. This guide provides short and accessible introductions to poststructuralism for undergraduate readers.

References

Barthes, R. (1957) *Mythologies.* London: Paladin.

Barthes, R. (1964) *Elements of Semiology.* New York: Hill and Wang.

Barthes, R. (1972) The structuralist activity. In *Critical Essays* (trans. R. Howard). Evanston, IL: Northwestern University Press.

Barthes, R. (1977) Death of the author: structural analysis of narratives. *Image–Music–Text.* London: Fontana Books.

Baudrillard, J. (1993) The order of simulacra (trans. P. Beitchman). In *Symbolic Exchange and Death.* London: Sage.

Deleuze, G. and Guattari, F. (1977) *Anti-Oedipus* (trans R. Hurley, M. Seem and H. Lane). New York: Viking.

Deleuze, G. and Guattari, F. (1987) *Thousand Plateaus: Capitalism and Schizophrenia* (trans. B. Massumi). Minneapolis. MN: University of Minnesota Press.

Derrida, J. (1976) *Of Grammatology* (trans. G. Spivak). Baltimore, MD: Johns Hopkins University Press.

Foucault, M. (1972) *The Archaeology of Knowledge* (trans. A. Sheridan Smith). London: Tavistock.

Foucault, M. (1984a) Truth and method. In P. Rabinow (ed.) *A Foucault Reader.* Harmondsworth: Penguin.

Foucault, M. (1984b) Nietzsche, genealogy, history. In P. Rabinow (ed.), *A Foucault Reader.* Harmondsworth: Penguin.

Irigaray, L. (1985) *The Sex Which Is Not One.* Ithaca, NY: Cornell University Press.

Kristeva, J. (1986) *The System and the Speaking Subject.* In Toril Moi (ed.), *The Kristeva Reader.* New York: Columbia University Press.

Kristeva, J. (1989) *Language: The Unknown.* New York: Columbia University Press.

Lacan, J. (1957) The insistence of the letter in the unconscious (trans. J. Miel). In J. Ehrmann (ed.), *Yale French Studies* 36/37, 1966.

Lacan, J. (1981) *The Four Fundamental Concepts of Psycho-analysis* (trans. A. Sheridan). New York: W.W. Norton.

Lévi Strauss, C. (1963) *Structural Anthropology.* New York: Basic Books.

Lévi Strauss, C. ([1962]1966) *The Savage Mind.* Chicago, IL: University of Chicago Press.

Nietzsche, F. ([1911]1954) On truth and lies in an extra-moral sense. Fragment from *The Nachlass* (1873: 1) in *The Viking Portable Nietzsche* (trans. W. Kaufmann). New York: Vintage Books.

Peirce, C. ([1894]1998) 'What is a sign?' In *The Essential Peirce: Selected Philosophical Writings,* Vol 2 (1893–1913). Bloomington and Indianapolis, IN: Indiana University Press.

de Saussure, F. ([1907–1911,1916]1983) *Course in General Linguistics* (trans. R. Harris). La Salle, IL: Open Court.

Warhol, A. (1962) *Marilyn Diptych.* Tate Gallery London.

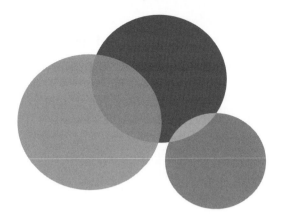

FIFTEEN

Semiotic structural and poststructural analysis (deconstruction)

This chapter takes the theory mentioned in Chapter 14 to a more practical level. Documentary analysis moves along a fluid dimension between structuralism and poststructuralism. These two forms of analysis involve determining how the meanings of signs and symbols are constructed and how they can be read. Structural approaches involve identifying the commonly accepted layers of meaning within texts while poststructuralism calls on Jacques Derrida's processes of deconstruction to illuminate the many possibilities of meaning.

KEY POINTS

- Semiotics is the study of signs, sign systems and their meanings
- Structuralism assumes that signs have a limited range of meanings, which can be identified
- Poststructuralism assumes that superficial and static meanings provide only one layer and deconstruction can reveal many more options as meaning slips away into multiple possibilities

---

1. Structuralism

When to use: When it is important to identify the language forms, structures and processes of meaning transmission.

Type of research questions best suited: What are the commonly accepted meanings of signs within a particular culture?

Strengths: The approach helps to clarify broad cultural values.

Weaknesses: This form of precision signifier – signified may not sufficiently represent complexities of meaning (see Chapter 14 for criticisms of structuralism).

Process

- Seek the way effects are created through metaphors, repetition and binary opposites.
- Identify meanings of signs in context and in the culture.

This process can most easily be seen within research examples:

Research examples

An example of the imposition of a structure for testing can be seen in Sigrun Karlsdottir's (2010) use of Rick Altman's structural classification of the American film industry to test three 'types' of film musical, namely: 'fairy tale', 'show' and 'folk' musicals. Altman defines musicals as having a dual-focus plot with a couple of protagonists who after many scenes emphasising their differences, finally come together and in coming together things change for the better. Also present is diegetic music (music that adds to the narrative).

1 In the *fairytale* musical, the protagonists often come from different social classes or the obstacles to coupling lie within themselves. Sex as desire/battle/adventure spices up the action and when the couple finally come together, order is restored.
2 In the *show* musical, the coupling (which is often centred around a tense triangle of an earthy and an energetic individual plus one other) accompanies the creation of a work of art – usually a show and the male usually gets the girl who is best for him not the one who could further his career or make him rich.
3 In the *folk* musical, set in some romanticised past era/geographical location with a strong values of family, community and honour, true love is usually found with a long-term friend and after the usual dramas the final couple formation restores harmony and extends community connection/communion with the environment.

In order to see if various musicals fitted Altman's classification the approach involved listing themes, patterns and the use of repeated signs and symbols to create particular meanings. An analysis of *My Fair Lady* put it into the 'fairy tale' category, similarly *Grease* and *Mamma Mia* fitted the 'folk' grouping and *Pal Joey* went into the 'show' musical genre. The assumption that certain signs have particular meanings enables this classification to occur.

2. Poststructuralism (deconstruction)

When to use: When deconstruction of the text/texts is desirable.

Type of research question: What are the deeper meanings of and links for this text?

Strengths: The capacity to go beyond superficial meanings.

Weaknesses: Too much pulling apart of the text can lead to meaninglessness.

Background

One of the major aspects of poststructuralism, the notion of deconstruction of the text through the critique of its structural integrity, was introduced by Jacques Derrida in 1976.

The word 'deconstruction' itself has been subject to different forms of interpretation but the meanings as Derrida understood them are clarified in a 'Letter to a Japanese friend' (1985) where he explains the orientation of this term by utilising several dictionary definitions:

> Deconstruction: action of deconstructing. ... Disarranging the construction of words in a sentence. Of deconstruction, common way of saying construction ... To disassemble the parts of a whole ... To deconstruct verse, rendering it, by the suppression of meter, similar to prose ... (1985: 1–5)

Thus the deconstruction of text appears to be a positive and a negative process of change, although it has been argued by some that it is more a destructive process (Habermas, 1987: 161). However, 'Rather than destroying, it was also necessary to understand how an "ensemble" was constituted and to reconstruct it to this end' (Derrida, 1985: 1–5). Deconstruction is less a method or stage-by-stage approach and more a natural unravelling which the text invites by presenting this opportunity within its own structure. The word 'deconstruction', like all words, is not a unity in itself but is also subject to deconstruction. Its value is relative to the other words, sentences and concepts against which it appears in context and to which it is linked.

Unravelling

Most systems constructed during the era of structuralism were seen as centred and self-referential (see Chaper 14) and all meaning emanated and referred back to this centre. One of the strengths of structuralism was its capacity to 'naturalise' or normalise through history and conditioning so that 'truths' were unquestioned. According to Derrida, in poststructuralism 'the center is, paradoxically, within the structure and outside it' (1978: 279), allowing 'the freeplay of its elements inside the total form' (pp. 278–9). Derrida talks of the hidden areas inside systems, perhaps in some 'eccentric corner' which can be accessed by various approaches. He uses the analogy of his own veins – their internal action can be viewed by various pieces of medical imaging equipment but if cut they reveal their action outside the body – an action that will display the workings of the circulatory system (the pumping of blood), but can lead to loss of the original form or death (www.iep.utm.edu/derrida/ accessed 21 April 2012).

Binary oppositions and 'difference'

Centered systems are usually created and maintained on the basis of binary oppositions, for example 'God' and the 'Devil', 'Good' and 'Evil', etc., where one reflects a positive value and the other a negative value in society. These central concepts provide meaning and the sense of something existing beyond the system – something indefinable – the 'constant of a presence ... consciousness or conscience, God, man, and so forth' (1976: xxi). For Derrida, hierarchical oppositions cannot be absolutes as each contains a trace of the opposite term. Derrida uses the binary opposition of 'presence' and 'absence' to clarify this. He saw presence and absence as being unable to be easily separated. Presence is only meaningful in the context of the notion of absence and because in each present there is a trace – a sign left by the absent thing. The concept of **'différance'** ([1972]1982), which has two aspects: difference (to differ, linked to identity) and deference (time and the constant deferral of meaning), which serve to break down the power of such oppositions. Every sign is a signifier and every signifier is linked to other signifiers in a never-ending process.

The overall purpose of deconstruction is to erase the boundaries of these binary oppositions in order to illuminate the similarities and interdependency between each oppositional pair. This is done by demonstrating that each member of the pair is not a complete opposite and to show how the marginalisation of one member has in fact centred it. This exposure of societal values causes rigid boundaries to blur and collapse and the oppositions to become meaningless.

Deferral of meaning

Thus both deconstruction – boundary removal – and construction – putting into free play the relationships among signs and allowing new possibilities of meaning to emerge – have occurred. Rather than developing new binary oppositions, conclusions become infinite with the constant referral/deferral of multiple interpretations of meaning. Sometimes a 'hinge' (*la brisure* – an internal device such as double meaning, trace, statement) can break open the text and put differance into play (1976: 65). Many meanings thread together to make up the discourses within any one text. With deconstruction, one thread leads to another and to another and slowly the text unravels. Roland Barthes has said that 'In the multiplicity of writing, everything is to be *disentangled*, nothing *deciphered*; the structure can then be followed, "run" (like the thread of a stocking)' (1977: 147).

Each sign carries traces of references to many other signs in an interconnected (rhizomatic) network of possibilities. Language and meaning depend on 'différance' (from other signs) and deferral of meanings. Interpretations are thus intertextual, differing among the author, the text, and the viewer, as well as constantly shifting and subject to revision. The viewer is empowered and both viewer and creator are part of the 'jubilant multiplicity of self-references' (Derrida, 1984: 174). Closure or finite meanings are impossible.

Deconstruction: indications of process

Derrida is quite clear that there is danger in formalising a method of deconstruction:

> I would say that deconstruction loses nothing from admitting that it is impossible; ... For a deconstructive operation *possibility* would rather be a danger, the danger of becoming an available set of rule-governed procedures, methods, accessible practices. Deconstruction is inventive or it is nothing at all; it does not settle for methodological procedures, it opens up a passageway, it marches ahead and marks a trail; its writing is not only performative, it produces rules – other conventions ... Its *process* involves an affirmation, this latter being linked to the coming [*venir*] in event, advent, invention. (1992: 312-13).

Although the disentangling or unravelling process appears fairly simple as a visual construct, when you are faced with a complex text the actual process of locating a key thread could be fairly daunting. Rosenau (1992) has collated a number of principles from various sources and these have been expanded in an attempt to provide you with some suggestions for guiding the procedure.

1 Take the position of accepting nothing and rejecting nothing in a critical and sceptical reading, the overall outcome of which should be the production of an understanding of the text's structure, its content and its omissions.
2 In the seeking of threads to rupture the text:

   o find dualities or binary opposites
   o allow the arguments of the text to challenge each other; place argument against argument, find the exceptions
   o identify any contradictions and inconsistencies (ideas, metaphors etc.)
   o seek out and disentangle the complexities of all dichotomies, binary oppositions and hierarchies
   o locate any generalisations and use these to undermine any principles used
   o try reading against the grain of the document to discover alternative readings
   o seek out links with other texts.

3 Examine the margins and identify marginalised or missing voices, concealed information and underrepresented arguments.
4 In writing up:

   o write so as to allow as many interpretations as feasible
   o avoid making any absolute statements
   o stay close to the language of the text
   o cultivate ambiguity and ambivalence.

5 Remember that this is a transitional not a finite text that you are creating – it should resist closure.
   (Adapted from both Rosenau, 1992: 120–21 and Boje and Dennehy, 1994: 340)

Research examples: causal layered analysis

Within the focus of poststructural deconstruction Sohail Inayatulla (1998) has introduced the technique of causal layered analysis, as part of the agenda of problematising units of analysis to 'open up the present and past and to create alternative futures' (1998: 815). This approach seeks the complex layers of the system, which provide the various perspectives framing the construction of an issue or event. The focus is deconstruction, the tracing of historical discourses and the reordering of knowledge. The first level sought is the *litany* – the public discourse often created and maintained by the politics of the day or the media; the second layer is concerned with *social causes* – the technical and academic discourses derived from social, economic, historical and cultural factors; the third level contains the deeper discourses that maintain structural *worldviews,* which maintain the underlying inequalities in society – the religious, cultural and historical views from which alternative discourses can be derived. The fourth and final level contains *metaphor and myth*, the unconscious often visual dimensions of emotive and intuitive thought.

As examples of how this would work in research, Inayatulla presents several case studies focusing on analysis of particular questions or workshops: a UNESCO workshop; a workshop for senior university management; and a seminar on advocacy for people with disabilities. Taking the last example in more detail; at the *litany* level, and regarding the debate around housing people with disabilities in institutions, the public debate focused on institutions as settings of neglect and abuse with 'feel-good' media highlighting government actions to improve this 'problem'. At the level of *social causes*, the focus on individual patients rather than structural imbalances of power within the institutions was noted. At the *worldview* level, the 'othering' of people with disability because of their difference from 'normal' people was an issue and at the *myth and metaphor* level, fear of difference was seen in terms of inclusion/exclusion of these people in society. Alternative future scenarios centred on societal change, removal of difference through genetic technology, and continued ghettoisation resulting from media-led campaigns (1998: 821-4). This approach allows for the development of alternative action plans based in a deeper recognition of the dominant discourses constituting a particular field.

Further research examples of deconstruction

- Researchers who have attempted deconstruction have employed various approaches to display or re-present data for the reader such as:

  o placing texts against each other in order to trouble them
  o interrupting texts in an attempt to prevent them closing and avoiding finite interpretations
  o creating another structure to allow a freer play of language.

Placing texts adjacent to each other

David Boje (2000) has attempted this juxtaposition to portray two different perspectives on the same community, presenting two opposing versions to beat against either side of the eardrum (see Figure 15.1). The two sources – a *Popular Mechanics* article and research data – are placed alongside each other to provide a contrast and to start a debate. The whole article can be viewed at http://web.nmsu.edu/~dboje/pmdecon9705.htm (accessed 1 May 2011) and the first couple of paragraphs and accompanying visual images can also be seen in Chapter 24. Boje has placed an article from *Popular Mechanics* on the left side of a two-column page demonstrating the 'dangerous community' – one that protects drug dealers and requires high level law enforcement, against researcher-collated reports of

Figure 15.1 Example of 'tympanum'
Image juxtaposition from the work of David Boje (2000) Postmodern detournement analysis: Nickerson Gardens V *Popular Mechanics*

'community action and celebration' on the right. This juxtaposition allows the joyousness of community life to be put into hard relief against the aggression of police in the maintenance of order in urban culture, thus dislodging threads for unravelling.

Avoidance of closure

The impact of childhood sexual abuse on the perpetrator and his now adult victims can be seen in an article by Karen Fox (1996) that involved placing several different sets of data in three columns. The first column has the voice of the perpetrator discussing his feelings, in the centre is the voice of the author (reflecting on the interview and on herself as a victim of childhood sexual abuse by a priest) and in the third column is the voice of the now-adult victim of the relationship under interview. The juxtaposition of these three voices provides the reader with a complexity of continuous interacting threads to pursue.

Ben sex offender

I love her you know. You see

We really had a good relationship.

She loves me, She told me that

Karen researcher

I want to believe him I guess

I always hoped I meant

something to my abuser

That he really did love me,

that he really did feel I was

special

Sherry victim

I never felt romantic love for

him. That area disgusts me .... I've had

feelings of love for him, like for a

father.

(Fox, 1996: 339)

Ben: sex offender	Karen: researcher	Sherry: victim
I love her you know. You see	I want to believe him I guess	I never felt romantic love for
	I always hoped I meant	him. That area disgusts me ... I've had
We really had a good relationship.	something to my abuser	feelings of love for him, like for a
	That he really did love me,	father.
	that he really did feel I was	
She loves me,		
	special	
She told me that		

(Fox, 1996: 339)

Creating another structure

Martin Wood (2010) investigated how academic health service researchers disseminated research information to those in daily practice in the United Kingdom National Health Service. Four exploratory case studies with 70 interviews plus 376 surveys provided information about how health service researchers operate.

The original thematic analysis of the data suggested that there was a mix of academic-based and socially based answers in community health services research in the UK, with tension between the two but with the greatest influence being toward an academic emphasis. Wood used Boje and Dennehy's guidelines for deconstruction (1994: 340), involving:

searching for dualities

reinterpreting the hierarchy of the story

querying existing voices

seeking the other side of the story

changing the plot, for example, from dramatic to romantic

seeking exceptions and reading between the lines

restorying to remove dualities and margins

so the voices of the health service researchers were more easily heard.

This process of deconstruction shifted critical attention away from organisational and policy factors and outcomes and emphasised the multiplicity of embedded and contextual experiences, meanings and values of individual researchers. This means that the strategies used by health services researchers to try to connect healthcare research information with those in daily clinical practice, could be more clearly seen in terms of the indefinite play in the field of human experience.

Structuralist and poststructuralist analyses: a comparison

It is possible to show the different emphases between structuralist and poststructuralist analyses by contrasting these two approaches using a simple nursery rhyme example such as 'Jack and Jill':

Jack and Jill went up the hill

to fetch a pail of water;

Jack fell down and broke his crown,

and Jill came tumbling after

Up Jack got and home did trot

as fast as he was able;

He went to bed to mend his head,

with vinegar and brown paper.

Structuralist analysis

Here the signifiers are presumed to have meanings that are easily recognisable and easily interpreted within the cultural language. In the first stanza we can then assume that Jack is a male person and Jill a female person. The fact that Jack is referred to first may indicate that males are of greater importance in the culture. Going up a hill to fetch a pail (older name for a bucket and probably made of metal) of water suggests also that water is a valued in this story and that getting it involves effort (climbing a hill) or that as water collects in low-lying areas it was necessary to get over higher ground in order to descend to a water collection point. Water as the basic constituent of life on the planet is clearly a resource worth travelling for. Jack's fall and the breaking of his 'crown' – either his head or a crown, suggesting he may be a member of the royal family – indicates his ultimate lack of success in achieving the goal of gaining water resulting in a painful outcome – either a broken skull or a fall from grace. Equally unsuccessful in their quest, Jill tumbles and falls after him. Their fortunes appear to be linked.

In the second stanza only Jack is mentioned, reinforcing the lesser importance of Jill, whose fate we now know nothing about. Jack is sufficiently intact as to get himself home at a fair speed (trot) and to put himself to bed and to treat his head with a mixture of vinegar and brown paper. This combination produces DMSO (dimethyl sulphoxide) which is currently under trial for its medical uses and a dilute form has been used in the past as a topical analgesic because it was viewed as having the capacity to reduce pain and inflammation almost immediately through its ability to enter the body quickly. The overall rhyme of the poem falls into a walking/trotting rhythm supporting the narrative.

Poststructuralist analysis

The first two verses of the nursery rhyme 'Jack and Jill' can also be used to provide a contrasting and simple poststructural analysis, where deconstruction of the text is the main aim.

a Identify arguments and challenges

Both going up a hill to fetch a pail of water
Jack falling down and breaking his crown
Jill tumbling after him
Jack trotting home fast
Going to bed to mend his head

b Identify oppositional elements, hierarchies, contradictions

Jack	v	Jill
up	v	down
pail of water	v	empty pail
head	v	crown
out of bed	v	in bed
broken	v	mended
out of home	v	in home
vinegar	v	water

c Identify ideas, metaphors, meanings

crown	=	head
water	=	life (for life maintenance or as a medium for new life – sperm)
tumbling	=	(sexual metaphor)
up the hill	=	moving up in status

Simple reading

It is possible to climb high but such a climb may lead to a fall with personal/political damage as the outcome.

Alternative readings

Nordic mythology   There are several versions of this tale in old Norse legends (Harley, 1855). One involves the Moon God Mani (male) taking from earth two children, Hjiki (pronounced Juki, which has a close resemblance to Jack), a word that also means to assemble and increase in amount, and Bil (also close to Jill), which means to break down or dissolve. Mani put these two on the moon. Both children are visible at the full moon, but Jack 'falls' and can't be seen as the moon wanes, and Jill comes 'tumbling after' as the new moon appears.

A reading of this could be that cycles of change are inevitable but that all things are renewable.

Gender   'Jack' and 'Jill' have often been used as generic masculine and feminine terms linked to water, as can be seen in Act III Scene ii of William Shakespeare's *A Midsummer Night's Dream*:

> And the country proverb known,
>
> That every man should take his own,
>
> In your waking shall be shown:
>
> Jack shall have Jill;
>
> Nought shall go ill;
>
> The man shall have his mare again, and all shall be well.

Returning to the nursery rhyme, the breaking apart of the text through the identification of oppositional elements allows for a straight sexual reading where the monarch has dallied (with a female) whom he may or may not have made pregnant (breaking the royal line 'head') and is obliged to retreat and lie low (from his wife? or from the public gaze?) until things are calmer. Or another version could view the queen (Jill) dallying and becoming pregnant elsewhere creating the need for a carefully managed situation. The rhyme can also be read as political/economic dalliance with ideas/another country/a particular project – in all cases some damage appears to have occurred, requiring caution and the outcomes are unclear.

Economics/politics   In the 1640s, King Charles I of England attempted to reduce the liquid measure of a 'jack' (two jiggers or two mouthfuls) which also impacted on the measure of a 'gill' (pronounce 'jill') (2 jacks = a gill) in order to increase tax revenue to balance some fairly severe fiscal mismanagement. The jack/jackpot was a particularly relevant measure for the sale of ale. After a reign of heavy taxation and civil war, Charles was beheaded.

In the late eighteenth century another monarch, King Louis XVI of France, also initiated a system of heavy taxation and reforms to deal with a financial crisis. The bourgeoisie of France resisted the reforms and the angry populace rose in revolt, and imprisoned the royal family in the Tuilleries. Louis and his wife, Queen Marie Antoinette, were beheaded.

The major theme of aggregating and building up and then losing what has been gained permeates all the stories from the waxing and waning of the moon to the perceived unfair extraction of money from the population by a powerful monarch followed by loss of position, power and life as the population take control through civil insurrection.

Reading against the grain

A positive reading against the grain of *disaster* could see Jack and Jill, as male and female representatives of the population, seeking new and powerful knowledge which they gain but in doing so they need to break with traditional ways of thinking in order to implement new ideas. A reading against the grain of *patriarchy* could point to the weaker more easily damaged male of the species in contrast with the more resilient female, while another reading might assume that Jack and Jill were both male and both female, making the narrative a warning tale about public displays of same-sex relations.

Transitional conclusion

The poem can be read as relating to either gaining or losing by individuals, pairs or heads of state and these gains/losses may be further linked to mythological/sexual/political/economic/social readings. One potential outcome indicated is that when losses are achieved it may be possible to retrieve or mend some of the damage if you retreat and lie low but the reverse may also be true because lying low may need to become a lifetime occupation. No finite conclusions are possible.

Summary

Semiotic approaches to textual analysis fall into two broad categories: *structuralism*, where there is an assumption that signs have clearly recognisable meanings and that binary opposites will serve to clarify these meanings; and *poststructuralism*, where meaning is seen as more complex, deferring endlessly to many possibilities which are only limited by the imagination of the writer and the reader. In structuralism your analytic process is straightforward involving identifying the construction of language and documenting the accepted meanings of words in order to make sense of them. A poststructuralist analysis involves you in a sceptical reading to identify arguments, challenges and metaphors, as well as unravelling binary opposites, seeking alternative interpretations, reading against the grain and presenting your conclusions in such a way as to avoid closure.

The overall implications for research with the advent of poststructuralism lie in a refocus on:

- *Intertextuality* – the impact of the text on others in terms of the appearance of particular signs and the linking of ideas from one text to another.
- *Intersystem linkage* – here change dominates.
- *Multiple selves* and many voices including the display of those previously marginalised or inaudible.
- *Referentiality* – many complex meanings at different levels.
- *Declining metanarratives* (an abstract idea or 'theory' that is thought to be a comprehensive theoretical explanation of culture, ideology and knowledge).

Student exercise

Taking 'Jack and Jill' as a model, choose any nursery rhyme (apart from 'Jack and Jill') and undertake and compare a structural and a poststructural analysis. Use Google to trace alternative readings.

Further reading

Structuralism and poststructuralism

Chaffee, D.G. and Lemert, C. (2008). Structuralism and post structuralism. In *New Blackwell Companion to Social Theory*. Chichester: Wiley–Blackwell, pp. 124–40. A good introduction.

Coller, J. (2006) *Critical Concepts in Literary and Cultural Studies*. London: Routledge. This four-volume collection explores the key areas of structuralism.

Gutting, G. (2011) *Thinking the Impossible: French Philosophy since 1960*. New York: Oxford University Press. A focus on Derrida and Foucault, and the ideas that changed structuralism.

Hawkes, T. (2003) *Structuralism and Semiotics*. London: Routledge. A compact volume that summarises the complex theories that have been labelled structuralist.

Palmer, D. (2007) *Structuralism and Poststructuralism for Beginners*. Hanover, NH: Steerforth Press. This is a comic book for beginners written by a professor of philosophy – Donald Palmer.

Deconstruction

Peters, M. and Biesta. G. (2009) *Derrida, Deconstruction and the Politics of Pedagogy*. New York: Peter Lang Publishing. Useful background to Derrida's ideas.

Royle, N. (2000) *Deconstruction: A User's Guide*. London: Palgrave. This book shows practical applications of deconstruction at work, illustrating what it is not and linking it to feminism, poetry, psychoanalysis, love and drugs.

References

Barthes, R. (1977) Death of the author: structural analysis of narratives. In *Image–Music–Text*. London: Fontana Books.

Boje, D. (2000) Postmodern détournement analysis of the *Popular Mechanics* spectacle using stories and photos of the festive community life of Nickerson Gardens. In *EJ-ROT Electronic Journal of Radical Organization Theory*, 6 (1). Retrieved from http://web.nmsu.edu/~dboje/pmdecon9705.htm (accessed 1 May 2011).

Boje, D. and Dennehy, R. (1994) *Managing in the Postmodern World: America's Movement Against Exploitation*. Dubuque, IA: Kendall/Hunt. Retrieved from http://business.nmsu.edu/~dboje/mpw.html (accessed 8 August 2011).

Derrida, J. ([1972]1982) *Margins of Philosophy* (trans. A. Bass). Brighton/Chicago: Harvester/University of Chicago Press.

Derrida, J. (1976) *Of Grammatology* (trans. G. Spivak). Baltimore, MD: Johns Hopkins University Press.

Derrida, J. (1978) *Structure, Sign, and Play in the Discourse of the Human Sciences: Writing and Difference* (trans. A. Bass). Chicago: University of Chicago Press.

Derrida, J. (1984) Living on: borderlines. In H. Bloom et al. *Deconstruction and Criticism*. London: Routledge & Kegan Paul, pp. 75–176.

Derrida, J. (1985) Letter to a Japanese friend (10 July 1983). In D. Wood and R. Bernasconi (eds), *Derrida and Differance*. Warwick: Parousia Press.

Derrida, J. (1992) *Psyche: Invention of the Other. Acts of Literature* (ed. D. Attridge). London: Routledge.

Fox, K. (1996) Silent voices. In C. Ellis and A. Bochner (eds), *Composing Ethnography: Alternative Forms of Qualitative Writing*. Thousand Oakes. CA: Sage.

Habermas, J. (1987) *Lifeworld and System: A Critique of Functionalist Reason* (trans. Thomas McCarthy). Boston, MA: Beacon Press.

Harley, T. (1885) *Moon Lore*. London: Swan, Sonnenschein, Le Bas and Lowry. Retrieved from http://books.google.com.au/books?id=hYm6vr7j5gEC&pg=PA68&lpg=PA68&dq=harley+1855+moon&source=bl&ots=XapZiT4Mnu&sig=kvdoISXiaasiWyn1FuyEOoj17Tc&hl=en&ei=1Vw_Tpa9AoPZrQeHjoUc&sa=X&oi=book_result&ct=result&resnum=5&ved=0CDgQ6AEwBA#v=onepage&q=harley%201855%20moon&f=false (accessed 08 August 2011).

Inayatullah, S. (1998) Causal layered analysis: poststructuralism as method. *Futures* 30 (8): 815–29.

Karlsdottir, S. (2010) A cold blooded murderer calls for a revision: Rick Altman's subgenre division of the American film industry. Thesis, University of Iceland. Retrieved from http://skemman.is/stream/get/1946/6275/17947/1/almost_there_sk_prenta.pdf (accessed June 2011).

Roseneau, P. (1992) *Postmodernism and the Social Sciences: Insights, Inroads and Intrusion*. Princeton, NJ: Princeton University Press.

Wood, M. (2010) Reluctant bedfellows or model marriage? Postmodern thinking applied to mainstream public sector health services research settings. University of York: The York Management School Working Paper No. 55. Retrieved from http://eprints.whiterose.ac.uk/11236/1/55_Working_Paper_Martin_Wood_2010.pdf (accessed 8 August 2011).

SIXTEEN

Content analysis of texts

In this chapter you will be introduced to two major forms of content analysis: the **enumerative version** with its focus on researcher imposition of categories and the use of computer tools such as word frequencies and key words in context, and **ethnographic content analysis**, where culture and context are important interpretive aspects and both enumerative and thematic analysis can be undertaken. In content analysis 'documents' can include written texts, audio and visual media.

KEY POINTS

- Content analysis requires up-front decisions regarding:
    - analytic techniques (enumerative/ethnographic/combined approaches)
    - the size and aspects of the data set to be analysed
    - sampling approaches
    - any predesigned protocols
    - any inter-rater reliability

Introduction

When to use: When you have large sets of existing written or visual documentation which require analysis.

Type of research questions best suited: What is the percentage of occurrences of 'X' words, events, types of approaches etc. How have particular concepts been used in context and why? And for what purpose?

Strengths: The different approaches – enumerative and ethnographic – provide different information regarding what is in the documents, with enumerative providing a numbers-oriented overview, while ethnographic provides not only a numerical overview but the addition of thematic analysis with more depth of explanation as to why and how words have been used in particular cultural contexts.

Weaknesses: Enumerative data alone provides only a superficial overview and thematic contextual interpretation alone lacks the detailed numerical information to situate and structure the data.

Background

Content analysis is a systematic coding and categorising approach you can use to explore large amounts of existing textual information in order to ascertain the trends and patterns of words used, their frequency, their relationships and the structures, contexts and discourses of communication. You can use this approach to analyse a broad range of written, audio or visual *'documents'*. These can come from memos, minutes of meetings, policy documents, census data, court case transcripts, case histories, newspaper articles (use LexisNexis to locate these), advertising brochures, books, radio programmes, speeches, websites, television programmes and movies, as well as personal records such as diaries, letters, emails and blogs. The researcher's creation of coding frames highlights certain aspects of the text providing the reader with one particular view, but other views are possible with the application of different protocols and the use of different sampling strategies. Enumerative approaches have tended to dominate content analysis but in many cases these have been combined with thematic forms of analysis.

Content analysis: general process

Six questions need to be addressed in every content analysis:

1 Do you have sufficient documents to make this form of analysis useful? And which aspects of these documents are to be analysed? All of the documents? Part of the documents? And pertaining to what topics?
2 What sampling approach will be undertaken? In the case of large numbers of documents you will need to judge whether random, stratified, cluster or non-probability approaches to sampling will be of benefit or whether this may mean that certain key documents get left out of the data set.
3 What level of analysis will be undertaken and what particular concepts or situations will be coded for? You may need to develop a prior protocol, for example a matrix that can then be imposed on subsequent documents in order to gain ennumerative data. And how will you incorporate any thematically analysed data: as a basis for the generation of codes? As a basis for cross-checking? To identify discourses? Or to provide depth information and case studies?
4 How will the protocol and/or your codes be generated? Will you seek these from the database via preliminary data and thematic analysis or will you impose a predecided (a priori) coding frame derived from the literature and your own experiences of this field? And if the latter, what inclusion or exclusion criteria will you use to develop predecided codes?
5 What relationships between concepts, codes and their contexts will be taken into account? And how will this be managed? Will you look at context? Or stay with a broad numerical overview?
6 How reliable is the approach or protocol that you have decided on? Can a high level of intercoder reliability be sustained? Can validity be achieved through cross-referencing to other documents or through triangulation and the inclusion of qualitative data?

Enumerative content analysis: tools

As the repetition of words in content analysis is assumed to indicate their level of importance in the document, enumerative information is favoured. These enumerative quantitative processes are based in seeking dictionary-based 'key words in context' and 'word frequency' indexes as well as 'space measurement' (of the columns in newspapers) and 'time counts' (of pauses and amounts of time given to particular topics in radio and television presentations). These tools provide a quick way of breaking into particular data.

Word frequency: this helps you to identify how often key words are turning up in your documents. It is sensible to exclude such words as 'a', 'the', 'of', 'and', 'in', 'like', 'because' and 'which' as well as any other joining words which are being widely used in your document set. Having identified the frequency of key words you might like to select several other tools to identify the contextual use of your chosen key words.

Key word in context or concordance: this approach shows each word in the document (apart from those you have excluded) in alphabetical order and in context – usually with a few words on either side.

Category frequency or cluster analysis: this is where other related words (synonyms) will also be picked up, for example, if you identify 'economy' then related words like 'employment', 'unemployment' and 'inflation' will also be searched for. Equally, 'family' would pick up 'mother', father', sibling', 'son', daughter', 'parent' and grandparent etc. The computer then shows how often each category occurs in the document.

Lemmatisation: this is another tool where the base form of the word and its variations are gathered, for example. 'go' picks up 'goes', 'gone' and 'going'.

Co-occurrence: you might look for particular words, such as 'security' and 'terrorism' for example. Or you might decide to start out with a list of words that you want to check on to find out how often they occur in proximity to each other.

Computer programs

To facilitate your enumerative content analysis there are a large number of computer programs available for your consideration. Most use the dictionary word approaches – whereby defined words can be tagged for word frequencies (which can be sorted alphabetically and by frequencies), key word in context (single words, word roots or multiple word combinations) can be shown with 8–10 words on either side to clarify the context, cross-references and concordances, and vocabulary comparison of two texts is also possible. Links to most of the available software for quantitative content analysis, audio, image and video analysis and management, and the generation of statistical information can be perused at http://bama.ua.edu/~wevans/content/csoftware/software_menu. html (accessed 28 April 2011). As well, a number of the second-generation qualitative data management programs such as ATLAS.ti, MAXQDA and NVivo also have some content analysis capacity.

Word frequency: rank ordering

The rank ordering of the frequency of words in the election speeches of key politicians from various political parties will clarify how often these people refer to such issues as health, education or national security and how the frequency of use of these terms may change from party to party and election to election.

In the following example, the top 100 words from Project Gutenberg (free English e-books online) are taken from these books in alphabetical order and are listed:

a · about · after · all · and · any · an · are · as · at · been · before · be · but · by · can · could · did · down · do · first · for · from · good · great · had · has · have · her · he · him · his · if · into · in · is · its · it · I · know · like · little · made · man · may · men · me · more · Mr · much · must · my · not · now · no · of · on · one · only · or · other · our · out · over · said · see · she · should · some · so · such · than · that · the · their · them · then · there · these · they · this · time · to · two · upon · up · us · very · was · were · we · what · when · which · who · will · with · would · you · your

A masculine trend can be detected even from this limited sample and many of these joining words ('a', 'the', 'about' etc.) could well be omitted from your content analysis.

The *Hermetic Word Frequency Counter* (free trial version available at www.hermetic. ch/wfca/wfca.htm) will allow you to scan a file and produce a rank order and frequency count of words and phrases that looks like the one in Figure 16.1.

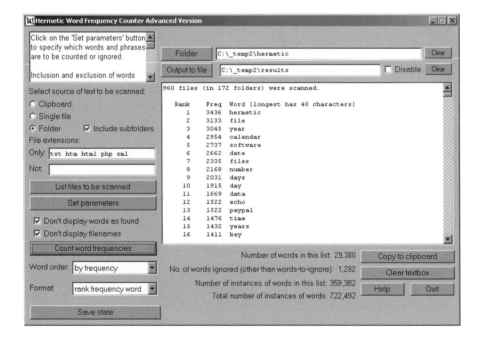

Figure 16.1   Word frequency counter image

Wordle at www.wordle.net/ can produce visuals of clouds of words for any text you enter, with the most-used words enlarged: This example comes from Martin Luther King's speech ' I have a dream …' and clearly the most frequently used word in this speech is 'freedom', followed by 'Negro' and so on. Another way to display word frequency using the size of words can be seen using Wordle as in Figure 16.2.

Figure 16.2   Wordle image

Key words in context (KWIC)

If you go to http://khnt.hit.uib.no/tactweb/doc/TWDisply.HTM (accessed 26 April 2011) you will find a simple illustrative program using *TACTWeb* 1.0 experimental software in which you can undertake a search for word frequency and KWIC in William Shakespeare's *A Midsummer Night's Dream*. From this site I have chosen 'love' using TACTWweb to locate words on either side of 'love' whenever it appears in order to provide greater detail about the contexts in which 'love' has appeared. A small selection of the 99 occurrences of 'love' in this play together with their script location, appear in the example below:

Database title: *A Midsummer Night's Dream*

Query: love Key Word in Context

love (99)

I.1/577.1 thee with my sword, | And won thy **love**, doing thee injuries; |

I.1/577.1 feigning voice verses of feigning **love**, | And stolen the

I.1/577.2   The sealing-day betwixt my **love** and me, | For everlasting

I.1/578.1   You have her father's **love**, Demetrius; | Let me have

I.1/578.1   Lysander! true, he hath my **love**, | And what is mine my

I.1/578.1   my **love**, | And what is mine my **love** shall render him. |

I.1/578.1   as he, | As well possess'd; my **love** is more than his; |

I.1/578.1 I'll avouch it to his head, | Made **love** to Nedar's daughter,

You could then undertake further classification of the use of the word 'love', for example the following four groupings, which can be imposed or generated from your data, provide thematic groupings:

- 'in love'
- personal loves – 'my love', 'his love', 'thy love'
- 'make love'
- 'Love' as a force in its own right.

Another example of key word in context can be seen below using the program *Concordance* (www.concordancesoftware.co.uk/; (accessed May 2011). The printout in Figure 16.3 gives some indication of the program's capacity.

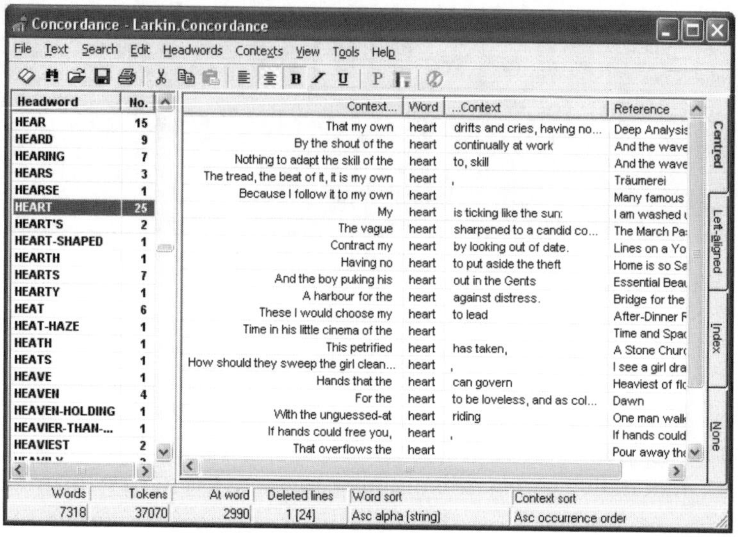

Figure 16.3   Concordance image

If you are seeking greater depth in contextual information you might like to display several lines surrounding your chosen word rather than just a few words. Simply type in your word and specify the lines to appear – in this case several lines above, and below the word 'love' in *A Midsummer Night's Dream* have been requested from *TACTWeb*.

Database title: A Midsummer Night's Dream

Query: love

love (5/99)
[Exit PHILOSTRATE]

Hippolyta, I woo'd thee with my sword,
And won thy **love**, doing thee injuries;
But I will wed thee in another key,
With pomp, with triumph and with revelling.

-- I.1/577.1
Thou, thou, Lysander, thou hast given her rhymes,
And interchanged love-tokens with my child:
Thou hast by moonlight at her window sung,
With feigning voice verses of feigning **love**,
And stolen the impression of her fantasy
With bracelets of thy hair, rings, gawds, conceits,
Knacks, trifles, nosegays, sweetmeats, messengers
-- I.1/577.1

My soul consents not to give sovereignty.

[THESEUS] Take time to pause; and, by the next new moon--
The sealing-day betwixt my **love** and me,
For everlasting bond of fellowship--
Upon that day either prepare to die
For disobedience to your father's will,
--- I.1/577.2

Research example

Daniel Coffey (2005) used the program TEXTPACK to analyse the annual addresses in 2000 and 2001 of 56 US state governors to determine the different ideological content. Two prior categories 'liberal' and 'democratic' were chosen as well as a further eight policy categories: budget, economic development, health and social welfare, law and order, education, environment, state regulation, morality and civil rights. The two initial categories were identified by TEXTPACK on individual word appearance from a predefined dictionary created by the author to include words most used in previous political party platforms but the results still had to be manually sorted to clarify ideological position and exclude extraneous data. The same process had to be applied to the eight policy categories in order to identify and apply words that would be useful in separating out statements into one group or another. The quality of the dictionary available will obviously be of importance here. You can see that although these programs can give quick insights of a simple nature the user has to do a fair bit of predefining and post sorting in order to ensure that results fit the defined categories.

Ethnographic content analysis

Ethnographic content analysis (ECA) refers to a method for retrieving and analysing documents for their significance and meaning in context. The emphasis is description, the search for contexts, explanatory meanings, patterns, and processes (Altheide, 1987, 1996). Apart from enumerative tools already discussed, thematic analysis and analytical approaches from grounded theory (see Chapter 7) are sometimes used to contextualise action and behaviour from documentation.

The basic steps include:

1 Locate all relevant documents – sample if desirable.
2 Identify the units to be analysed.
3 Develop and test a protocol from the intensive analysis of a few documents.
4 Revise and further refine the protocol as analysis proceeds.
5 Interpret meaning within content and culture.

Research example

Research focus: David Altheide (1987) undertook an ethnographic content analysis of television news coverage of the Iranian hostage crisis (November 4, 1979 – January 24, 1981), which involved 52 Americans who were held for 444 days. The major research focus was the role of formats in the television news coverage of an international crisis.

Formats were defined here as organisational devices: the rules and procedures for presenting information as news, such as visual imagery, narrative form and aural information. Other foci included accessibility (of events for journalists); visual quality of the events, encapsulation and thematic capacity for summarising the event and linking it meaningfully to others as well as the relevance of such events to a mass audience.

Documentation and units: 925 news reports were collected. Random and stratified sampling were rejected on the basis that this would distort the coverage to be assessed because of the interlinking of newscasts where each day builds or borrows from the news of the previous day.

Protocol development: this involved viewing several reports, identifying through preliminary data and thematic analysis the major themes of: hostages; families; the Shah of Iran; Iran (government operation); Iran (internal problems); Iran (external problems); the USA (government); international responses; and Iranian students in the United States. This process revealed clusters and groupings that were linked to the origins of reports and to the visuals, and which would have been missed in a solely enumerative analysis. The protocol was further extended to collect both numeric and descriptive data on other aspects of the research question: the network; the presenter; length of report; origin of report; news sources; names and status of individuals presented/interviewed; their dress, appearance and facility with English; what was filmed, and the correspondence between film, speech and overall emphasis.

Apply protocol: Altheide utilised a constant comparative process (going from data to theoretical explanation – see grounded theory, Chapter 7) to further break open the text to discover its complexity. For example, by transcribing a news broadcast down the left-hand column of a page with identification of the speaker in the centre column and descriptions of the accompanying visuals in the right-hand column, greater insight as to the messages being constructed could be obtained through the juxtapositions that comparisons between the left and right columns naturally offered. The visuals were then further broken down into the three categories:

1 What was shown?
2 Who was shown?
3 What were they doing?

Enumerative data were manually collated in an iterative style (allowing one set of documents to feed into the themes of another set).

Intepretation: Altheide found that moving reflexively between enumerative data, contextual themes and literature provided greater depth of understanding of media process and particularly of the role that the families of hostages played in such crises.

Key word in context and grounded theory   *Research focus*: Thomas Mowen and Ryan Shroeder (2011) investigated the extent of patterns of opposition to the death penalty from victims' families following an apparent increase in retribution and closure arguments in support of capital punishment.

Documentation and units: They sourced 3892 American newspaper articles from 1992 to 2009 through LexisNexis and sampled 119 that provided the most in-depth coverage of a murder trial.

Protocol development: They selected four key words and phrases – 'closure, murder victim's family'; 'victim's family'; 'family'; 'closure' – and added 'capital punishment' and 'death penalty' in various combinations and decided to use grounded theory to collect contextual data of the views of the victims' families within categories of pro-death and anti-death penalty.

Protocol application: using KWIC they showed that anti-death penalty sentiment had increased over the two decades. The results also showed a significant increase in victim family opposition to capital punishment over time; however, newspaper representations of capital cases in which the families support the execution of the offender received more words per article and greater exposure than cases where families were against the execution. The grounded theory investigation found five ideological positions:

- The victim's family does not support state-endorsed executions and does not believe a 'circle of killing' will bring closure.
- The victim's family is against using the death penalty for personal or religious reasons and therefore does not believe closure can be obtained by capital punishment.
- The victim's family is pro capital punishment but does not want to go through numerous years of trials and appeals and therefore requests a plea bargain.
- The victim's family is for the death penalty but does not believe it brings closure.
- The victim's family is for the death penalty and believes it brings closure.

The advantages of a combined analytical approach are that both enumerative and narrative descriptive approaches can provide different perspectives in the analysis of the text and can serve to illuminate other critical questions and issues.

Advantages of content analysis

- Can simplify very large documents into enumerative information (enumerative).
- Can identify intentions, attitudes and emotions as well as reveal lines of propaganda, inequality and power (ethnographic).
- Can combine both enumerative and ethnographic approaches to look at relationships between numbers, relationships and the cultural context.

Disadvantages of content analysis

- Can be criticised for being too positivist and too decontextualising in orientation, particularly when only enumerative approaches are used.
- Limited or poor sampling strategies can lead to bias.
- Words and meanings for inclusion may be limited by the dictionary capacity of the computer program.
- Can often be a-theoretical with minimal interpretation on the assumption that numbers say it all.

Summary

Content analysis uses enumerative and ethnographic approaches. The computer-based tools of word frequencies, key word in context and other graphical representations of occurrences within documents, are a useful way of turning a large set of written or visual documentation into something manageable and meaningful. These processes are extremely valuable in their own right but the addition of preliminary data and thematic analysis permits mining down much deeper into this documentation to provide other levels of interpretation and theorising and a more complete picture of what is happening within the defined context/culture.

Student exercise

Part 1: Data collection

Select two magazines – one directed at women and one directed at men.

Part 2: Data analysis

1 Add up the total number of advertisements in each
2 In each magazine, calculate the percentage of ads devoted to each of the following three categories: 'diet', 'skin products', 'exercise'.

Part 3: Data interpretation

Examine the data and analyse your findings addressing the following questions:

1 Are there differences in advertising emphasis for the two magazines?
2 What patterns are evident?
3 How do the cultural norms for men compare with those for women?
4 How would you explain your results in terms of your own cultural values?

Further reading

Content analysis background and practice

Franzosi, R. (2008) *Content Analysis*. London: Sage. A four-volume set in the Sage Benchmarks in Social Methods series. These provide a comprehensive and detailed history and discussion of techniques linking to a range of disciplines.

Hesse-Beber, S. and Leavy, P. (2010) *Handbook of Emergent Methods*. New York: The Guilford Press. ch. 5 by Lindsay Prior and ch. 6 by David Altheide et al. on researching documents are particularly relevant to content analysis.

Krippendorf, K. (2012) *Content Analysis: An Introduction to Its Methodology* (3rd edn). Thousand Oaks, CA: Sage. Currently one of the more detailed books available (the first edition was published in 1980).

Content analysis: research examples and computer programs

Budge, I. (2001) *Mapping Policy Preferences. Estimates for Parties, Electors and Governments, 1945–1998*. Oxford: Oxford University Press. An interesting example of the application of content analysis methods in political science, dealing with political parties and their impact on electoral systems.

Mayring, P. (2000) Qualitative content analysis. *Forum: Qualitative Social Research* 1 (2). Available at www.qualitative-research.net/fqs-texte/2-00/2-00mayring-e.htm (accessed 26 April 2011). Provides a discussion about qualitative content analysis including: history, basic ideas, procedures, inductive category development, deductive category application, computer programs and examples of projects.

http://academic.csuohio.edu/kneuendorf/content/cpuca/ccap.htm (accessed May 2011). Link to a range of computer programs for content analysis.

References

Altheide, D. (1987) Ethnographic content analysis. *Qualitative Sociology* 10 (1): 65–77. Retrieved from www.public.asu.edu/~atdla/ethnographiccontentanalysis.pdf (accessed 16 November 2011).

Altheide, D. (1996) *Qualitative Media Analysis*. Newbury Park, CA: Sage.

Coffey, D. (2005) Measuring Gubernatorial ideology: a content analysis of State of the State speeches. *State Politics and Policy Quarterly*, Spring: 88–103.

Mowen, T. and Schroeder, R. (2011) Not in my name: an investigation of victims' family clemency movements and court appointed closure. *Western Criminology Review*, 12 (1): 65–81. Retrieved from http://wcr.sonoma.edu/v12n1/Mowen.pdf (accessed 30 May 2011).

SEVENTEEN

Content analysis of visual documents

This process of understanding and interpreting the world uses visual images rather than words and these images are seen as reflections of reality in particular contexts. This chapter will look at four forms of visual analysis: ethnographic visual analysis, historical analysis through iconography and iconology, structuralist and finally poststructuralist analyses of visual images.

KEY POINTS

- Visual images, either alone or in conjunction with other data, provide a rich source of research information
- Depending on your research question, any of the following analytic approaches may be useful
  - ethnographic content analysis
  - historical (iconography and iconology) analysis, or
  - semiotic structural or post structural analysis

Visual data

Visual records fall into three groupings.

1 *Visual records currently in existence*, such as:

- film
- newspaper images
- artwork (paintings, posters, cartoons)
- computer images
- architecture and all forms of design
- videos
- photos
- aspects of material culture such as clothing, graffiti etc.

Analyses of these visuals are complicated by their location and the devices of presentation and re-presentation contrived for consumption by particular audiences. Many are embedded in non-visual contexts such as words and link to a multiplicity of other texts within cultural and structural settings. Our earliest visual research records were undertaken by anthropologists and comprise black-and-white photography and moving films. A structuralist approach involving classification and the development of taxonomies formed the dominant analyses of these historical records.

2 **Visual records collected by you as researcher**. The capacity to capture conversations, interactions and events as they occur in natural environments is enormous although the presence of visual recorders may well disturb routines if they are intrusively located or left in place by you for only short periods.

3 **Visual records collected by your participants** separately or together with you in a collaborative approach. Participants are usually involved in using static image or video cameras, or mobile phones for the collection of personal narratives (auto photography) where there is an inbuilt notion of power transfer or empowerment. Sometimes filming is directed into data collection of specific events and situations that have been predefined or suggested by you and sometimes these are at the discretion of the participant. Collaborative approaches can lean more toward you collecting data with direction from your participants as to what aspects should be highlighted. Photo elicitation – the provision of photos, captured by you or your participants for further interview discussion – is another approach. The collection of verbal or written responses and participant authored drawings and paintings can provide an adjunct to visual data allowing one to complement or comment on the other.

Who should interpret visual images? You? Your participants? Your participants can provide considerable insight here regardless of who has collected the data. Conversational analysis, content and context, spatial movements and interaction can provide specific analyses here although thematic analysis and deconstructive approaches are more common. The positioning of you and your audience also needs to be taken into account as visual images have the capacity to create the audience (readers) as consumers.

Data analysis

Regardless of their origin, you can analyse visual records through a range of approaches. The four most common are:

- ethnographic content analysis
- historical analysis: iconology and iconography
- structural analysis
- poststructuralist analysis.

The chapter will look at each of these in turn.

Ethnographic content analysis

Ethnographic content analysis seeks to identify the signifiers/signs within visual images and to understand their accepted meanings within the culture in which they are located.

When to use: When you have access to visual images and you want to contextualise these within the culture.

Type of research questions best suited: What aspects of the cultural context or social organisation are reflected in these images?

Strengths: Enables visual images to be 'read' within cultural or historical contexts.

Weaknesses: The origin and the purpose of the construction or collection of the images may be unclear limiting readings.

The following steps will enable you to undertake an ethnographic content analysis.

Content and context

- What is the image of?
- What is the context of its production? Who was involved in the production? And for what purpose?
- How do the outcomes convey meaning within the cultural context of origin? Today?

Links (of images to other signs)

- Each image will be linked to/embedded in a variety of other signs through intertextuality. What are these other signs?
- How do other signs impact on/affect the image?
- How does this image reflect or depart from dominant cultural values?

Interpretation

- What is the most obvious reading of the image?
- What alternative readings can be made?

Research example A

An ethnographic content analysis of representations of psychiatric disability in 50 years of Hollywood films was undertaken (Levers, 2001). Twenty-one films were assessed in a cross-case cultural context analysis to identify the following aspects:

- *structured narratives (content and context)* which included credit information, description of main theme/setting and plot, stereotypical portrayals and context
- *the presence of previously identified stereotypes (links – images that can be read)* – dangerous people, objects of violence, atmosphere, pitiable and pathetic, asexual or sexually deviant, incapable, comic figures, their own worst or only enemy and 'super crips' or burdens
- *the frequency of icons (links of images to meaning)* associated with the traditionally historical portrayal of madness in art, especially through images of: lighted window/door, seated, caged, restrained, held/guided by warders, carrying a staff (long stick), eyes cast down, music icons, and holding hands.

Interpretations were cross-checked with a psychiatric rehabilitation professional, a sociologist, a psychologist and a filmmaker. There was a change in terminology from 'insanity' or 'madness' to 'mental illness' after changes in the production code in 1968 allowing mental illness to be used as a major theme in films. This resulted in more positive portrayals and more serious explorations of relevant issues being undertaken, although iconography (icons with recognised meanings) and greater use of stereotypes also increased. The icons most noted overall in the 21 films were: hospital white, bandages, wheelchairs, glazed stare and locked doors/keys. The stereotypes identified were: dangerous people, passive objects of violence, atmosphere, pitiable and pathetic, asexual or sexually deviant, incapable, comic figure, own worst/only enemy, 'super crip', burden, artistic/creative genius and pathology.

Research example B

Content and context   This image relates to the 7th War loan and was published in *The New Yorker* in 1945 by F. and M. Schaefer Brewing Company (Figure 17.1). The image comprises four men striving to raise a flagpole with the flag of the United States unfurling upon the top of it. The foreground appears to be covered in broken wood in shapes reminiscent of the bones of the dead. A helmet also lies in the foreground. From behind a cloud, the sun's rays illuminate an elevated gilded statue of a soldier holding a gun. The purpose is clearly to remind the public that the people who have given their lives for

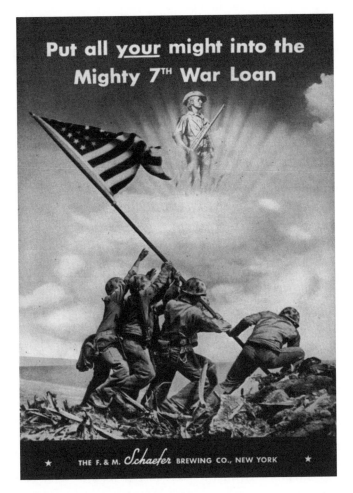

Figure 17.1   A World War II poster (*The New Yorker*, 1945)

freedom should not be forgotten and that the public should continue to support those who are struggling to win and maintain democracy by contributing financially to the war effort.

Links (symbols)

Clouds have the capacity to hide and to reveal

Graven images suggest immortality, glory, youth captured, perfection sustained, and adulation of those remaining

Sun illuminates, warms, glorifies, gives life

Wood/bone remains suggest death, altruism, sacrifice for the better good

The flag and pole link to national pride, identification and power

Water links to cleanliness, peace, tranquillity

Men pulling together links to strength in numbers and team work

Interpretation: obvious reading   The clouds move back to reveal the statue of the soldier caught by the sun's rays. His elevated image beyond the struggle symbolises hope and provides intimations of glory, perfection and immortality – caught in time and providing an ongoing memory. This contrasts with those still alive and still struggling to lift the flagpole, reflecting the battle to win, to conquer and to retain the values that the flag represents. The forward-looking face of the statue focuses on a distant future – one of peace and security, also emphasised by the expanse of water flowing tranquilly in the background.

Interpretation: alternative reading   War is destructive; it leads to death and decay. Peace through physical fighting is costly in terms of lives lost and difficult to gain and maintain. Those who have given their lives will soon be forgotten, remembered only by generic images reflected on special occasions.

Iconology/Iconography

Iconology tends to refer to the interpretation of art and religious images while iconography refers to the meanings of these symbols, but in practice, the two have become closely interwoven.

When to use: When you have access to images from art or religion.

Type of research questions best suited: What are the meanings of the signs in this painting?

Strengths: Enables the identification of the meanings of the icons/signs being used.

Weaknesses: Interpretations may change over time so the original meaning is lost.

Erwin Panofsky (1974) proposed three levels of analysis for these kinds of images – primary, secondary and tertiary:

- *primary level* (description of factual and expressional representations)
- *secondary level* (representation at a more abstract level – iconographical analysis)
- *tertiary level* (iconological interpretation involving seeking the deepest meaning reflecting the underlying principles or period).

Example: Mona Lisa

Primary level (*description of factual and expressional representations*): Leonardo da Vinci's *Mona Lisa* (Figure 17.2) is painted in oil on a wood panel using the *sfumato* (blended smoke) method in which translucent layers of paint are applied in such a way that the transitions between colour changes on the clothing are hard to detect. The chiaroscuro technique of using light and shade for skin contrast is also used. The portrait is of a Florentine woman (thought to be the wife of Francesco del Giocondo) dressed in the

Figure 17.2 *Mona Lisa (La Gioconda)*, Leonardo da Vinci (1503–7), oil on poplar, 77 × 53 cm, Paris, Musée du Louvre

fashion of the sixteenth century, hands folded, with a face that appears to be made up of two not quite matching halves and a half smile (lips closed) portrayed against a mountainous, watery landscape.

Secondary level (representation at a more abstract level – iconographical analysis): Here symbols are linked with accepted meanings or themes. This painting represents beauty and the enigmatic power of women – the complex smile can be both alluring and mocking at the same time. The complexity of the composition seen through the male/female face is another (somewhat contentious) theme. Other signs lie in numbers and measures, particularly the geometry of the figure (comprising 12 circles and the pyramid-like placement of the figure in the landscape) providing a possible link to ancient cultures and to astronomy. Other signs lead to a form of numerology and to myths, for example – using a simple Latin code of values for particular letters 'Mona Lisa' and 'La Gioconda' and 'Leonardo' all come to the same number value – 84 – suggesting some connection. Numerology has counted the numbers to 84 (8 + 4 = 12), 12 (1 + 2 = 3). The number 3 refers to creative, artistic, optimistic and imaginative people. Going into mythology, the title 'Mona Lisa' has been seen as a rebus (a code) for sol + anima or sun and moon or male and female, again giving support to the argument regarding the male–female dimensions of the face providing a global human rather than a gender-specific portrait.

Tertiary level (iconological interpretation involving seeking the deepest meaning reflecting the underlying principles or period): Here the focus is on the links between nature, mythology, astronomy, mathematics. and the power and beauty of women/men and females/humans in the dual creation of human life and the environment. The primary link between nature and beauty characterises the major value of the Renaissance period. An alternative feminist reading could emphasise the power and longevity of the presence of women with their strong link to the earth and to nature and their capacity to produce the future (children, food) and their strength to survive all that the patriarchal society imposes upon them.

Example: Guernica

A more detailed analysis of a single painting can be undertaken using Pablo Picasso's *Guernica* (Figure 17.3). At the *primary level* the painting falls within the synthetic cubist tradition with its grey, brown, white and black colours and its incorporation of geometrical experimental constructions of collage-forming layers which can be seen through to create and impart other, less obvious, meanings. The purpose is to represent images as the mind rather than the eye sees them. The painting, which measures approximately 350 × 770 cm, was undertaken for the Spanish pavilion at the Paris Work Fair for the Spanish Republican government. It represents a massacre of civilians in the town of Guernica in the Basque region of Northern Spain. The massacre occurred as the outcome of German military practice and the attack on the town was permitted by the Nationalist leader General Franco in exchange for military aid against the Republicans in the Spanish Civil War. German aircraft bombed the town and surrounding area for three hours on 27 April 1937. Sixteen hundred people were killed or wounded and the town burned for three days. The painting uses two- and three-dimensional imagery to depict dead and

An image of pain and brutality depicts the fascist bombing of the town Guernica in Spain (1937)

Figure 17.3 *Guernica*, **Pablo Picasso (1937), oil on canvas, 349 × 776 cm, Museo Nacional Centro de Arte Reina Sofía, Madrid. (Reproduced with permission.)**

wounded people and animals – some dismembered, others mutilated. The agony and horror experienced by the victims is evident on their faces. A woman wails, head thrown back holding an inert baby, another woman with outstretched arms and head thrown back weeps, body split. A bull's head looks impassively over the scene while a horse's head is open mouthed in horror and pain. In the centre is a representation of Hitler impaled by a spear.

A fallen warrior lies in crucifixion position holding a broken sword. A hand holds a flower in the foreground. Another hand holds out an oil lamp to the exploding electric lamp that occupies a central position on the top of the painting. Rays of light penetrate the dark and lines intersect at points creating apparent explosions. There appear to be layers within the painting; a Lucifer is present as well as a second bull's head goring the horse, and a human skull penetrated by a spear can be deciphered beneath the wounded horse. The horse has been stabbed by a spear which has a diamond tip – the symbol of a Harlequin. A Harlequin, mouth open, looks down on the scene and four other hidden harlequins can be seen when the painting is inverted.

At the *secondary level* and according to Picasso any analysis of the painting lies solely within the meanings that the observer takes from the symbols. Some suggestions: the bull may represent fighting in general but more likely represents Franco and the gored (sexual imagery) and speared horse, the Spanish Republic. The weeping women symbolise suffering and loss while Lucifer is often the bringer of light/evil – the light of the bomb explosions. The crucified warrior with the broken spear is Christ or the incapacity of good to reign over or to combat this situation. The surviving flower represents hope and peace. Harlequins are often seen as having power to combat death.

At the *tertiary level*, the major reading is a negative representation of the horrors of war through the portrayal of a barbaric act, the death of hope and goodness, the self-serving duplicity of political leaders, and the resulting pain and suffering of innocent people and animals. An alternative meaning is difficult to find in the face of such destruction except perhaps a hope that it will never recur or that hope survives all and peace will prevail.

Structural analysis

The signs and patterns of visual symbols are viewed as being directly related to concepts within particular cultures, which have meanings that can be read. The signifier (image) is connected to the signified (meaning).

When to use: When you wish to identify the commonly accepted meanings of signs.

Type of research questions best suited: What do these signs represent? What are the meanings of these images for participants?

Strengths: Enables visual images to be 'read' and understood by a broad population, within cultural contexts.

Weaknesses: The static nature of sign and signifier doesn't allow for rapid changes in meaning.

There are different kinds of symbols:

- a realistic representation or strong resemblance between image and object (*iconic*), for example, a picture of a horse
- a learned symbol such as a crown (*symbolic*) – representing royalty and the power of the monarchy
- a symbol that links to natural events via a strong physical connection (*indexical*) – for example, steam to hot water, or a red sky at night relating to good weather the following day.

Clearly all of these signs or symbols can operate on more than one level and the boundaries may overlap. For example, a crown is both iconic, indexical (sign of a particular kind of administrative organisation) and symbolic (power). In addition, signs are often not just single entities, they can be made up of other signs. The openness and widespread availability of visual images means that those viewing images may well come up with a range of analyses but the underlying assumption is that these will have common codes (systems to which signs refer and into which they can be organised) identified through similarities and oppositions and categorised.

Example: the Apple Macintosh '1984' AD

Content and context: This commercial advertisement, which can be seen at http://video.google.com/videoplay?docid=-715862862672743260# (accessed 26 April 2011), provides a useful basis for a semiotic structural analysis (Moriarty, 1995) (Figure 17.4). The 60-second advertisement was shown to a Superbowl audience in 1984 regarding the advent of the Apple Personal Computer.

The first frame of the advertisement features a line of marchers or walkers in identical grey prison style clothing moving along a circular enclosed tunnel while an Orwellian 'Big Brother' figure's face on a screen continuously speaks in the background in an idealistic, sloganeering style. There is a flash of white as a woman in a white singlet and red shorts

Figure 17.4 Stills from the Apple Macintosh commercial aired during the Superbowl, 22 January 1984 (director Ridley Scott, running time 1:00 min)

carrying a sledgehammer runs into view followed by guards with face shields. The Big Brother image is then seen speaking to a hall of grey-clad, passively seated and unmoving people with elevated faces and trancelike expressions. The woman, lit from behind, comes into this hall and runs to the screen She swirls the hammer and throws it into the screen as the Big Brother figure says, 'We shall prevail'. An explosion occurs, flooding the scene with white light. Then a voiceover explains that Apple will introduce Macintosh on January 24, 1984 and that '1984 will not be like *1984*'. There are clear links to the original Orwellian text (the rightsholders of *1984* considered it to be a copyright infringement and subsequently prevented its further broadcast), to Fritz Lang's film *Metropolis*, to Ridley Scott's own *Blade Runner* and negatively to the conformity of the IBM culture.

Symbols and interpretation: In an analysis of this advertisement undertaken in 1991 (Moriarty, 1995), 200 undergraduate students were asked to observe the commercial and complete a short survey. The survey comprised open-ended questions designed to identify the symbols evident, to capture meanings and to understand the messages students were receiving. Content analysis of the responses clustered the meanings identified and categorised them. All responses were grouped as *iconic, indexical* or *symbolic*. A question regarding the dominant images revealed that 92% of responses mentioned a woman, a hammer and a TV screen. The woman was seen as a bright (white in colour), an athletic runner (iconic), a change agent, a representative of the future, a saviour and a metaphor for freedom (symbolic). The sledgehammer was viewed iconically as a tool and symbolically as a destructive force and creator of new possibilities. The TV screen was iconically linked to various other screen technologies and symbolically linked to the power of the media, control and censorship. The researcher concluded that, overall, iconic images impacted more than symbolic or indexical images and that people and objects had greater impact on viewer's impressions than did dynamic or audio elements.

Poststructuralist analysis: deconstruction

When to use: When you have access to visual images and their deconstruction/unravelling will enhance the clarification of your research questions.

Type of research questions best suited: What is the meaning of the sign components of this visual image?

Strengths: Enables in-depth analysis of visual images as they are deconstructed within cultural and historical contexts.

Weaknesses: Multiple readings and multiple conclusions mean there are no finite answers, everything is transitional.

Taking the guidelines for deconstructing written texts presented in Chapter 15, the process of deconstructing visual images involves a sceptical reading together with an identification of the arguments that will need to be positioned against each other to clarify ideas, metaphors, contradictions, generalisations and binary opposites. Images present, images missing and absent voices, also need identification. Alternative readings and multiple interpretations are essential in the recognition of the transitional and open ended nature of images.

Art example: *The Three Sphinxes of Bikini*

Arguments and challenges: Within the poststructuralist tradition, layers and complexity should be sought. In Salvador Dali's painting *The Three Sphinxes of Bikini* (Figure 17.5) the notion of a sphinx in the title first needs exploration. In Greek mythology the Sphinx was a creature with a lion's body, the wings of an eagle and the head and breast of a human female. This animal–female–bird combination emphasises strength, flight and fertility and was seen as both a guardian (protector) and a destroyer. In the plays of Sophocles around 400 BCE the Sphinx was to be found on a high rock near a road into Thebes where it posed a riddle to passers by: '*What is it that has one voice and yet becomes four-footed and two-footed and three-footed?*' (Apollodorus (trans. Frazer), 1921: 1.349). Those who failed to solve the riddle were killed. Only Oedipus was able to answer correctly that it was man, who crawled on four legs in infancy, then walked on two and

Figure 17.5 *The Three Sphinxes of Bikini,* **Salvador Dali (1947), 30 × 50 cm, oil on canvas. Geneva, private collection.**

resorted to a stick in older age. The Sphinx committed suicide on the rocks below when its riddle was correctly answered. So are **Dali's** sphinxes voiceless? Dead? Waiting for enlightenment or sentinels for future knowledge and/or survival or what?

Contradictions, complexities and generalisations: In terms of the atomic bomb test explosions around Bikini Atoll from 1946, the two human sphinx heads portrayed face away from the viewer (silent, hidden power, hard to decipher) and in contrast to the image of the tree, which may represent life and knowledge (transparent, but fragile), reflect the dual capacity of the sphinx for destruction (man) and regeneration, within a particular landscape (earth, tree, mountains and sky).

Marginalised voices: Humans, animals, sphinxes, nature and scientists.

Transitional interpretation: In avoiding finite interpretation, many questions arise creating intertextual links. Why is the front head severed and bloody but set upon the earth? Why is the tree one entity but comprised of two parts? And what does the situation of the distant head on the mountains mean? Is man really creative and intelligent or just destructive (lemmings following each other to self-destruction?). Do the mountains reflect the rocks upon which the Sphinx suicided when Oedipus answered the riddle correctly? What is the connection between the similar shapes of the mushroom cloud hair and the hair-shaped leaves of the tree – is it man's individuality that is dangerous compared with the power of nature? Why are the human heads solid while the tree can be seen through to a blue mountain vista and the front head looks toward a fading reflection of itself in the distance placed in a whitened landscape (denuded by atomic fallout?)

with a bright white sky. The colours of the earth and foliage – green and gold brown stand out more than the black sky and the shadows cast. This reading would appear to indicate that man's destructive capacity may well terminate his/her own existence but an alternative reading would point to the continuing capacity of man to survive despite blindness, and lack of vision. Can the creative power of man, which as knowledge has increased has produced so much destruction, also use this creative power to save the earth? Or does humankind have no real capacity to emulate nature?

Or is there no real message just an ironic postmodern play by an intelligent artist who likes to combine the bizarre for visual effect but with no particular message except that created by the reader? And what would be the reading today, 50–60 years later? That the human–science combination produces great beauty and unexpected outcomes?

Photo example

A poststructural analysis of a family photo of a young woman from an earlier generation was undertaken by Karen Crinall (1999). She collected family stories about the person in the photo, who is pictured as a lively young woman, dressed as if for a formal social occasion and smiling – face made up, lipstick, pearls and earrings on (Figure 17.6).

The author attempted to understand the layered constructed narratives regarding this person and how these had changed over time. First the location of this photo (on grandmother's walnut-veneered buffet) is contextualised. The photo is of her grandmother's

Figure 17.6　Crinall family story photo (Crinall, 1999)

child – the author's aunt. The narratives regarding the person in the photo shifted over time from identification as 'a lady I knew once' to 'your aunty' and eventually the silenced stories started to emerge. Intimations of 'talent ' and 'struggles' and 'victimisation' within a family context of violence and despair leading to the young woman's final escape to homelessness and death by accidental means. Crinall interlinks this photo with other photos of homeless women which she has previously analysed in order to see further into the smiling face portrayed.

Example: attempting a comparative structural and a poststructural analysis of the same photo

1. Structural content analysis

Content and context: Figure 17.7 a photo of Barbara Hoffman, a Swiss woman who has set up a charity in order to provide for children in Mozambique who are abandoned, orphaned or abused (www.asemworld.org/eng/opere.htm#manga) to provide them with education and a safe haven. She is central to the photo and stands head and shoulders above the group of children. The children are watching the camera and are close to her but not in contact with her. There is a building with meshed windows behind the group. The *symbols* are:

- White woman closed mouth smile, averted gaze, above the crowd – modest saviour, elevated above the masses
- A large group of children of colour – deserving poor?
- Meshed windows – protection? or imprisonment?

Figure 17.7 Photo taken in Beira, Mozambique, in January 2010. Swiss woman, Barbara Hoffmann, with orphaned children. Since 1989, after seeing the reality of war, Barbara set up a charity to provide shelter for children. (Caption adapted from http://cutcaster.com/photo/800954697-African-children/royalty free photo accessed 30 May 2011)

Interpretation: A European woman of high ideals and commitment has made it her life's work to raise money in order to improve the lives of children at risk in war-affected Mozambique.

2. A poststructural interpretation

Allow the arguments to challenge each other:

- Elevated woman set above the group modestly avoiding the camera's gaze while young children mill about. They are close in proximity but closeness with her is not evident.
- The black and white race mix emphasises the social and political contrasts between Switzerland and Mozambique.
- Educated and privileged contrasts with uneducated and economically poor with the assumption that educated is desirable to provide options.
- Financially endowed versus financially unendowed individuals.
- Poverty seen as bad, education seen as good or as having higher value in the marketplace.

Identify any contradictions and generalisations:

- There is an assumption that this is a good thing to do – but what about colonialism?
- What about the plans of the Mozambique government?
- Is there room for private charities to intervene in these ways? Does this cast a poor reflection on the government's policies/capacities?

Disentangle the complexities of all dichotomies:

- Should white Europeans interfere in the politics of black Mozambique?
- Is it right for Europeans to impose their cultural ideals on a developing emerging African country?
- Is Hoffman actually filling a need (hers? or theirs?) or is she creating one for purposes of self-aggrandisement?

Seek marginalised voices: The children's voices, their carers at the orphanage (Mozambiqueans), any living parents/extended family are not represented.

Avoid closure and seek alternative readings: What is Hoffman seeking to achieve here? Who really benefits? What are the outcomes for these children potentially caught between the values of two societies? Are her good deeds improving the lives of these children or imprisoning them in the values of European culture – a culture with ideals that may not be the same as those of emerging African nations. Is this white European woman seeking to increase her status in both European and Mozambique societies by rescuing children in need and housing and educating them in the hope that she may 'do good' within the Christian ethic and increase her chances of adulation in this life or preferment in another life?

Summary

You can analyse visual images using different approaches but your choice will depend on your desired outcome. You might choose ethnographic content analysis – where cultural meanings are important; or iconological and iconographical approaches – where historical icons are present; the structural approach – where the commonly accepted interpretations of signs are sought; or the poststructural approach where deconstruction through a sceptical reading is seen as useful.

Further reading

Visual methods

Rose, G. (2011) *Visual Methodologies: An Introduction to Researching with Visual Materials* (3rd edn). London: Sage. A comprehensive overview of: semiology, psychoanalysis, discourse and content analysis as well as an introduction to visual material, data analysis and data interpretation.

Stanczak, G. (2007) *Visual Research Methods: Image, Society, and Representation.* London: Sage. A good cross-disciplinary text with emphasis on photography.

Van Leeuwen, T. and Jewitt, C. (eds) (2002) *Handbook of Visual Analysis.* Thousand Oaks, CA: Sage. Methods for visual analysis, content analysis, historical analysis, structuralist analysis, iconography, psychoanalysis, social semiotic analysis, film analysis and ethnomethodology are included.

References

Apollodorus (1921) *Apollodorus: The Library* (trans. Sir James Frazer), 2 vols. Cambridge, MA/London: Harvard University Press/William Heinemann Ltd.

Crinall, K. (1999) My aunt, our mother, their face: sharing identity in a family photograph. *Visual Anthropology Forum.*

Levers, L. (2001) Representations of psychiatric disability in 50 years of Hollywood films. *Theory and Science.* Retrieved from http://theoryandscience.icaap.org/content/vol002.002/lopezlevers.html (accessed 26 April 2011).

Moriarty, S. (1995) Visual semiotics and the production of meaning in advertising. Paper presented at the Visual Communication Division of Education in Journalism and Mass Communication Conference. Washington. Retrieved from http://spot.colorado.edu/~moriarts/vissemiotics.html (accessed 26 April 2011).

Panofsky, E. (1974) *Meaning in the Visual Arts. Views from the outside: a centennial commemoration of Erwin Panofsky (1892–1968).* Princeton, NJ: Princeton University Press.

EIGHTEEN

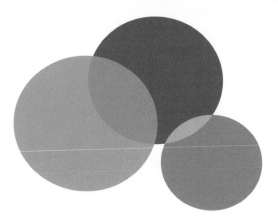

Narrative analysis

Narrative analysis focuses on stories told by participants. The story aspect is seen as a complete entity in itself with a beginning, middle and an end. There is an underlying presumption that much of our communication is through stories and that these are revealing of our experiences, interpretations and priorities. Eliciting narratives of personal experience is seen as a more natural form of communication than face-to-face interviews although it is possible that the question and answer format of this approach may elicit often lengthy responses in the form of a story. In this chapter we explore the structure and sequence of personal events portrayed by the speaker, their content and context, how things are portrayed and by whom, how people make sense of events, how these relate to the original event, how, in the analytical process one story compares with other accounts, and how story construction conveys meaning to the receiver and to the reader.

KEY POINTS

- There are two main versions of narrative analysis
  - sociolinguistic, which focuses on 'plots' or the structure of narratives and how they convey meaning
  - sociocultural, which looks at the broader interpretive frameworks that people use to make sense of particular incidents in individuals' lives
- Although these two approaches tend to be used separately, their combined use provides a powerful analytic tool

---

Introduction

When to use: When you are collecting stories from participants.

Type of research questions best suited: Those that explore either the structure of narratives or the specific experiences of particular events, such as marriage breakdown or finding out information that is life-changing; undergoing procedures (social/medical); or participating in particular programs.

Strengths: Gives insight into how individuals structure communication for effect and how they construct meaning from their life experiences.

Weaknesses: When only one approach (sociolinguistic/sociocultural) is used the perspective is limited.

Historical definitions and changes

How can we define a narrative? It is evident that the term can cover a wide variety of textual possibilities, from fairy tales, myths and legends, paintings, movies, books and from journalistic articles to personal autobiography. The key defining feature appears to be that the stories are narrations of events which unfold sequentially over time. The definition of what constitutes a narrative and how it should be treated has shifted and polarised over the past half century. Drawing on a detailed review of narrative approaches (Franzoni, 1998: 519), it is evident that a structuralist approach dominated the middle of the twentieth century. This approach was strongly influenced by Russian formalists, who emphasised the difference between the '*story*' (the actual action or event which occurs) and the '*plot*' (the orderly arrangement wherein events are presented to the reader). This distinction was further emphasised by French structuralists, who introduced different terminology but with a similar meaning: 'histoire' (story) vs 'discourse' (the actual textual narration). In English-speaking countries the events of the story and their textual presentation have continued to be separated through the 'plot' work of Labov (1972, 1997), which emphasises structure through clauses while at the other extreme, personal narratives focus on content and contextual interpretation.

Narrative genres

These encompass a broad range of presentations and representation and are usually tailored for particular audiences. In addition to the broad sociolinguistic and sociocultural styles already identified, Catherine Reissman (2008) has further suggested that *interactional* narratives (where the focus is the content of the interaction and the power plays therein) and *performative* narratives where the narrative becomes a dramatic performance to be shared with/to convince others, provide subnarratives within the sociocultural domain.

Three of the more widely accepted types of texts – *lyrical*, *dramatic* and *essayist* – have largely been constructed by a narrator, who is not the actor, in the form of re-presentation. The fourth – *narrative* – is where the actor who has had the actual experience has control of its telling. Because they are told for a purpose it is possible to classify narrative stories into particular types. Northrop Frye (1957) identified four conventional narrative forms or generic plots: *tragedy, comedy, romance* and *satire/irony*. Despite being separate in purpose, these depend on contrast or the incorporation of other genres. For example, tragedy and comedy form a contrast, as do romance and irony, but comedy can blend into either satire or romance. Equally, romance may become comic or tragic while tragedy can also be romantic or ironic.

Apart from these broad genres of narrative, which are more applicable to literary conventions, it is possible for you to identify particular narrative styles in the telling of personal stories. Stevens and Tighe Doerr (1997: 523-38) found three types of narratives in the subjective responses of women to being informed that they were HIV-positive:

1 *Epiphany* (a revelation which suddenly clarified for them the meaning of their lives often leading to dramatic changes such as geographical relocation, the re-seeking of contact with family members or leaving a job and pursuing more meaningful ways of living).
2 *Confirmation* (of something suspected leading to more matter-of-fact or more resigned responses based in recognising their own contribution to the diagnosis through drug habits, prostitution, own sexual preferences or practices, or those of partners).
3 *Calamity* (a sudden and unexpected event causing considerable distress, extreme fear, shock, terror and panic as well as feelings of anguish occasionally involving consideration of suicide).

Continuing the trend to label and classify types of narratives, Catherine Reismann (2008), in her work on women's experiences of relationship breakdown and divorce, has identified the narrative styles of:

- *habitual* narrative (when events are repeated again and again with no peak in action, often seen in patterns of grieving)
- *hypothetical* narratives (presentation of events that did not happen)
- *topic-centred* narratives (snapshots of events that have occurred and are linked in to current discussions as exemplars).

Further styles were evident in the narratives of managers and workers in different organisations that were attempting to improve organisational performances through management of human resources (Beech, 2000):

- the '*heroic director*' involved a story of transformation through aggressive individual action taken by a heroic leader which was successful in managing a conflict situation to the benefit of all but especially enhancing the honour and glory of the manager
- the '*romantic ward manager*' involved a story of an assertive type of manager who pushes ahead team individuals and the group and, despite setbacks, is positive, pragmatic and maintains direction toward an improved future for all
- the '*tragic skilled worker*' occurred where individual action by workers is viewed as personally costly, often leading to alienation, and passivity is viewed as the safest path
- the '*ironic response to human resource management*' involves a story of passive resistance of workers to what is viewed as pointless, top-down organisation-directed change which will not benefit them.

Your purpose in identifying different styles of narratives is to generalise them to other settings. The '*habitual*' and '*hypothetical*' styles can clearly be applied to a number of story types in a range of settings as can the '*epiphanous*', '*calamitous*' and '*confirmatory*' narratives of Stevens and Tighe Doerr while those of Beech are more confined and are probably most relevant to organisational settings where change is being attempted.

Analysis of narratives

Two major orientations are currently available for you to consider: a structuralist sociolinguistic approach and a sociocultural approach. Following the historical division into plot and story this dichotomy now dominates analysis in the field. There has been a recent re-emphasis toward stories in the shift toward postmodern ways of thinking which has led to a focus on the subjectivity of the author as the person either writing (autobiography) or transmitting the narrative – we now ask questions like Who is this person? What is their background and socialisation? Why are they doing this? For what purpose? and Who benefits?

1. The sociolinguistic approach

This approach came to the fore with the research of William Labov and Joshua Waletsky (1967), who were interested in looking at the speech narratives of African American people. These researchers became fascinated by the structure of these narratives, in particular the match between the reported chronological verbal sequencing of personal events compared with their order as they actually occurred, as well as how their construction conveyed meaning to the receiver. Labov assumed that sequential ordering of narrative clauses would form the basis of the narrative while Todorov ([1978]1990) has added in to this the element of transformation. He suggested that narratives usually involve some form of disruption and in order to demonstrate change in equilibrium, tend to move backwards and forwards between changed events, usually ending with the achievement of a final state of equilibrium.

According to Labov (1972: 360–61), the most basic narrative comprises at least two clauses which are sequentially ordered, for example:

1 I usually shop at X
2 Last week the girl at the checkout overcharged me
3 I complained and gained a refund

Clause 1 is a free clause because it can be moved to any position without changing the meaning of the story while clauses 2 and 3 are narrative clauses that need (in this case) to stay in this order for the story to make sense.

From Labov and Waletzky's research on African American narratives they concluded that a well-developed narrative displays a macrostructure of ordered recurring patterns comprising six elements. These elements are as follows:

- *Abstract*: an initial clause that reports or summarises the entire sequence of events of the narrative
- *Orientation clauses*: the time, place and events of the narrative
- *Complicating action clauses*: these clauses form the main body of the story and provide the next sequential event to respond to the question 'and what happened then?'
- *Evaluation*: interpretation of the significance of events and meanings and also the importance of the narrator's situation, socialisation, experience and views
- *Result* or resolution: the final outcome of the narrative
- *Coda* (often missing): ties narrator and audience back to the present.
  (Adapted from Labov and Walensky, 1967; Labov, 1972: 370; Labov, 1997)

The underlying assumptions here are that it is possible to break down all narratives into units of meaning and to map them in such a way that their common properties will be revealed.

Example

She gave birth after a long labour (*orientation*)

She went into labour on Thursday (*complicating action*)

On Friday they said she would have to have a caesarean (*complicating action*)

I think they should have let her have a normal birth, but these gynaecologists won't work weekends (*evaluation*)

And she had a lovely baby girl (*result*)

They're all fine now (*coda*)

Process of detailed analysis   A more detailed analysis can be provided by identifying the classes of narrative clauses and examining each in terms of their range and impact (Labov, 1997):

- The *range* of a narrative clause is the number of preceding clauses it is occurring simultaneously with (left subscript) and which it is followed by and linked to (right subscript). The range is then the sum of the two.
- A (temporarily) *bound clause* is an independent clause with a range of 0.
- A *free clause*, defined semantically as non-sequential, refers to a condition that remains unchanging throughout the narrative – it cannot be a sequential clause.
- A *restricted clause* is sequential with a range greater than 0.

Identifying temporal types of narrative clauses   The following is an example of this form of analysis:

Interview with Harold Shambaugh

Range	Elements	Type of clause	Transcript
$_0a_2$	OR	restricted.	Oh I w's settin' at a table drinkin'
$_1b_0$	CA	restricted.	And - this Norwegian sailor come over
$_0c_0$	CA	bound	An' kep' givin' me a bunch o' junk About I was sittin' with his woman.
d	OR	free	An' everybody sittin' at the table with me were my shipmates.
$_0e_0$	CA	bound	So I jus' turn aroun'
$_0f_0$	CA	bound	An' shoved 'im,
$_0g_0$	CA	bound	An' told 'im, I said, 'Go away',
$_0h_0$	EV	bound	[and I said,] 'I don't even wanna fool with ya.' An' nex' thing I know
$_0i_2$	CA	restricted.	I'm layin' on the floor, blood all over me,
$_1j_0$	EV	restricted.	An' a guy told me, says, 'Don't move your head.'
$_0k_0$	CA	bound	[and he said,] 'Your throat's cut.'

In the first column, the lines are all given letters in sequence (a–k) except for the fourth and tenth lines which are not independent (not sequential) clauses. The subscripts for line (a), $_0a_2$, indicate that (a) is not simultaneous with any preceding events, but does overlap with the two following (and with the free clause (d)). But (a) is not simultaneous with (e), since at that point Shambaugh has moved beyond just sitting and drinking at the table.

In the second column, the orientation (OR) clauses are picked out (a,d,) as are the evaluation (EV) clauses (h,j) there is no abstract or coda, and the other sequential clauses are all complicating action (CA).

In the third column, each sequential clause is identified as free, bound or restricted.

In the fourth column, the narrative is transcribed.

(Adapted from Labov, 1997)

Labov has constructed the causal sequence of events of this narrative as follows:

Shambaugh is sitting with his mates at a table drinking (*orientation*).

A Norwegian sailor comes over to complain to Shambaugh about his sitting with the Norwegian sailor's woman (*complicating action*).

Shambaugh rejects the complaint (*complicating action plus evaluation*).

Shambaugh shoves the Norwegian the sailor and tells him to go away (*complicating action*).

The sailor cuts Shambaugh's throat (*complicating action and result*).

Shambaugh is warned not to move by another person (*evaluation*).

Criticisms of the sociolinguistic approach

- The focus is the text and the sequence of events and what is missing is the interaction between the actor and the audience; the power relations; the shifts in meaning; the outcomes in terms of impact on the listener; and the development of shared understandings. Only the plot, its performance via clauses and the structure of its construction, is analysed.
- The assumption that language represents reality does not take into account the arguments that language is power laden, embedded in culture and socialisation contexts, and actually constitutes and constructs reality.
- Narratives are complex constructions of meaning linking personal lives, community and culture and should be preserved intact, not fractured.
- The context is completely omitted and the impact of the issues of race, class, gender and hierarchy are not considered.
- Narratives may not follow a chronological sequence in a linear way through time, they may be linked by themes that are not necessarily sequential.

2. The sociocultural approach

Here lives and stories are narrated as meaningful, coherent entities; however, the sociocultural approach goes beyond language structures to the broader interpretive frameworks that people use to make sense of everyday happenings/episodes, usually involving past–present–future linking. These personal narratives tend to be fairly concise and relate to specific incidents that have been observed or experienced. The segmentation of data into themes and other forms of fragmentation such as coding is avoided in this process as the stories that are told are complete entities in themselves and resist such processes. The assumptions underpinning this approach are that stories reflect not only culture, ideology and socialisation, they also provide insights to the political and historical climates impacting on the storyteller's lives – like stones dropped into water, the ripples reach out in ever-increasing circles.

Process of detailed analysis

- *Identify the boundaries* of the narrative segments in the interview transcript. These may be entire life stories or specific life episodes recorded in interactive talk or interviews.
- *Explore the content and context* of the story. How do people make sense of events? What emotions and feelings are displayed?
- *Compare different peoples stories* (if examining similar events).
- *Link stories* to relevant political structures and cultural locations.
- *Interpret stories* being aware of your own positions and reactions and how these shape the final text.

Example

In response to the question *'How did your mother respond to you becoming a father at home?'* (data set, Grbich, 1987):

> Well mum thought I was being taken for a ride by an older woman when she first found out I was going to be a father. Her first reaction was horror that I wasn't still a virgin, which shows where her thinking lay. She's now good, she's come round a lot. She gets on very well with Dan [his partner's child by another relationship), and she gets on well with Jen [partner]. Once she got over the problem of Jen being a terrible woman – a single mother who wanted someone to hang her bloody hat with – they got on very well, so that's been a substantial change.

Identification of boundaries: Using Labov's framework, this narrative appears in structure to be bounded by an orientation clause, complicating action, a result and a coda to bring it back to the present. This approach allows us to see that it is a fairly well developed narrative, with a beginning, a middle and a resolution.

Interpretation of content, political and social context: The context of gaining the narrative was that it emerged from within the bounds of research interviews of men who stay at home to rear young children while their partners take on the breadwinner role. This is a narrative response identified in the first of several interviews. These interviews recurred at intervals over a period of five years and were backed up by further interviews with the partner and the househusband's parents. In this narrative we have John, a male in his late twenties, who 18 months previously left his job as a manager of a small credit union to become a househusband to look after two children – his stepson, Dan, who is two years old and his own child, Emily, who is three months old. Jen, his partner, who is in her early 30s, is a social worker. They share a house with a priest, another couple and a baby. John's mother lives in a rural town in a fairly remote area and the emotions reported here indicate that she initially had a negative response both to the relationship and to the role change involved.

Other interview data confirm that the mother's views stem from a strongly conservative Catholic upbringing. Her husband died when John was 20 and she is close to her son, who is her third and youngest child, despite the fact that they live about 3,000 kilometres apart. Her expectations for her son were very high as he was the only child to go to university, even though he only attended for five weeks. It appears that her initial reaction reflected the socialised expectations of many Western cultures, that the male should be the older partner (or at least not the younger partner) and that the female partner should not be the breadwinner, particularly in a situation where there was a young baby at home still being breastfed. Her indicated concern that John wasn't still a virgin at 26 is also a reflection of earlier moral standards no longer seen as relevant to metro males in Western societies who are well past their teens.

Further indications are that this initial response from John's mother also stems from geographical distance and it was interesting to note that prior to the birth of their shared child the couple had travelled to spend time with her and this face-to-face contact had obviously allowed other factors to impinge on her view of the situation. Having met both Jen and Dan, she realised that they were likable people and that Jen was not just out to capture her son for her own selfish wellbeing. A young child and a future new baby to whom she would be Grandmother were undoubtedly also an influence here, but in addition Jen's very practical no-nonsense and down-to-earth nature would also have provided reassurance that despite being a 'city girl', Jen was in fact very close in character to many country women and therefore probably the right person for her son.

Contrasting stories: John's frustration and anger at his mother's response that Jen was just 'taking him for a ride' and looking for 'someone to hang her bloody hat with' is revealed in the language he uses and suggests he feels strongly about the relationship being seen in a truer light. The strength of his response also indicates that his mother's views are important to him. These emotions probably prompted the long trip with a pregnant wife and a one-year-old child to demonstrate to his mother that she was wrong. He later stated that he was 'very fond of her … she doesn't understand what we are doing … but we get on well. We're good mates; we love each other very much.' The stories presented – his mother's and implicitly his own views, which are quite different from hers – provide the contrast in the story and match Todorov's aspect of transformation: the disruption of equilibrium through change and the movement over time to another form of equilibrium.

Positioning of the actor and the researcher: But what about the position of the actor and the interviewer? The actor had strong ideological views about the importance of relationships and the need to avoid allowing workforce requirements to dominate and to undermine the time and energy levels available to develop these relationships. Commitment to community, social action and personal growth were also important. This was summarised later in this interview, when he said '*When you work in the fast lane, you live in the fast lane …we found that we just were not enjoying our life, it was too empty, too much going on.*' Choosing to live in a group household with people who were equally committed to such views, reinforced and supported this situation. The researcher was also largely committed to these values: she was undertaking her doctoral thesis on the topic of househusbands because she believed that this form of role change was important to allow the development of greater equality in the home division of labour and also because in being the breadwinner herself while her partner was the househusband at home to their three young children, she was interested to see how other couples were coping given that there was little research on this topic at that time and none of it had been undertaken longitudinally. Her own position, which had been clarified to each participating family, undoubtedly placed her inside this group and facilitated acceptance but may also have resulted in a belief that there was shared ideology and therefore too much elaboration was not required (the 'insider' dilemma).

The narrative and in fact the whole interview needs to be seen as a dramatic performance. The use of the word 'bloody', often used as an expletive by men in this culture, emphasises the fact that despite his mother's views and the traditionally 'feminine' role he is inhabiting, he is definitely a male and the statement that he 'wasn't a virgin' emphasises that he is sexually experienced, with the implication that he also knows what he is doing regarding his choice of partner and role change. The language used to portray his partner (from the perspective of his mother – 'taken for a ride by an older woman', 'a single mother who wanted someone to hang her bloody hat with') serve to position the mother at a different end of the spectrum from himself and his partner and make the resolution involving 'substantial change' more impressive. Using other information from the interview, the narrator can be seen as positioning himself as a heroic and powerful knight in shining armour galloping forth to the ends of the earth with partner and child in hand to right wrongs and mitigate the impact of his mother's negative opinions on his immediate family unit.

In choosing to display and to analyse this narrative, the researcher is highlighting her own views that although parents may not initially respond positively to their sons' choice to take on what has previously been seen as the 'female' nurturing role, it is very likely that eventually such parents may abandon negative views, particularly if these are challenged. These views then change and become subsumed into a desire to accept, to justify and to protect their offspring from the responses of others by taking an accepting position. Another researcher might have chosen to omit the father's voice or to report it minimally while highlighting the voices of the partner and mother for consideration.

Interpretations: Each narrative is subject to many readings and interpretations. A feminist reading might focus on a generational clash between two women and their capacity to resolve this, viewing the role of the male as diminished except as one perspective on the situation. A reading based on power relations would look at male, female and intergenerational relations between the son and his mother, while an emphasis on the concept of socialisation might view this male as deviant or suggest that the socialisation toward traditional gender roles has not been enduring either for himself or his partner. But even without the utilisation of theoretical concepts, the reader brings to the open narrative a considerable amount of background knowledge which they will use to add their own interpretations, which may be quite different from those presented by the researcher/writer. This allows the text to be further produced in the reading process in an ongoing and transformative process (Eco, 1979).

Longer narratives   Longer or more complex narratives may be reduced to their elements by grouping lines that relate to a single topic then linking these to form scenes each of which represents a geographic, temporal or reported voice shift in the narrative. An illustration of this from the above short example would then look something like:

Question: How did your mother react to you becoming a father at home?

Scene 1

Well mum thought I was being taken for a ride by an older woman

when she first found out I was going to be a father.

Her first reaction was that I wasn't a virgin, which shows where her thinking lay.

Scene 2

She's now good, she's come round a lot.

She gets on very well with Dan (his partner's child by another relationship),

and she gets on well with Jen (partner).

Once she got over the problem of Jen being a terrible woman

– a single mother who wanted someone to hang her bloody hat with –

they got on very well,

so that's been a substantial change.

This form of division helps to distinguish the sections that serve to build the narrative and to clarify their sequencing.

Variations of process

Despite guidelines, there is no right way to undertake sociocultural narrative analysis. There are many creative processes (Richardson and St Pierre, 2005) that can be used. Writers such as Cassandra Phoenix et al. (2010) have suggested that narratives can be divided into three researcher approaches: the first is *structural*, where the focus is primarily on *what* has been said and the classification of this into a particular typology or narrative type which can be named. The second approach is termed *performative*, with a focus on the *how* of the story, in particular how it has been constructed in the dialogical process between interviewer and interviewee and how it has been communicated and interpreted both between the two and between the writer and the audience. The third type is *autoethnography*, where both the *what* and the *how* of the narrative come into play as the researcher crafts and shapes their own story for the audience as they move inward to share often very personal aspects of their lives and then step outside to pursue another more distant but critically self-interpretive view.

Kathleen Wells (2011) has taken a *structural* approach in order to expose the surface and deep manifestations of the maternal identity of a mother who had lost and regained her children. In order to transform a 76-page transcript of an interview into a narrative, she focused on statements of attitudes and beliefs, and on recurring contrasts and binary oppositions in order to define the deep structures of the narrator's identity.

She used a four-stage process (Gregg, 2006):

1 Divide the text into episodes (here five) which comprise the plot/sequence of the story.
2 Eliminate material irrelevant to the plot (often facts).
3 Identify the stanzas in each episode which comprise a single theme or embedded story.
4 Identify contrasts, binary oppositions and mediating terms (a blend of the shared features) within and across each episode.

In this manner she was able to uncover the 'what' of this person's identity. The danger of this approach is that imposing a unifying/academifying label of 'identity construction' may obscure other aspects of the story, particularly those that may be of greater importance to the narrator.

Within the more *performative* tradition of engaging an audience, a range of visual, and textual re-presentations have been incorporated in consultation with the interviewee. Kip Jones (2004) presents a *biographic ethnographic narrative interview* with Mary Gergen which mixes visuals and text, as you can see from the following extract:

The omnipresence of the war

Everything in that small town [Balaton] was orientated toward the absence of the sons

I was in a little group of children that were all born at the same time there were four in this family where I was oldest and the oldest **girl**, and there were two younger **girls** and then the rest were **boys** and me. I was in these little **boys**. So, I never had this sort of inordinate respect for **boys** my age or younger. I also [pause] was [pause] one of the best students in our class. But I do think that I had this real sense of ownership and belonging and ah, you know that I was somebody in this little town.

When I was 12 we had to *move* to Minneapolis because [my **FATHER**] had been promoted.

[He was not very self-promoting and I think that was a problem].

We had to leave, it was very hard.

No! it wasn't hard, I was looking **forward** to it,

I thought it would **great,**

I thought it would be like *Balaton,*

Only b i **g g e r**.

I started

to collect movie

star pictures.

(From Jones (2004) www.qualitative-research.net/index.php/fqs/article/viewArticle/ 554; accessed June 2011)

In this example, the mix of visuals, including photos, pictures, different-sized fonts and varied text placements, lead the reader to 'hear' the voice of the narrator more accurately than traditional textual presentations.

The **autoethnographic** form of narrative (previously detailed in Chapter 10) can be seen in Ainslie Yardley's (2006) biographical authoethnographical narrative of her friend 'Lindy', who commits suicide. The reader is drawn into the text by a photograph of a pool at night, a brief insight into the mind of 'Lindy' through recalled conversation, then the author's story in the third person helps the reader to 'see' Lindy, her disappearance, the discovery of her drowned body, the despair of her male friend and the memorial service the two remaining friends organised. Although the 'data' is formed by memories and the events that occurred after the life of Lindy ended it is a highly evocative homage to this person.

Summary

There are two major approaches to narrative analysis of existing documentation: sociolinguistic and sociocultural. The latter can further be seen as having a predominantly structural, performative or autoethnographic focus. These polarisations, however, are merely trends that shift, change, merge and reform in the fluid amalgam that comprises qualitative research.

So which approach is preferable? Sociolinguistic or sociocultural? You need to choose here. The literature has polarised the two orientations and it is clear they both operate on different principles and produce very different readings. However, it may be possible for you to use both together in the one study, but for different purposes. Although Labov's segregation has been criticised, it provides one way of gaining insight into the structure of a narrative while the sociocultural approach allows the contextual constructions and interpretations of the actor and the researcher to emerge.

Student exercise

Take the following segment of an interview and analyse it

1   Sociolinguistically, in terms of identifying the clauses (orientation, complicating action, evaluation and result) and see if you can identify the notation of clause positioning in terms of range.
2   Socioculturally, in terms of identify political and social context, contrasting stories, researcher and actor positions, reader position and interpretation.

He was 14 months old and my husband virtually had to threaten the doctor at X hospital to tell us what was wrong. We knew there was no sign of him [child] trying to sit up at the time. Very quiet, didn't move a lot , hardly cried – more a sort of a whine. The doctor was very evasive and my husband said 'We're not leaving until you tell us and you're not leaving until you tell us.' Then he called another doctor behind a screen and they had a whispered conversation. Then he came back. He felt 'there was a certain degree of retardation but no specific reason why'. He told me to continue on with what I was doing and he told me that once a month for four and a half years

Please visit the companion website **www.sagepub.co.uk/grbich2** for possible answers.

Further reading

Sociocultural narratives

Boje, D. (2000) *Narrative Methods for Organisation and Communication Research*. Thousand Oaks, CA: Sage. In this book, Boje sets out eight analysis options for dealing with storytelling and recognising the complex natures of stories. The notion of poststructuralism can be seen in the introduction of ' anti-narrative' methods, where fragmented and collective storytelling can be interpreted.

Herman, L. and Vervaeck, B. (2005) *Handbook of Narrative Analysis*. Lincoln, NB: University of Nebraska Press. These authors look at the ideas and approaches of various theorists and their practices with regard to narrative analysis.

Reissman, C. (2008) *Narrative Analysis: Methods for Human Sciences*. Thousand Oaks, CA: Sage. Sociocultural principles and techniques are accessibly presented with central examples from feminist research and further examples from medical sociology.

Sociolinguistics

Milroy, L. and Gordon, M. (2003) *Sociolinguistics: Method and Interpretation* (2nd edn). Language and Society Series. Oxford: Blackwell. Covers models and methods, data collection and language variation in the social world: issues in analysis and interpretation, social relations and social practices, phonology and style and code shifting.

Wardhaugh. R. (2002) *An Introduction to Sociolinguistics* (4th edn). Oxford: Blackwell. This is useful as a comprehensive advanced undergraduate text focusing on four major areas: Languages and Communities, Inherent Variety, Words at Work, and Understanding and Intervening.

References

Beech, N. (2000) Narrative styles of managers and workers: a tale of star crossed lovers. *Journal of Applied Behavioural Science*, 39 (2): 210–28.

Eco, U. (1979) *The Role of the Reader: Explorations in the Semiotics of Texts*. Bloomington, IN: Indiana University Press.

Franzoni, R. (1998) Narrative analysis – or why (and how) sociologists should be interested in narrative. *Annual Review of Sociology*, 24: 517–54.

Frye, N. (1957) *Anatomy of Criticism: Four Essays*. Princeton, NJ: Princeton University Press.

Grbich, C. (1987) Fathers as primary caregivers: a role study. Doctoral thesis, Monash University, Melbourne, Australia.

Gregg, G. (2006) Gregg: the raw and the bland: a structural model of narrative identity. In D. McAdam, R. Josselson and A. Lieblich, *Identity and Story: Creating Self in Narrative*. Washington, DC: American Psychological Association. pp. 63–87.

Jones, K. (2004) 'Thoroughly Post-Modern Mary' [A Biographic Narrative Interview with Mary Gergen]. *Forum: Qualitative Social Research*, 5 (3), Art. 18. Retrieved from at http://www.qualitative-research.net/index.php/fqs/article/viewArticle/554 (accessed 14 March 2011).

Labov, W. (1972) *Language in the Inner City*. Philadelphia, PA: University of Philadelphia Press.

Labov, W. (1997) Some further steps in narrative analysis. *Journal of Narrative and Life History*, 7 (1-4): 207–15.

Labov, W. and Waletzky, J. (1967) Narrative analysis: oral versions of personal experience. In J. Helm (ed.), *Essays on the Verbal and Visual Arts*. Seattle, WA: University of Washington Press. pp. 12–44. Retrieved from www.clarku.edu/~mbamberg/LabovWaletzky.htm (accessed 10 August 2011). Classic work focused on the importance of evaluative statements in first-person narratives.

Phoenix, C., Smith, B. and Sparkes, A. (2010) Narrative analysis in ageing studies: a typology for consideration. *Journal of Ageing Studies*, 24 (1): 1–11.

Reissman, C. (2008) *Narrative Analysis*. Thousand Oaks, CA: Sage.

Richardson, L. and St Pierre, E. (2005) Writing, a method of inquiry. In N.K. Denzin and Y.S. Lincoln (eds), *Handbook of Qualitative Research* (3rd edn). London: Sage.

Stevens, P. and Tighe Doerr, B. (1997) Trauma of discovery: women's narratives of being informed they are HIV infected. AIDS *Care*, 9 (5): 523-38. Retrieved from www.ncbi.nlm.nih.gov/entrez/query.fcgi?cmd=Retrieve&db=PubMed&list_uids=9404395&dopt=Abstract PubMed (accessed 10 August 2011).

Todorov, T. ([1978]1990) *Genres in Discourse*. Cambridge: Cambridge University Press.

Wells, K. (2011) A narrative analysis of one mother's story of child custody loss and regain. *Children and Youth Services Review*, 33 (3): 439–47.

Yardley, A. (2006) Living stories: the role of the researcher in the narration of life. *Forum: Qualitative Social Research*, 9 (1). Retrieved from http://www.qualitative-research.net/index.php/fqs/article/viewArticle/990/2154 (accessed June 2011).

NINETEEN

Conversation analysis

The central goal of conversation analysis is the exploration, through the use of the spoken word, of the procedures that speakers use to communicate in a variety of socially mediated situations. Your analysis needs to focus on the forms of exchange in naturally occurring conversation sets and how any accompanying visuals and non-verbal interaction add to this.

> ### KEY POINTS
>
> - Transcriptions of naturally occurring conversations form the substance of the data in conversation analysis
> - Identification and discussion of the 'devices' used by participants in the communication process provides the major focus
> - Structures and social systems are reflected in interactive behaviours
> - Analytical approaches include
>   - exploring the mundane in everyday conversations
>   - reading the language of environmental settings
>   - understanding chat room conversation

Introduction

When to use: When you have access to naturally occurring conversations that can be transcribed.

Type of research questions best suited: How do people interact through the medium of conversations within particular environments?

Strengths: Clarifies the dynamics of interaction by looking at the minutiae of turn-taking.

Weaknesses: When we have access only to transcriptions of spoken dialogue the revealing facial expressions and non-verbal communications are missing.

Background

Conversation analysis (CA) is a research tradition that grew out of ethnomethodology – a theoretical position developed by Harold Garfinkel (Lynch and Sharrock, 2004). Ethnomethodology is a study of the ways in which people make sense of what other people do in the processes of social interaction. Such study should illuminate not only the micro level of interaction but also the broader social systems which are in place and which constrain or enable our behaviour. As much of our interaction is carried out through conversations with others, the study of ordinary conversations as they occur has become an important area of research. In particular, ordinary conversations shed light on the rules of social behaviour and indicate what is acceptable and what happens when these rules are broken or bent. In studying conversations, every aspect becomes significant, from the smallest pause to the loudest yell and all that goes in between. The dynamics of interaction are also relevant. What happens when a person of higher status talks to a person of lower status? How do conversations between women and between men differ from those when the genders are mixed? How do we manage both our own and others' emotions and impressions?

Purpose

The underlying assumptions here are that the conduct of society is socially organised and that much of this organisation is reflected, reinforced and shifted into new dimensions by both verbal and non-verbal interaction. The objective of CA is the description of the procedures by which conversationalists produce their own behaviour and understand and deal with the behaviour of others. A basic assumption throughout is that these activities – producing conduct and understanding and dealing with it – are accomplished as the accountable products of common sets of procedures. Thus the central goal of CA is the description and explication of the procedures that ordinary speakers use and rely on in participating in intelligible, socially organised interaction.

Analysis and data presentation

The focus on a conversation (defined as at least two turns, that is, two people interacting verbally) provides you with a fairly precise way of analysing the organisation of verbal interaction. The sociocultural content and context of conversation or interactive talk in the construction of meaning-making can be explored through a detailed inspection of tape recordings and their transcriptions. Analysis focuses on conversation sets, visuals, non-verbal interaction and environmental and social structures that impact on everyday behaviour as well as individual conversations.

Most practitioners of CA tend to refrain, in their research reports, from extensive theoretical and methodological discussion but this varies from discipline to discipline. As researcher you will tend to use your habitual expectations, derived from established social-scientific practice, as a frame of reference. A CA report will not generally have an extensive a priori discussion of the literature, or details about research situations and the subjects and participants who have provided the data, no descriptions of sampling techniques nor coding procedures, no testing and no statistics. Instead, the reader is confronted with a detailed discussion of transcriptions of recordings of (mostly verbal) interaction in terms of the 'devices' used by participants.

Speech acts, patterns and devices

In the process of conversation several recognised patterns of interaction or 'devices' have been documented. In the analytical process, the presence or absence of these is sought in order to provide insight into what is happening in particular texts.

Assertions are statements that state, describe, predict, announce or speculate. For example:

'It is cold today.'

'I wonder what the weather will be like tomorrow?'

'I think it will be fine.'

'There are long flakes of snow catching on the leaves and sliding to the ground.'

A stronger form of assertion is the *declaration*:

'I pronounce you man and wife.'

'You're hired/fired/redundant.'

'I sentence you to 10 years of imprisonment.'

Directives attempt to produce some form of action/response in another person, through requests, commands, questions, suggestions and orders. For example:

'Do this.'

'Tell me what happened.'

'Would you like to come with me?'

'Why did you do that?'

Commissives involve the elicitation of guarantees and vows of the order of 'Promise not to tell anyone else.'

In *expressive statements* the speaker's feelings are shared through apologies, thanks, greetings, acknowledgements and compliments. For example:

'I'm really sorry about that.'

'I think that definitely suits you.'

'Thank you so much for ...'

Sequential features

Turn-taking interaction in the display of interactional meaning can be more specifically indicated by the investigation of timed gaps and overlap between or among speakers. It is assumed that one speaker will dominate at a time, although various people may speak at different times and no set order can be predicted. There are occasionally gaps and overlaps in turn transition and most conversations will tend to occur in pairs called *adjacency pairs* which are expected paired interactions of matching responses, such as:

'Congratulations!' and 'Thank you very much.'

'Promise not to tell anyone,' and 'I promise.'

"I wish to complain about...' and 'I'm very sorry about...'

'How are you?' and 'I'm well, thank you.'

'Are you responsible for this?' and 'No I had nothing to do with that.'

They may also be question and answer type pairs, such as:

'Can I come round to visit you this evening?' and 'Yes/No.'

Some question answer pairs are more complex and contain conditional interactions, such as:

'Shall we go for a walk this evening?'

'Do you think it will rain?'

'No.'

'Then I'd love to.'

Silences in conversation can be interpreted in one of several ways: as natural gaps between speakers, as significant pauses because of the content and one person's response to this, or as a lapse in the continuity of the conversation. Another aspect worthy of note is *alignment*, which provides an indication that mutual understanding has occurred. This can be seen in echo/reinforcing statements, such as:

'I had a terrible time ...' and 'That must have been terrible for you.'

and in exclamatory reinforcers such as 'Really!', and 'Uh huh', or when one person completes the sentences of the other, for example 'I wonder if I might have a ...' '... cup of coffee?' It is when the conversation does not take an expected turn or responses don't match that interaction becomes more complex and from the conversational analyst's point of view, more interesting.

Researcher options

The term 'conversation' can be used very broadly and often involves (as well as language), visuals, non-verbal interaction, the environmental structures that impact on everyday behaviour as well as individual pushing of behavioural boundaries.
You can:

- examine situated activities with audio/video equipment, seeking order and mundaneity in the constructed interaction of everyday happenings

- attempt to make sense of information/visuals that are very different from those of the usual conversational interactions, such as reading the language of a coffee bar that converses with its patrons both in terms of signs and through the layout of tables and counter
- put yourself in unusual situations where routine sense-making may not work, for example following non-sequential conversations recorded in chat rooms.

A general model of CA's research practices

1 *Select episodes to be analysed,* such as: a consultation – the opening conversation, or 'discussions' about the understandings of the client regarding their particular problem; the casual conversations that occur between and among people who meet in public places; gatherings of family and friends; talkback radio etc. An episode will generally consist of one or more sequences, in which an interactant initiates an action and (the) other(s) react(s) to it. Only ordinary conversation as it is naturally occurring should be included, no interviews nor staged scripts. Record the material to be analysed.

2 *Transcribe recordings.* The following information should be included for complete analysis of the conversation:

   time, date and place of the original recording
   participant information
   words and sounds as uttered
   spaces, silences
   overlapping speech and sounds
   pace, stretches (::), stress(es) (underlining), volume (CAPS indicate increased volume)
   visual information.

3 *Check the episode carefully in terms of turn-taking.* Note the construction of turns, pauses, overlaps, etc.; make notes of any remarkable phenomena, especially any 'disturbances' in the fluent working of the turn-taking system.

4 *Look for sequences* and note any phenomena such as repair initiators, or actual repairs (recognition and correction of a speech error by self or others). On a more structural and contextual level, how do speakers manage sequences and turns? What patterns are evident? What adjacency pairs can be identified?

5 *Try to make sense of the episode,* using informal understandings of what utterances 'mean'. Your analytic interests will tend to 'predispose' you to certain hearings and these may need to be checked with the participants and their sense-making must be taken into account. Interpretation is directed at a typification of what the utterances that make up the sequence can be held to be 'doing' and how these 'doings' interconnect with other instances.

6 *Interpret the material in a comparative manner* and if desired use any of the concepts/theories/explanations which are meaningful in your own discipline.
   (Adapted from ten Have, 2007; Wang, 2011)

A useful way in which you can gain an overview of a total conversation would be to identify the kind of conversation that has occurred:

- Is it amicable, a heated discussion, or an outright argument about personal or political issues?
- Is it an equal exchange? or is one person leading?
- What happens when one person moves to a dominant questioning or declarative mode and how does this structure or impact on the conversation?

- Are any misunderstandings evident?
- If there is any tension, how is it created? Maintained? Reflected in the structure of the conversation?
- What is your response as a reader to this conversation?

Notation for conversational analysis

Notation is important in that it gives life to the conversation and allows it to be read in the manner in which it was spoken. It provides clarification as to where pauses have occurred and where the voices have risen, fallen, added emphasis, become very quiet or where overlapping speech has occurred. It also indicates where breath and laughter have been audible. The following table contains the major notational signs currently in use:

	Notation for conversation analysis
(.)	Just noticeable pause
(.3), (2.6)	Pauses in seconds
↑word, ↓word	Rise or fall in pitch/intonation
.hh, hh /.hhh	Indicates in-breath (note the preceding full stop)
hhh	out-breath respectively.
	(sometimes more than two h's are used)
wo(h)rd	(h) is a way of showing laughter within the word
wor–	The dash shows a sharp cutoff in speech
wo:rd	Colons indicate a stress on the preceding sound.
or word =	The equals sign indicates that there is no discernible pause between
= word	two speakers' turns or shows that they run together for one or for two speakers
word,	Underlined sounds are louder
WORD	Capitals are louder still
°word°	Material between signs is quietly spoken
word: word:	A colon indicates an extension of the sound it follows
word,	A comma indicates intonation
word?	Question marks indicate a rising inflection
word	Underlining indicates emphasis
( )	Unidentifiable speech
< >	Talk between these signs is rushed/compressed
[	Two separate successive brackets on 2 lines with utterances from dif-
[	ferent speakers indicates the same thing
]	A right bracket bridging two lines indicates overlapping or simultane-
]	ous utterances at this point
//	One speaker overlapping with another speaker
*	Indicates end of overlap
.	Indicates falling intonation
<	Talk starts with a rush
(( ))	Transcript creator's descriptions of events, e.g. ((cough))

Example: conversational interaction

The following (Jeffersen, 1989) is an example of a brief interaction using the notation from above:

```
1        Carol:        Victor

2        Vic:          Ye:h?

3        Carol:        Come here for a minute.

4                      (1.0)

5        Vic:          You come he[: r e] please?]

6        Carol:        [↑You can] come  b]a:ck=

7        Vic:          =I ↑have to go to the ba:th↓room.=

8        Carol:        =°Oh:.°
```

In terms of analysing this you can see that Carol emphasises the 'i' in Victor's name and that his response of 'Yeh' is drawn out. Her directive to him to come to her results in a one-minute pause where no interaction appears to occur. Victor issues a counter-directive to her to come to him which is qualified by a softer 'please' in a questioning tone. Carol raises her voice to emphasise that Victor could/should be the one to move but modifies the word 'back' by drawing it out and saying it quietly. Victor provides an excuse for the fact that he is heading not back but in the direction of the bathroom and Carol gives up at that point with a quiet overlapping 'Oh' of resignation/acceptance. Adjacency pairs can be seen in the relatively expected response patterns of Victor to Carol except for the last response when he veers off in another direction and it is unclear whether this terminates the conversation or whether it will continue after he returns from the bathroom. If the researcher wanted to go further into an analysis of gender relations it is clear from this short extract that power lies with Victor and that tension is provided by Carol attempting to get him to meet her demands while he successfully resists.

An example of an unscripted interaction using notation between a mother (Lyn) and her daughter (Zoe) in a situation where Lyn is sitting at a table (possibly studying) in front of a video camera when her daughter enters the room can be viewed as video clip 2 at www-staff.lboro.ac.uk/~ssca1/imagepage.htm (Charles Antaki, 2009, accessed 26 April 2011). The notated version of this interaction is presented below.

```
17                                    (6.0)
18  →    Zoe            th' camera's on.
19       Lyn                >yes<
20                                    (1.8)
```

```
21          Zoe          w'(h) are you ta(h)lking to it while you
22                                        wORK?
23          Lyn                           no:,
24                                         (.5)
25          Lyn                    [heh heh °heh heh°=
26          Zoe                    [hh what ye' DOINg then
27          Lyn                    =hahh hahh hahh
28                                         (1.0)
29          Zoe                  what's the ↑point:h
30                                        (1.5)
31          Zoe          ↑oh ↑god (.) look what ↑I'm wearing
32                                        (.3)
33          Lyn                   eh hehh huh [↑HUhh=
34          ?Zoe                             [(heh)
35→         Lyn          =you look like (.) ↑Fa:gin
36                                         (.5)
37          Zoe                  eh HUHh HAhh h[ahh
38          Lyn                               [>heh hah hh< (.) ↑H=
39                                ((squeaky at end))
40          Zoe                   =w' maybe I am.
41          Lyn          y' just need th' little gloves, with
42                               th' ↑fingers out.
43                                         (.8)
44          Zoe                    (°v' funny°)
45                                         (1.2)
46          Zoe                   (°d'y wan' one.°)
```

Analysis of the interaction   Lyn is sitting at a table looking down, apparently thinking for some considerable period of time before Zoe comes in and notices that the camera is recording. Lyn's response is a very compressed 'Yes' and her disinclination to clarify why the video is going can be seen in the pause of over one and a half minutes. Zoe again attempts to find out what Lyn is doing with the camera but again no explanation is forthcoming and Zoe's questions regarding the point of having the camera recording are met initially with laughter followed by silence. Zoe then notices that her voice, appearance and actions are also being recorded and comments on her clothes which leads to much louder laughter from Lyn and a response that Zoe looks like Fagin. This leads to combined laughter except that Lyn's additional comment that all Zoe needs are fingerless gloves to complete the Fagin image are met by a quiet response 'very funny' and a distracter/terminator of the discussion from Zoe who offers Lyn a cigarette.

One central part of the interaction is Lyn's response to Zoe's perception that she sees herself as looking like Fagin that maybe she is like Fagin. But instead of reassuring Zoe that she really doesn't look like Fagin, Lyn takes her teasing response further by suggesting that all Zoe lacks are the gloves. Although Zoe has been happy to laugh at her own criticism of her clothes up to that point, she suddenly stops laughing and indicates that things have gone too far 'well maybe I am'. It has been all right for her to comment on her own clothes sense but not alright for others to take it further, however light the teasing might be.

More detailed conceptual analysis could examine mother–daughter interaction in terms of question–response, resistance, teasing and shifting power dynamics.

Three types of conversational analysis

There are many possibilities for CA and three different examples are provided for you:

1 mundane conversations
2 the 'conversations of public places'
3 internet chat rooms.

1. The mundaneity of everyday conversations

Sally and Stephen Hester (2010) have documented and analysed a dinner table squabble between older brother (R) aged 12 and younger sister (M) aged 7 in the presence of their mother (J), who audiorecorded the conversation:

1. J: Have some chee-put some cheese on your potato now and it will melt (10.0)

2. ((Maggie starts to get up)) Sit down I'll get you a drink

3. R: And me please

4. M: *Milk*

5. J: Milk or water Russ?

6. R: Water please (1.0) *SIT DOWN*

7. M: *I KNOW I SLIPPED*

8. J: *Ok* there's no need to [shout] at her

9. R: [If you] slipped you're just standing there goin'=

((does action of Maggie's claimed slipping))

10. M: =[*No*]=

11. R: =[Ooh] [I slipped!] ((mimicking))

12. M: [*I went back*]*wards like that*

13. (1.5)

14. R: *SIT DO::WN*

15. M: *I KNOW* [*don't talk*] *with your mouth open*

16. J: [She is love]ly ((s.v.))

17. R: Hmm How am I meant to talk then?

18. J: *Russell*

19. M: You've got a m[outhful]

20. J: [*Russell*]

21. R: Ner ner ner ner ner [ner] (('talking' with mouth closed))

22. J: [J– Ma]ggie just leave him alone – ignore him he's being

23. purposely (3.0) Kevinish

24. M: Mm

25. R: I'm not

26. J: And you *are* eati'- er talking with your mouthful (11.0) what did Harry say when

27. he phoned then?

28. R: Erhm h-he was leaving somewhere and he'd be back in ten minutes

(Hester and Hester, 2010: http://dis.sagepub.com/content/12/1/33, accessed June 2011)

Analysis was divided into four main areas:

1 *Direction, degradation and resistance* (lines 6 and 7 with reference to line 2) in the construction of their category (here sibling relationship), where the older child imitates the powerful parental role and the younger child resists blame.
2 *The fallacious account* (lines 9–12), where the younger child explains her 'transgressions' as accident related.
3 *Resistance and mockery* (lines 14 and 15, and 19–21), where the younger child hits back but is mocked by the elder.
4 *Ending the argument* (lines 21–28), where mother steps in and terminates the argument.

Jo-Anne Perry et al. (2005) studied nurse-patient interaction with patients with advanced dementia recorded in a residential care home in the United States during a social group session. Analysis of audiotaped resident interactions across 10 socialisation groups indicated that nurses mainly utilised three types of questions: *exploratory, clarifying* and *validating* while the resident's responses produced a taxonomy comprising six types of responses: *discourse markers, limited engagement, expanded response, personalised response, self-initiated participation* and *disconnected participation*.

One conversational example follows using the three types of questions:

Nurse: You said you have a problem with your leg? (**Exploring**)

Resident 1: Well it's my left leg. [pause] I have a little trouble, left always. Just, well not at this time, I don't know [long pause]. But anyways, it bothers me. Not all the time, just sometimes.

Nurse: Yeah, (Discourse Markers) how about you [Resident 2] (**Exploring**)

Resident 2: What?

Nurse: How are your legs [question directed to Resident 2]? (**Clarifying**)

Resident 2: How are what?

Nurse: Your legs. (**Clarifying**)

Resident 2: I don't know. [shouting] They're all right.

Nurse: They're all right? (**Clarifying**)

Resident 2: Yes.

Nurse: That's good, you're lucky. (**Validating**)

(Perry et al., 2005)

2. Visual/non verbal 'conversations' in public places

Public places such as cafés create their own forms of conversation with the public through signs and symbols indicating that coffee and various forms of food can be purchased and imbibed or eaten on these premises. They also use written directions to patrons such as 'enter here' or 'close the door' or 'please order before you sit down', indicating how the establishment runs as well as menus to show what is on offer. But other forms of 'conversation' can be seen in the arrangement of tables with which clients will interact. Pathways between the tables encourage patrons to move in a particular direction and the types of tables also encourage/restrict interactive possibilities. For example if there are only two-person tables available a larger group entering will tend to put tables together to form one to fit their numbers or seek out another café. If only long tables are available then some singles will use the opportunity to mix with others but other singles will seat themselves in such a way as to minimise interaction – perhaps by leaving a gap between themselves and the next person, and this separation will be reinforced by gaze avoidance, by reading a book or by positioning a newspaper in such a way as to screen the individual from others and to make several adjacent chairs inaccessible.

Other non-verbal forms of conversation can be seen on the tables themselves when individuals 'take' or reserve a table by leaving a coat/keys or some other possession to show they have just gone to order/or to visit the restroom and will be back soon. Empty glasses and plates and the absence of possessions indicates the table is vacant and waiting to be cleaned and taken.

Cultural settings such as cafés invite and reinforce certain interactions and the extent and type of social order that has been established can only be ascertained by pushing the boundaries of indicated expectations; for example sitting down and reading but refusing to order, or shifting tables to quite different areas of the inside or the outside of the café without seeking permission, or going and sitting opposite a single patron at a two-person table without seeking their permission or checking whether the seat is already taken, and/or talking loudly to oneself.

3. New forms of conversation: chat rooms

Online communities have been seen as having the following characteristics in common:

- active participation and regular participants
- shared history, purpose, culture, norms and values
- solidarity, support, reciprocity
- criticism, conflict and means of conflict resolution
- self-awareness of group as entity distinct from other groups
- emergence of roles, hierarchy, governance, rituals.
  (Herring, 2004: 351–2)

In chatrooms the neat assumptions that turn-taking and agency pairs will dominate inter-action in a linear progression are thrown by the intertwining nature of the 'conversations' where one statement/question may not be responded to until several players later. Responses in between will be read by all the interactants and will tend to dilute later responses or act as intersection points for a number of conversation streams.

Terrell Neuage (2004) examined the dialogues from seven chatrooms to discover:

- a truncated form of writing and grammar, for example:
  - LOL – laughing out loud
  - PLZ – please
  - ROFL – rolling on the floor laughing

- the use of graphical/textual avatar images to enhance the portrayal of the writer

- the use of text graphics

- and the use of word 'emoticons' to communicate emotions

s, *S*, <s>, = smile   *g*, <g> = grin   xoxo = hugs and kisses   huggggggssssss = hugs

See www.web-friend.com/help/lingo/chatslang.html for an extensive list of word emoticons.

- the insertion of chatroom graffiti by non-regular participants leaving political messages
- the silence of lurkers and the discomfort they can create
- the complex braiding and overlapping of threads as the reader/writer responds to multiple threads.

Neuage found that although chat was more deliberate and contrived than normal conversation, overall it did not differ dramatically from it. He utilised a combination of conversational, semiotic, discourse and cyberethnographic approaches to clarify similarities in the patterns of each chatroom case study.

The focus of much chatroom research has been in the construction and maintenance of discursive identities in online communities and self/other management and accountability in the maintenance of the community.

Managed accountability of discursive identities can be seen in a German eating disorder website, the Hungrig-Online forum, where Wyke Stommel (2008) uncovered the role of moderator in enforcing the rules of the site:

Extract 4 (thread no. 31)

1	#Sylvia: am I in danger?
2	Hello you forunners…
3	
4	so I don't actually know what I should write here exactly
5	actually I want to know whether others find my thoughts abnormal
6	so I've never really revealed my thoughts to anyone on this subject
7	
8	don't really know where to begin. I weigh myself [*] times a day.
9	[21 lines omitted]
10	
11	now is that ill? I mean somehow it is actually ill…but is it REALLY
12	ill?
13	is it ill to think to hope that one somehow will eventually get
14	thinner????
15	
16	thanks in advance
17	
18	[Dear Sylvia. Please don't give any figures for your weight or
19	anything to do with it and no descriptions of how you harm yourself.
20	Read through the rules again. Love Marcia]
21	
22	#Sylvia
23	@Marcia: I'm sorry, I had read the rules, but somehow I didn't really
24	pay attention… well, I did try but this one thing I must have
25	overlooked
26	

The moderator controls and maintains the aims and intent of the forum, keeping vulnerable contributors safe within the rules of participation.

Charles Antaki et al. (2005) examined the delicacy of turn-taking and manipulation of accountability in a Spanish online forum via a single case study of one initial thread message – a declaration of love – and the first response which ratified it. The focus of the analysis was the first participants' apparent and displayed concern with accountability while actually bypassing the rules. The forum's expectations required conversational moves (such as declarations) to be 'occasioned' by previous talk but this initiator managed to set up an oblique statement of love so that it would not be accountable in the usual way:

Statement

For you, who already know who you are, my love, from your Lourdes.
(with apologies to all the members of this forum).

Response

What a way to make us green with envy, girlie ... well,
we're gonna have to live with it, I guess!!!!
kissy-kiss to both of you.

In these examples you can see that when voices can only be read not heard, notation and timing become irrelevant and sociocultural analysis dominates.

Summary

The assumption in conversational analysis is that in a structured society with rules of interaction and behaviour that reflect social conventions, conversations can be read and analysed regardless of whether these interactions are with environments or face-to-face or occur as audio, video, radio, TV or online interactions. It is also assumed that these conversations will reflect and consolidate the values and behaviours that make up this society.

Student exercise

Use the following six-stage model of conversation analysis:

1   Select episodes to be analysed.
2   Transcribe recording and notate.
3   Check the episode carefully in terms of turn-taking.
4   Look for sequences.
5   Try to make sense of the episode.
6   Interpret the material in a comparative manner.

The answers to stages (1) – (4) are provided below. Combine (5) and (6), making sense and interpreting the interview extract below.

1   Select episode to be analysed and (2) transcribe and notate interview response to:

Q. How are others responding to you in your father at home role?

Answer: Its the per:ception of the divi:sion between MALE and FEMAle roles that I find a ↑KEY to most of the INJUSTICE I've encountered ↓ during this past year. When it comes to the crunch most ma:les prefer to be ↓ breadwinners; they see this as the more important role(.). This has also to do with money ↓ and title and status.

I remember when my wife graduated from ↓ Medical School, (::)amongst the group she was part of what struck me as odd(.) even then(:) was that the men all looked forward to their futures as ↑doctors ↓ and that's natural enough, but there was never any question that they wouldn't work ↓ full time. Several were in stable relationships and their partners had started ↑careers of their own. But none of the graduates (::)↑male (.) or ↓ female ↑ever ques:tioned who would stay ho:me ↓ should they start a family. There was ↑NO question of whose career was expendable. As soon as they had children ↑both the wives of doctors AND the female medical graduates would all give up work and ↓ retire to the house.

3   Check the episode carefully in terms of turn-taking. *Strictly question and answer.*
4   Look for sequences. *None, as this is a sole response.*

Please visit the companion website **www.sagepub.co.uk/grbich2** for possible answers.

Further reading

Conversation analysis – introductory

Antaki, C. (2009) An introductory tutorial in Conversation Analysis. Online at www-staff.lboro.ac.uk/~ssca1/intro1.htm (accessed on 25 June 2011). This site provides several examples (one of which has been used in this chapter) of conversational analysis in tutorial format. It also provides links to other teaching and learning resources

Ethno/Ca news www.paultenhave.nl/ (accessed 25 April 2011) is a site that provides information and accessible examples and links on both ethnomethodology and conversational analysis.

Hutchby, I. and Wooffitt, R. (2008) *Conversation Analysis* (2nd edn). Cambridge: Polity Press. An introduction to the field, theory, methods and practical examples including human–computer interaction, political communication and speech therapy.

Schegloff, E. (2007) *Sequence Organization in Interaction: A Primer in Conversation Analysis*, volume 1. Cambridge: Cambridge University Press. The first in a series of texts defining the state of CA art.

Sidnell, J. (2010) *Conversation Analysis: An Introduction.* Chichester: Wiley–Blackwell. An authoritative and readable account.

ten Have, P. (2007) *Doing Conversation Analysis* (2nd edn). London: Sage. A comprehensive introduction.

Conversational analysis – advanced and practice

Arminen, I. (2005) *Institutional Interaction: Studies of Talk at Work.* Aldershot: Ashgate. This book in the Directions in Ethnomethodology and Conversation Analysis series (Series Editors D. Francis and S. Hester) provides a fairly advanced discussion of conversation analysis and looks at talk and interaction in institutional settings, in particular the classroom, counselling settings, the courtroom and the doctor's surgery.

Nevile, M. (2004) *Beyond the Black Box: Talk-in-Interaction in the Airline Cockpit.* Aldershot: Ashgate. This book, also in the Directions in Ethnomethodology and Conversation Analysis series (Series Editors D. Francis and S. Hester), looks at the organisation of talk in a complex technological work setting and examines how airline pilots use language and gestures linked to the equipment they are using to build action and to share meanings. 24 pictures and 23 video stills are included.

Seedhouse, P. (2004) *The Interactional Architecture of the Language Classroom: A Conversation Analysis Perspective.* Oxford: Blackwell. This book comprises a compilation of work from Seedhouse's doctoral thesis together with various journal articles, to explore classroom discourse as institutional interaction. He describes the interactional architecture of the language classroom across cultures and the teaching of different languages in different institutions.

Wooffitt, R. (2005) *Conversation Analysis and Discourse Analysis: A Comparative and Critical Introduction.* London: Sage. Clarifies the similarities and differences between conversation and discourse analysis.

References

Antaki, C. (2009) Conversation analysis discourse and rhetoric groups. Loughborough University. Retrieved from www-staff.lboro.ac.uk/~ssca1/intro1.htm (accessed 23 April 2011).

Antaki, C., Ardévol, E., Núñez, F. and Vayreda, A. (2005) 'For she who knows who she is': managing accountability in online forum messages. Journal of Computer-Mediated Communication, 11 (1): Art. Retrieved from http://jcmc.indiana.edu/vol11/issue1/antaki.html.

Herring, S.C. (2004) Computer-mediated discourse analysis: an approach to researching online behavior. In S. Barab, R. Kling and J. Gray (eds), Designing for Virtual Communities in the Service of Learning. New York: Cambridge University Press. pp. 338–76.

Hester, S. and Hester, S. (2010) Conversational actions and category relations: an analysis of a children's argument. *Discourse Studies*, 12 (33). Retrieved from http://sagepub.com/content/12/1/33 (accessed June 2011).

Jeffersen, G. (1989) Preliminary notes on a possible metric which provides for a 'standard maximum' silence of approximately one second in conversation. In D. Roger and P. Bull (eds), *Conversation: An Interdisciplinary Perspective*. Clevedon: Multilingual Matters.

Lynch, M. and Sharrock, W. (eds) (2004) *Harold Garfinkel.* Sage Masters of Modern Social Thought series. London: Sage.

Neuage, T. (2004) Online discourse analysis method ODAM: conversational analysis of chatroom "talk". Doctoral thesis, University of South Australia. Retrieved from http://s126867739.onlinehome.us/neuage/thesis.pdf (accessed June 2011).

Perry, J., Galloway, S., Bottorff, J.L. and Nixon, S. (2005) Nurse–patient communication in dementia: improving the odds. *Gerontological Nursing*, 31 (4): 43–52. Retrieved from www.slackjournals.com/article.aspx?rid=4446 (accessed June 2011).

Stommel, W. (2008) Conversation analysis and community of practice as approaches to studying. Online Community, vol. 5. Retrieved from http://www.languageatinternet.de/articles/2008/1537 (accessed June 2011).

ten Have, P. (2007) *Doing Conversation Analysis* (2nd edn). London: Sage.

Wang, L. (2011) Introduction to Language Studies. Singapore: Pearson.

TWENTY

Discourse analysis

There are several approaches to the location of discourses (patterns of speech and writing that define, determine and influence disciplines and the general population). Two dominant approaches to identifying and analysing discourses are Foucauldian discourse analysis and critical discourse analysis (CDA), and both of these will be discussed.

KEY POINTS

- Discourses are the spoken or written practices or visual representations that characterise a topic, an era, or a cultural practice. They dictate meaning and upon analysis may indicate their hidden impact and the individuals or groups whose views have dominated at a particular point in time
- Discourse analysis spans a broad field from formal linguistic approaches through Foucauldian analyses to cultural and critical communication studies and has been used in many disciplines including: linguistics, psychology, education, information technology, sociology, health, management and administration, and communication
- Foucauldian discourse analysis identifies statements and tracks their changes and challenges historically in the mapping of the creation and maintenance of power-laden discourses
- Critical discourse analysis (CDA) seeks how discursive practices within societal structures secure and maintain power over people
- Various hybrid approaches to discourse analysis, combining with other forms of analysis and interpretation, continue to be developed

---

Introduction

When to use: When the identification, tracking and operation of powerful discourses is useful.

Type of research questions best suited: How did this particular way of thinking/behaving/writing/talking eventuate? What are the outcomes? What other ways of knowing have been marginalised?

Strengths: The capacity to track the historical origins of accepted ways of thinking and writing and to identify marginalised or missing voices.

Weaknesses: Incapacity to do much beyond record the dominance of powerful discourses unless feminist/action research attempts to redress the situation other ideas.

Discourse analysis

Discourse analysis is a way of questioning in both social and scientific areas, the ways of thinking, writing and speaking about particular topics in order to discover the rules, assumptions, ways of seeing, hidden motivations, conditions for development and change, and how and why these changes occurred or were resisted. In short, how a discourse developed (historical formation and powerful groups); how it works (ordering and exclusion); and what the outcomes have been.

Foucauldian discourse analysis

The Foucauldian approach uses historical and political tracking of documentation over time and tends to utilise the conceptual preconceptions of power as a basis for interpretation. Michael Foucault was concerned with the ways in which knowledge had been created and sustained within cultures. In whose best interests was this knowledge developed? And in its creation had powerful interests obscured its origins as well as any protests, or challenges put up by others with an interest in this piece of knowledge? According to Foucault, discourses are 'practices that systematically form the objects of which they speak. ... Discourses are not about objects; they do not identify objects, they constitute them and in the practice of doing so conceal their own invention' (Foucault, 1972: 49).

Once a discourse has been established, Foucault suggests that it disperses throughout society. He uses the metaphor of the body to represent society in order to show discourses filtering through the arterial and venous systems of the populace and then being fed back in a cyclical process through the capillaries, enabling maintenance and reinforcement. The binary opposites of structuralism, in particular notions of 'right' and 'wrong', serve to persuade the population that truth is singular and notions of 'confession' further serve as a micro form of control, confirming individual alignment alongside the dominant discourses that control and constrain thoughts and actions. Meaning and myth then become products of power relations.

Power is a key aspect of discourse. In his books on madness, sexuality, prisons and medical clinics Foucault traces the development and institutionalised control of the population both physically and mentally through technologies of power. The interlinking of sovereign power (monarchy) with dominant modes of disciplinary power (legal system) is seen as being managed through the 'normalisation' of particular discourses maintained by surveillance and monitoring, and enforced by the law, police, warders and the courts. At the micro-level, normalisation can be observed through the image of the Panopticon, a model prison designed by Jeremy Bentham in the nineteenth century, but one that was never actually built. Foucault used the Panopticon as a metaphor for the articulation of powerful discourses and the technologies of their maintenance in society. The Panopticon

ANALYTIC APPROACHES FOR EXISTING DOCUMENTATION

is a circular structure with internal and external glass windows – to let light into each cell from outside and to give access to each cell from a central watchtower. The wardens can observe activity but the prisoner cannot distinguish when he is actually being observed. Each cell becomes a stage and the performance is a public one for those under surveillance. All this anticipated observation is said to produce self-monitoring – the most effective form of discipline maintenance and one for which, once established, minimal observation by 'watchers' is required.

From this, two areas need to be addressed in undertaking a Foucauldian approach:

1 The outside looking in: historical development and tracking of a discourse over time, identifying the players and the social, economic, and political climate which fostered its development. Locating challenges and seeing what happened to these – where did they come from? Why? And if they were rejected, how were they dispensed with? And by whom? For what purpose?
2 The inside looking out: to identify constituents in terms of statements, themes, arguments, traces of challenges and traces of ideas that changed directions. Seeking disunity and the limits to the discourse, monitoring dispersion and tracking discontinuity.

From the *outside*, in order to record the emergence of the object of a discourse you need to first map the surfaces where the object has emerged. In identifying the location of an object such as 'sexuality' the mapping of perceptions and their interplay would involve investigation of the family, social groups, work, religion, medicine, art, literature and pornography. Then the clarification of the rules of cultural institutions such as education, medicine and law in dealing with sexuality/ies will need explanation as will the identification of who has been responsible for these rules. In tracing the paths of sexuality as they are named, redefined, challenged and erased, it is important to identify disunity, dispersion and discontinuity. For example, different kinds of sexuality need to be 'divided, contrasted, related, regrouped, classified, derived from one another as objects of psychiatric discourse' (Foucault, 1972: ch. 3: 2). However, you should be very critical of statements and groups of statements that appear to have become grouped and bounded within a particular discipline and should seek their use elsewhere. Foucault takes the example of 'madness' and indicates that such a word will be used differently when it appears in psychiatry from when it appears in the legal system, in police action and in the media etc. Following this, the transformation, replacement and type of connection of groups of statements and their concepts needs defining. The final regrouping of statements, their interconnection, their consolidation in particular fields, the persistence of particular themes and their systems of dispersion within which regularities may be evident, can then be undertaken.

From *inside* the text the process involves tracking the historical processes by which the discourse has been constructed, and the influences that have constituted its production 'history is that which transforms documents into monuments. In that area where, in the past, history deciphered the traces left by men, it now deploys a mass of elements that have to be grouped, made relevant, placed in relation to one another to form totalities' (Foucault, 1972: 7). The process now becomes like an archaeological dig, a searching among the traces left, now erased 'like a face drawn in sand at the edge of the sea' (1970: 387), seeing how material remains have become grouped into meaningful entities, comparing them in order to decipher the gaps, and locating the interruptions or discontinuities that may indicate missing pieces, erased voices or obliterated events which may have occurred between 'epistemes' (major systems of knowledge documented over time).

In the archaeological dig of discourse analysis, the artefacts found comprise a set of statements that can transform and change over time with new knowledge, exclusion of challenges, and maintenance of powerful interests. Notions of discontinuity and dispersion underpin this process. Unity is unlikely to be a feature of any discourse, so the task of the researcher is to discover the rules that define the discourse, not to interpret it, but to identify the limits to unity and forms of disunity which hold groups of discursive statements in a particular pattern.

Thus, the researcher should be seeking from the inside out:

- forms of succession (particular arguments of the discourse)
- forms of co-existence (relations among all statements – accepted or excluded)
- procedures of intervention (the rewriting and ordering of information into systems of ideas, usually by powerful individuals or groups).

Guidelines for Foucauldian discourse analysis

The following broad guidelines have been drawn from Foucault's writings:

a   Track the historical development of the discourse over time and identify the players and the social, economic and political climate which fostered its development.
b   Identify constituents in terms of objects, statements, themes, arguments, traces of challenges, traces of ideas that changed directions.
c   Seek disunity and discontinuity and the limits to the discourse. Monitor dispersion in other fields.
d   Locate challenges and see what happened to these: Where did they come from? Why? And if they were rejected, how were they dispensed? and by whom? for what purpose?

Example of Foucauldian discourse analysis

The following extract from the BBC TV political comedy series *Yes Minister* provides a brief illustrative example of how a Foucauldian discourse analysis might be attempted:

The Minister: Humphrey's system for stalling. According to Tom, it's in five stages. I made a note during our conversation, for future reference.

Stage One: Humphrey will say that the administration is in its early months and there's an awful lot of other things to get on with.

Stage Two: If I persist past Stage One, he'll say that he quite appreciates the intention, something certainly ought to be done – but is this the right way to achieve it?

Stage Three: If I'm still undeterred he will shift his ground from how I do it to when I do it, i.e. 'Minister, this is not the time, for all sorts of reasons.'

Stage Four: Lots of Ministers settle for Stage Three according to Tom. But if not, he will then say that the policy has run into difficulties – technical, political and/or legal. (Legal difficulties are best because they can be made totally incomprehensible and can go on for ever.)

Stage Five: Finally, because the first four stages have taken up to three years, the last stage is to say that 'we're getting rather near to the run-up to the next general election – so we can't be sure of getting the policy through'. ... He also warned me of the 'Three Varieties of Civil Service Silence', which would be Humphrey's last resort if completely cornered:

1 The silence when they do not want to tell you the facts: *Discreet Silence*.

2 The silence when they do not intend to take any action: *Stubborn Silence*.

3 The silence when you catch them out and they haven't a leg to stand on. They imply that they could vindicate themselves completely if only they were free to tell all, but they are too honourable to do so: *Courageous Silence*.

(Lynn and Jay, *The Complete Yes Minister*, 1989: 93–4)

Let's look at this example working through the guidelines for Foucauldian analysis set out above:

a Track the historical development of the discourse over time and identify the players and the social, economic and political climate which fostered its development.

This is a standard historical discourse played out by officials in the British Civil [Public] Service to keep new government ministers, regardless of which party they represent, in a state of inaction. The players are the new Labour 'Minister of Administrative Affairs', the Head of the Civil [Public] Service, the naturally conservative Sir Humphrey, and Bernard, a civil servant to whom the Minister is talking. 'Tom' was the previous incumbent of the same ministerial position who has decided to enlighten his successor regarding the mechanisms by which Sir Humphrey controls ministers.

b Identify constituents in terms of objects, statements, themes, arguments, traces of challenges, traces of ideas which changed directions.
c Seek disunity and discontinuity and the limits to the discourse. Monitor dispersion in other fields.

Power relations: The endless conflict between a new minister bent on bringing about change and the established system of the Civil Service which maintains the status quo via resistance and obfuscation to ensure that minimal transformation occurs.

Discourses evident: Power of the system in maintaining the status quo through resistence and stalling techniques. These stalling techniques are stage-based and may also include types of silence. The limits to the maintenance of power are becoming obvious as the Minister becomes more informed about the methods of resistance he is to encounter. Information from a previous minister provides a challenge to the smooth maintenance of the officials' obstructive discourse. Ministerial knowledge could potentially have the capacity to break service resistance and enable the new minister's desire for change or even allow the needs of the general populace to be met.

d Locate challenges and see what happened to these: Where did they come from? Why? And if they were rejected, how were they dispensed? and by whom? for what purpose?

Challenges are coming from the Minister via Tom (whose agenda is unclear but he may have challenged previously or has decided to challenge Sir Humphrey indirectly through the current minister) – not only to create change but also to use insider knowledge to pre-empt the five stages (too early, positive support, wrong timing, policy in difficulties and too late to do anything) together with the techniques of discrete, stubborn and courageous silence) as he identifies Sir Humphrey attempting these. At this point success is unclear.

A more detailed analysis would track these processes much more precisely both in terms of other ministers' experiences and the success or otherwise of their challenges, and the long-term impact of stalling techniques on policy and practice.

Foucauldian discourse analysis: research examples

Julie Hepworth (1999) used a Foucauldian approach to examine over 100 years of published medical articles relating to *anorexia nervosa* – all those published since the emergence of the term in 1874 – in order to identify relevant discourses. She also conducted interviews with current health professionals. The cultural and historical underpinnings of the diagnosis were situated in the view that the illness appeared as a result of the failure of middle-class women to move without fuss into their pre-ordained domestic roles (Hepworth and Griffin, 1990). In the rapid orientation of the documentation toward psychological aetiology and over time, five discourses were exposed:

1 *femininity* – women as emotional, deviant, irrational and perverse psychological, mental and reproductive entities
2 *medical* – the search for scientific organic causes
3 *clinical* – the prescriptive treatments and the (moral) quality of relationships
4 *discovery* – the link between medicine and psychiatry
5 *hysteria* (the link between femininity and the psycho-medical framework through the notion of femininity.

The power of medicine in the maintenance of the enduring discourse of femininity (irrational female behaviour) was revealed. The conclusion was that the coherent set of linguistic practices evident since the late nineteenth century has been very influential.

Gemma Yarwood (2011) undertook a structuralist Foucauldian discursive analysis of fathering and masculinity talk in the United Kingdom. She interviewed nine employed first-time fathers over four years to investigate how the aspect of paid work and traditional familial roles presented challenges in the daily negotiation of fathering–work identities. She unearthed a multiplicity of identities for these men as they negotiated the dominant and powerful constructs of masculinity in terms of breadwinner fathers which continued to challenge the increasing notions of men as nurturers and carers of their children. She found these men to be discursive agents utilising fluid identities in the struggle to manipulate the institutional norms of fatherhood.

Limitations of Foucauldian analysis

- The focus on language has been seen to exclude other contextual experiences that may be relevant.
- Language may also be problematic depending on whether it is seen as structuralist in meaning or poststructuralist (transitional) as well as having single or multiple meanings.

ANALYTIC APPROACHES FOR EXISTING DOCUMENTATION

- Feminists have criticised Foucault for not addressing the social position of women as being different from powerless groups in general, noting that this has impacted on the historical production of gender relations and a range of associated discourses.
- The absence of praxis – actually doing something about any imbalances of power that have been uncovered – is another criticism but Foucault has made it clear that he was only seeking to expose the complexity and discontinuity of the discourses that dominate Western culture.

2. Critical discourse analysis (CDA)

Norman Fairclough initiated CDA in 1989. This form of discourse analysis takes an aspect from Michael Foucault and develops it; if social practices are discursively shaped and enacted, then linguistic analysis should help to clarify the relationships among discursive practices, texts and events, and social structure and process (see Figure 20.1). In this analysis we would expect to uncover not only these connections but also social inequalities, hierarchies of power and non-democratic practice (Fairclough, 1993).

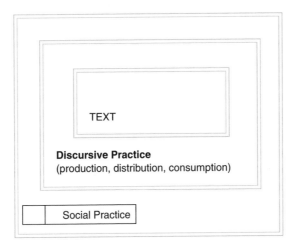

Figure 20.1   Three-dimensional conception of discourse (Fairclough, 1992)

The theoretical underpinnings to CDA come out of the critical theorist tradition – Karl Marx to Jürgen Habermas as well as positions from Michael Foucault and Pierre Bourdieu which imply that knowledge can lead to power or at least to empowerment.

The basic premise of CDA is that discourse is shaped by social groupings, culture and constructs, and has the power to limit our knowledge and beliefs. On a practical level three things interact (Fairclough, 2000):

the text (representing facts, beliefs and events, identity construction and interpretation)

discursive practices (the rules, norms, behaviours, speech, social identities and hierachies that maintain power and create responses to the text, for example, doctors have white coats and stethoscopes and are highly educated regarding complex literature which baffles those not educated in this language); and

the broad social context (hospital, surgery etc.).

The basic principles that underpin CDA (adapted from Fairclough and Wodak, 1997: 271–80) are as follows:

- The focus in CDA is social problems.
- Power is developed and maintained in society by discursive practices.
- Discourses reproduce historical inequalities.
- A sociocognitive approach can expose the links between text and society.
- Systematic discourse analysis involves investigation and interpretation of content and context.
- Social action is part of CDA.

Like Foucauldian discourse analysis, CDA has no clear stage-by-stage strategies only some general guidelines. This allows you considerable flexibility in how you approach the task. Past researchers have used a mix of approaches from conversational analysis, narrative analysis, ethnographic content analysis and semiotic linguistic approaches. Fairclough (2007) interwove three approaches: language textual analysis, processes of discourse production and analysis of events as instances of sociocultural practice. Interpretation involved *micro* (syntax and metaphor); *meso* (text production and consumption and power relations); and *macro* (intertextual understanding of the contemporary societal situation).

In attempting to put this into a usable form Thomas Huckin (1997) has suggested the following guidelines may be helpful:

- **Identifying framing**

    o Read the text twice: first in a general manner, next more critically within the expected structure of its genre
    o Identify strategies of placement (headings, graphs, pictures, keywords, etc.)
    o Note what could have been said (but wasn't)
    o Identify whose voices are used and whose are missing?

- **Interpretation**

    o Note use of sentences – how many on one aspect of a topic how many on another?
    o Who is depicted as powerful? Who is passive? Why?
    o Note use of passive verbs to focus on one aspect.
    o Question statements the author is taking for granted.
    o Note insinuations to take power from people (minimising, comparing with others).
    o Note connotations, such as 'terrorist' versus 'freedom fighter'.
    o Note use of uncertainty (may, might, should, could) to slant information.
    o Register: Is it optimism? Is it scepticism? Does it use direct quotes (more legitimate) or third-person comment (less powerful)?

Example of CDA

We will take again the *Yes Minister* extract used earlier in this chapter to demonstrate Foucauldian discourse analysis and attempt a critical discourse analysis on it:

> *The Minister*: Humphrey's system for stalling. According to Tom, it's in five stages. I made a note during our conversation, for future reference.

Stage One: Humphrey will say that the administration is in its early months and there's an awful lot of other things to get on with.

Stage Two: If I persist past Stage One, he'll say that he quite appreciates the intention, something certainly ought to be done – but is this the right way to achieve it?

Stage Three: If I'm still undeterred he will shift his ground from how I do it to when I do it, i.e. 'Minister, this is not the time, for all sorts of reasons.'

Stage Four: Lots of Ministers settle for Stage Three according to Tom. But if not, he will then say that the policy has run into difficulties – technical, political and/or legal. (Legal difficulties are best because they can be made totally incomprehensible and can go on for ever.)

Stage Five: Finally, because the first four stages have taken up to three years, the last stage is to say that 'we're getting rather near to the run-up to the next general election – so we can't be sure of getting the policy through'. ... He also warned me of the 'Three Varieties of Civil Service Silence', which would be Humphrey's last resort if completely cornered:

1 The silence when they do not want to tell you the facts: *Discreet Silence*.

2 The silence when they do not intend to take any action: *Stubborn Silence*.

3 The silence when you catch them out and they haven't a leg to stand on. They imply that they could vindicate themselves completely if only they were free to tell all, but they are too honourable to do so: *Courageous Silence*.

(Lynn and Jay, *The Complete Yes Minister*, 1989: 93–4)

Structure, placement and voice   This text is structured in stages 1–5 to emphasise the progressive shifts as the Minister moves into his role and how each stage can be counteracted. The types of silence are also numerically ordered from 1 to 3. The use of numbers provides a focus for the reader/listener, keeps their attention and provides emphasis. The first three stages are of similar length and quite short while stages 4 and 5 are increasingly longer. The three varieties of civil service silence follow the same pattern, with the third one being considerably longer than the first two.

The only voice heard is that of the Minister reporting to Bernard what he has heard from Tom.

Interpretation   Power is central to this debate and is complex; it appears to lie with the Civil Service and Sir Humphrey but this may shift and change now the Minister has inside information regarding approaches to creating stalemates and he plans to use it to become more powerful than Sir Humphrey. Tom has also shared his powerful knowledge with the current Minister. Another complicating factor in the power retention area is that the Minister is talking to Bernard, a civil servant in the employ of Sir Humphrey, so he may well shift/support the balance of power in one of two ways – he may inform Sir Humphrey of the Minister's knowledge and thus set in train a new set of strategies or he may say nothing, leaving power with the Minister. The Minister, however, may well be deliberately telling Bernard this information to cut short Sir Humphrey's strategies as they will now be recognisable to them both. The future location of power is very unclear.

The passive and active verbs are neatly balanced into an 'if this then that' mode of situation and strategic action. Connotations are legal – obfuscation and delay.

The overall tone is optimistic and positive without uncertainty – the Minister is on a high at having discovered the strategies of the Civil Service and is planning to use this information to his benefit.

CDA: Research example

Catherine Compton-Lilly (2011) tracked discourses about literacy and schooling as they impacted on one African American middle-school student and members of her family. The study took eight years of interview transcripts and field notes. Compton-Lilly found that the discourses of space, school, literacy and literacy practices shifted and changed over time as they were selectively taken up, challenged, negotiated, and/or abandoned. Aspects of uncaring teachers, fairness, sharing books, getting pushed through school, the community as a 'ghetto', inequities between suburban and urban schools, identity, and the need for parental agency involving letter writing and school visits on behalf of the student, all contributed to these discourses. Further, multiple, intertextual language resources of familial members' past life experiences were used to create meanings and understandings of present discourses and the current student's experiences at school. Again, these intertextual meanings were negotiated rather than linear entities for explanation, comparison or for discarding.

Criticisms of CDA

- If action and emancipation are core to CDA how will they be evaluated as outcomes?
- How systematic is CDA analysis, linguistically speaking?
- Is the political analysis actually derived from systematic analysis of the language or is this shaped and used to further researcher political interests?
- Are people active agents who can identify and resist oppression or can they recognise it but are too conditioned to act effectively?
- Has the dynamic and multiple nature of individuals and their different interpretations over time been adequately recognised?

Summary

From this you can see that CDA tends to focus more on words and language structure but ultimately the analyses between the two approaches would not be dissimilar in outcome. Although Michael Foucault and Norman Fairclough did not provide specific directions for the process of undertaking their forms of discourse analysis, guidelines can be derived from their writings and applied to the identification of discourses and to a clarification of which discursive practices have held particular discourses in place in a particular discipline or in society. However, like all forms of qualitative research, discourse analysis has had its share of creative adaptation by researchers, resulting in the dilution of method and the development of hybrid approaches through the addition of content, narrative, conversational, feminist, critical, grounded theory and other analytical entities. In some cases the aspects of power, hegemony and language in context have been lost, leaving the label 'discourse' attached to what is largely thematic analysis.

Further reading

Discourse analysis: method and practice

Andrejevic, M. (2004) *Reality TV: The Work of Being Watched*. Lanham, MD: Rowman and Littlefield. Critical Media Studies: Institutions, Politics, and Culture series. This is a detailed explanation of the discourses of reality TV: its history, its seductive interactivity with audiences and the notions of the use of surveillance.

Cordella, M. (2004). *The Dynamic Consultation: A Discourse Analytical Study of Doctor–Patient Communication*. Amsterdam: Benjamins. The focus here is the dynamic interaction and forms of talk used by both doctors and patients during consultations in an outpatient clinic in Chile.

Levine, P. and Scollon, R. (eds) (2004). *Discourse and Technology: Multimodal Discourse Analysis*. Washington, DC: Georgetown University Press. Looks at the complexities of multimodal discourse including: cell phones, video recorders, visuals, Internet chat rooms, online journals, speech, gesture and the landscape of text making.

Speer, S. (2005) *Gender Talk: Feminism, Discourse and Conversation Analysis*. London and New York: Routledge. This text links feminism, gender and discourse with ethnomethodology, conversation analysis and discursive psychology.

Thiesmeyer, L. (ed.) (2003) *Discourse and Silencing: Representation and the Language of Displacement*. Amsterdam: Benjamins. The filtering of knowledge in discursive language communication is the focus here. Examples are provided from courtroom trials, domestic violence, censorship, marital discussions, news media and penal institutions.

Critical discourse analysis: method and practice

Bayley, P. (ed.) (2004) *Cross-cultural Perspectives: Parliamentary Discourse*. Amsterdam: Benjamins. This collection of nine papers focuses on parliamentary talk in Western democracies – European (British, Swedish, German, Italian, Spanish) and United States and Mexican settings are examined from a cross-cultural perspective. Using functional linguistics and critical discourse analysis.

Fairclough, N., Cortes, G. and Ardizzone, P. (eds) (2007) *Discourse and Contemporary Social Change*. pp. 281–316. Bern: Peter Lang. CDA within contemporary social changes.

van Dijk, T. (ed.) (2007) *Discourse Studies*, 5 vols. Sage Benchmarks in Discourse Studies series. London: Sage. The critical discourse studies or sociocognitive approach to discourse analysis is detailed here.

Wodak, R. and Meyer, M. (eds) (2009) *Methods of Critical Discourse Analysis*. London: Sage. This book provides an introduction to Critical Discourse Analysis (CDA), appropriate for both novice and experienced researcherś.

Wooffitt, R. (2005) *Conversation Analysis and Discourse Analysis: A Comparative and Critical Introduction*. London: Sage. This is specially helpful for students grappling with the difference between CA and the many varieties of discourse analysis.

References

Compton-Lilly, C. (2011) Literacy and schooling in one family across time. *Research in the Teaching of English*, 45 (3) : 224–51.

Fairclough, N. (1989) *Language and Power*. London: Longman.

Fairclough, N. (1992) *Discourse and Social Change*. Cambridge: Polity Press.

Fairclough, N. (1993) Critical discourse analysis and the marketisation of public discourse: the universities. *Discourse & Society*, 4 (2): 133–68.

Fairclough, N. (2000) *Language and Power* (2nd edn). New York: Longman.

Fairclough, N. (ed.) (2007) *Discourse and Contemporary Social Change*. Bern: Peter Lang.

Fairclough, N. and Wodak, R. (1997) Critical discourse analysis. In Teun A. van Dijk (ed.), *Discourse as Social Interaction*. London: Sage. pp. 258–84.

Foucault, M. (1970) *The Order of Things*. Random House: New York City.

Foucault, M. (1972) *The Archaeology of Knowledge* (trans. A. Sheridan Smith). London: Tavistock.

Hepworth, J. (1999) *The Social Construction of Anorexia Nervosa*. London: Sage.

Hepworth, J. and Griffin, C. (1990) The 'discovery' of anorexia nervosa: discourses of the late nineteenth century. *Text* 10: 32138.

Huckin, T.N. (1997) Critical discourse analysis. In T. Miller (ed.), *Functional Approaches to Written Text*. New York: Wiley Interscience. Available at http://eca.state.gov/education/engteaching/pubs/BR/functionalsec3_6.htm (accessed 25 July 2011).

Lynn, J. and Jay, A. (1989) *The Complete Yes Minister*. London: BBC Books.

Yarwood, G. (2011) The pick and mix of fathering identities. *Fathering*, 9 (2): 150–68.

PART 5

Data management using qualitative computer programs

This section discusses the advent and uses of coding versus themes as a preliminary introduction to an overview of the computer packages that support the management of larger qualitative databases.

The two chapters in this section are:

TWENTY ONE

Coding

Coding involves the grouping and labelling of data in the process of making it more manageable both for display and to provide answers to the research question/s. However, in the language of qualitative research 'codes' and 'themes' have become interchangeable and researchers need to be transparent about how they are utilising such labels in the data analytic process.

KEY POINTS

- Coding is a fairly recent phenomenon and has been reinforced by:
  - grounded theory methods
  - computer management of data

Introduction

When to use: When using qualitative computer management programs or if, when and as decided by the researcher.

Type of questions best suited: any, but most useful where a large amount of data has been collected.

Strengths: One way of breaking into the data set.

Weaknesses: Can decontextualise data.

Background

The process of analysis in qualitative research is one that moves from description to interpretation via some identified process. The advent of the notion of coding as opposed to just identifying the dominant themes in your database (thematic analysis, see Chapter 5) occurred in the mid 1960s with Barney Glaser and Anselm Strauss's publication of their text on grounded theory (see Chapter 7). Possibly in order to separate out this new approach from more generic qualitative approaches the terms 'coding' and 'categories' were used. Coding in this context referred mainly to specific processes of open coding with its intensive critiquing of the data, and axial coding with its grouping or consolidating of related data segments around a central concept or label or category. From this time the twin notions of coding and thematic analysis have tended to be enacted either:

- *separately* or
- *sequentially*, with either thematic analysis preceding coding or, more recently,
- with coding preceding thematic analysis.

The advent of computer management programs in qualitative research in the mid-1980s placed further emphasis on the notion of coding as an essential process of breaking the data up into segments (be it words, phrases, sentences, lines or paragraphs) to suit the capacity of the program to be used.

So where does this leave the researcher? Several questions spring to mind:

- If not undertaking grounded theory or using computer management, do you need to code? (*Answer: No*)
- Is coding an essential and mandatory part of undertaking qualitative data analysis? (*Answer: No*)
- Can coding be undertaken without thematic analysis? (*Answer: Yes*)
- Where does thematic analysis fit? It is the preferred approach when data themes are allowed to emerge naturally without categorical imposition. Can it be undertaken without coding? (*Answer: Yes*)
- Have the terms 'codes' and 'themes' simply become different terms for similar processes? (*Answer: Yes – in some cases*)

It is impossible to give finite responses to some of these questions because it is really up to you the researcher to decide what terms you are planning to use, to explain how you are using them and to make your processes and justifications transparent to the reader. But do be aware that there are no set rules here.

That is not to say that there are no guidelines as to how the terms 'coding', 'categorising' and 'thematic analysis' are being used, nor that there are no detailed exposures of what researchers do in the analysis of their data.

Processes: thematic analysis/coding/ categorising/seeking patterns

A fairly extensive exploration of terminology usage within published articles using qualitative approaches without computer assisted data management leads this author to the conclusion that although individual researchers have often provided detailed definitions and complex stage-based guidelines for their analytic processes there appears to be considerable slippage of terminology across the field between what constitutes themes and codes and how these two elements might be achieved. Equally, there is considerable diversity of process demonstrated, with some researchers going from codes to themes, others from themes to codes and yet others using only themes or only codes. However, stepping back, the general process of data analysis appears to involve some basic stages, regardless of which terms are being used.

Stages of qualitative data analysis

1 The process is an iterative or recursive one, involving you becoming familiar with your completed database through moving backwards and forwards across it, reading, re-reading and comparing aspects until you are sure of what it contains.

2 Bearing in mind your research aim, the research questions which have provided the prime focus of your study, any relevant theoretical frameworks previously identified and the literature you have reviewed, go though your transcribed database and block/underline/colour key segments and write descriptive comments alongside in the margins. In particular seek to let the data speak for itself, allowing you to identify informants' statements about beliefs, attitudes, values, explicit ideas and ideologies as well as behaviour patterns, actions and events.

3 These identified segments are then matched with relevant like segments across the database and grouped.

4 Within these groupings, overarching labels are attached and sub-groupings identified.

5 These groupings are then conceptualised and linked more directly with literature and theory as you move to data display and writing up.

Theme identification

Themes have variously been referred to as: groupings; outcomes of coding/conceptualising; abstract constructs; and analytic patterns. Few texts provide instructions about how to undertake the discovery of themes but Gery Ryan and Russell Bernard (2003) have detailed the potential sources of themes as: *repetition* (repetition = theme); *indigenous typologies* – meaningful terms from the data, e.g. 'D dees' (dead democracy) referring to rubber stamp type management meetings; *KWIC* – seeking examples of key words in context; *metaphors*, e.g., 'work as a prison'; *change events and their impact on participants*; *comparison* (between text segments); *contextual explanations*; *participants causal explanations for events*; and *participant silence* on issues of relevance.

Coding

There is overlap here with theme identification, where coding is seen as a grouping and labelling process or identification of themes via a labelling process.

What is involved in coding?

Aspects of the data are coded (assigned a letter, a number, or phrase tag) for identification, later amalgamation and finally for ease of retrieval along with related elements.

What skills do you need to code?

- **A broad view** – the capacity to stay above your data to see it in the wider context rather than to become bogged down in every quotable quote or story.
- **Theoretical sensitivity** – the capacity to link your data to theory/your literature – for interpretation.
- **A love of ordering** but the capacity to understand that not all data will fit neatly into your developing coding system.
- **An unfazeable personality** when your messy data ends up fitting into many codes.
- **A good memory** to recall where you have come across something similar in another part of the data.

What is usually coded?

- themes
- theoretical concepts
- key words
- participants' narratives/stories, behaviours, values, interpretations, situations, relationships and states of mind
- events
- policies
- methodological issues
- researcher's views
- settings/environments
- metaphors and similes or setting-related language
- strategies.

How are these codes identified?

Kathy Charmaz has suggested asking the following questions of your data to understand better what is going on in the environment and to facilitate code formation:

- What is going on?
- What are people doing?
- What is the person saying?
- What do these actions and statements take for granted?
- How does structure and context serve to support, maintain, impede or change these actions and statements?
  (Charmaz, 2003: 94–5)

Coding terminology

Various computer programs and textbooks use a variety of terminology from:

nodes for codes (NVivo)
in vivo coding (using words in the text to create the code)
automatic coding (develop a code, define the parameters and use the query function to locate other like segments – using a dictionary to identify like terms)
free coding (assigning any code to a segment of data)
contextual coding (coding the words that give meaning and context)
supercodes (in ATLAS.ti–saved data queries)
memos (additional notes added to coded segments)
landscape coding (coding the physical features of the landscape)
intensive coding (using many codes in a small fragment of data).

Coding options

You can choose to:

1 code everything of relevance and develop themes/categories or major codes using computer/non-computer management programs

2 develop broad themes via thematic analysis approaches and then code all your data as a microcheck

3 summarise your data, edit and present in narratives or case studies (minimal/no coding)

4 Query the data on the basis of your predefined research question and develop some broad overall themes (minimal/no coding).

With such approaches as Phenomenology and Autoethnography, 3 or 4 would be the most likely options.

Taking one response to the question *'When did you first realise your child had a disability?'* you could attempt the first option and develop and attach codes (tags/labels) to all relevant aspects of the database, in this case part of an interview response. Each code can be marked/coloured to indicate the boundaries of the coded area and the extent of double/triple/quadruple coding and overlap.

Example

Response 1	*Codes*
He was 14 months old and my husband virtually had to threaten the doctor at X hospital to tell us what was wrong. We knew there was no sign of him (child) trying to sit up at the time. Very quiet, didn't move a lot, hardly cried – more a sort of a whine. The doctor was very evasive and my husband said 'We're not leaving until you tell us and you're not leaving until you tell us.' Then he called another doctor behind a screen and they had a whispered conversation. Then he came back. He felt 'there was a certain degree of retardation but no specific reason why'. He told me to continue on with what I was doing and he told me that once a month for four and a half years	**Parent behaviour to doctor** (P1 = Father, P2 = Mother, D = Doctor) P1→D (threatening) D→P1 (Poor communication) CC = Child Capacity (at 14 months) D→P1 (evasive) P1→D (threatening) D→P1 (self protective) MD (Medical Diagnosis) D→P1 & P2 (poor communication) D→P1 (advise) Use as quote

Once all labels and letters are attached, you will need to organise your codes into a coding list. You may develop up to several hundred codes in a large project but these will need to be reduced via amalgamation into broader categories/themes/codes and subcategories/subthemes/subcodes for writing up, data display and interpretation.

Coding for qualitative computer data management

Taking the three most popular 'theory generating' computer management programs – NVivo, ATLAS.ti and MAXQDA (see Chapter 22) – we can take a take a quick look at what is involved in coding in these programs.

NVivo

Documents can either be imported from word and coded on screen *or* they can be coded off screen and then imported and sent to files. The boundaries of the segments you are coding can be marked in the margin with coding stripes which are colour-coded. Memos can also be written at the same time and attached to coded segments.

Figure 21.1 illustrates what this process looks like on screen. This screenshot comes from online QDA data analysis learning on the web. Here the researcher is working within the free nodes option to develop a 'dancing' node. The other nodes that have already been attached to the surrounding transcript are shown on the right-hand side. Other coding approaches within this program could involve using word frequency for individual words such as 'dancing' or undertaking a text search for more complex issues like 'carer's allowance'. Automatic coding involves pre-defining a

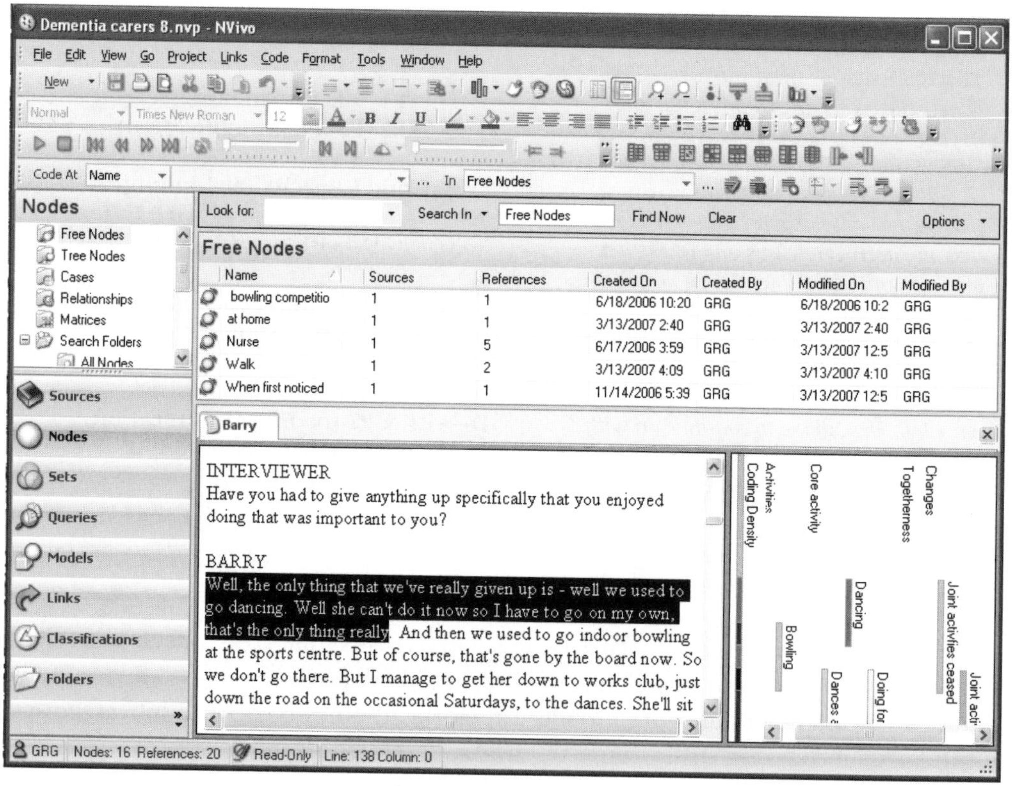

Figure 21.1   NVivo screenshot http://onlinegda.hud.ac.uk/Step_by_step_software/NVivo/NVivo8/NVivo8_coding.php (accessed 1 August 2012)

node, say responses to a particular question such as 'joint activities ceased', and coding and storing the responses under that node for later examination and sorting.

MAXQDA

Using MAXQDA (Figure 21.2) the same processes occur and files, including PDFs, can be imported and interviews coded on or off screen. Coding on screen occurs by highlighting sections, choosing names and code colours and attaching memos. Pre-assigned or in vivo (from the text) codes are options and all codes are hierarchically arranged and can be displayed in a matrix. Here the code is 'colonialism', and the issues of 'identity', and 'expert' and 'general' views are being coded.

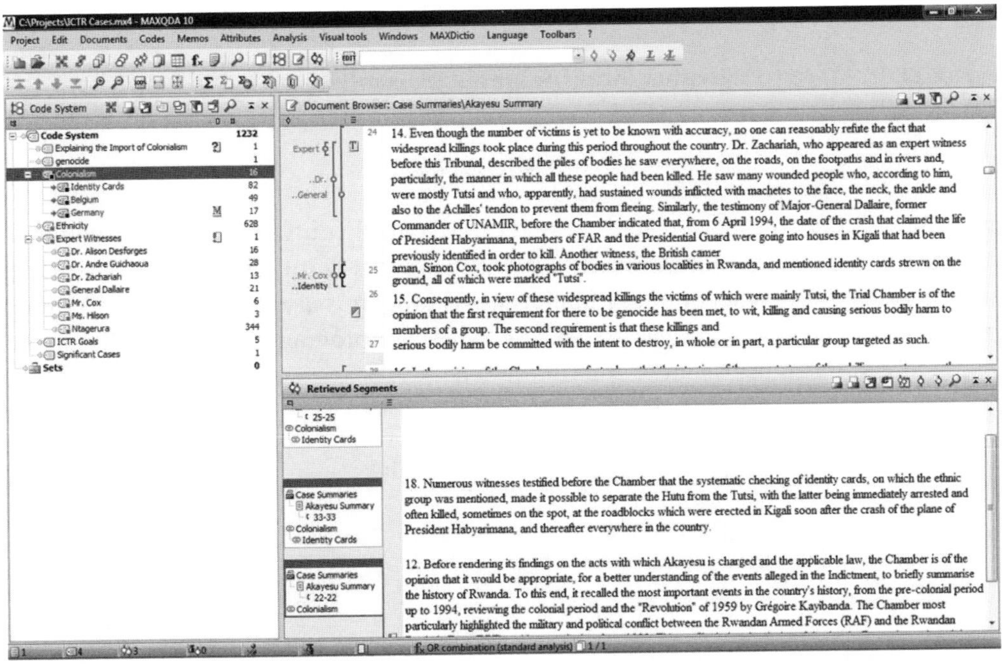

Figure 21.2   MAXQDA 10 screenshot (http://www.maxqda.com/products/screenshots)

ATLAS.ti

The ATLAS.ti program (Figure 21.3) has the same capacities as MAXQDA and NVivo including the importation of PDF files and video, graphic and Google Earth documents. Data is placed on the left and codes and notes on the right. Here a newspaper article about a Welsh road sign containing an email reply instead of a translated warning is being coded for location and placed under the code 'lost in translation'.

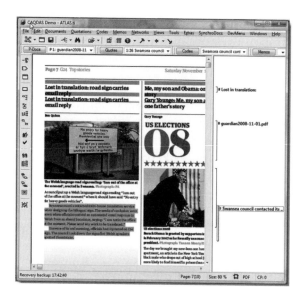

Figure 21.3 ATLAS.ti screenshot (http://www.soft-go.com/view/ATLAS-ti_79845.html)

Summary

The advent of coding has created some terminological confusion between the terms 'themes' and 'codes' but this can be dealt with by you clarifying how you are using these terms. Coding via computer management programs also has some terminological variation and you will need to get to know these programs and their idiosyncrasies before you can use them to the fullest extent.

Student exercise

Assume you want to code most of the information in the following interview transcript:

Transcript	Codes
It just happened. It's complicated because D came from England and couldn't get a work permit and couldn't get permanent residency so that I took over the breadwinner role and I became pregnant and he became very excited about that and he wanted to be with the baby and it didn't worry me because my job is very convenient and I enjoy doing it. We just stayed as we were. I could just get six months leave of absence not 12 months because I hadn't been employed long enough full-time, so I went back to work when G was only four months of age. But I was able to come home at lunchtimes. So it was really financial and political reasons why we swapped roles.	

Please visit the companion website **www.sagepub.co.uk/grbich2** for possible answers.

USING QUALITATIVE COMPUTER PROGRAMS

Further reading

Coding

Bernard, R. and Ryan, G. (2010) *Analysing Qualitative Data*. London: Sage. Clear and accessible for novices, with a particular focus in interviewing, thematic analysis and coding.

Liamputtong, P. (2009) *Qualitative Research Methods* (3rd edn). Melbourne: Oxford University Press.

O'Leary, Z. (2010) *The Essential Guide to Doing Your Research Project*. London: Sage. How to code and develop themes.

Saldaña, J. (2009) *The Coding Manual for Qualitative Researchers*. London: Sage.

Coding for qualitative computer management programs

Bazeley, P. (2007) *Qualitative Data Analysis with NVivo*. London: Sage.

Richards, L. (2009) *Handling Qualitative Data: A Practical Guide* (2nd edn). London: Sage. Data analysis with a focus on NVivo computer management.

References

Charmaz, C. (2003) Grounded theory: objectivist and constructivist methods. In N.K. Denzin and Y.S. Lincoln (eds), *Strategies of Qualitative Inquiry* (2nd edn). Thousand Oaks, CA: Sage. pp. 249–91.

Ryan, G. and Bernard, H.R. (2003) Techniques to identify themes. *Field Methods*, 15: 89–105. Retrieved from www.analytictech.com/mb870/Readings/ryan-bernard_techniques_to_identify_themes_in.htm (accessed 17 November 2011).

TWENTY TWO

An overview of qualitative computer programs

This chapter will detail a brief history of the development of qualitative computing packages and will list a number of available programs and indicate their capacities while also providing a critical assessment of the impact of such packages on the qualitative analytical process. The chapter is illustrated with a number of screenshot examples, which are taken from individual program websites unless otherwise stated.

KEY POINTS

- Qualitative computing packages comprise three main types:
  - code and retrieve
  - theory generation
  - content analysis
- These programs provide useful tools but you need to be aware of their pitfalls and limitations

---

A brief history

The development of computing packages has undergone three distinct developmental eras since their emergence around 35 years ago:

1 Systematisation: code and retrieve
2 Theory generation
3 Analysis of content

1. Systematisation: code and retrieve programs

The notion of systematic data emerged in the 1970s following an earlier push for more rigorous data that included moves toward quantification and justification of findings. The major focus of these earlier programs was the storage, retrieval of data and the provision of sub-views of the data through the assigning of codes and categories (often termed 'code and retrieve' programs). Systematisation programs are usually *single file systems* (data) and require the marking of (often program-predefined) text segments and the attaching of codes to segmented data (either on or off screen). This process follows preliminary data analysis. Thematic data analysis can be undertaken before, after or instead of coding (see Chapter 21). The coded passages are then filed and stored with identification tags and sometimes memos are attached. These files can then be retrieved and printed out for further examination and consolidation. One of the more popular programs with researchers within this group is The Ethnograph, and this and another program, SuperHyperQual, are discussed below.

The Ethnograph 6.0 (PC) (www.qualisresearch.com/) is the most well developed of the cheaper code and retrieve programs. It can create and import data files, format the file and automatically save it as an 'ETH' file, import and number the file, and assign it to a project, with no limit on the number of data files. It can also rename, move, merge, duplicate, delete or back up projects as desired. The screenshot in Figure 22.1 shows the coding of segments relating to life change.

SuperHyperQual 1.4 (PC) (Mac) (http://hyperqual.on-rev.com/hyperqual/) handles structured and unstructured interviews, observations, documents and research memos. It can undertake manual, semi-automatic and automatic text tagging (coding) as well as flexible retagging of text chunks, editing of tag lists, management of multiple windows and the maintenance of a bibliographic database for literature reviews.

In terms of function, code and retrieve programs have largely been superseded by the more complex theory generation programs.

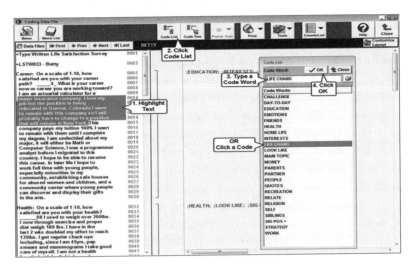

Figure 22.1   Ethnograph 6.0 screenshot

2. Theory generation programs

During the 1980s researchers at qualitative computing conferences recognised the benefits of the first generation of code and retrieve programs but pointed out their limitations, particularly their inability to address issues of 'validity', 'reliability' and 'generalisability', which some researchers still regarded as problematic. Another perceived limitation was the incapacity to facilitate combinations of qualitative and quantitative data and the lack of any capacity to undertake theory generation. These debates resulted in the development of a second generation of programs. These 'theory generation' programs comprise a *two-file system* (data and literature) and are often underpinned by the structural framework of grounded theory (in particular the constant comparative process that the researcher can operate between the two files). Relationships among coded categories in different folders within one file can be sought using the Boolean logic of 'and', 'or' and 'not' and conceptual and theoretical explanations for these can be sought in the other file. These processes can lead to proposition testing and the development and application of theoretical concepts. MAXQDA, NUD*IST, NVivo and ATLAS.ti have been popular programs within this tradition.

The development of these more sophisticated programs prompted further discussion regarding the methodological and theoretical implications of the use of computers to manage qualitative data (Fielding and Lee, 1991). Initial concerns expressed included the possible impact on the 'craft' of qualitative research and the moves toward 'control' rather than 'diagnosis' and toward 'explanation' rather than 'interpretation' (Lyman, 1984: 86–7). The potential for minimising the gap between variable-oriented (quantitative) and case-oriented (qualitative) research was also noted with concern, as was the potential for method to define substance (Friedham, 1984). Another concern was that computer-managed data would encourage 'quick and dirty' research or research that is over-interpreted through the abuse of complex indexing systems (Fielding and Lee, 1991: 7–8).

Theory generation programs: a brief overview of six

1. ATLAS.ti 6.2 (PC) (www.atlasti.com) has an object-oriented graphical user interface for processing large file formats – rtf, doc, txt, pdf, graphical, audio and video data, on-screen coding (drag and drop), no fixed definition of data segments, can highlight without coding, uses rhizomatic rather than hierarchical coding and groups codes into 'families'. It can simultaneously display data segments in context, can handle virtually unlimited numbers of documents, including codes and memos, and can integrate all relevant material: primary texts, codes, annotations and theories into separate files. It facilitates 'mind mapping', multiple visual documents, graphical network editing, semi-automatic coding with multi-string text search and pattern matching, Word frequency counts and an SPSS interface are included. It can also manage hypertext links, hypotheses, survey data, word frequencies, and has end-on SPSS and a networking capacity. Figure 22.2 shows a list of research questions relating to the financial crisis of 2008–2009 organised in ATLAS.ti Memo Manager showing lists of major memo groups.

2. Rocket FolioVIEWS (Mac, PC) (www.thefiengroup.com/np-views.html) is used for browsing and editing graphic, sound and video objects but particularly books. It supports memo writing, hypertext linking of text segments and some theory building. Figure 22.3 shows a screen displaying an overview of books listed and their contents.

3. HyperRESEARCH 2.6 (Mac, PC) (www.researchware.com/) can deal with rich text and has advanced multimedia capabilities for text, graphic, audio and video data. The screenshot in Figure 22.4 shows a general screen display for coding organisation.

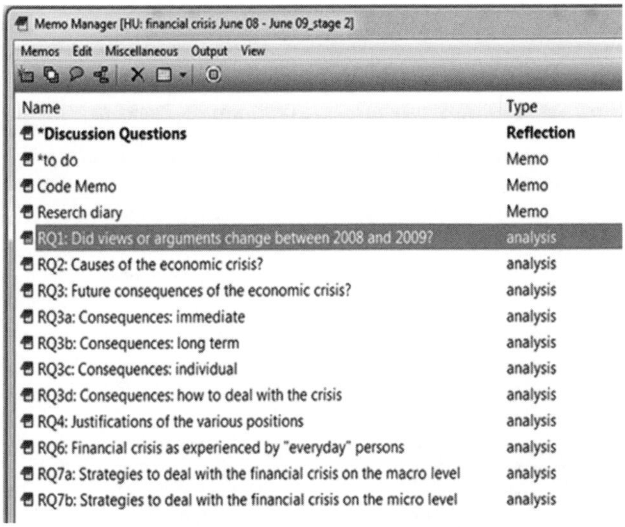

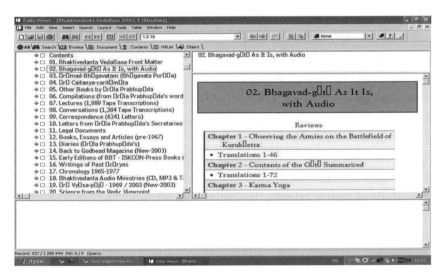

Figure 22.2   A screenshot of ATLAS.ti Memo Manager from a study by Susanne Friese (Friese, 2011). Research question memos start with the prefix RQ

Figure 22.3   Rocket Folio VIEWS screenshot

4. MAXQDA 10 (PC) (www.maxqda.com/maxqda-eng/index.htm) is the successor of the software package winMAX. It has a theory testing and theory generating capacity, is user-friendly, can cope with large volumes of data and is stable and fast. It links to SPSS and content analysis packages (word frequencies and dictionaries) as well as to MS Office and MS Internet Explorer. Its general coding screen is shown in Figure 22.5.

5. NVivo 9 (Mac, PC) (www.qsr.com.au/) is designed for multimedia data and allows researchers to import and export data to and from statistical packages and to merge

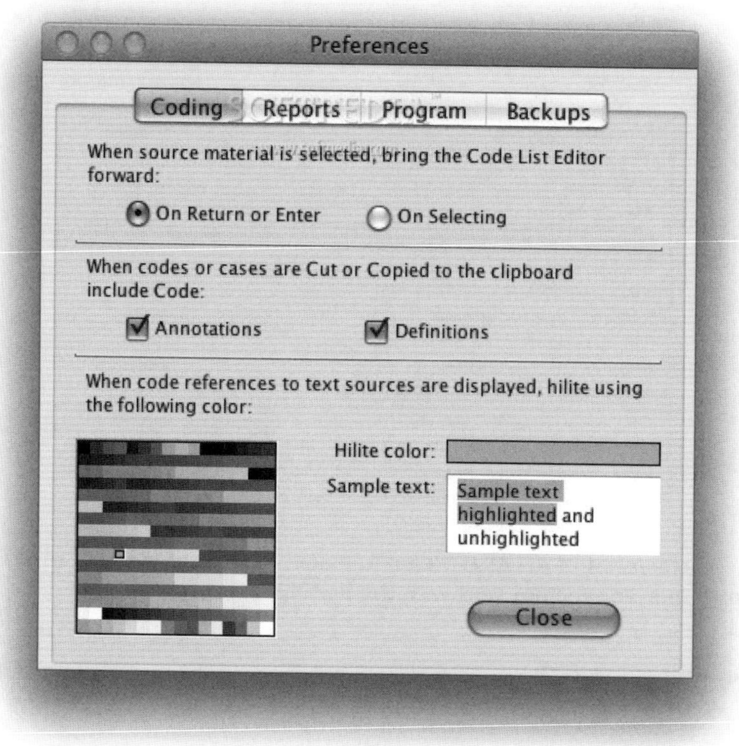

Figure 22.4 HyperRESEARCH screenshot (image from http://mac.softpedia.com/ progScreenshots/HyperRESEARCH-Screenshot-1777.html)

projects. It facilitates rich text analysis, flexible interpretations, memos, development of matrices, modelling and framing. It uses hierarchical coding but there is a free category. *NVivo Server 9* enhances teamwork and has tools for managing, monitoring and comparing contributions of team members. The screenshot shown in Figure 22.6 places coded interview data next to a visual image of the area being discussed.

6. NUD*IST N6 (Mac, PC) (www.qsr.com.au/) is a heavy-duty program with an old Windows 2 interface, used for large-scale projects and mixed methods allowing the import and export of data to and from statistical packages. It allows rapid coding, pattern seeking and hypothesis testing.

Although some of the theory generating programs have incorporated content analysis functions, content analysis programs are becoming increasingly sophisticated in their own right.

3. Content analysis

These packages are useful tools for breaking into text. Most have the capacity to undertake:

- *word frequencies* – indicating how often each word occurs in a document
- *category frequencies* – where synonyms are grouped into categories and the program shows how many times each category occurs in the document

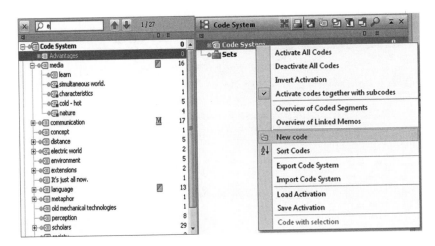

Figure 22.5   MAXQDA 10 screenshot

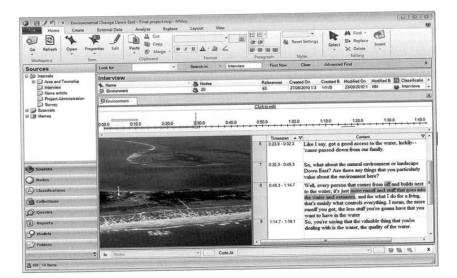

Figure 22.6   NVivo screenshot

- *KWIC* (key word in context) – which displays, in alphabetical order, each word together with a number of words on either side to provide information on its context in the document
- *cluster analysis* – where groups of words can be identified as being utilised in similar contexts
- *co-occurrence of pairs* of words – the more sophisticated of these programs are developing the capacity to attempt semiotic analysis and often include cultural grammars.

Content analysis programs: a brief overview of six

1. askSam 6 (www.asksam.com/solutions/research.asp) imports word processing documents, email, spreadsheets, webpages and PDF files. It sets up fields for keywords, categories, subjects and dates etc. and undertakes wildcard, fuzzy and proximity searches. Figure 22.7 illustrates the saving of webpages directly from Internet Explorer.

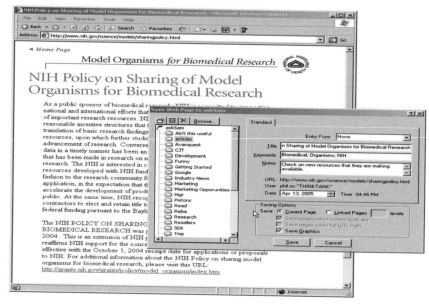

Figure 22.7 askSam screenshot

2. QDA Miner 3.2 (PC) (www.provalisresearch.com/QDAMiner/QDAMinerDesc.html) stores and edits documents in Rich Text format. Cases can contain up to 2,030 variables, including multiple documents, numeric nominal/ordinal data and Boolean values. Easy Windows handling and file importation can occur from Excel, Access, Paradox and dBase. Pictures embedded in text files can be retrieved and drag and drop assignment of codes with memos is facilitated, as is some automatic coding and coding by variable. An inter-coder agreement tool exists, and the WordStat program for data mining and SIMSTAT for statistical analysis are both attached. Visualisations of word maps can occur. QDA Miner is available in English, French and Spanish with multi-user and merge features. Codes can be suggested by the program and on the basis of acceptance or rejection the program 'learns' the orientation of the researcher. An explanation of a typical interface is shown in Figure 22.8.

3. TEXTPACK 7 (PC) (www.gesis.org/en/services/data-analysis/software/textpack/) under-takes word frequencies, keyword in context and keyword out of context, cross-references, concordances and word comparison of two texts. Figure 22.9 shows a table from a study by Daniel Coffey (2005) comparing US state governors' speeches using Textpak.

4. Wordcruncher 7.1 (PC) (www.wordcruncher.com/wordcruncher/default.htm) can index multiple texts up to ten levels. These can be either hierarchical (play, act, scene, line, etc.) or non-hierarchical (speakers, themes, etc.). Searches consist of words, phrases or multiple word searching using Boolean logic. An image library manager allows for the inclusion of graphics, and image maps with hyperlinks to other images can be created. Hyperlinks can also be created between graphics and text and for cross-referencing texts. Bookmarks and user notes allow for annotation. Figure 22.10 shows a list of typical search features.

USING QUALITATIVE COMPUTER PROGRAMS

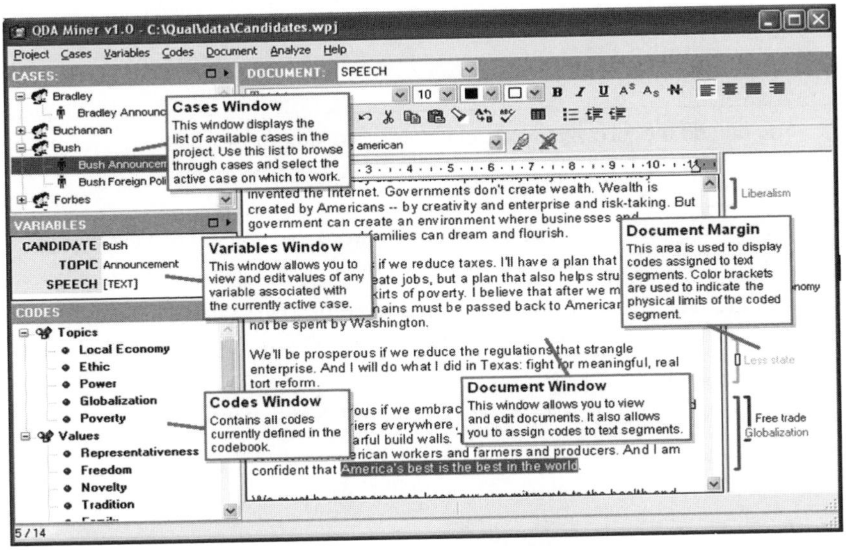

Figure 22.8   QDA Miner screenshot

Table 2.   Factor Loadings for Policy Categories on Dimensions of Gubernatorial Ideology

Ideological Category	Economic Dimension	Social Dimension
Budget	.54	.39
Economic development	.57	.19
Health and welfare	.74	−.08
Education	.61	.00
Law and order	.30	.38
Morality and civil rights	.01	.73
Environment	.01	.71
State regulation	.12	.15
Eigenvalue	1.94	1.09
Percentage of variance explained	24.30%	13.59%
N	93	

Note: These entries are rotated factor loadings from a principal-components factor analysis with varimax rotation. A third factor had an eigenvalue greater than one (1.06). This factor was not used to create an issue dimension since only one variable (state regulation) had a high loading on it.

Figure 22.9   Table from a study using TEXTPACK (Coffey, 2005)

5. WordStat 6.1 (PC) (www.provalisresearch.com/wordstat/wordstat.html) is used for content analysis and focus group transcripts, it undertakes Boolean and proximity searches, development of a dictionary tree and keyword frequency pages in and out of context. An 'unknown words' finder allows quick identification of misspelled words, acronyms, technical words and proper nouns. Cluster analyses and proximity searches are available for two keywords. Figure 22.11 shows a graphical display of words.

Type	Description
Single Word	You can do the following types of single word searches:

Source	Description
Text Window	Double click on any word and you will see every occurrence of that word.
Word Wheel	Double click on any words in the WordWheel and you will see every occurrence of that word.
Typed search	Type a word in the Search Edit Box and press enter. You will see every occurrence of that word.

Type	Description
Phrases	You can do the following types of phrase searches:

Source	Description
Text Window	Highlight a small block of words and right click. You will see a menu where you can select the type of search you wish to execute.
Word Wheel	You can highlight a group of words (single click the first word, [Ctrl] click the other words. You can press insert and add or replace all the words in the search edit box. Then if you press the Search Execute button you will see all the occurrences of all these words (they are OR'd together)
Typed exact phrase	Double quotes around a group of words finds all the occurrences of this group as an exact phrase (e.g. "and it came to pass").
Typed partial phrase	Putting single quotes around a group of words finds all the occurrences of this group within 7 words of the first word (e.g. 'faith hope charity').
Complex phrases with custom logic	Type individual words and insert custom logic between each word token (e.g. faith &.5,0 hope)

Type	Description
Wild Card Searches	You can do the following types of wild card searches:

Source	Description
Typed single word	There are two types of wild card characters: (1) Asterisk – it stands for 0 through n characters; (2) Question Mark – it stands for a single character. Some examples: *ing would find every word than ends in "ing"; re?d would match read, redd, reed, reid, and rend.
Typed phrases with custom logic	You can incorporate a wild card word into a complex search (e.g. hope &.3,0 *ing would find every word that ends in ing that comes within 3 words of hope

Figure 22.10   Wordcruncher table of search features

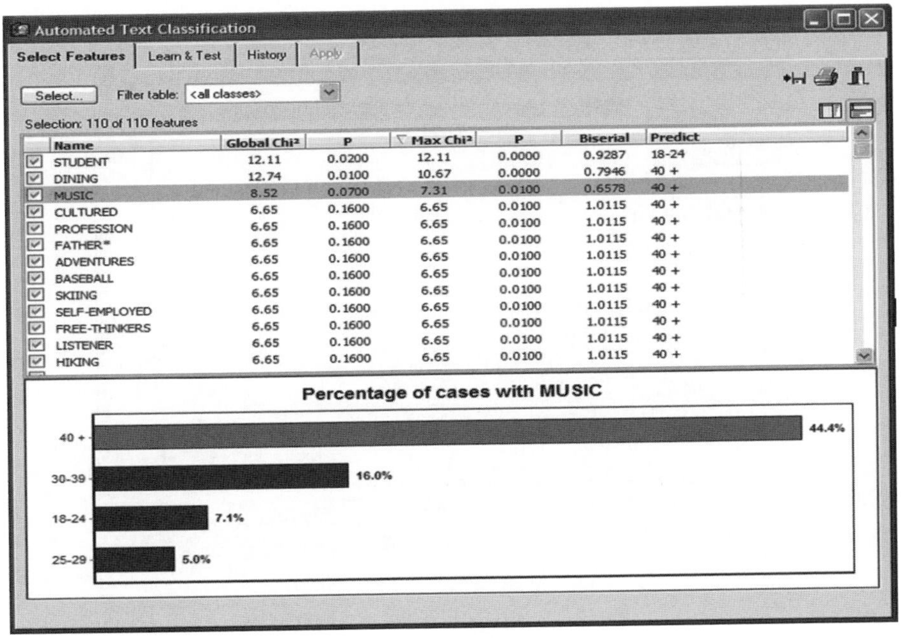

Figure 22.11   WordStat screenshot

6. ZyIndex (PC) (www.searchtools.com/tools/zyindex.html) provides a research tool for complete recall, appropriate in situations where any missing data could be catastrophic. Fast indexing of over 250 file formats, including HTML, PDF, Word, Excel, PowerPoint and Outlook, can occur. It integrates with ZyScan to make scanned documents searchable. Translated products for English, German, French, Dutch, Spanish, Italian, Danish, Swedish, Norwegian, Finnish, Portuguese, Turkish, Greek, Cyrillic and Arabic frequency and visual mapping capacities exist. The screens in Figure 22.12 demonstrates its word frequency and mapping capacities.

Visual data

Two of the available packages are discussed.

1. C Video (http://homepage.mac.com/jeremyroschelle/CVideo/index.html) can locate any video scene or segment in a 2-hour tape, take notes in any form and attach video start and end times to textual notes at the touch of a key. It can also link unlimited notes, transcripts and content logs to each video scene, search texts for any word or phrase, plug in to any TV, and can import and export notes to other Macintosh applications including NUD*IST.

2. Transana 2.4 (www.transana.org/) is freeware software for analysis of digital video or audio data. Keywords can be assigned to clips, creating complex collections of interrelated clips and allowing exploration of relationships between applied keywords. Multiple simultaneous users with multiple media files are easily managed. Figure 22.13 simultaneously shows a code in context and a visual clip with written transcript.

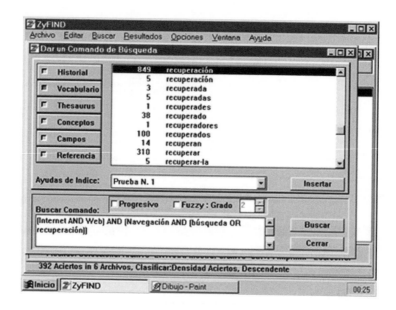

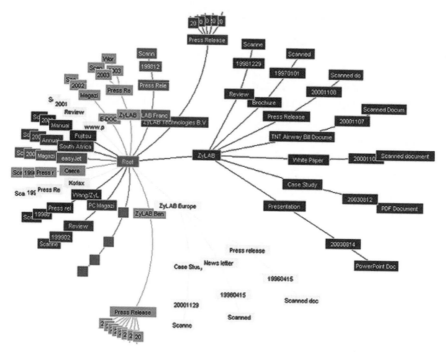

Figure 22.12 ZyIndex screenshots

Qualitative computing packages:
continuing concerns

Despite their obvious usefulness in the management of large databases, the concerns that emerged in the 1980s regarding these packages have persisted. The following is a summary of the major issues.

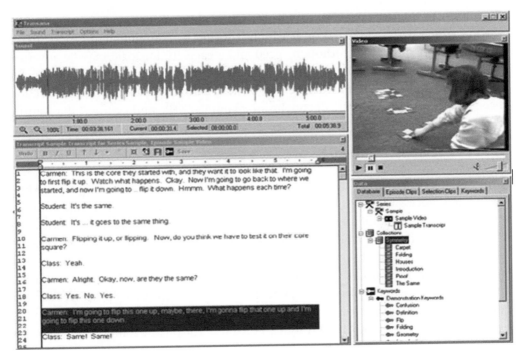

Figure 22.13 Transana screenshot

The tools of computer programs

In non-computer managed research data analysis and interpretation is a continually changing process that occurs from the initial stages of data collection to the final stages of data presentation. In placing a database into a computer package and separating it into program-specific coded portions, these fluid and overlapping processes are necessarily truncated, omitted or made invisible by the specific requirements of data segmentation and the structured coding, categorising, relinking and reinterpreting performances required by the computer program.

Tools constructed for a particular program must inevitably impact upon the data. Technologies carry with them symbolic meanings and divisions of labour (Pfaffenberger, 1988: 11–24). They texture our ways of thinking, reading and writing (Idhe, 1990: 141–3, 182–3). In creating computer tools for the management of data, we cannot avoid shaping both the outcomes of our data interpretation and our perceptions of these outcomes. Each tool creates artefacts and metaphors (frames) that are not neutral in effect and that change our ways of thinking and seeing. 'Reality' has to be segmented, truncated and textured to prepare data to 'fit' a particular form of programming. These procedural aspects are fundamentally reductionist and affect our views of the data as it moves from a complex, multifaceted reality of intersecting aspects embedded in rich contexts, to a simplified rational, decontextualised version that can be viewed as discrete groups of representations and subrepresentations.

These processes also promote procedural thinking (Rozak, 1994: 190) and high frequency logic, and have the capacity to enhance the distortion of time. The speed at which one can interact with data, atomising it and shifting it around, far exceeds the speed at which it was collected or at which it would be contemplated in a reflexive framing process off screen. Although speed and a capacity for logic may be advantageous in coping with computer technology, these may well foster superficial interpretations of qualitative data. The tendency for decontextualisation, massive overproduction of codes, and spurious theoretical conclusion abounds (Kelle and Laurie, 1995; Laurie, 1992; Seidel, 1991).

The framing of knowledge

In the framing of knowledge, frames can be seen as storage systems bounding areas, while the framing process is seen as formal and restrictive or as active, dynamic and ongoing with flexible frame boundaries. Two of the theory generating programs, NUD*IST and ATLAS.ti, reflect these possibilities. The inverted-tree framing structure of NUD*IST is very formal, bearing a close relationship with Metzing's (1980) cognitive frames for knowledge. Here, networks of 'nodes and relations' hang off a defined aspect or category. Adaptation of nodes and replacement frames are part of the continuing process of gaining new knowledge through processes of matching and accommodation. More flexible and in a non-hierarchical fashion, ATLAS.ti uses a horizontal rhizomatic frame, the boundaries of which are constantly evolving.

Despite this dynamic potential, one major limitation of any framing structure is its potential to gain a reified status, creating in the researcher a preference to confine and order, rather than to allow for constant transformation and change. The sequential and procedural approaches which are intrinsic to individual programs must inevitably structure thought processes and texture the data in particular ways. The act of enclosure within framing processes confines the data at an early stage within coded segments. Enclosure also serves to separate out the data from both the researcher and the context. Discovery then tends to be linear rather than chaotic and complex. It seems inevitable that these procedures must texture and simplify what we see, limiting the potential for change and transformation of both researcher and data in the research process (Grbich, 1998).

The texturing of reality

Currently, the programming languages that have been used as a basis for qualitative computing packages are either the very basic first- and second-generation languages with mechanical functions, or the third- to fifth-generation languages incorporating Boolean logic and true–false dichotomies. True–false dichotomies are based on the Boolean concept of minimisation that 'corresponds to the variable oriented experimental design' (Huber and Garcia, 1993: 145) in which single cases are compared. These rigorous mathematical approaches differentiate 'subjectivity' and foster the appearance of 'objectivity' (Guattari, 1984) through diagnosis and control. Units of data are treated as inert objects or 'input' (Murphy and Pardeck, 1988), further reinforcing the abstract model of segmentation, categorisation, comparison and relinking of data. Further, the rule-based approaches of computer programming have much in common with positivism. Views of reality are 'formal, discrete, reductionist, algorithmic, sequential, deterministic, mechanical, computational, atomised, digitalised, logical and rational' (Henman, 1992: 1). A close examination of qualitative computing packages supports this view. The separation of parts from the whole is a positivist rather than a qualitative approach.

The representations of 'reality' that are produced are based primarily on discreet objects, although fuzzy logic (where variables are less precise and can overlap) has been used in AQUAD (www.aquad.de/eng/index.html), a program developed by a psychologist to access implicit theories of an individual's view of self. Fuzzy logic allows movement from the narrow true–false dichotomy based in probability to the wider 'possibility' of truth (Zadeh, 1988), but this possibility, found in overlapping boundaries, is still seen as quantifiable.

The generation of theory in qualitative research requires intact thick description for thick interpretation (Denzin, 1988: 432). Much of the more recent 'impressionist' work (Van Maanen, 1988), done within postmodern ethnographic fieldwork, phenomenology and feminist approaches, requires minimally atomised data. Although re-presentations do occur, these are carefully reconstructed from rich, intact texts, a process that would not benefit from computer procedures.

Impact on knowledge

Computing programs are known for their capacity to texture reality. The gendering of technology through 'masculine' logic (Wajcman, 1991) is one area where texturing of reality has been identified as having the potential to distance women from involvement. The privileging of logic and rationality above lateral, multiperspective and creative thinking and the elevation of this form of information as authoritative (Nye, 1990) has led to a change in the nature of knowledge (Lyotard, 1984). The narrow focus on what stands as 'knowledge' has resulted in a silencing of female voices and a fragmentation of 'reality' (Bruhn and Lindberg, 1995; Henman, 1992). There is considerable potential for such minimal and decontextualised fragments to be hammered into a shape convenient to the purposes of the manipulator (Eco, 1994).

The capacity of programs to handle larger and larger data sets frees up researcher time but encourages more and more data to be collected. Although this may be advantageous in terms of allowing researchers access to both greater numbers and increased funding, it does beg the question of whether the collection of larger volumes of information will actually result in increased meaning. Baudrillard has argued that more information does not produce more meaning, it simply wears itself out in staging it through a 'bombardment of signs' (1980: 140). The continual coding and counting of what may be becoming increasingly decontextualised data (Henman, 1992) leads to the GIGO principle, 'Garbage In, Gospel Out' (Rozak, 1998) where this now meaningless information becomes trusted as 'gospel' findings. Jean Baudrillard (1980: 139) has pointed to the danger of the development of the hyperreal. Here the elevation of a particular approach to interpreting data (such as one involving complex coding and subcoding) serves to disguise the loss of meaning which is also involved. The outcomes of the imposition of this new frame appear more real than the original 'reality', which then becomes lost in the process.

Communication

Although networking facilities are available, especially for the more developed programs from the stables of MAXQDA, NUD*IST/NVivo and ATLAS.ti, these structured forms of communication (person-to-computer, computer-to-computer) bear little resemblance to the more usual processes of collaborative research. Here, face-to-face processes comprise spontaneous verbal arguments, hands-on data interaction and high-level theoretical/ conceptual discussions. These lose not only speed but flavour in the laborious type–send–wait–read/type–send–wait cycle of computer interaction.

Reification (or the glorification of the status of computer management)

The concept of reification emerges often within criticisms of qualitative computing packages. The first concern is the reification of the computer as a preferred way of defining the social world concisely and logically, where individuals become depersonalised and events neutralised (Dupuy, 1980). The second concern with reification is the relationship between the researcher and the data (Seidel, 1991). Once codes have been developed, they have a tendency to become objectified and treated as major explanatory foci. In addition, the reification of codes has led to them being regarded as variables to be looked at in terms of frequency of occurrence. This leads to inappropriate conclusions from the data (Laurie, 1992; Seidel, 1991).

Quantitative interfaces

The quantitative interface that has been developed in some programs through end-on statistical programs such as SPSS, also imposes additional frames, especially in relation to the differing paradigms of origin. Where the same data set is involved in both quantitative analysis and qualitative interpretation, issues of different sampling techniques and lack of variable control become relevant (Hesse-Biber, 1995; Laurie, 1992). The emphasis in qualitative research on diversity, non-representativeness, small numbers, minimal stratification, self-selection and the focus on thick ethnographic description, suggests that drawing quantitative from qualitative data is contraindicated and that such a transformation produces unrealistic versions of the original. Where the quantitative data is from a separate data set with appropriate design and sampling strategies, the above comments do not apply.

Users' comments

Although many qualitative researchers have found computing packages essential in assisting with the management of larger databases, providing a more rigorous analytic style with the systematic use of certain tools and a useful easily accessed digital storage system (Cresswell, 2007), there is ongoing discussion centring around users' concerns. The following issues have been highlighted.

Idiosyncrasies

Many of the programs are idiosyncratic in nature, originally developed by individual academic researchers to help manage their own databases (Fielding and Lee, 1991). This poses the question as to how translocatable they really are to the different and equally idiosyncratic data sets of other qualitative researchers.

Time

Considerable time is required for the processes of setting up the data and learning to operate the program efficiently (Baugh et al., 2010); the larger the sample the more time will be required. One researcher compared the time she took interpreting qualitative data from a large British survey of household practices manually and by using The Ethnograph. She discovered that project analysis and interpretation took the same amount of time by hand as it did with computer assistance and that on-screen coding limited this researcher's view, encouraging and resulting in less complex coding patterns with fewer overlapping and nested codes (Laurie, 1992). Jim Vander Putten and Amanda Nolen (2010) also compared manual and computer analysis and discovered that they created 51 codes and 2 coding levels (manually) versus 728 and 6 coding levels (via computer management), and although greater depth of analysis was also produced by computer means, more knowledge about the phenomenon under investigation was required to adequately weigh up the relevance of this extra information.

Decontextualisation of data

Computing packages targeted at qualitative research tend to emphasise the common and shared properties of a large number, rather than variations in the minutiae of detail of small numbers (Agar, 1991). Cutting up the text interrupts the chain of reasoning. Utterances have multiple actions and events embedded in them and segmentation disrupts the ethnographic process, tending to drive the research (Agar, 1991). The off-screen reading and re-reading of data in context produces starkly different interpretations (narrower but data focused) compared with tool-driven on-screen analysis (broader but decontextualised) where generic dictionary meanings may obscure the original meanings so that researchers have to go back and find out which are insightful and which irrelevant (Vander Putten and Nolen, 2010).

Etic view

Particular program structures influence analytic results. The various processes of labelling, pattern-making and synthesis, and pattern-searching leading to thick description, must inevitably structure outcomes (Walker, 1993). In this manner, it seems likely that the etic (outsider, 'objective') rather than the emic (insider, 'subjective') approach to interpreting meaning will be fostered by the use of qualitative data management programs (Manwar et al., 1994). The dangerous ease with which one can move into enumerative mode in large databases, counting frequencies and undertaking variable analysis, is problematic (Bruhn and Lindberg, 1995). Automatic and semiautomatic coding of predefined areas doesn't take into account that people do not speak in predictable nor predefined language patterns and words; so much of the subtlety and 'in between the lines' communication is lost and if the researcher does not immerse him/herself in the data, will be irretrievable or go unnoticed (Evers, 2011). In addition, on screen there is a likelihood of the loss of the 'untypeable' – the off-screen fleeting notes and doodles that often encapsulate researcher insight (Richards and Richards, 1994).

Best practice

In terms of trustworthiness, a variety of processes (more) is viewed as better – and multiple analytic approaches (manual plus computer-managed) should enhance dependability of results (Leech and Onwuegbuzie, 2007). In addition, particular programs are best used for particular methodologies – it is not a matter of convenience nor one size fits all. The trend appears to be toward careful management; researchers still need to think and undertake some manual coding/noding and spend time identifying themes off screen. This is more likely to result in the researcher staying close to the data, developing sound interpretations and producing reputable results (Baugh et al., 2010). If you are using computer management it is crucial to be a competent methodologist prior so you have control over the process. These programs are tools for the experienced researcher to use wisely, not substitute tools to cover lack of expertise (Friese, 2011).

Audiovisual data

Although several programs have recently developed the capacity to deal with audiovisual data and they have the capacity for sorting and sequencing, they have been viewed as 'blunt tools' in a fairly primitive state, useful only if code-based methods and linear formats are sought. They also need to develop other output options apart from quantifying data if they are to become more useful (Silver and Patashnick, 2011).

There is clearly a need for a more in-depth conversation regarding the processes of qualitative computing (Boy, 1992; Bruhn and Lindberg, 1995) and their impact on researchers and on data. It appears that computer-aided qualitative research may have lost its connection with the theoretical and methodological debates of the disciplines of sociology, psychology and philosophy, and that these links would benefit from reconstruction (Boy, 1992), as would the newer approaches of mixing qualitative and quantitative data.

Which program is better?

Comprehensive analyses are in their infancy and have focused largely on the theory generation packages. Kus Saillard (2011) and Walter Schonfelder (2011) have independently compared NVivo and MAXQDA and both found MAXQDA with its integrated code, comment and memo functions supported the interrelationship among data, coding and memoing far better in regard to design, ease of use and theory generation than did NVivo. (One of my own doctoral students trialled NVivo, ATLAS.ti and MAXQDA in a desperate search to manage a large unwieldy database and MAXQDA won hands down in terms of capacity, stability, ease of learning and use.) In a more negative vein, comments have been made on the homogenisation of output both NVivo and MAXQDA. Evers (2011) and Schonfelder (2011) both noted that there seemed to be a general over-focus on quantifying qualitative data rather than on the display of diverse individual views.

Summary

The way knowledge is constructed in our society is important, as is the hegemony of logic, which determines which statements become knowledge. As human beings we have the capacity to create an inner representation of life which is multidimensional, complex and characterised by spontaneous reflexive actions. Processes involving segmenting and ordering data have the capacity to distance us as researchers, to limit perspectives and to favour outcomes of homogenisation and standardisation. These forms of control constrain the normal (non-computerised) framing processes of interpretation but despite this the flexibility of mind processes helps mitigate against too narrow an interpretation. The tyranny of a system, however useful, that has the capacity to direct and simplify the construction of the views of researchers and ultimately those of readers, will always be problematic.

Student exercise

Go to the following websites for the data management programs: MAXQDA, ATLAS.ti and NVivo:

www.maxqda.com/maxqda-eng/index.htm
www.soft-go.com/view/ATLAS.ti_79845.html
www.qsr.com.au/

and using a piece of your own data or data from any other source, go to the demo models and play with your data and see what you can achieve with the available tools. Try coding on and off screen to see if there are any notable differences.

Further reading

Program comparison

Koenig, T. (2009) CAQDAS comparison. www.restore.ac.uk/lboro/research/software/caqdas_comparison.php#text (accessed June 2011). This article on the CAQDAS site provides a detailed comparison of a number of functions of the currently available computer packages.

Bazeley, P. (2007) *Qualitative Data Analysis with NVivo*. London: Sage.

Welsh, E. (2002) Dealing with data: using NVivo in the qualitative data analysis process. *Forum: Qualitative Social Research*, 3 (2). Available at www.qualitative-research.net/index.php/fqs/article/view/865/1880 (accessed 18 July 2011). A researcher's experience in using NVivo – advantages and disadvantages.

Forum: Qualitative Social Research (2011) Volume 12 No. 1. Thematic Issue on current qualitative computing packages and their capacities. Available at www.qualitative-research.net/index.php/fqs/issue/view/36.

There are other more detailed listings of computer programs at the following sites:

www.textanalysis.info/qualitative.htm

http://bama.ua.edu/~wevans/content/csoftware/software_menu.html

Impact of computers on research

Ragin, C. and Becker, H. (1989) How the microcomputer is changing our analytic habits. In G. Blank, J. McCartney, and E. Brent (eds), *New Technology in Sociology: Practical Applications in Research and Work*. New Brunswick, NJ: Transaction. pp. 47–55. An examination of the changes that computer technology has made upon social research.

Kelle, U. (ed.) (1995) *Computer Aided Qualitative Data Analysis: Theory, Methods and Practice*. London: Sage. The impact of computer-assisted analysis is discussed together with the fundamental methodological and theoretical issues involved in using computers in qualitative research.

Using your computer but not qualitative computer management programs

Hahn, C. (2008) *Doing Qualitative Research Using Your Computer: A Practical Guide*. London: Sage. A useful book for those who want to format transcripts, code, develop themes, memos, and store using Access and Excel.

References

Agar, M. (1991) The right brain strikes back. In N. Fielding and R. Lee (eds), *Using Computers in Qualitative Research*. London: Sage. pp. 181–94.

Baudrillard, J. (1980) The implosion of meaning in the media and the implosion of the social in the masses. In K. Woodward (ed.), *The Myths of Information Technology and Post Industrial Culture*. New York: Coda Press. pp. 137–48.

Baugh J., Hallcom, A. and Harris, M. (2010) Computer assisted qualitative data analysis: a practical perspective for applied research. *Revista del Instituto Internacional de Costos*, No. 6 (June).

Boy, P. (1992) Introductory remarks: Current trends in computer-aided qualitative analysis. Paper presented at the Qualitative Research Process and Computing Conference, Bremen, Germany.

Bruhn, A. and Lindberg, O. (1995) Computer-aided qualitative data analysis: some issues from a Swedish perspective. Paper presented at the Australian Association of Social Research Conference, Victoria, Australia.

Coffey, D. (2005) Measuring gubernatorial ideology: a content analysis of State of the State speeches. *State Politics and Policy Quarterly*, 5 (3): 88–93.

Cresswell, J. (2007) *Qualitative Inquiry and Research Design: Choosing among Five Approaches*. Thousand Oaks, CA: Sage.

Denzin, N. (1988) Review of the book *Qualitative Analysis for Social Scientists. Contemporary Sociology*, 17 (3), 430–32.

Dupuy, J. (1980) Myths of the informational society. In K. Woodward (ed.), *Myths of Information: Technology and Postindustrial Culture*. New York: Coda Press. pp. 3–17.

Eco, U. (1994) *Interpretation and Overinterpretation*. Cambridge: Cambridge University Press.

Evers, J. (2011) From the past into the future: how technological developments change our ways of data collection. Transcription and analysis. *Forum: Qualitative Social Research*, 12 (1): Art. 38. Retrieved from www.qualitative-research.net/index.php/fqs/article/view/1636/3161 (accessed 3 April 2012).

Fielding, N. and Lee, R. (1991) *Using Computers in Qualitative Research*. London: Sage.

Friedheim, E. (1984) Field research and word processor files: a technical note. *Qualitative Sociology*, 7 (1–2): 90–97.

Friese, S. (2011) Using ATLAS.ti for analysing the financial crisis data. *Forum: Qualitative Social Research*, 12 (1): Art. 39. Retrieved from www.qualitative-research.net/index.php/fqs/article/viewArticle/1632/3149 (accessed 25 July 2011).

Grbich, C. (1998) Computing packages for qualitative data measurement: what is their real impact? *Australian Journal of Primary Health – Interchange*, 4 (3): 98–104.

Guattari, F. (1984) *Molecular Revolution*. Harmondsworth: Penguin.

Henman, P. (1992) Grounding social critiques of computers: The world-view embodied in computers. Paper presented at the Australian Sociological Association Conference, Adelaide, South Australia.

Hesse-Biber, S. (1995) Unleashing Frankenstein's monster? The use of computers in qualitative research. In R. Burgess (ed.), *Studies in Qualitative Methodology: Computing and Qualitative Research*. London: JAI Press. pp. 25–41.

Huber, G. and Garcia, C. (1993) Voices of beginning teachers: computer assisted listening to their common experiences. In M. Schratz (ed.), *Qualitative Voices in Educational Research*. London: Falmer Press. pp. 131–56.

Idhe, D. (1990) *Technology and the Life World: From Garden to Earth.* Bloomington, IN: Indiana University Press.

Kelle, U. and Laurie, H. (1995) Computer use in qualitative research and issues of validity. In U. Kelle (ed.), *Computer Aided Qualitative Analysis: Theory Methods and Practice.* London: Sage. pp. 19–28.

Laurie, H. (1992) Using the ETHNOGRAPH: Practical and methodological implications. Paper presented at the International Conference on the Qualitative Research Process and Computing, Bremen, Germany.

Leech, N. and Onwuegbuzie, T. (2007) An array of qualitative data analysis tools: a call for data analysis triangulation. *School Psychology Quarterly*, 22: 587–94.

Lyman, P. (1984) Reading, writing and word processing: towards a phenomenology of the computer age. *Qualitative Sociology*, 7 (1-2): 75–89.

Lyotard, J. (1984) *The Postmodern Condition: A Report on Knowledge.* Minneapolis, MN: University of Minnesota Press.

Manwar, A., Johnson, B. and Dunlap, E. (1994) Qualitative data analysis with hypertext: a case of New York City crack dealers. *Qualitative Sociology*, 17 (3): 283–92.

Metzing, D. (ed.) (1980) *Frame Conceptions and Text Understanding.* Berlin: deGruyter.

Murphy, J. and Pardeck, J. (1988) The computer micro-world, knowledge and social planning. *Computers in Human Services*, 3 (1): 127–4l.

Nye, A. (1990) *Words of Power: A Feminist Reading of the History of Logic.* London: Routledge.

Pfaffenberger, B. (1988) *Microcomputer Applications in Qualitative Research.* Qualitative Research Methods series, Volume 14. Newbury Park, CA: Sage.

Richards, T. and Richards, L. (1994) Using computers in qualitative research. In N.K. Denzin and Y.S. Lincoln (eds), *Handbook of Qualitative Research.* Thousand Oaks, CA: Sage. pp. 445–62.

Rozak, T. (1994) *The Cult of Information: The Folklore of Computers and the True Art of Thinking.* Berkeley, CA: University of California Press.

Saillard, K. (2011) Systematic versus interpretive analysis with two CAQDAS packages: NVivo and MAXQDA. *Forum: Qualitative Social Research*, 12 (1): Art. 34.

Schonfelder, W. (2011) CAQDAS and qualitative syllogism logic – NVivo 8 and MAXQDA 10 compared. *Forum: Qualitative Social Research* 12 (1): Art 21. Retrieved from www.qualitative-research.net/index.php/fqs/article/view/1514/3134 (accessed April 2012).

Seidel, J. (1991) Method and madness in the application of computer technology to qualitative data analysis. In N. Fielding and R. Lee (eds), *Using Computers in Qualitative Research.* London: Sage. pp. 107–16.

Silver, C. and Patashnick, J. (2011) Finding fidelity: advancing audiovisual analysis using software. *Forum: Qualitative Social Research*, 12 (1): Art. 37. Retrieved from www.qualitative-research.net/index.php/fqs/article/viewArticle/1629/3148 (accessed 22 July 2011).

Vander Putten, J. and Nolen, A. (2010) Comparing results from constant comparative and computer software methods: a reflection about qualitative data analysis. *Journal of Ethnographic and Qualitative Research*, 5: 99–112.

Van Maanen, J. (1988) *Tales of the Field: On Writing Ethnography.* Chicago: University of Chicago Press.

Walker, B. (1993) Computer analysis of qualitative data: a comparison of three packages. *Qualitative Health Research*, 3 (1): 91–10l.

Wajcman, J. (1991) *Feminism Confronts Technology.* University Park, PA: Pennsylvania State University Press.

Zadeh, L. (1988) Fuzzy logic. *Computer*, 21 (4): 83–93.

PART 6

Interpreting and presenting qualitative data

In this final section we will deal with interpreting and presenting qualitative data innovatively. Regardless of the methodological approach you have taken, once you have assembled your data into groupings several decisions have to be made so you can move into writing up. The first is to see if it is possible to develop a more abstract explanation regarding the results you have gathered. The depth to which you undertake this will depend on whether the method you have pursued has a particular philosophical underpinning that you would like to follow or that you can build on. You may of course decide to minimise your theorising and to display your data in creative ways so that the reader can decide where your findings fit with their knowledge and experiences, or you may decide on a position midway between these two and combine theorising with interesting displays but in such a way that the reader is clear about what you have found and where it all fits (in your view). If you have collected some quantitative data to provide a broader overview, you will need to decide if, when and how you will combine it with your qualitative data. The two chapters in this segment attempt to help you with these decisions by discussing theorising and the variety of data display options which are available.

This final part contains two chapters:

Chapter 23 Theorising from data
Chapter 24 Writing up and innovative data display

TWENTY THREE

Theorising from data

This chapter will help you undertake the process of developing a more abstract theoretical explanation of data collected through the range of approaches that have been covered in this text to date. The interpretive process can be initiated early and should have strong links to the research question, to the literature and to any specific forms of data analysis that have been undertaken. Sometimes this is an almost seamless process where, at one extreme, previously identified theories are applied (theory testing/theory directed), while at the other emergent explanation closely linked to a range of theoretical positions (theory generation) occurs. In between these two extremes, light theoretical interpretations of a conceptual nature and the development of models of best practice may occur.

KEY POINTS

Your choices regarding theorising range from:
- Being directed by your chosen theoretical underpinnings from the beginning
- Closely following the theoretical underpinnings of your method
- Linking your emerging findings to any relevant theories/concepts to generate something new
- Minimising theorising (postmodernism)

Theorising

The process of theorising involves you in taking the results you have collated and looking at them again through the lens or frame of one or several theoretical (Marx, Freud etc.) or conceptual positions (power, gender etc.) or models in order to make further sense of them and to lift the analytical discussion to a more abstract level. The whole notion of theorising from qualitative data can be looked at from one of four options.

1 The first relates to your *pre chosen theoretical positions*, which will drive your research and against which you will place your findings (theory direction). Here your relevant theories have been

stated early, the implications for the study drawn out, the data collected to meet these implications and in effect to 'test' the theory. Critical ethnography and feminist research are examples of this.

2   The second option relates to your *methodological underpinnings*, which may constitute the orientation and processes of data collection, for example the grounded theory approach has elements of symbolic interactionist theory which may lead you toward this theory or toward some related form of interactive theorising. Phenomenology has a variety of philosophical theoretical possibilities that may be called upon.

3   The third option, *researcher choice*, allows you to call upon the huge variety of conceptual models and theoretical ideas that exist across all available disciplines in order to provide a more abstract explanation of your findings and to generate some new model or pathway or theoretical proposition (theory generating).

4   The final option, *theory minimisation*, lies in the postmodern tradition where minimal interpretation but maximal display of data occurs so the reader can get close to the participant's experiences and make their own interpretive decisions based on their own life experiences.

Theory testing versus theory generation

One other complicating factor is trying to decide whether you have adopted a *theory directed/theory generating* type of approach, because it is easy to slide from one into the other when the implications and explanatory power of the former cannot be sustained in view of your research findings. This may lead you to draw on a range of relevant theories/concepts from the literature and to combine these with what is emerging from your data to form the basis for new theoretical explanations and models of practice.

What is theory?

But what is *theory*? Theory is abstract knowledge that has been developed as an account regarding a group of facts or phenomena. It is derived from the exploration of phenomena, the identification of concepts and the interrelationships between concepts surrounding phenomena from which an explanatory framework can be developed.

There are different levels of theory: micro, middle range and grand.

- At the *micro* level theoretical framing is mostly provided by *the concept*. Concepts are a simple unit of abstract thought which identify the common aspects of phenomena. Examples would be 'power', 'socialisation', 'masculinity' and 'locus of control'. Various concepts are combined with *propositions* (i.e., that x and y explain z) to form the next level up.
- Theories of the *middle range* are explanations with a narrow or particular discipline focus, such as Nursing or Architecture or Business.
- *Grand* theories combine concepts, propositions and *statements* to provide an abstract overview with the capacity to be meaningful to a range of disciplines and even across cultures (although this is contentious).

Example: levels of theory

At the *micro* level we have concepts that refer to limited aspects of social organisation, for example, 'Women carry the burden of care in our society.'

Lifting this to the *middle range* level we have concepts – gender roles, burden etc. – plus propositions, for example, 'women of low socioeconomic class, as less powerful members of the culture, will carry the burden of care in some societies.'

Taking this further to the level of *grand* theory this would involve an abstract statement/explanation of the uniformities of social behaviour, organisation and change and would comprise definitions, concepts, variables, statements and theoretical constructs, for example, using a Marxist analysis our concept could become 'In capitalist societies, women's powerless lower class position will ensure they always have lower status work. Strong socialisation into nurturing roles means they will continue to be unwaged domestic slaves.'

Thumbnail sketches of examples of how other researchers have dealt with theory, chosen from within the particular methodological approaches previously outlined in earlier chapters, are provided for you below.

Classical ethnographic approaches

The in-depth exploration of a culture – however this has been defined, whether it be the operation of tribal groups or the culture of a classroom or department – can be undertaken in either a theory directed or theory generating manner.

Theory directing

Some of the older ethnographies closer to the original anthropological tradition fall into the theory directing mode. For example, Margaret Mead in her work in Samoa set out to apply the concept of 'adolescence' to the group under study. This can be seen in her initial application for funding to do the research, which she titled: 'A study in heredity and environment based on an investigation of the phenomenon of adolescence among primitive and civilised people'. Later, in *Life as a Samoan Girl*, she states 'I had been sent to the South Seas to study … the life of Samoan girls. I was to find out what sort of life girls lived in Samoa, whether they, like American girls, had years of tears and troubles before they were quite grown up' (1931: 94). She did discover that in fact the concept of adolescence had little value in Samoan culture:

> So, the sum total of it all is – Adolescence is a period of sudden development, of stress, only in relation to sex – and where the community recognizes this and does not attempt to curb it, there is no conflict at all between the adolescent and the community, except such as arises from the conflict of personalities within a household (and this is immediately remedied as I have shown by the change to another relationship group) and the occasional delinquent – of any age from 8–50 – who arouses the ire of the community. I think I have ample data to illustrate all these points. (Letter from Margaret Mead to Franz Boas her supervisor, March 14, 1926)

This concept of adolescence had come from the American culture and what Mead was doing was simply testing it and seeking substantiating data to confirm the more universal application of this concept in another setting. Some would argue that this form of theory testing is inappropriate, running the risk of influencing findings and that a more theory generating approach involving extensive exploration with no imposition of a priori researcher generated concepts would have been a better way to go and more in line with the traditional anthropological approach of extensive documentation and categorisation, allowing the data to speak for itself. Yet despite strong direction from the concept of adolescence, Mead was able to come up with sufficient data to challenge the universality of the concept.

Theory generating

An example of theory generation within the ethnographic tradition can be seen in Laud Humphreys's (1970) exploration of impersonal sex between consenting males in public toilets. Here Humphreys, in taking the position of the 'watch queen' or lookout, was able to observe hundreds of acts of fellatio, writing up 53 in detail. In addition, 30 further detailed records were kept by one of the participants. This information was added to by the dozen respondents who consented to be interviewed, and by identification of other participants through a car number plate search enabling the researcher to include 100 of them in a health survey interview. From all this, Humphreys generated four major profiles of these men: trade; ambisexuals; gay guys; and closet queens. The development of theory was limited to the micro level and the exploration of the concepts 'stigma', 'deviance', 'deviant behavior' and 'deviant adaptation' as at that time such acts were illegal. He concluded that society had provided very few 'legitimate' sexual outlets for men so that turning to the 'tearooms' had became one of the few options available.

Newer ethnographic approaches

The move into postmodernism has resulted in an explicitly subjective orientation where fragmentation and the rejection of grand theories as power laden discourses, dominates. Extensive display of data rather than elaborate theorising is seen as the best way to bring your reader close to the experiences you wish to transmit. However, many researchers draw on a range of theoretical perspectives, usually at the micro level and with a strong focus on the transitional nature of any conclusions. Pamela Autrey (1995) used autoethnography to study her own experiences as girl and woman, both as a student and as a teacher. She utilised feminist theory, the issues of gender and the cultural icon of 'Barbie' as well as the concepts of depression and adolescence to help clarify her findings, ending up with a 'menopausal' theory of curriculum that focuses on the issues teenage girls face in American society.

Some autoethnographic research tends to display the story first then generate particular concepts to lightly frame it. Shamla McLaurin (2003) positions herself and her view of self under the conceptual framework of 'recovering homophobe' after exposing how her bias against homosexuality can be connected to the context of her upbringing as poor, female, black and Baptist living in the southern United States. Cultural changes and several epiphanies changed her views in a roller-coaster ride from supportive to aggressively attacking any mention of homosexuality and finally to a more accepting position, particularly with regard to lesbianism.

In a similar manner, Elena Maydell (2010) chronicled the autoethnographic experience of being a researcher and collecting stories of identity of Russian migrants and of self (also a Russian migrant) in New Zealand. She developed three conceptual/theoretical frames to explain her part in the creation of data:

- positioning theory, both self-positioning (own perspective) and other-positioning (wider societal perspective)
- the insider–outsider dilemma where different versions of her identity were co-constructed across the two cultures with and by participants during each interview
- social constructionism, which was used to clarify the interplay between the self and other during the knowledge production enterprise.

Grounded theory

Here is where the focus is your observation of the minutiae of interaction in the understanding of social patterns, social structures, social processes and social behaviours. The structure of data collection through the *constant comparative process* means that theory construction from data is put in place very early. You need to compare each data segment not only across the database with other segments but also with existing literature (if you have undertaken a review) and with the concepts/theories (theoretical sensitivity) that may shed light on what is emerging in terms of data groupings. This movement between data, literature and theory serves to consolidate data and theory in the theory generation process.

Glaser and Strauss (1967) indicated that the processes of comparison tend to clarify differences and patterns that can generate explanatory concepts and propositions to form part of a general discussion of the results gained. Two levels of theory can ultimately be generated:

- *substantive theory*, which is specific to a particular focus in the research, for example, teenage pregnancy, learning styles in school settings, or the care of the dying; and
- *formal theory*, which develops out of this and concentrates on the further development of broader emerging explanatory concepts such as socialisation, gender roles, class structure etc.

In order for one concept to move to the realms of formal theory, this particular concept will have to be linked to all like situations. For example, the concept of 'status passage' related to earlier work by the two researchers on transitions to dying. In order to elevate this concept to the level of formal theory, all kinds of transitions needed to be sought from a range of literature and research, such as transitions from adolescence to adulthood, from bachelorhood to marriage, from hidden homosexuality to overt homosexuality, from wellness to illness, from imprisonment to freedom, from marriage to singlehood etc., so that the concept could be widely substantiated and its properties identified. For example, the properties of status passage were that they were considered desirable/undesirable; inevitable; possibly reversible; repeatable/non-repeatable; could be undertaken alone, in pairs or groups as well as in different styles such as calmness or anger; where communication with others may/may not occur; where variable control over the situation may occur; where levels of choice and degree of control will vary; and where legitimation of entry may be needed and clarity of signs may also vary (adapted from Glaser and Strauss, 1971).

In an example of *substantive theory* generation regarding corporate turnaround (Pandit, 1995), a number of concepts and categories were constructed during the processes of open and axial coding and the development of core categories such as 'recovery strategy content' occurred during selective coding. These recovery strategies were found to be related to six contextual factors: the causes of decline; the severity of the crisis; the attitude of stakeholders; industry characteristics; changes in the macroeconomic environment; and the firm's historical strategy. The content of recovery strategies was further divided into operational and strategic level actions and a process dimension was also uncovered. From this, actions for recovery were seen to be: management change; retrenchment; stabilisation; and growth. These findings led to the generation of 53 propositions linking the concepts and categories that were tested to identify levels of support within the database for the models of recovery strategies developed.

Phenomenology

Implicit assumptions do underpin this approach, in that you as researcher have the capacity to access in-depth life experiences of the self and also of the other – through an assumption of interconnectedness and processes of intuition, exploration and thematic analysis. Another assumption is that people who have these experiences have particular ways of making sense of them within their own lives and not only can articulate this but it is acceptable that these meanings will differ. The findings draw on these and many other theoretical assumptions and are presented to readers by you as the final authority, with some theories/concepts generated to provide broader explanations. More recently, interview and observational data have been presented in different forms – poetry, drama, pastiche and narrative – as well as other creative forms of display from within the postmodern tradition where there is minimal formal theorising.

Jan Pascal (2010) explored the lived experiences of cancer survivorhood of 15 people using Heideggerian phenomenology. Two in-depth interviews, spanning a 6-month interval, were conducted with each. The study found that temporality and relationships of care were intimately entwined in aspects of survivorhood but that these relationships involved reciprocity and were not just with family but also with community. Another essential factor in surviving appeared to be having a passionate commitment to a project beyond one's self and leading a good life by transcending the acquisitive demands of the world and returning to a more compassionate space. Explanations drew on the Heideggerian notion of *being-in-the-world* in a holistic, interconnected and meaningful way.

Feminist research

Although the principles of feminist research can be applied to a range of approaches from ethnography through to poststructuralism, they tend to operate within the theory directed tradition of presuming they are relevant explanatory tools. Sarah Smith (2009) took an initial position of challenging the widespread assumption implicit in the literature and also held by feminists that care relationships between disabled and non-disabled partners were closed roles; that is the caregiver was a carer only (albeit predominantly female and a victim of exploitation by the system) and the disabled partner was a care-receiver only. These assumptions desexualised both roles and allowed no insight into the possibility of reciprocity. As she sought to include the marginalised voices of people involved in disabled/non-disabled intimate relationships she found the boundaries between caregiver and care-receiver dissolving, with reciprocal caregiving and care-receiving occurring and with sexual intimacy often being a part of physical care.

Content analysis

The variety of theory directing and theory generating or data-driven approaches that have been used in content analysis of personal construct psychology have been collated by Bob Green (2004).

- *Theory directed approaches* have included: the imposition of limited categories defined a priori by the researcher, for example, 'people' or 'problems', or 'time' – past present/future; or 'degree' – high/low; word co-occurrence using cluster or factor analysis of word frequency matrices; and the use of psychological scales weighted for intensity or magnitude of anxiety, hostility, and alienation.
- *Theory generating approaches* have involved the generation of personal constructs relating to a variety of life experiences.

Concept generation is also evident in a study by Dina Borzekowski et al. (2010), who undertook a systematic content analysis of 180 online sites pertaining to eating disorders. They examined site logistics, site accessories, images and prose intended to inspire weight loss, tips and tricks, recovery, themes and perceived harm. Eighty-four per cent of the sites offered pro-anorexia content, and 64% provided pro-bulimia content. Few sites focused on eating disorders as a lifestyle choice but images and prose intending to inspire weight loss appeared on 85% of the sites and overt suggestions on how individuals might indulge in eating-disordered behaviours occurred on 83% of the sites, while in contrast only 38% of the sites included recovery-oriented information or links. The dominant concepts generated were success, control, perfection and solidarity.

Conversational analysis – chat rooms

More than one approach within theory generation can be used on a data set and this is illustrated in computer-mediated communication (Shi et al., 2006), where the primary purpose was to view the interaction patterns in online discussions (computer-mediated communication) using a grounded theory approach to generate a conceptual model which was termed 'thread theory' which then acted as a framework to make sense of relationships between individual thinking processes and group interactions. This framework was then used to undertake a discourse analysis of the content of the postings. These authors took the chaotic transcripts from online discussions and displayed them to show the actual order of interaction and identified ongoing themes such as 'course project' and ongoing 'noises off', which interrupted the flow of conversation. These threads (related messages on a particular topic) were then tabled and schematically visualised to show the non-linear, non-sequential appearance of the messages more clearly; to indicate where individuals were contributing simultaneously to particular threads, as well as the life, intensity and magnitude of a thread; where threads break; and where new threads emerge. This theory could then be used to interpret both qualitative and quantitative data relating to processes of learning and outcomes in computer-mediated communication.

Semiotic analysis of visual images

Within semiotic analysis, there is an assumption that visual codes will be able to be read (although perhaps not interpreted) in an almost identical manner by all observers from a particular culture. Paul Carter (2000) has explored front page photographs in three leading newspapers: *The Guardian* (a broadsheet with detailed news and articles), the *Daily Mail* (a more subjective tabloid) and *The Sun* (a judgemental tabloid). On one particular day, the first two papers ran articles about the death of a white farmer in Zimbabwe, murdered by vigilantes over disputes about land, while *The Sun* ran a story about Madonna claiming that the sex of her unborn baby was male. The analysis covers the choice of news/entertainment for the front page, the size of the photo compared with the amount of type. *The Guardian* was 50/50, with the headline 'Death at dawn: the agony of Zimbabwe' and a photo of the body of the dead man and surrounds; the *Daily Mail* used under half the page for the same photo of the body only but with a directional headline, 'Have a happy birthday Mr Mugabe'; while *The Sun* used a sexual type photo of Madonna, mid-torso up, to take up most of the page, with a caption: 'Madonna: it's a boy'. The signifiers of size of type, photo composition, lighting, visual depth and symmetry as well as headings are said to be used to direct the reader's attention. These help to clarify and generate the conceptualisation of each paper's ideological thrust: balanced and objective (*The Guardian*), subjectively judgemental the *Daily Mail*, or opinionated and populist (*The Sun*). Theoretical interpretation was at the micro (concept level) of generation.

Theory direction more toward the middle range occurred in Siân Davies's (2002) use of the theoretical concept of 'constructed femininity' as the centre of interpretation for a semiotic analysis of teenage magazine covers. Two magazines, *19* and *More*, were analysed by their titles, fonts, layout, colours, paper texture and the language used as well as how these magazines target the readership sought, influence readings and feed desires. The presentation of female icons and role models was seen to influence young females into particular notions of femininity (beautiful and sexy – perfect features, blond, tanned, tall, slim, sassy and attractive to males). To fulfil this notion of femininity, young women should also be interested in fashion and knowledgeable about the trivia of the lives of famous people. Thus a particular form of femininity is constructed through subliminal education via information reinforced by visual representations of desirable characteristics.

The general hermeneutic qualitative approach can also be theorised at any level. Isabel Brodie (2000) has provided an example of conceptual theorising in social work with regard to the school experiences of children looked after in residential accommodation. She uses the concept 'exclusion' to build up a picture of 'exclusion by non-admission', 'exclusion on admission' and 'graduated' and 'planned' exclusion to build up her interpretation of 'exclusion as a social process'.

Theory building through metaphor

Metaphor has also been used to build theory, via analogical mapping (where graphic symbols portray features), to explore the nature of a school system. One example of this would be the application of the term teacher as *nomad* (Aubusson, 2002), providing a possible comparison between the teacher and the nomad in terms of journey, gains and losses, obstacles to be overcome, survival etc. and providing a link to another domain of knowledge which may serve to shed light on the life of the teacher and to provide another level of interpretation. The main metaphor used to provide comparison with the school system was that of an *ecosystem*. This term allowed the introduction of such terminology as: *adaptation, complexity, homeostasis, succession, fitness, generation and re-generation, opportunism, reproductive maturity, fragility, evolution purpose and knowledge*, which could be applied to generate new insights to the results.

Ammina Kothari (2010) in undertaking a comparative analysis of six years of newspaper articles in Tanzania on HIV/AIDS found that although the war metaphor dominated, others were also important in clarifying cultural orientations, in particular a masculinist discourse that focused on the power and wisdom of men, even those HIV-positive, by implying that men have the capacity to stop the epidemic. This reinforces the existing patriarchal power structure, disempowering females and the gay community by omitting their experiences. This silence and the use of the plague metaphor implicitly places women as deviant and stigmatised in spreading the disease (plague) to innocent men and children. In this manner, the role of culture, gender and sexual practices are left out of information on the spread of AIDS in Africa.

Summary

From the above it should be clear that apart from situations where theory/principle direction is occurring, the most usual forms of theorising in qualitative research occur along a spectrum from the use of concepts in micro-theorising, to the theory generation of middle range theory and or the development of formal/grand theory, as in grounded theorising. These processes are not exclusive and may shade into each other. Postmodernism lightly calls on multiple concepts or avoids theorising altogether.

Student exercise

Read the following excerpt and, using dot points, list the interpretative labels you might apply to it.

First Story

It's 1969. She's on her high school senior trip to Florida. She's a white girl from a small, rural, southern town, attracted to Jesse, one of only two African American males on the journey. Prior to lights out the first night, students go for a walk on the beach. Immersed in talking about being Black in a White world, she and Jesse wander away from the others.

'You always remember you're Black,' Jesse says. 'People's responses remind you.'

'What was it like growing up?' she asks.

'We had no money. My father left when I was a baby, so I was raised by my ma and grandma. Then my mother remarried. Once I woke up and my step-daddy had a butcher knife to my throat.'

(Continued)

(Continued)

'Oh, my God. What did you do?'

'I ran outside. In the freezing cold, with no shoes, in my underwear. I got frostbite on my toes.'

'What had you done to make him so angry?'

'Nothin'. He was drunk. And he was always jealous that my mother loved me more than him. That's all. Just jealous.'

'We better go back in,' she says, noting that everyone else has disappeared. She wonders what people will think about their being out in the dark … together … alone.

She leads the way into the room where the other students have gathered. She feels she has nothing to be embarrassed about since her time with Jesse was so innocent. What she feels does not matter when all eyes turn on her and she experiences the deadly silence of all voices stopping – at precisely the same time. She has never felt such hostile attention before. Jesse, who has, hesitates before walking into the same treatment a few minutes later. In those few silent, enraged moments, she knows viscerally a little of what it feels like to be Black in a White world – just a little.

(Excerpted from Ellis, 1995a: 152–3)

Please visit the companion website **www.sagepub.co.uk/grbich2** for possible answers.

Further reading

Using theory

Alvesson, M. and Karreman, D. (2011) *Qualitative Research and Theory Development Mystery as Method*. London: Sage. These authors view the research process as one of theory–data interplay, allowing creative empirical material to challenge established theory in a constructive process.

Becker, H. (1993) Theory: the necessary evil. In David J. Flinders and Geoffrey E. Mills (eds), *Theory and Concepts in Qualitative Research: Perspectives from the Field*. New York: Teachers College Press. pp. 218-29. Available at http://stuff.natehaas.com/pub/TheoryThe%20Necessary%20Evil.htm (accessed 3 April 2012). A good discussion on the need for theory and theorising.

Pascale, M. (2011) *Cartographies of Knowledge Exploring Qualitative Epistemologies*. London: Sage. This text examines theoretical and historical foundations that shape qualitative research. Issues of social justice, agency, subjectivity, and experience are covered within feminist, critical race and poststructural literature.

Flinders, D. and Mills, G. (eds) (1993) *Theory and Concepts in Qualitative Research: Perspectives from the Field*. New York: Teachers College Press. This is one of the few texts that actually addresses the issues relating to theorising.

Kelle, U. (1997) Theory building in qualitative research and computer programs for the management of textual data. *Sociological Research Online*, 2 (2). Available at www.socresonline.org.uk/2/2/1.html (accessed June 2011). This article looks at the processes of theory building and challenges the idea that the use of computer management of qualitative data will inhibit these processes.

www.csudh.edu/dearhabermas/theory.htm (accessed June 2011). An eclectic website with a range of theory links, theory journals, theorists and various research articles using theory.

References

Aubusson, P. (2002) Using metaphor to make sense and build theory in qualitative analysis. *The Qualitative Report* 7 (4). Retrieved from www.nova.edu/ssss/QR/QR7-4/aubusson.html (accessed June 2011).

Autrey, P. (1995) The trouble with girls: autoethnography and the classroom. Doctoral dissertation, Louisiana State University. Retrieved from http://etd.lsu.edu/docs/available/etd-0708103–131111/ (accessed June 2011).

Borzekowski, D., Schenk, S., Wilson, J. and Peebles, R. (2010) e-Ana and e-Mia: a content analysis of pro-eating disorder Web sites. *American Journal of Public Health*, 100 (8): 1526–34. Retrieved from www.ncbi.nlm.nih.gov/pubmed/20558807 (accessed June 2011).

Brodie, I. (2000) Theory generation and qualitative research: school exclusion and children looked after. *Theorising Social Work Seminar Series*. London: ESRC. Retrieved from www.scie.org.uk/publications/misc/tswr/seminar6/brodie.asp (accessed June 2011).

Carter, P. (2000) A semiotic analysis of newspaper front-page photographs. Retrieved from www.aber.ac.uk/media/Students/pmc9601.html (accessed June 2011).

Davies, S. (2002) Semiotic analysis of teenage magazine front covers. Retrieved from www.aber.ac.uk/media/Students/sid9901.html (accessed June 2011).

Glaser, B. and Strauss, A. (1967) *The Discovery of Grounded Theory*. New York: Aldine Publishing.

Glaser, B. and Strauss, A. (1971) *Status Passage: A Formal Theory*. Chicago, IL: Aldine–Atherton.

Green, B. (2004) Personal construct psychology and content analysis. *Personal Construct Theory and Practice*, 1: 82–91. Retrieved from www.pcp-net.org/journal/pctp04/green04.pdf (accessed June 2011).

Humphreys, L. (1970) *Tearoom Trade: Impersonal Sex in Public Places*. Chicago, IL: Aldine. Retrieved from http://www.angelfire.com/or3/tss/tearoom.html (accessed June 2011).

Kothari, A. (2010) War and plague: a semiotic analysis of HIV/AIDS metaphors in the Tanzanian daily news. Doctoral thesis, School of Journalism, Indiana University. Retrieved from www.natcom.org/uploadedFiles/Content/Education/Kothari%20-%20War%20and%20Plague.pdf (accessed June 2011).

Maydell, E. (2010) Methodological and analytical dilemmas in autoethnographic research. *Journal of Research Practice*, 6 (1): Art. M5. Retrieved from http://jrp.icaap.org/index.php/jrp/article/view/223/190 (accessed June 2011).

McLaurin, S. (2003) Homophobia: an autoethnographic study. *The Qualitative Report*, 8 (3): 481–6. Retrieved from http://www.nova.edu/ssss/QR/QR8-3/mclaurin.pdf (accessed 3 April 2012).

Mead, M. (1931) Life as a Samoan girl. In *ALL TRUE! The Record of Actual Adventures That Have Happened to Ten Women of Today*. New York: Brewer, Warren & Putnam.

Mead, M. (1926) Letter to Franz Boas, March 14, 1926. Retrieved from http://sociology.uwo.ca/mead/March14,1926.htm (accessed June 2011).

Pandit, N. (1995) Towards a grounded theory of corporate turnaround: a case study approach. Doctoral thesis, University of Manchester, UK.

Pascal, J. (2010) Phenomenology as a research method for social work: contexts: understanding the lived experience of cancer survival. *New Scholarship in the Human Services*, 9 (2).

Shi, S., Mishra, P., Bonk, C., Tan, S. and Zhao, Y. (2006) Thread theory: a framework applied to content analysis of synchronous computer mediated communication. Retrieved from www.itdl.org/Journal/Mar_06/article02.htm (accessed June 2011).

Smith, S. (2009) Love, sex, and disability: the ethics and politics of care in intimate relationships. Doctoral thesis, The Ohio State University. Retrieved from http://gradworks.umi.com/33/75/3375902.html (accessed 3 April 2012).

TWENTY FOUR

Writing up and innovative data display

The display of your results is as important as consolidating the data into manageable forms. It should enable you to bring the reader close to what you and others have experienced. This chapter will demonstrate some of the forms of display that are available for you to consider.

KEY POINTS

- Your final writing up and display of data will be influenced by:

  - the audience to which the results are targeted
  - your position in your research study

- Styles of display include:

  - graphic summaries
  - case studies
  - hyperlinks
  - vignettes
  - layers
  - juxtapositions
  - fiction
  - narratives
  - aural approaches (audio)

  - quotes
  - mixed methods (graphics and quotes)
  - interactive approaches
  - anecdotes
  - pastiche
  - parody and irony
  - poetry
  - drama
  - visuals (photos, videos)

- The type of research approach taken should not dictate nor limit the form of data display you choose

---

Writing up

Your decisions regarding when to use which particular forms of writing up will depend largely on the following issues:

- the audience for whom you are writing
- the position you have taken as the researcher.

Audience

If you are writing for a particular *research journal* it is wise to familiarise yourself with the variety of styles that have appeared in issues over the past few years. If you are writing a *report for a government agency* then an executive summary of not more than four sides of $2 \times A4$ pages needs to include: the approach taken, techniques employed, analytical paths taken, and a summary of results as well as recommendations for change where these are relevant. In other words what you have done, how you did this, what you found and what the authority needs to consider because of your findings.

Format   If you are writing a *thesis* there is a general format, which mirrors that of many journal articles:

Abstract: Comprising a summary of up to 200 words, which should clearly identify your research question, how you undertook your study, what you found and the implications of this for the field.

Introduction: This is your opportunity to reveal (but only in a thesis) how you came to choose such a topic, your personal biases with regard to this topic (work/personal experiences or directions from previous research) and what the research journey has involved for you. For example, in my thesis on stay at home fathers I expected to find somewhat similar results to earlier researchers, which were that these men were prepared to stay in the home role with young children as a temporary measure for no more than two years after which they would move fairly rapidly back into the workforce. I was quite surprised when I discovered that all the men in my group continued to inhabit the role for at least five years. Few seemed in any hurry to rejoin the full-time workforce after this time, with most preferring to set up a part-time business to be run from home while they continued to contribute heavily to the home and parenting roles.

Literature review and theoretical/conceptual frames: A critical review of current literature (updated just prior to submission of the thesis) occurs here, allowing you to identify, catalogue and even dismiss previous research in an effort to clear a space for your crucial (but previously missing) perspective on the field. Exposure of the theories/conceptual frames previously used by others as well as those that you as researcher plan to use or think may be of relevance, should also occur here.

Study design/methods: What particular approach has been undertaken? Just *naming* one is not sufficient. Aspects that need to be discussed in this section include:

- Which approach was chosen or adapted and why? In addition, if adapted how? Moreover, for what particular purpose? And did this adaptation work? What issues arose and had to be dealt with?
- Access to participants – how was this gained? What permissions were sought – to tape? to video? to observe? To gain access to personal documents? etc.
- What sampling approaches were used and at what stage of the project? Why were these chosen? Were they effective?
- What ethical issues were addressed? And what ethics permissions were gained from which authorities?

- Were any agreements made with funding authorities or the major organisations that were accessed? If so, what was the outcome of such negotiations/agreements?
- Recording of information – how was this undertaken? How was data stored? And for how long will it be stored?
- What checks and balances were put in place to enhance design and data reliability?
- What forms of data analysis were undertaken?

Results: What forms of display were used and why were these seen as the most appropriate? Display may depend on your position, that of the reader and the extent to which you have decided to allow the participants to speak for themselves.

Discussion traditionally involves two things: a more abstract discussion of the results utilising the theoretical perspectives, as previously indicated in Chapter 23 and the location of the findings within current literature. This can often be intertwined within the results section (as in grounded theory and in postmodern and poststructural approaches where researcher interpretation is minimised in favour of reader interpretation) or the Results and Discussion sections can be kept separate.

Conclusions and Recommendations: A final summary of what has been found, together with what needs to be done about this ends the thesis, together with a brief discounting of the data – identifying its limitations (such as size of study, time available to do it, problems of access to participants etc).

Researcher position

If the researcher has taken a more traditional position involving an authoritative voice along the lines of 'I went, I saw, I found', then display will tend to be limited and will support conclusions already drawn. This display may well include thick ethnographic description (content, context and values) but the voices of participants are often limited to key quotes that illustrate the findings gained. This has been termed a *'realist'* display (Van Maanen, 1988).

If the researcher has taken a *subjective* position the 'I' 'eye' of his person will be heard/seen at some point in the text as he/she moves to upfront personal experiences or to address the audience directly before shifting offstage to enable the voices of participants to be heard. Author decentring allows the re-presentation of data in a range of formats from poetry to dramatic dialogue, fictionalised versions, polyphonic presentation and visual displays. The authoritative or subjective/decentred positions are two ends of a continuum along which a variety of mixes may occur.

Research approaches

Although some of the more established approaches such as grounded theory and classical ethnography have tended to use more conventional forms of data display (descriptive graphics, quotes and case studies) there are no rules that suggest one form of display is more appropriate to any particular approach than another. The notion of a toolkit of possibilities with appropriate author justification is a better reflection of what is currently going on in the field, always bearing in mind the targeted audience. The type of data that is being collected should not limit the forms of display possible. For example, an analysis of chat room conversation could be displayed as any or all of the following:

- tables of ranked word frequencies and keywords in context
- individual case studies
- threads
- illustrative quotes
- a poetic form of one particular story
- an author/participant voiced vignette
- a dramatic dialogue.

The only limitations would lie in the lack of audio and visual data available to the researcher.

Despite this, in order to take, for example, a subjective approach that would require large chunks of personal data to be available for re-presentation it would be necessary to design the study so that this data is collected either in the form of very detailed journal records or in the form of an autoethnography. Equally, if graphic displays are the preferred option then the data needs to be more substantial than just a handful of people. If you have collected six in-depth case studies over time, constructed from a number of interviews, this data would be better used as a base for thick descriptive display using quotes, case histories, narratives, poetic form, pastiche, vignettes etc.

Display options – the toolkit

1. Graphical display

- Social networks
- Bar graph
- Matrix
- Table
- Decision tree modelling
- Flow chart
- Ladder
- Metaphorical visual display
- Modified Venn diagram
- Scatterplot
- Taxonomy

All of these, illustrated below, provide a quick summary of considerable chunks of data, producing an overall snapshot which can then be more fully explained and illustrated with other forms of qualitative display such as quotes, case studies or other visuals.

Social network   See the section 'Social network analysis' and Figure 4.1 in Chapter 4 for a graphic example from the work of William Whyte (1956) showing the relationships among members of a street gang.

Bar graph   The use of a bar graph to display data is illustrated in Figure 24.1. Here, for example, the display makes evident the dominance of male finishers up to the age of 40.

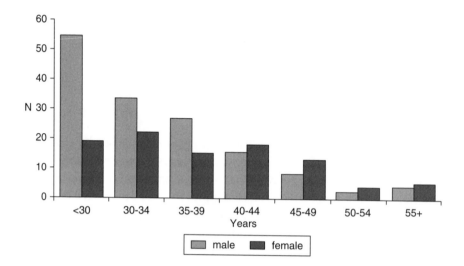

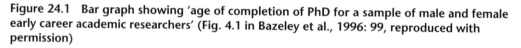

Figure 24.1   Bar graph showing 'age of completion of PhD for a sample of male and female early career academic researchers' (Fig. 4.1 in Bazeley et al., 1996: 99, reproduced with permission)

Matrix   The example of a matrix in Figure 24.2 demonstrates the choices in pregnancy based on a couple's relationship. In this situation the choices are similar for both the male and female of the couple. In some matrixes the choices will be quite different.

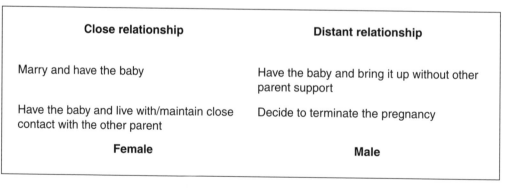

Figure 24.2   Matrix

Table   In Figure 24.3 a table gives a quick insight into where three groups – locals, tourists and hippies – might meet in a small rural town.

TABLE X *Showing places where interaction occurs*

	Locals		Hippies			Tourists
	Men	Women	Men	Women	Children	
Grocery	X		X	X	X	X
Post office	X		X	X	X	
Cafe	X		X	X	X	X
Garage	X		X			X
Bar	X		X			X
Church	X	X				
School		X			X	
Laundry				X		X
Art Centre		X				
Inn						X

Figure 1. Patterns of association in downtown Jax. (Cavan, 1974:332). This table gives a quick insight into where the three groups: locals, tourists and hippies might meet in a small rural town.

Figure 24.3   Tabular display showing 'patterns of association in downtown Jax' (Fig. 1 in Cavan, 1974: 332)

Decision tree modelling   Decisions trees (Figure 24.4) can be created in Excel using dialog boxes. They are useful for demonstrating the outcomes of sequential decisions made.

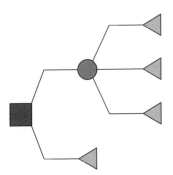

Figure 24.4   Decision tree modelling

Flow chart   Figure 24.5 gives an example of a flow chart, here demonstrating the stages in clinical decision making with regard to osteoporosis.

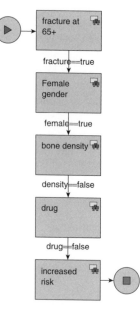

Figure 24.5   A flow chart (Huser et al., 2011: 43)

Ladder   The ladder (see Figure 24.6) is a useful tool for demonstrating incremental stages in the evolution of some aspect of your research question.

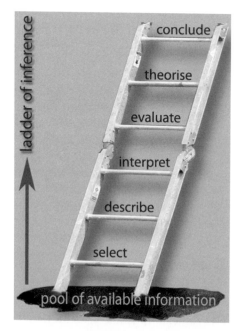

Figure 24.6   The 'ladder of inference', demonstrating stages in the qualitative processes (Robinson and Lai, 2006; https://www.det.nsw.edu.au/proflearn/der/htmods/thinking/ladder.html. © 2009 Commonwealth of Australia.)

Metaphorical visual display   In Figure 24.7 a participant, Carlos, has chosen a metaphorical image of the solo voyager to reflect the stage his career is at:

> It is a person standing up in a small boat looking out over a large body of water. He's feeling a little bit unsure about how things are going to go, not knowing what he's going to encounter as he sets out, but still knowing where you want to go is where you want to get to … The horizon is a little clear, but with my experience with boats, there are going to be some things that you don't see along the way. He is by himself … so it's a little bit scary, because I know that I have to make this decision on my own and determine what's important to me.

Figure 24.7   Metaphorical visual display – a man in a boat (Barner, 2011, http://jcd. sagepub.com/content/38/1/89.full.pdf+html)

Modified Venn diagram   The distribution of response patterns for males and females from two focus group questions (see Figure 24.8) can map gender dominance. Here the same male responded to both questions first (Capital letters) and five of the males responded to both questions, while only one female responded to both questions. It appears that males were dominating the responses to these two questions.

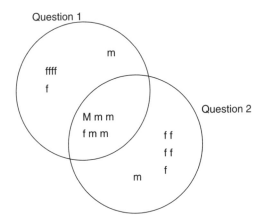

Figure 24.8   Venn diagram comparing the response patterns of the male and female focus group members for two questions (Onwuegbuzie et al., 2009, reproduced with permission)

Scatterplot   Figure 24.9 example shows use of a scatterplot for comparison of exam scores and quiz scores in the teaching of research methods.

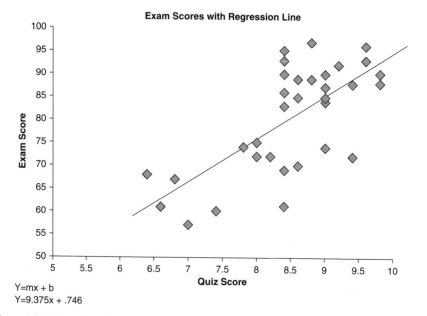

Y=mx + b
Y=9.375x + .746

Lindner, A.M. 'Teaching Quantitative Literacy through a Regression Analysis of Exam Performance' in *Teaching Sociology* 2012; 40: 50-59.

Figure 24.9   Exam scores with regression line scatterplot (Lindner, 2012)

Taxonomy   The taxonomy in Figure 24.10 shows the levels of knowledge required for different levels of personnel in information technology firms.

	Core	*Advanced*	*Innovative*	
Structural Capital	Software Quality Processes eg. Six Sigma etc. Documentation	Advanced Hardware Knowledge Repository BCP (Business Continuity Plan)	R&D	Internal
	Manufacturing Units Logistics Test Labs Development Centers	Patents Certifications		External
Human Capital	Programmers/Analysts Marketing/Sales Testers	Domain Experts/ Architects Experts System Designers	Researchers	Internal
	Contract Employees	External Consultants		External
Relational Capital	Customers Suppliers Distributors Outsourced Vendors	Legal Advisory Good will	Branding	External

This taxonomy shows the levels of knowledge required for different levels of personnel in Information Technology firms (Sharma et al, 2010)

Figure 24.10   Tabulation of knowledge taxonomy for IT services firm (Sharma et al., 2010, reproduced with permission)

Other display forms   A number of display forms available via Google programs are presented at: www.smashingmagazine.com/2007/08/02/data-visualization-modern-approaches/.

2. Textual display

- Boxed display
- Quotes
- Vignettes
- Case studies
- Mixed methods
- Anecdotes (researcher's gestalt)
- Layers (different perspectives)
- Pastiche (quilting of perspectives)
- Juxtaposition (of voices)
- Fiction, poetry, drama
- Interactive
- Hyperlinks
- Parody and irony

Boxed display   This is often used to illustrate issues and concerns the researcher has during the research project and is displayed alongside gathered data or to illustrate a point.

An example of minimal community support

I was becoming concerned about the ethics of non-intervention. Our research purpose was to see where/how carers of family with terminal cancer in the home situation accessed community help and support. Effectively we were evaluating the function of the outreach palliative care team in addition to the interaction of community nursing and care groups in 20 case studies. It was becoming obvious that minimal interaction with those support groups was occurring. All appeared siloed in their own worlds. But it was the case of X, a 78-year-old man proudly caring for his (now) incontinent 82-year-old wife at home in winter with hand-washed sheets hanging everywhere drying by the heat of a two-bar electric heater (very costly for a pensioner of minimal means), that really threw me. Shouldn't we tell him of the sheet service offered by Domestic Care? Why hadn't this group or one of the other groups noticed and offered this? I agonised for a couple of weeks waiting, hoping someone would intervene but they didn't and on our next visit I decided to contact Dom Care on his behalf. On our next visit the carer was so pleased to have received this help – although he said quite firmly that he had been managing but that it did leave him more time with his wife and after all that was what counted most. I justified my intervention by saying to myself that we already had enough data to show the poor interaction amongst the various care groups and at least we had done something to improve things if only for one person.

(Grbich, diary record)

Quotes   This is one of the most common approaches and involves the display of key quotes. For example, in a study on early career researchers (Bazeley et al., 1996: 29), immediately under the heading of 'Networking and becoming known' appears this quote from an interviewee:

> You can't afford to be introverted, in other words just stay in the four walls here, you have to get out there and particularly internationally. That would be the most important single key to success I believe ... it allows you to benchmark yourself.

And from a study on the experience of caring for a family member with terminal cancer (Grbich et al., 2001), under the heading 'View of the role' come two quotes. The first refers to the factor of time – the luxury of having time to say proper farewells – while the second refers to how one caregiver viewed herself in the caring process:

> You know this has been a gift, if you like, for us. The fact that he really now understands how much he is loved and how much people really think of him.

> I was like a duck – calm on top and paddling like mad underneath, but he was so good. I couldn't sit down and show how I felt you know ...

When more than one quote is displayed, the purpose is to demonstrate the variety in responses or to emphasise the concordance of a range of views on a particular issue. In both cases, the display acts as a starter for more detailed explanations or discussions.

Vignettes   A vignette is like a photo with blurred edges, and it provides an example or small illustrative story, which can clarify a particular point or perspective regarding some finding in the data. Vignettes can be author-voiced or participant-voiced and tend to be formed either from compressed data or from consolidation of different data sources. Laud Humphreys' (1975) study of impersonal sex in public places has an initial scene-setting vignette derived from his observation of these settings:

> At shortly after five o'clock on a weekday evening, four men enter a public restroom in a city park. One wears a well-tailored business suit; another wears tennis shoes, shorts and tee shirt; the third man is still clad in the khaki uniform of his filling station; the last, a salesman, has loosened his tie and left his sports coat in the car. What has caused these men to leave the company of other homeward-bound commuters on the freeway? What common interest brings these men, with their divergent backgrounds, to this public facility?

> They have come here not for the obvious reason, but in a search for "instant sex". Many men – married and unmarried, those with heterosexual identities and those whose self-image is a homosexual one – seek such impersonal sex, shunning involvement, seeking kicks without commitment. (Humphreys, 1975. Copyright © 1975 Aldine Publishers. Reproduced by permission of Aldine Transactions, a division of Transaction Publishers.)

Susan Bell and Roberta Apfel (1995) have consolidated different sets of their data into three substantial vignettes to display very different participant-voiced perspectives on the topic of women's experience of DES (diethylstilbestrol)-related cancer. This drug was given to pregnant women in the 1950s to prevent miscarriage but predisposed their female children to cervical cancer. The first vignette is a summarised transcript of a conference presentation given by a feminist health activist of the process of teaching women vaginal self-examination as part of an empowerment process. The second vignette likewise is a summary of an oncologist's conference presentation involving displaying a DES-infected vagina to his medical colleagues. The third vignette is in the voice of a woman who has experienced DES-related cancer and who is sharing her experiences and clarifying the impact of this cancer on her sexual relationship. This last presentation is in poetic form and is derived from interview transcripts.

Case studies   These tend to be either consolidated narratives in the voice of a participant or author-voiced summaries of a typical or extreme situation or individual experiences, or, as in the following case study of a man excluded from the processes of decision making upon entry into a nursing home, a combination of author and participant voices are presented:

Mr Barclay

Mr Barclay was 70 years old and had never married. A loner throughout his life, he drifted from one boarding house to another. He had few friends. Although he had two brothers and three sisters, he had not kept in touch with them 'for years'. He lost contact when his mother died 20 years ago. He said he feels close to no one. For Mr Barclay, life after retirement was different from expectations. Without a job to go to, he no longer felt useful. With failing eyesight, he could not read the newspaper or watch television. Eye surgery was refused by his doctor unless Mr Barclay moved into a nursing home. Mr Barclay had never thought about living in a nursing home. In fact he held some very negative views about nursing homes:

> Some of them are like hovels. All they are interested in is taking old people's money. The government has closed some of them down because of abuses to patients, for ill treatment, neglect and all that ugly business. Well I was very wary of them.

Without consultation, the social worker announced the decision. Mr Barclay 'was not given a choice'. He was unhappy, had no knowledge of nursing homes, nor had he the opportunity to visit the home selected for him, prior to his admission.

> You just do not walk into places like this. You go to the doctor and he makes enquiries. It works just like going into a hospital. You just do not arrive at their doorsteps and say you want a bed. I did not choose to come here. They sent me here. If I had my way, I'd still be living in a boarding house.

(Minichiello,1990: 323–51, reproduced with permission)

Mixed methods – data complementary presentation   Here survey results are presented in graphical form and the findings elaborated on through numerical explanations and quotes. See Figure 24.11 regarding evaluating client satisfaction with police response.

TABLE X *Satisfaction with the response of the police*

	Satisfied No.	%	Total answering the question
Time to attend	296	82.7	358
Details taken	429	88.1	487
Further action	305	64.2	475
Attitude towards the offence	397	81.5	487
Attitude towards the victim	424	87.8	483
Decide whether to proceed	121	78.1	155
Advise on preventing re-victimisation	327	82.8	395
Information on available assistance	176	67.4	261

Although the majority were satisfied (64.2%) with further action taken by police, a quarter (24.4%) of victims were not satisfied. The main complaints were either 'nothing being done' (44.8%) or 'no feedback' (30.2%). Comments illustrating the latter view are as follows:

'Police said would follow it up and haven't, would like to know what happened' (assault victim)

'Don't know what's going on, not enough contact. Expected them to get back' (assault victim)

'Want to know what's gone on since then.' (break and enter victim)

Figure 24.11 Mixed methods presentation of data using table and quotes (Gardner, 1990: 22, reproduced with permission)

Anecdotes An anecdote is a subjective story that is often used as a reflective tool to show a particular event in the data collection. Van Maanen (1988: 20) has indicated that an anecdote is a very short and simple story, usually relating to one incident which is close to the central idea of the research question. It includes important concrete detail, often contains several quotes, requires a punch line and closes quickly after the climax. In the following case, the anecdote illustrates the impact of one particular event on the prevailing view of the researcher:

I had surveyed the literature on caregivers of family members/friends with a terminal illness and everything pointed to the 'burden' of care and its negative impact on carer's health and well-being. My first foray into data collection involved a focus group with a bereavement support group almost a year after the death of their loved one. Much of the discussion did centre around issues of burden until one man said 'It was an absolute privilege to care for her and I am so pleased that I had the opportunity and that I was able to do it well'. This opened my eyes to other possibilities and we were ultimately able to gather sufficient data to challenge the 'burden of care' literature with a more positive perspective. (Grbich, diary record)

Layers Presenting data in layers can help the reader to see more easily what you have sighted. These layers may involve the deliberate interweaving of different voices to juxtapose their views, for example sequential narratives on how an accident happened or how a marriage was broken or who saw what in a particular incident or event. The following example comes from separate interviews with a couple who had decided to reverse primary caregiving roles for their young children. The two stories provide different perspectives on the topic '*How did you come to change roles?*' and serve to enrich knowledge.

Joe:	It springs from a desire to integrate more fully the different facets of my life – of our lives – a concept of the union of your personal and political lives. One of the things we have found is that if your work life does not reinforce your personal life and doesn't reinforce your interests, everything goes in a different direction. Your work life dominates and takes up too much time in your life thus leaving less time for your relationships, less time for other people, less time for the things you want to do, less time for yourself, less time for your family so everything goes against each other. We both had extremely high powered demanding jobs, our relationship was suffering and at that stage we had one child. We had both made the decision to leave work before we knew the second child was on the way.
Mary:	Well we started off with me staying home with the first child and him working and I found that very difficult to cope with because I'd been a very independent person with my own career and I really got stuck being at home and I had so many other things I wanted to do which I had tried to squeeze in at the same time. I was only on maternity leave, it was always intended that I would go back to work. So I stayed home for 10 months then I went back to work. Various people helped look after our child – that worked – it made me feel as though I was getting back into life again. When I was at home I had the feeling that Joe was out doing all the vital and vibrant things and I was bogged down with the nappies and it made me feel awful, I just didn't cope with it at all. At least when we were both working it was equal; we both had exciting things to talk about. The more I stayed home the less he talked to me about his work.

(Grbich, data)

Mary mirrors Joe's comments about the problems of both working and although she agrees that both had decided to give up work and rear their children together, a preference for her workforce role sent her back to work as soon as their second child was born. In these extracts, it is clear that Joe rationalises the decision for both of them from an ideological perspective while Mary is clearly unhappy in the home situation and decides to stay in the workforce leaving Joe with the home role.

In another version of layering, Mary's transcript could be displayed and different fonts used to tease out the different positions she takes. For example, her dislike for the limitations of the home role could be highlighted one way perhaps by using a different font while her statements about the problems of family relationships when partners have high pressure jobs could be highlighted in another way to further emphasise the differences in the two views.

Pastiche This more complicated version of layering involves 'quilting' or the display of many voices centring on a particular issue. A collage of fragments is presented which together help to build a more complete picture.

Figure 24.12 presents a pastiche of a number of comments, which have been drawn from various interviews and from the researcher's own journal in order to build up a snapshot of the views of the family and friends of 'Tony' – a long-term father at home caring for a young child. Tony's own voice is juxtaposed with these comments and a separate collage of his views over the years he was in the role could have been developed and displayed to show changes over time. The use of different sized fonts and spacings as well as emboldened information that you want to highlight, help focus the presentation of such information

Sue (wife)

I do think I missed out on a lot of the baby stuff. I still remember driving off the first day – he was standing at the front door with this little baby and I was feeling absolutely terrible and thinking 'how could I ever let this happen' ... But because we're very different personalities I think Jane has gained immensely – in that he's much more willing to spend a lot of time with her – those things I'm not very good at doing, so she's got a lot more contact than if I'd stayed home. I think I probably would have come to the decision of going back to work ...

Sue's mother (Sue's report)

My mother never really encouraged us to be at home mothers, she wanted us to be professional women ... I think she was pleased that I was going to continue on with my career

Tony's view of mothers' at home

If you get talking to women at home at any length you often find that they hate it and they themselves wonder why anyone else would want to do it.

Female friends (to Sue)

Isn't he wonderful, I'd really like to have that opportunity.

How could you do it? How could you go back to work when she's so young?

Tony's parents (to Tony)

Mother: I think it's a great idea, but no doubt when Sue gets sick of working you'll go back to work. If you're not prepared to support your wife and child, I'll disown you. I have a brother-in-law who never worked from the day he got married, she [her sister] worked, and none of us thought much of him because of that.

Father: You don't mean you're going to go on and do this forever? You may find that when you want to go back to the workforce, you can't.

Women in community playgroup (to Tony):
Aren't you marvellous!

Tony:

'It's the most demanding job I've ever had; isolated, unstructured. People tend to downplay it but after I've talked to them they realise there's a lot more to it than they thought. But being a man who feels a naturalness in that sort of role, you can be made to feel emasculated. From some men there's the attitude that I'm doing a female, lesser role

Tony's parents (to the researcher):
Mother: Well our reactions were commonsense, that one or both or each of them were going to earn money. Sue was going to earn a lot more than Tony. Tony had the sort of temperament that I believe was capable of being a father. I think he was soft, he was quite – not quiet, he was softly spoken – he was intelligent and he had a deep love for that kid ... But I do wonder getting right back to the primitive thing of it – is it a natural thing – isn't it more of the woman having the nesting instinct, deep down – if she doesn't do it she is missing out. Aren't they going against nature of things? A woman is a woman, that's their function – motherhood, and nothing, no matter what they do can take that away and if its undeveloped, she's not much of a mother, if it is developed its most rewarding. Although there's no doubt about it, you get tired of being in the house all the time, you can't live for housework.

Male friends (to Tony);
How's the holiday?
Getting lots of golf?

Parking attendant's response (to Tony): At least I've got a job!

Tony's view of Sue

**She feels she couldn't do this job at home, that she'd get too angry ...
but she's also very sensitive to me being overwhelmed by it.**

Researcher's journal. Tony moved into the father at home role at the age of 39. His most recent workforce position was that of a real estate valuer – a job he didn't enjoy. When Tony and Sue had been married for some years, it became apparent they were unlikely to have children so Sue had decided to pursue medical qualifications and gain a career in medicine. At the end of her studies she became pregnant. It was decided that as Tony didn't like working and Sue had just spent a lot of time becoming a doctor (a job she liked), Tony would stay at home long term with Jane and Sue would share the early morning and evening childcare tasks.

Figure 24.12   Pastiche of responses by and to 'Tony' in the father at home role (Grbich, 2004: 115)

Juxtaposition   The placing of one set of information against another in an echoing/mimicking manner in order to bring out the differences can be seen in the beginning of an article by David Boje (2000) (Figure 24.13).

Here Boje uses the imagery of the 'tympan' – juxtaposition of texts in order to strike the ear from two perspectives. He presents two distinctly different views of the community of

The noise of the city at daybreak mixes with the sounds of the locking and loading of Heckler and Koch MP5 submachine guns and the slamming of double banana-clip magazines into CAR-15 assault rifles as nearly 60 cops mill about a rooftop in Los Angeles. They are preparing for urban combat. Lt. Tom Runyen, commander of the Los Angeles Police Department Special Weapons and Tactics (LAPD SWAT) platoon, walks confidently amid his men. Wearing grayish-blue fatigues, black Kevlar vests and Fritz helmets, they fill their Benelli automatic 12-gauge shotguns with 00-buckshot magnum shells, pack hand-toss flash-bang devices into the pouches of their body armor and recheck voice-activated helmet radios.

The noise of the community after school mixes with the sounds of size 24 clown shoes thumping and slamming on the sidewalk and the joyous chatter of Nickerson Gardens mothers, kids, and students from Loyola Marymount University as the festive parade of nearly 60 people wind their way through the streets and backyards of the gardens. Professor Boje, clown-professor of the College of Business and consultant to the Nickerson Gardens Resident Management Corporation (NGRMC) walks confidently amid his children. Wearing blue hair, red and white checkered jacket and a red clowns' nose, he has filled his pockets with lolly pops, bubble gum, and a squirt gun disguised as a lapel flower. He does hand-tosses of the candies from his clown shorts pockets...

Figure 24.13   Juxtaposition: image comparison presenting different views of a community (Boje, 2000; http://web.nmsu.edu/~dboje/pmdecon9705.htm)

Nickerson Gardens – one from *Popular Mechanics* (Samuel Katz, 1997), called 'Felon Busters: when the cops are outgunned, LAPD SWAT breaks up the party', which sees Nickerson Gardens as a dangerous and drug-ridden community inhabited by criminals. This is contrasted with a view drawn from David Boje's nine years of data collection in this community representing it as a strong cohesive group. The reader is instructed to move the cursor between the two texts and to read them in any way they prefer.

Fiction   The 'fictionalising' of qualitative data does not mean glancing at the data and then going off on a tangent that is only vaguely related. It generally means turning carefully collated data into a fictional form, as Caroline Ellis has done in her 'ethnographic short story' where she documents a subjective account of a meeting with a former colleague who was now dying of AIDS (Ellis, 1995).

Steven Banks (2000) has created what he terms a 'weak form of fiction' or 'accidental fiction' – a fictional story loosely based on the pseudo 'joyful' annual summer holiday letters which eventuate each year from holidaymakers – here constructed through the central character and 'writer' of these letters, a fictional wife and mother, Ginny Balfour. In addition, Banks constructs and displays five of these letters, written over a period of six years, in order to share his understanding of the structural properties of such letters, their display of human struggles and values, and to create emotional responses in the reader.

Poetry   Gaining the essence of what is said in interview and maintaining the rhythm, tone and diction, pauses and repetition used by the interviewee is regarded as essential in turning transcripts into poetic form. These factors help to give the proper flavour of what might be a condensed form of many hours of interview. For example, from the following short interview two poems could be started:

> My primary concern in the role is looking after Jane and attempting to relate to her, and the rest is in my view quite an adjunct. I don't see this as having anything to do with housework, I object to the term 'housewife'. I came into it fairly worried because I figure that no one is taught how to be a parent, we just don't do anything about that.

> Six weeks after the birth came, she (Sue, wife) drove off and it was just terrifying and I thought 'My god, what am I going to do when she (Jane, daughter) wakes up!' I think I managed to struggle on for the first few weeks.

(Grbich, data set)

Poetic form 1

I came into it fairly worried

No one is taught how to be a parent

It was just terrifying

I think I managed to struggle along for the first few weeks

> My primary concern is looking after Jane
>
> The rest is quite an adjunct
>
> I object to the term 'housewife'

The orientation chosen will depend on whether the major focus of the poem is to be the experience of early stage caring or the father's view of the role.

Narrative   Moving beyond the editing of transcript data, the narrative poem often has the elements of a short story, with location, characters and situation around which the poem moves. It can be broadly 'fictional' (loosely based on data), factual, subjective or historical. The narrative as a story (with a beginning, a middle and an end) can be either participant- or researcher-voiced or can allow the 'I' 'eye' of the researcher to move in and out of the story permitting other voices to speak in their own right and providing the reader with access to all players.

Margery Wolf (1992) has taken a set of data and presented different aspects in three juxtaposed narratives. The original data was collected 30 years previously and centred on an incident in a Taiwanese village where a women appeared either to be experiencing madness or had become a conduit for spiritual voices (a position of considerably higher status than the former.

Narrative 1 is taken from Wolfe's own research journals, a confessional tale of heat, dust, precise observations minutely recorded but interspersed with frustration, ambiguity and the problems of interpreting the event under observation through barriers of language and culture:

> I also realised that for the last half hour I had forgotten the weight of the hot sodden air. It came back to me in full force as I went out the back door and made my way down the dusty road toward the Tan house. The sun reflected cruelly off the hard yellow earth path, and even when I turned into the shade of a large old tree that guarded the courtyard there was relief only from the glare.

Narrative 2 is constructed from the field notes of the Chinese research assistant and provides cultural insights:

> March 15, 1960
>
> 154 (F 3 I) to Wu Chieh: 'Very early this morning 48 came here and told my mother that she wanted to bai-bai to that god today and make 60 turtles and give one to every family in the village. She said that today the god is going to open his mouth and say something so that everyone in the village will believe in him. My mother told her that she had already spent a lot of money and that she wasn't rich and that her husband wasn't working now, so why didn't she just use a little pork and a little fish and make 12 turtles and then have a big bai-bai when the family has more money. So finally, 48 went to her mother with the money to buy the things.

Narrative 3 comprises the authoritative author-voiced article written about the event for an anthropological journal:'

> IN THE SPRING of 1960, in a then remote village on the edge of the Taipei basin in northern Taiwan, a young mother of three lurched out of her home, crossed a village path, and stumbled wildly across a muddy rice paddy. The cries of her children and her own agonized shouts quickly drew an excited crowd out of what had seemed an empty village. Thus began nearly a month of uproar and agitation as this small community resolved the issue of whether one of their residents was being possessed by a god or suffering from a mental illness. (Wolf, 1992)

Drama   Dramatic performances of data can be seen in Carolyn Ellis and Art Bochner's dialogue (gained from their own diary records) on this couple's separate experiences of Carolyn's pregnancy and her abortion. Each speaker faces the audience then turns his/her back so the other can speak without the expressions on their partner's face being visible. The following is an extract from the beginning of this performance:

Voiceover Alice:	Ted arrives and plays with the dogs before he looks at me. He knows I bought the test. Does he suspect I'm pregnant? "Well what do you want to name it?" I ask, and immediately wonder if this is a good way to tell him. I feel none of the lightness that my words are supposed to convey.
	Ted: What? You are? (Yes Pregnant?
	Yes the tests are 99% effective)
	Oh god. What are we going to do?
Ted:	I feel myself drifting away. Memories flash through my mind. I recall conversations with former lovers in which I fantasised the birth of a "love child" created during a nearly perfect, mutually orgasmic sexual encounter and nurtured to birth by the compassion and tenderness characteristic of idealistic love. I particularly recall the brief moments during our passionate romance when Alice and I had played with the idea of having a child, more jokingly than seriously, but nevertheless opening possibilities that simultaneously were threatening and thrilling. I remember how easily and innocently we flirted with danger by finding reasons not to use condoms. I conjured up sweet images of fathering that had been buried by the despairing experiences of three relationships in which the timing was never quite right or the love never quite sufficient. My head is spinning as I try to concentrate on the immediate circumstances, but my mind is crowded with memories and fantasies. Part of me wants to scream with joy, another part to howl in agony.

(Ellis and Bochner, 1992: 79–101)

Confrontational theatre performances based in research (ethno drama) have been used for some time to bring about emotional catharsis in the audience.

The assessment of visual representation, be it drama, film, video etc., lies in:

- the capacity to develop meaningful dialogue with the audience
- whether the interaction developed can encourage the audience to engage with wider social issues

(adapted from Agar, 2004)

Interactive   Techniques that can prompt an active response from the reader are only just starting to be introduced into research from literature and films and can include feedback mechanisms – for example a questionnaire to gauge the reader's responses or experiences with regard to a particular display of data. The responses gained can become part of the ongoing collection and display of data from different phases in a research project. Another approach includes directions to the reader to go at a particular point in the text to a visual/aural display – such as a video clip or sound track of relevance to the conclusions being drawn. Paintings completed by researcher or researched can also be appended in hard copy or on CD to demonstrate emotions or experiences toward particular aspects of the research under study.

Another approach to prompting active reader interaction is the technique of leaving gaps in the narrative for the reader to fill from their own life experience or from commonsense expectations. Care needs to be taken here as this is difficult to do successfully and may simply prompt reader frustration or, at worst, reviewer/examiner fury.

Hyperlinks   This involves the placing of raw data (interviews, observations and documents) at a hyperlinked point on the World Wide Web to allow the reader access to the complete transcript from which the quote has been drawn or the case study derived. The reader has now moved light years from the position where they are told what to think by the authoritative researcher. Processes of interpretation and re-presentation thus become transparent. Hyperlinks can also be used to promote a multimedia experience (videos, photos, film clips, scanned documents, audio and digital media), allowing the reader to move from site to site and from textual to visual images. Aspects of design, analysis and ethics can become issues; for example when the borders between writing up and analysis become blurred, when issues of writing for a particular audience dominate, or when the ethics of displaying data to a broad audience where participants can never be anonymous is occurring (Coffey et al., 2005; Dicks et al., 2005).

Parody and irony   Parody involves the mimicking of the work/roles of others for a particular effect while irony can convey a meaning opposite to that to which the words actually refer. These techniques have often been used to clarify what has been privileged and what has been marginalised in society. In written texts and films the juxtaposition of male–female relations (typically portrayed as couples of similar ages) are contrasted with young males (teenagers) in love with female octogenarians (Eco, 1993). In research, one example might be an article on men who stay home written in the heroic tradition with day-to-day father–child routines being presented as though they were major battles involving life-threatening situations.

3. Aural and visual displays

- Pictogram
- Videos, self cam, YouTube, computer links
- Photos, photo collages
- Films
- Aurals
- Drawings, paintings

The inclusion of audio tapes and video clips are options to enhance the reader's understanding of a particular issue, story or experience.

The display of static visual data from photographs or videos can easily be incorporated into the paper-based text. Additional CDs of synchronised audio-tracked visual data can also be presented as moving images, either as a two-way split screen, a four-way split screen, action indicator augmented display (with graphical monitoring system visualised in a corner of the monitor and activated by participants' actions) or as a pentagram where multiple sequences of events are represented (Gamberini and Spagnolli, 2003)

Photo collage   The benefits of photo collages (see Figure 24.14) are that you can tell a story quickly with a broad spread of multiple images.

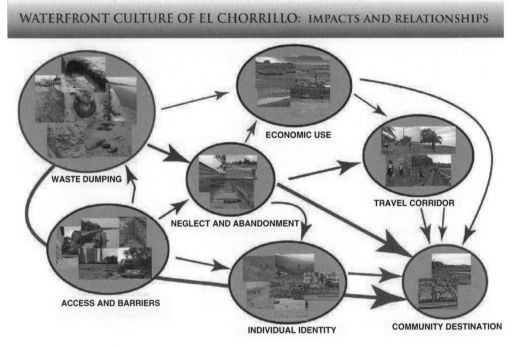

Figure 24.14 Bubble diagram of relationships providing a visual exposure of a waterfront culture in Panama (Powell, 2010)

Summary

Although the final writing up and display of data will be influenced both by the audience for which you are writing as well as your own position, there are no hard and fast rules as to which particular form of data display should be attached to any given research approach. However if particular styles are preferred then it is wise to work out early whether the design you have developed will provide the kind of data that you can utilise for your favoured forms of display.

Student exercise

When your database is complete attempt a number of ways of presenting and re-presenting segments of your data.

For example, in a study by Williams (1994), the finding that Aboriginal health workers were unhappy with the accessibility of the manual provided for them was trialled initially in two ways:

1. Firstly as several quick short *quotes*:

   The vast majority of Aboriginal health workers' initial comments on the manual were as follows:

   > 'Too many words'
   > 'Too many big medical words – too complicated for us'
   > 'All these Western medical words are like white fella secrets'

2. Secondly, as a *vignette* (compressed data, researcher-voiced sourced from researcher observation) in order to provide more detail to the reader:

   At one health centre I asked the AHW's to show me an example of the 'hard words'. An experienced male health worker opened the page to 'conjunctivitis'. We discussed the fact that 'conjunctivitis' could be changed to 'pussy red eye'. He, however, was referring to the next line which stated 'document visual acuity'. It was obvious that this style of language was not generally used in conversation and is an example of the concise nature of the written medical word. Over the phone during a medical consult the doctor is far more likely to say 'have you checked the vision with the eye-chart?' It was this type of 'complicated jargon' that AHW's found difficult to understand and it discouraged them from reading the manual. (Williams, 1994)

Further reading

Innovative ethnographic displays

Atkinson, P. and Delamont, S. (2008) *Representing Ethnography Reading, Writing and Rhetoric in Qualitative Research.* Four-volume set. London: Sage. The focus is postmodern qualitative research, its controversies, analyses, voice and representation.

Dicks, B., Mason, B., Coffey, A. and Atkinson, P. (2005) *Qualitative Research and Hypermedia: Ethnography for the Digital Age.* Thousand Oaks, CA: Sage. The theoretical implications of writing and researching for the electronic screen are discussed.

Ellis, C. and Bochner, A. (eds) (1996) *Composing Ethnography: Alternative forms of Qualitative Writing.* Newbury Park, CA: Sage. Lots of good examples of innovative ways of displaying the newer forms of ethnography.

Writing qualitative research

Ely, M., Vinz, R., Anzul, M. and Downing, M. (1997) *On Writing Qualitative Research: Living by Words*. Bristol, PA: Falmer Press. A comprehensive, detailed overview of how to go about transforming collected words into qualitative research displays such as narrative turns, metaphors, drama and poetry.

Wolcott, H. (1990) *Writing Up Qualitative Research* (2nd edn). Newbury Park, CA: Sage. Lots of examples, reader friendly, with practical tips.

Modern display forms

www.smashingmagazine.com/2007/08/02/data-visualization-modern-approaches/ presents a number of display forms available via Google programs.

References

Agar, M. (2004) We have met the other and we are all non-linear. Ethnography as a non-linear dynamic system. *Complexity*, 10 (2): 16–24.

Banks, S. (2000) Five holiday letters: a fiction. *Qualitative Inquiry*, 6 (6): 392–405.

Barner, R. (2011) Applying visual metaphors to career transitions. *Journal of Career Development*, 38 (1): 89–106. Retrieved from http://jcd.sagepub.com/content/38/1/89.full.pdf+html (accessed July 2011).

Bazeley, P., Kemp. L., Stevens, K., Asmar, C., Grbich, C., Marsh, H. and Bhathal, R. (1996) *Waiting in the Wings: A Study of Early Career Academic Researchers in Australia*. Canberra: Australian Government Publishing Service. Commissioned Report No. 50.

Bell, S. and Apfel, R. (1995) Looking at bodies: insights and inquiries about DES-related cancer. *Qualitative Sociology*, 18 (1): 3–19.

Boje, D. (2000) Postmodern détournement analysis of the *Popular Mechanics* spectacle using stories and photos of the festive community life of Nickerson Gardens. In *EJ-ROT Electronic Journal of Radical Organization Theory*, 6 (1). Retrieved from http://web.nmsu.edu/~dboje/pmdecon9705.htm (accessed 1 May 2011).

Cavan, S. (1974) Seeing social structure in a rural setting. *Urban Life and Culture*, 3 (3): 329–46.

Coffey, A., Dicks, B., Mason, B., Renold, E., Soyinka, B. and Williams, M. (2005) Methods Briefing 8. Ethnography for the digital age. Retrieved from_http://64.233.179.104/search?q=cache:c_c-C41tGJIJ:www.ccsr.ac.uk/methods/publications/documents/coffey.pdf+interactive+qualitative+data&hl=enon (accessed 1 May 2006).

Dicks, B., Mason, B., Coffey, A. and Atkinson, P. (2005) *Qualitative Research and Hypermedia: Ethnography in the Digital Age*. London: Sage.

Eco, U. (1993) *Misreadings*. Orlando, FL: Harcourt and Jonathan Cape.

Ellis, C. (1995) Speaking of dying: an ethnographic short story. *Symbolic Interaction*, 18 (1): 73–81.

Ellis, C. and Bochner, A. (1992) Telling and performing personal stories: the constraints of choice in abortion. In *Investigating Subjectivity: Research on Lived Experience*. Thousand Oaks, CA: Sage.

Gamberini, L. and Spagnolli, A. (2003) Display techniques and methods for cross-medial data analysis. *PsychNology Journal*, 1(2): 131–40.

Gardner, J. (1990) *Victims and Criminal Justice*. Adelaide: Office of Crime Statistics South Australian Attorney General's Department.

Grbich, C. (2004) *New Approaches in Social Research*. London: Sage.

Grbich, C., Parker, D. and Maddocks, I. (2001) The emotions and coping strategies of caregivers of family members with a terminal cancer. *Journal of Palliative Care (Canada)*, 17 (1): 30–46.

Humphreys, L. (1975) *Tearoom Trade: Impersonal Sex in Public Places*. Chicago: Aldine. Retrieved from http://www.angelfire.com/or3/tss/tearoom.html (accessed June 2011).

Huser, V., Rasmussen, L., Oberg, R. and Starren, J. (2011) Implementation of workflow engine technology to deliver basic clinical decision support functionality. *BMC Medical Research Methodology* 11: 43. Retrieved from http://www.biomedcentral.com/1471-2288/11/43/abstractFull (accessed August 2011).

Katz, S. (1997) 'Felon Busters': when the cops are outgunned. LAPD SWAT breaks up the party. *Popular Mechanics*, May.

Lindner, A. (2012) Teaching quantitative literacy through a regression analysis of exam performance. *Teaching Sociology*, 40: 50. Retrieved from http://tso.sagepub.com/content/40/1/50.full.pdf+html (accessed 1 March 2012).

Minichiello, V., Alexander, L. and Jones, D. (1990) A typology of decision-making situations for entry into nursing homes. In *In Depth Interviewing: Researching People*. Melbourne: Longman Cheshire.

Onwuegbuzie, A., Slate, J., Leech, N. and Collins, K. (2009) Mixed data analysis: advanced integration techniques. International Journal of Multiple Research Approaches, 3 (1): 13–33.

Powell, K. (2010) Making sense of place: mapping as a multisensory research method. *Qualitative Inquiry*, 16 (7): 539–55. Retrieved from http://qix.sagepub.com/content/16/7/539.full.pdf+html (accessed July 2011).

Robinson, V. and Lai, M. (2006) *Practitioner Research for Educators: A Guide to Improving Classrooms and Schools.* Thousand Oaks, CA: Corwin Press. pp. 45, 47.

Sharma, R., Chia, M., Choo, V. and Samuel, E. (2010) Using a taxonomy for knowledge audits: some field experiences. *Journal of Knowledge Management Practice*, 11 (1). Retrieved from www.tlainc.com/articl214. htm (accessed August 2011).

Van Maanen, M. (1988) *On Writing Ethnography*. Chicago, IL: University of Chicago Press.

Whyte, W. (1956) *The Organisation Man*. Philadelphia, PA: University of Pennsylvania Press.

Williams, N. (1994) An evaluation of the Central Australian Rural Practitioners Association Standard Treatment Manual (CARPA Manual). Masters thesis, Flinders University, Adelaide, Australia.

Wolf, M. (1992) *A Thrice-Told Tale: Feminism, Postmodernism, and Ethnographic Responsibility.* Stanford, CA: Stanford University Press.

Glossary

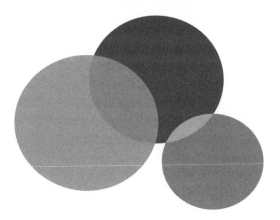

Analogical mapping A mapping process where graphic symbols apply information from one setting to another.

Basic hermeneutic approach A method of data gathering and interpretation that seeks to understand the meanings of parts within a whole by going out into the field, collecting data, interpreting it and using this interpretation as a basis for further data collection and interpretation in an iterative cycle.

Centred Where the researcher acts as the authoritative voice of the research, that is: this is how the research was conducted, these are the findings.

Decentred The process of removing oneself from a central authority (as author/ researcher) and allowing the views of others to be featured, often with minimal or no interpretation.

Differance Jacques Derrida used this term to clarify the way in which all words (signs) create meanings in terms of their differences from other words or aspects in terms of the constant deferral of meaning.

Discursive practices Michel Foucault used this to describe the ways that particular discourses are maintained, e.g. the power of the doctor in hospitals is maintained by hierarchies of education and status, case notes, and the rituals of examination and prescribing, which only doctors have control of.

Grand theory Often called meta narratives, large bodies of authoritative thought that dominate belief systems, cultures or disciplines.

Hermeneutic See basic hermeneutic research

Matrix analysis The development of a rectangular matrix, usually 2×2, to compare two different aspects.

Metaphor A figure of speech in which a name or descriptive word is transferred to an object/objects to which it is not normally applied in order to provide comparison.

Ontology The study of reality through the conceptualisations of essences (models, interactions and things written about the nature of being) that underpin the particular domain under study, e.g. relationships.

Postpositivism This follows and analyses positivism based on issues regarding the problem of unity of all science; the separation between facts and theory; and the assertion that reality is partially a social construction such that measurement and variable control become problematic.

Quasi-statistical Not quite but almost statistical – i.e., using descriptive (means, median, mode and standard deviations) rather than inferential statistics.

Realism The depiction of events and people as entities that exist independently of our conceptions.

Recursive spiral A repeated spiral that enables the researcher to go backwards and forwards between the collection and interpretation of data in the collation of a holistic view.

Transcendental realism The belief that social phenomena exist in both the mind and in the objective world and that the domains of the real (what exists), actual (events) and empirical (observable events) have reasonably stable relationships among them.

Typologies The classification or grouping of common traits.

Index

This index is in word-by-word order. Page references in *italics* indicate figures and those in **bold** indicate tables.

discourse analysis
  classical ethnography and 42
  critical discourse analysis 251–254, *251*
  critical ethnography and 57
  Foucault and 246–251
  investigative semiotic inquiry and 18
  overview 9, 245–246
dissertations 137–138
drama 124, 320–321

e-research 160–161
economics 110
emancipation
  critical ethnography and 56
  critical theory and 7
  ethnodrama and 144
  feminist research and 69, 70
  memory work and 76
empirical data 4
  See also data
empowerment
  critical ethnography and 56, 57
  critical theory and 251
  ethnodrama and 144
  feminist research and 68–69, 70–71
  reflective generative practice and 102
Enlightment 6
enumerative content analysis 191–195, *192,*
  193, 194
enumerative inquiry 18, 19
epiphanies 144
epistemology 4
equality 70
ethics
  cyber ethnography and 156–157, 161
  ethnodrama and 149, 150
ethnodrama
  autoethnography and 144, 150
  criticisms of 149
  evaluation of 12–13, 149–150
  new forms of 150–151
  overview 143–149
The Ethnograph (computer program)
  269, *269*
ethnographic content analysis (ECA)
  195–197, 201–204, *203*
ethnography 7, 8, 17
  See also classical ethnography; critical
    ethnography
ethnomethodology 8, 230

evaluation research 8, 17
event analysis 52–53
existential phenomenology 98–99
expressive statements 231

feminist participatory action research 71
feminist research
  constructionism/interpretivism and 8
  critical ethnography and 56
  critical theory and 7
  grounded theory and 89
  investigative semiotic inquiry and 18
  iterative inquiry and 17
  memory work and 71–76
  overview 68–69
  postmodernism and 8
  researcher and researched in 69–70, 72
  subjective inquiry and 17
  theorising and 294, 296–297
fiction 318
film
  ethnodrama and 151
  postmodernism and 110
Finding My Place (Saldaña) 147
flow charts 307, 308
formal theory 87
frame analysis 49–51
free verse 137
freelists 46

generalisability 5, 26
grounded theory
  constructionism/interpretivism and 8
  constructivism and 81–82, 88
  critical theory and 7
  data display and 304
  Glaser and 80–82, **81**, 87, 259, 295
  iterative inquiry and 17
  method modification 88–89
  overview 79–81
  postmodernism and 8
  Strauss and 7, 80–81, **81**, 82–87, 89,
    259, 295
  subjective inquiry and 17
  theorising and 295–296
Grounded Theory Review (journal) 82
Guernica (Picasso) 206–208, *207*

haiku 136
Hermeneutic Circle (Gadamer) 16